Haunted Liverpool 26

Tom Slemen

The Tom Slemen Press

Copyright © 2013 Tom Slemen

All rights reserved.

ISBN-10: 1514717158
ISBN-13: **978-1514717158**

DEDICATION

For
Thomas and Eleanor Cain, beloved grandparents of
Samantha Cain

CONTENTS

Mandy	1
Run For Home	16
Through the Time Barrier	19
Hugo	46
The List	61
The Black Angel	70
Some Weird Apparitions	92
Strange Abductors	108
Featherfingers	119
Walls Have Ears	126
Hadlow Next Stop	131
Zodius	138
Belle Vale Ghosts	146

Winslow Street Ghosts	168
The Seventh Step	180
What Are They?	186
The Golden Typewriter	214
A Trick of Time	217
Aintree's Ghostly Girl	223
Huyton's Faceless Child	227
Taxi in the Rain	232
Spooked Crooks	254
Hillfoot Road Haunting	275
Samaritan Superhero	278
Helpers From Beyond	282
Not Ours to See	289
Norris Green Hauntings	311
Some Haunted Churches	335
The Druid Boy	346
Ford Cemetery's Reaper	349

A Gateacre Mystery	353
Punch	357
Strange Caller	363
Smart Alec	375
Hard Knock Angel	385
The Saurians	394
Night Drive Terror	403
The Taured Mystery	409
Old Swan's Black-Eyed Children	415
Wither	418
Everywhere Eric	432
Beyond Explanation	438
The Humlorts	454
Cold Caller	465

MANDY

In the city centre of Liverpool one evening in June 2014 a 20-year-old Huytonian man named Corey Richardson was smiling inanely in front of a pub jukebox with a pint of Foster's in his hand as he swayed in the fog of intoxication with the dreamy Hammond organ of one of pop's greatest acid lullabies – Procul Harum's *Whiter Shade of Pale*. His friend Marlowe – a 19-year-old media student with high-hopes to direct a film one day that would (as she was always promising) 'change the form of film' – was mouthing a line from the Gladys Knight song *Midnight Train to Georgia*. 'Superstar but he didn't get far!' For some reason, probably the surrealistic out-of-context nature of the sentence and because of the large amounts of alcohol Marlowe had sloshing around in her brain, the line from the song made her laugh, and Corey, lip-reading her words in the din of the jukebox, also found it funny.

The song faded and the chaotic hubbub of the pub's clientele's myriad conversations returned; the periodic squeak of the door as outcast smokers came in and out, loud louche words of virgins boasting about imaginary conquests, the asymmetrical conversation of a bore droning out a blow by blow description of every childish stunt in last night's *Top Gear*, and nearby, a pale tall student was stood with half a pint of flat mild in his hand, with the tapering long fingers of his other hand waving about like the tentacles of an anemone as he explained the beauty of programming with the Python language. Marlowe brought up a YouTube vid of a compilation of funny cats on her Samsung phone and shoved the screen in Corey's face, and he looked past the phone and at his reflection – and the reflection of Marlowe – in the mirrors behind the bar. He admired his beard. 'Never mind looking at yourself you vain tosser, look at this!' Marlowe shoved the screen nearer to his bloodshot eyes.

'Do you think it defines my face – ' Corey enquired, pinching the chin hair between his finger and thumb.

'That beard could slow you down when you're swimming, mate,' Marlowe told him, annoyed because he wasn't watching the cats. 'You need a trim.'

And then suddenly, Corey saw this beautiful tall girl come out of the pub toilets, and she looked at him as if she knew him, and the weird thing was that Corey felt an overwhelming sense of déjà vu – as if *he* knew her from someplace. Even from a distance of about thirty feet he could see how blue her eyes were. Marlowe followed the line of Corey's spellbound sight and then looked back at him. 'You and redheads,' she said, with a flash of jealousy in her olive-green eyes.

'She's not a redhead,' Corey told her, and blushed. He tried to look away, to be cool, but he had to look at her again. She was confident, and pale, brown-haired and blue-eyed – but what type of blue? Corey asked Marlowe, as she seemed to have an accurate name for every colour in the visible universe.

'Majorelle Blue,' Marlowe decided upon.

'Shurrup – you just made that up,' Corey retorted, watching the beautiful stranger out the tail of his right eye now.

'You've never heard of Majorelle Blue?' Marlowe looked the redhead up and down condescendingly. 'You never heard of Jacques Majorelle and his Moroccan garden then?'

'No,' admitted Corey, and he didn't care about any painter now he had set eyes on this girl.

'He painted everything in the garden blue,' Marlowe told him, and then she bowed her head as she turned off her mobile. 'Why don't you go and talk to her?'

'Nah,' Corey screwed his nose up and shook his bearded head. 'Bit stalky that.'

'Go and talk to Miss Cobalt Eyes,' Marlowe advised him, and hurt her own heart in doing so.

'Her eyes aren't cobalt, they're like sky blue,' Corey opined, and asked: 'Cobalt isn't light blue is it?'

'Superstar but he didn't get far!' Marlowe quipped, and smiled, but Corey didn't even smirk – he was apparently mesmerised by the redhead.

'I might get off soon, my head's chocker,' Marlowe announced.

'I thought you wanted to go to the Kazimier?' Corey realised Marlowe was hurt by the way he was gawping at that girl.

'Nope, I'm going,' Marlowe told him, and her eyes glistened from unshed tears.

'I'm going too then,' Corey told her and plonked his half glass of lager on the top of the wall-mounted jukebox.

'No, you stay here,' Marlowe told him, and he could hear a trace of choked up larynx. 'You might get lucky with cobalt.'

'She's gone now anyway,' Corey replied, looking about. Each wall of the pub had a mirror, and it made the place look bigger, but to drunken eyes it was hard to ascertain who was real and who was mere reflection. 'God, is there any need for all these mirrors?' Corey grumbled.

'Looking for Miss Cobalt in the citadel of mirrors – make a good poem that,' said Marlowe, and she turned and headed for the door, and Corey was right at her heels as she stepped into the warm night outside. She began to march, but she swayed as she did and Corey thought it was funny. 'Come back, woman.' Corey shouted, all tongue in cheek, 'I'm with you tonight, baby, you don't have to gnaw the sheets!'

Marlowe turned and slapped his face and it literally sobered him in that instant.

He halted. 'What was that for?' He felt his cheek and moved his jaw with a chewing motion.

'Dunno,' Marlowe shrugged in an exaggerated fashion and turned away and began marching again, and then she started to wipe her eyes with the back of her hand. He followed her all the way back to her flat in the Georgian Quarter but she left him on the doorstep. He sat there watching the moon for some time, and twice he heard Marlowe attempting to buzz him in but he sulkily ignored the sounds of the rattling solenoid in the doorframe until she had to come down in nothing but her white 'Bottom' tee shirt, and she had to drag him into the hallway. He was too drunk to do anything sexual that night but he held her stiflingly close in bed till the morning rays of the sun crowned the belltower of the sandstone cathedral with its solar gold.

In September Corey and Marlowe were engaged, and by now, Corey had moved in with his fiancée at the flat at the Georgian house. An engagement party was thrown there and by 9.30pm the place was almost standing room only as friends of the couple brought along friends and their friends. Jackson, a former boyfriend of Marlowe, cornered her in the kitchen and began to brag about the big art shop he was going to open on Renshaw Street. 'We already have Rennies down in Bold Street though, don't we?' Marlowe reasoned out, sipping a perfectly made dark and stormy courtesy of her friend Amelia.

'Yeah, but there's room for more though,' was Jackson's poor riposte.

Around this time, the girl who had held Corey's attention in the pub appeared; the girl with the amazing blue eyes. She was dressed in some retro pink pea coat and matching pencil skirt combination reminiscent of a Jackie O outfit. Of all the times for her to appear, Corey thought – on the night when his engagement was being celebrated – and yet he felt he just had to go and talk to her – seeing as no one else was chatting to her. She's that beautiful, slim, tall and attractive they probably all think she has a fellah, Corey reasoned. He went over to her anyway and said,

'Hi.'

'Hello Corey,' she said in a strange voice devoid of accent – and how did she know his name? He asked her that. 'I knew you a long time ago, ' was her calm reply, and when she said these words her lips moved in quite an odd way, seemingly out of sync with the utterance. 'My name's Mandy.'

'Pleased to meet you,' Corey replied, and found himself grasping for her hand. Marlowe had smooth hands, but even she had slight traces of raised blue veins in the back of her hands – but Mandy had perfect hands, back and front – not a vein, and – it was hard to see with the lighting – apparently no lines in her palm. All of the fingers of the girl were perfectly straight, and there was no clamminess which *all* hands have to a certain degree – just well, it was hard to explain – there was just the sort of ambient temperature of a plastic knife handle to her hands. The blueness of her eyes was even more breathtaking close up, and although her eyelashes looked false, they really complimented the big eyes. Corey had never seen perfection in the face of a female like this before, not even in a Photoshopped cosmetic ad in one of Marlowe's magazines. Of course, statistically, from the millions of mingers in the world, Corey's street-philosopher friend Fletch used to reason, there had to be some fit people in circulation.

'Please sit down over here,' Corey pushed a drunken semi-conscious stoner lad of about fourteen off the padded yellow Ikea ottoman that Marlow usually meditated on, and the teenager groaned something and got up. 'Sit there, its quieter here too,' Corey said, patting the low seat, and the paragon gracefully parked her pink-clad derriere where he indicated.

'Can I get you a drink?' Corey asked, and there was a turmoil brewing in the back of his mind; he felt lousy because Marlowe would be gutted if she knew how he was feeling about Mandy and yet in his mind he already had Mandy stripped and in bed.

'Babycham, please,' Mandy replied, and she smiled, and that smile of perfect teeth and those cherry red lips did it. That's how shallow Corey was – that smile tipped him over the edge; he now had to make love to her. He knew it was wrong but he was finding that the old adage about forbidden fruit tasting sweeter certainly applied to him.

'I'll just go and see if he we have that in,' he said, and went to the kitchen, where Jackson now had Marlowe cornered, and now he was talking about his vague plans for a virtual studio.

'Ah, babe, come here!' Marlowe shouted to Corey as he looked through the bottles stacked in the fridge.

Corey cussed and then turned to Jackson and said, 'What's Babycham?'

'Eh?' Jackson thinned his eyes and looked Corey up and down sarcastically, before telling him: 'It's a band.'

Clive the Know-all, a spectacled student from next door suddenly spoke in the kitchen doorway with a bottle of Bud in his hand. 'Ah, no, you're thinking of Babyshambles,' he said to a deflated Jackson, and then he turned to Corey and informed him: 'Babycham is a rather light sparkly sort of perry with er, if I remember it rightly, a little baby fawn on the label.'

'Aww,' Marlowe screwed her face up, 'a little fawn?'

'Yes, but do we have it?' Corey asked.

Clive put his bottle down and said, 'Let me have a

look,' and he searched the fridge and then looked around at the crates on the kitchen worktops and the bottles on the chequerboard tiled floor, and shook his head of woolly hair. 'No Babycham here old chap,' he told Corey, but then optimistically added with a smile: 'But I can make some if you like – albeit a very close approximation.'

'Yes, please do,' Corey patted Clive on the back of his corduroy jacket and the student looked about for ad hoc sifters and glasses to mix the ingredients.

'It's all down to ratio and proportion...' he was telling an annoyed Jackson as Corey darted out of the kitchen to rejoin Mandy – who was still not being pestered by any of the red-blooded males or females.

'It's on its way,' Corey knelt by the yellow ottoman on one knee and looked at her pink shoes and her ankles, and then his eyes ran up her leg – right up to her smiling face.

'Hey Corey!' a loud deep voice somehow got through to Corey's ears, even though the party DJ, a vinyl-aficionado named Kyle was blasting out the old Primal Scream hit *Rocks*.

Corey turned and saw Jay, his sister Marianne's ex-husband, standing in the doorway.

'Come in Jay, man!' Corey shouted to him. He had always got on with Jay, a real great conversationalist and freethinker who had taken him on some 'intellectual safaris' as Jay used to call them. He had divorced Marianne after she had shacked up with a self-styled witched named Selena.

Jay grimaced, shook his head and beckoned him out of the room.

To Mandy, Corey said: 'Please excuse me, I won't be

a minute!' And he went to see what Jay wanted. When he reached his former brother-in-law, Jay carefully closed the door and in the hallway, he said to Corey: 'Your sister and that thing she's with [meaning Selena] are using some sort of spell to split you and Marlowe up.'

'What?' laughed Corey, but then he recalled his sister's obsession with witchcraft.

'The things she and her other half do really work, Corey, believe me,' Jay said earnestly. 'Remember the teacher who topped himself?'

Corey recalled the incident. Marianne had had a crush on her English Literature teacher at college, and had tried all sorts of love spells, and when the news of his engagement got out, Marianne asked Selena to kill him; if Marianne couldn't have the teacher, no one else could. Marianne made some plasticine effigy of the teacher and hanged it with a bootlace from a tree branch. Three days later the teacher was found hanged in his garage, and everyone had gone on about how he had seemed so happy with his life before the tragedy and how out of character his suicide was. 'What sort of spell has she used? How do you know she's doing this? How – ' Corey was full of questions.

'Someone in their coven told me,' said Jay, and he reached into his trouser pocket, and then he mumbled something. 'Where is it? I brought something to protect you – but where the hell is it?' He plunged his hand into his inside jacket pocket and shook is head. He couldn't find whatever it was. 'She's spirited the thing away!' he told Corey, wide-eyed, and angry. 'It was a little talisman thing, supposed to counteract – '

'Look, Jay, why don't you come in and have a drink?'

Corey suggested, and tugged at his sleeve.

'No, I've go an early start tomorrow. Listen, if I find that talisman I'll post it through your letterbox, okay?'

'Thanks for being concerned Jay,' Corey told him, 'I'm sorry the way things went with you and Marianne.'

Jay was already at the end of the landing, heading for the stairs. 'I'll post it through in the morning.'

'See you Jay!' Corey called after him, and he thought about what Jay had said. Marianne had always vetted his girlfriends, and he knew she wasn't keen on Marlowe, but how could she split him and Marlowe up? He wondered about this as he pushed open the door, but then he suddenly thought of Mandy. Had she been sent by his witchy sister? Oh, this was getting ridiculous, he thought, and Jay was known to be something of a drama queen; he'd probably exaggerated the whole spell thing. Talismans! What a load of crap.

'Corey!' Clive's head popped out of the kitchen doorway, and as Corey looked over at him he lifted a tumbler of clear liquid. 'Babycham! Freshly made.'

'Wow, thanks, Clive, I owe you one, but could you er, put some of it in a smaller glass? It's for a lady, see?'

'Ah, yes,' Clive returned to the kitchen. 'What you require – and I did see one before – is a little four-ounce champagne glass. There it is!'

That glass – with the alleged freshly-made Babycham – was presented to Mandy, and after all of the trouble Corey went to in procuring the drink, the girl didn't even drink a damned drop of it. She did put the glass to her lips and she plainly pretended to sip it, but not a molecule of it was consumed.

'Tell me,' Corey addressed Mandy, 'How did you

hear about the party?'

'I think some girl told me about it,' was Mandy's fuzzy reply.

'Not a girl called Marianne was it?' Corey asked. He knew he was being paranoid, but he had to ask.

Mandy winked at him, and Corey had never seen a wink like it. When most people wink the closed eyelid had some influence – usually miniscule – on the other eyelid, but Mandy's eyelid closed perfectly and well, almost *mechanically*.

Corey took out his phone and decided it was selfie time. He threw his right arm around Mandy, resting his hand on her right shoulder, and he thrust his other hand high in the air and tilted the phone's camera down at him and his new interest. Mandy looked at the screen when the selfie pic flew up on it.

'Mandy, you are even photogenic - perfect in every way, girl,' Corey said, and he looked about, and saw everyone - except Clive and some girl he was chatting to – was dancing now to Kyle's latest turntable hit: *Agadoo* by Black Lace. Now was the time while everyone was distracted. Corey nuzzled up to Mandy's face and kissed her cheek, and her skin felt very firm. His hand quickly groped her chest and it was smooth – all over. Not a single projecting mammary gland! How odd.

He tore himself away, his heart pounding now, and he felt sick with guilt, but when he reached the kitchen, he saw that Marlowe was still in that corner, and although she was hemmed in because Jackson was leaning against the wall, barring her escape with his arm – she didn't seem too bothered; she actually seemed lost in his eyes.

'What's good for the goose is good for the gander,' Corey muttered, and he quickly turned and hurried back to Mandy. He grasped her hand and almost yanked her off the ottoman. 'Come on,' he said, and looked about at the dancing inebriates. He went into the little spare room where Marlowe's young brother sometimes slept when he stayed over. The bed in there would do fine – but when Corey opened the door he saw two of the partygoers were already on it.

'Sorry! Sorry!' he said, and closed the door. He thought fast. Could he bring himself to do it in his own bed – the one he shared with Marlowe? He swore under his breath after looking at Mandy's beautiful eyes in the subdued light of the hallway. 'Come on!' he said, and he opened the door to the room and saw that the bed was still unmade. There was a make-up bag on that bed, discarded knickers, a sports bra, two coat hangers and a flip flop.

'You *do* want this?' Corey asked Mandy, and she just smiled and seemed blank across the eyes.

He dragged the unit stacked with books and DVDs across the carpeted floor until it was squarely in front of the door, and then he took his trousers off, and as he did, he caught a glimpse of himself in the dresser mirror – and on that mirror there was a printed selfie picture of him and Marlowe, taken in The Walkabout pub. He turned away from it, pushed all that from his mind. He drew a curtain to throw the room into semi-darkness, just so he could try and forget that this was the bed he shared with a girl he had loved. He walked over to Mandy and began to kiss her and run his hand through her hair – and for a moment he thought she had on a wig, for the hair did not feel as silky as

Marlowe's but artificial. He was too turned on now to think about this, and he took off her pea coat, and her white blouse – and then he pushed her onto the bed, and there, as she sat and looked at him with a shocked expression, he removed the rest of her clothes until she was naked. He lay next to her and kissed her neck and before long he was on her, but although he was rearing to go – he could not 'engage' with her – there was no way to!

He gave a little false laugh in the darkness and asked, 'Have you still got your tights on?'

There was no reply, just a sound of sobbing.

'Why are you crying? Mandy? You alright?' Corey got up and he switched on the bedside lamp.

On the bed lay Mandy, as naked as the day she had been made – no sexual organs, not a nipple to be seen.

Corey stood there, overcome with confusion. He swore and asked Mandy what she was, and she threw her perfect hands to her big blue eyes that were now streaming with tears.

'Corey!' came a male voice from behind the bedroom door.

Corey turned, and he saw that door steadily opening, and it must have been pushed by someone who was strong because he was pushing the unit over that had been placed in front of the door as a barricade. Jackson's face came around the door. 'What the f – ' he looked at Corey, standing there in his birthday suit.

Corey covered his manhood with his hands. 'Haven't you ever heard of privacy you cheeky – '

Marlowe's face came round the door and she seemed both shocked and amused when she asked: 'Corey, what are you doing?'

'I can explain,' Corey blabbered, his face crimson. He turned to look at the bed – and saw no one there. No Mandy, and not an item of her clothing either.

Corey now knew Jay had been right – this had to be the work of Marianne – or he was going insane. He checked his mobile and there was the selfie he had taken – of no one but himself. 'What are you supposed to be showing me?' Marlowe asked him, and Corey decided not to tell her. 'No wonder she never drank that Babycham,' he whispered to himself. He discreetly asked some of the partygoers if they recalled the girl in pink on the ottoman, but not one of them did. But surely, she had been real, Corcy thought, because he remembered how Marlowe had seen her in the pub when he had first set eyes on Mandy – but it transpired that Marlowe had seen a redheaded girl with deep majorelle blue eyes – not the light blue eyes Mandy had possessed, so she must have assumed he was looking at the girl with red hair who he faintly recalled. So who was Mandy? Corey eventually confronted his sister Marianne and asked her what she had done, and Marianne's partner Selena eventually told him; she said that Marianne and her had cast a spell – a bona fide spell taken from an old grimoire – so that the very first love of Corey would visit him – and that first love was not a real person at all, but Marianne's doll Mandy. Mandy with the big blue eyes and thick eyelashes – who could shed a tear when she was filled with water and would wink if she was tilted at the right angle. 'Remember her, Corey?' Marianne asked, and she produced the old doll – still in her little pink outfit – from a drawer. Corey recoiled in revulsion at the doll in his sister's hands – something from the innocent days of his early childhood when he would talk to that doll and promise to marry her one day.

'Aww, she remembers *you*, look,' Marianne touched the doll's face and droplets of tears stuck to her fingertip, 'she's crying.'

Corey left the dark parlour of the house shared by his sister and Selena, and as he hurried down the dark hallway, he heard the witches laughing hysterically.

RUN FOR HOME

I *know* from many personal experiences that there is much more to the human mind than the psychologists could ever know, that there are vast untapped powers within us all which could transfigure us and push this troubled world out of the dark ages. Zen Buddhists, Maharishis, and children of a certain age know this profound truth. In my youth I used to unknowingly bilocate – I was seen in two places at once, and never thought it strange. Half asleep one wintry morning, I stupidly closed my eyes as I walked to a corner sweetshop, just to see how far I could make it without vision. I estimated the turning correctly, entered the doorway of the shop, and opened my eyes as I pulled back my parka hood – only to discover I was in a shop which hadn't opened yet. The door was locked and bolted – yet there I was on the premises. The old shopkeeper said he saw me 'come in' and asked me how I did it - to which I shrugged – as I was as baffled as him by the incident. The old man was that impressed he gave me a free Lion Bar.

There are other latent human powers occasionally glimpsed by us dullards.

In the late 1990s, two men, Doug and Ritchie, both

fifty, sat in a café on Bold Street. Spectacled Doug was perusing the *Liverpool Echo*, and Ritchie asked him what he was reading. 'Just looking for my name in the obituaries,' came the grim reply. A confused Ritchie almost smiled. 'Eh?' he said.

'We're dead,' Doug told him, 'and all we need now is for Jenkins the undertaker to come through that door with the pine boxes and the pallbearers. The Grim Reaper has made a clerical error and allowed two corpses to continue walking the earth.'

'You've been like this ever since you turned fifty,' Ritchie told him. Doug said his life was a cop-out; that everything had gone downhill since his twenties. He hankered for the days when he routinely did something so magical and liberating – he would *run*. He would take flight, fleet-footed, racing ahead of his dog on errands, sprinting in the quicksilver of his youth, in his prime when the world was younger, and now he was fat-bound with a creaky closed mind and so utterly reliant on that glorified bath chair of a car to get around. 'I need to run again,' Doug said with such a sorrowful look, and Ritchie came back with: 'Those days my friend, are sadly gone.'

Vivid memories of running in the old neighbourhood haunted the dreams of Doug each night, and someone in those dreams said that just as the summers of the past are recorded as rings within the trunk of a tree, the fire of youth lies within the soul, and each person is like a Russian doll with earlier versions of that person contained within. Doug awoke and told his baffled wife that salvation from obsolescence was at hand, and that day he went out and bought a tracksuit and a pair of trainers.

'You should see the doctor first, love,' Doug's wife advised, but the next morning at dawn he set off, and the milkman helped him home from the end of the street. On the day after that, for inspiration, he drove to his old street in West Derby, and the past returned. He began to jog down Deysbrook Lane, and he heard the jangling glockenspiel melody – "Popeye the Sailor Man" - from an ice cream motor of long ago – and there was old Mrs Harris carrying a bag of washing on her head to the laundrette – but hadn't she died in the 1960s? Doug felt lighter, faster, smaller! Some 900 yards later he came back to the present at the end of Deysbrook Lane; he'd done it! He told his wife and Ritchie and the milkman what had happened and they all worried about Doug. 'Perhaps he's had a mini stroke,' Ritchie wondered out loud, but Doug didn't even hear what he said because he was gazing into space with a weird smile on his face.

'I'm going again in the morning,' Doug gleefully told Ritchie, 'and I may never come back – it's a better place back there.'

And the next day, a man walking his dog came across the body of a boy of about twelve or thirteen at the end of Deysbrook Lane, swathed in a tracksuit that was five sizes too large for him, and the white trainers on his feet looked like oversized clown shoes. When the paramedics arrived, they found the body of a man instead of a boy, but the man with the dog swore he had found a child's body. Doug lay there with a delicate Mona Lisa smile on his face. He'd died of heart failure.

THROUGH THE TIME BARRIER

The age of the mind is one of the most neglected areas in modern psychology, for the mind's inner age does not usually correspond to bodily age, hence, we often see men in their fifties and sixties gawping at girls of eighteen or even making passes at them, and people say, 'He must be insane to think he'd have a chance with her; he's old enough to be her grandfather.' Most of these men gape at much younger females because they feel – mentally - as if they are around their age group – until they look in the cruel mirror of course! The same is also true of some women who go for 'toyboys', only this phenomenon is admittedly a lot less common with females.

Some people will tell you that they feel as if their mind is years, or even decades, younger than their body, and the opposite is also true; many young people often feel older than they are, or act with a maturity that is well in advance of their physical age. This phenomenon was evident in eighteen-year-old Imogen Hayward, a Grassendale girl who opened a second-hand bookshop on Bold Street early in 1984. She looked about sixteen, but felt as if she was about forty. The girl's 39-year-old mother – Amanda – on the other hand, looked a lot younger than she was, and she was often mistaken for Imogen's older sister. Furthermore, Amanda felt as if her mind had stopped aging when she was sixteen, and she was very open-minded and thoroughly modern in her ways, much more so than her daughter. Amanda also had a young voice, and people who talked to her on the telephone often thought they were talking to someone aged about thirteen, whereas Imogen had a very strong and mature-sounding voice.

Early in February 1984, Imogen and her 22-year-old boyfriend Dafyd had finally opened their second-hand bookshop on Bold Street. They had cleaned and decorated the long-unoccupied little shop and fitted shelves and tall bookcases to the walls. The floorboards had been sanded and polished and ruby and black Persian rugs had been laid down here and there, and all of the books had been meticulously laid out on the shelves in subject-groups. Here and there on the chocolate-coloured walls were framed prints of Renoir, and a faint aroma of coffee – which floated in from the makeshift kitchen in the shop's backroom – usually hung in the air. Dafyd had bled the radiators early in the morning and now they were working perfectly to ward off the February cold of grey Bold Street, which wafted in every time the shop door was opened. Dafyd was presently up a ladder outside the shop, stencilling the letters "Imogen's Books" in gold paint on a 9-foot-long board he'd painted with black gloss the day before.

The radio on the shelf behind the counter was usually tuned to BBC Radio 3, as Imogen loved to sit in the shop, immersed in the works of the classical composers as she read books by favourite authors such as Anais Nin, Françoise Sagan, Virginia Woolf and Émile Zola. But on this day – the Tuesday afternoon of February 14 – Valentine's Day – Imogen's young-minded mum had volunteered to help out at the shop, and she had tuned the aforementioned radio to Steve Wright on Radio 1, and Nik Kershaw's latest offering - *Wouldn't It Be Good?* was blaring out of the radio.

'Ah, I love this,' Amanda said, clicking her fingers and doing a little slow twisting dance to the music, and a hippie in the Mind, Body and Spirit section turned around and looked at her over the top of his bifocals with a nettled expression.

'Mum, turn that rubbish off!' Imogen snarled out the side of her mouth.

'Oh alright, killjoy, ' Amanda said sourly, and she turned the volume right down. She then went to make three cups of tea for herself, Imogen and Dafyd. They all usually had tea and chocolate digestives or Kit-Kats at this time – 3.30pm. Imogen cast an annoyed glance at her disruptive mum as she pushed the curtain aside and went into the back room to make the tea, and she retuned the radio to Radio 3 just in time to hear Vivaldi's Concerto No. 4 in F minor – "Winter", which was rather appropriate on such a bleak February afternoon. A few minutes later, that radio was subjected to some sort of interference. It buzzed and hissed, and then came the voice of an American-sounding man singing *Shake, Rattle and Roll*. Imogen turned the tuning control on the radio and could not find BBC Radio 3. Instead, she heard nothing but old-fashioned swing music of the sort Glen Miller played decades back. She switched the radio off and asked

Dafyd to have a look at it.

Amanda was gone for an inordinate amount of time, and so Imogen left the counter and went to see why her mum was taking so long to make the tea. She went to the entrance of the backroom kitchen and threw back the curtain - and there was her mother, locked in a passionate embrace as she kissed a young man dressed in the attire of a 1950s Teddy Boy: lemon yellow jacket with black velvet trim, drainpipe trousers, suede crepe-soled "brothel creepers" – and a potent pongy aftershave which gave Imogen the sniffles. This young stranger had an enormous quiff of black oily hair, long thick black sideburns and a cheeky, handsome but impudent-looking face.

'Mum?' Imogen gasped, framed by the doorway, and her mother had to wrench herself from the lad's pressing lips before she stammered, 'It's not what you think; he's older than me. Don't tell your Dad!'

'See you later alligator!' the young Ted sung to Amanda, and he left the room and went into the backyard, making himself scarce. Imogen was flabbergasted and a little disappointed in her mother, who had now turned a nice shade of tea rose pink. Every word of what follows is true, as bizarre as it sounds. Amanda explained: 'That man you just saw is Frankie Ryden, and he was born in 1936, right? Now, I was born in 1945, so he's nine years my senior.'

'What are you talking about?' Imogen shook her head, perplexed, and simply unable to take in what her mother was saying. 'He looked my age, mum; why are you carrying on with him?'

Amanda straightened her disarrayed clothes. 'Love, he's from 1956, and I know that sounds far-fetched, but it's true – I've been back there with him. Don't tell your father, please.'

'Just tell me the truth, mum.' Imogen said, putting the kettle on, and her mother replied, 'Look, that break-in we had at this shop a month ago, was carried out by Frankie, and do you remember how we found the money from the till-float on the floor? That was because it was modern decimal money – it was no good to Frankie in 1956, so he left it. I caught him in here a week later, that night I came down here because the alarm had gone off, and when I said I'd call the police, he just laughed and asked me out. He had me pinned to the wall!'

Imogen didn't believe a word of it, and so her mother took the girl into the back yard, to a dark corner, where she touched the bricks in such a way that it seemed as if she was looking for the entry to some secret passage. 'He comes through here – damn, it's closed now, but listen!' And all Imogen could hear was a faint low-frequency humming sound, reminiscent of the noise a fridge makes at night, which proved nothing.

Amanda sighed and shook her head. 'I don't know how it happens, but there's like a hole here, and you can go back in time, Imogen, and I swear on your life that I am not making this up.'

Imogen was lost for words; she could now see a raw love-bite at the base of her mother's neck near to the collar bone, and the sight of it unsettled her – made her feet ill. The girl had seen younger men flirt and make passes at her mother in the past, for she was undoubtedly attractive and did not look anywhere near the age of thirty-nine, but this was different – she had kissed her admirer – and Imogen felt her stomach turn as she wondered if her mother had gone as far as having sex with this Frankie.

Amanda gripped her daughter's forearm, looking into her eyes as if she knew what she was thinking, and she resumed her strange narrative. 'If this hadn't happened to me and *you* were telling me the things I am now telling you, *I* wouldn't believe it either, but its true love,' she said, and was met with a brimming silence.

'Well, the sign's done,' Dafyd announced softly as he entered the makeshift kitchen with a tin of gold paint in one hand and a paintbrush wrapped in a rag in the other. His words did not evoke a reaction from the mother and daughter, and he instantly sensed something tense was hanging in the air between them. He put the paint can down and placed his fingers on the handle of the tin kettle on the gas stove and noted it was still cold. Amanda immediate filled the kettle with water in the big white marble sink and went about making the tea.

'I don't know what's up with the radio, by the way,' Dafyd admitted, 'but it's as if some pirate station is playing all stuff from the Fifties – nostalgic stuff. I tuned it to the FM band and it's deadly quiet; quite odd.'

As he said these words there was a loud blast of music from the radio, which made the browsers of the shop and Dafyd, Imogen and Amanda jump. It was *Relax* by Frankie Goes to Hollywood.

Imogen rushed out of the kitchen and grappled with the radio. She switched it off and apologised to her clientele.

On the following day, Amanda went missing for three days, and returned with love-bites on her neck. Her husband threatened divorce unless she stopped seeing her "fancyman". Imogen had not mentioned the Teddy boy but her father had certainly noticed the tell-tale lovebites on his wife's neck and breasts.

Amanda told her daughter she was thinking of going back in time with Frankie for good, and Imogen began to really worry about the state of her mum's mind. She told Dafyd about her strange 'fantasy' and he told Imogen to talk her mother into seeing her doctor. No one had linked the claims of the time-hopping Teddy boy with the way the radio had started playing backdated music that afternoon, and the timeslips of Bold Street were virtually unheard of in that day and age.

Imogen recalled her mother going missing for weeks at a time, and on one very memorable occasion Amanda turned up at the shop sporting a bouffant hairdo and she was dressed in a pencil skirt and tight pink sweater, and on her feet she wore a pair of black stilettos. This time, Amanda produced a purse from an elegant handbag and showed her doubting daughter crisp new ten-shilling and pound notes, as well as farthings, half crowns and other long obsolete currency.

'I've given him the big e,' Amanda said, cryptically, and Imogen asked what she meant and also asked her mother where she had been.

'I've given him the elbow, Frankie,' she said in a broken voice. 'Caught him with someone; I've finished with him.'

When Amanda went home, her husband George

brought a friend from Liverpool University to see her; he was Eric, an animal behaviourist who studied the mental processes of rats, dogs and monkeys; in essence, an animal psychologist. George had told Eric about his wife's affairs and of her bizarre explanations, and Eric was expected to psychoanalyse her to get to the bottom of Amanda's strange complex. He fired question after question at Amanda and began to jot down her laconic replies in a notebook until she swore at him, told him she was not insane and ordered him out of her house. Eric quickly left.

Amanda eventually stopped going to her daughter's bookstore and Frankie appeared at the shop several times, always asking for Amanda, and Imogen always told him to get lost. On one occasion Imogen and Dafyd saw the Ted literally vanish in the backyard, and believing Frankie was some sinister ghost, Imogen had the shop blessed by a priest and even called out a medium (who could not uncover the reasons behind the 'visitations'). Frankie was seen twice after this by Dafyd and several customers at the shop, and then he never showed up again. The bookstore was not a success and closed less than a year later. Many years later, Amanda read of the many accounts of timeslips in Bold Street detailed in my books and also in the local press, and she got in touch with me and described her experiences at the shop. She gave me the full name and address of Frankie Ryden and described his family and friends and even the cinema he had taken her to and what film had been playing there at the time, and all of this information was subsequently confirmed by examining records and the entertainment columns in archived newspapers on microfilm. Frankie had passed away from an illness in the 1960s, I discovered, and, if Amanda's story is true, it would have been amazing if Frankie would have visited the shop in 1984 in his older years, but the fact that he did not hinted to me that he had died before then. It would seem then, that Bold Street is riddled with 'holes in time' and that one of them was possibly in the backyard of a shop. I have been inundated with all sorts of accounts of timeslips across this city, and obviously only have room to feature some of the more intriguing ones. I have witnessed quite a few timeslips and I know from first-hand experience that there is a barrier of disbelief you pass through when you find that time has somehow reverted to some earlier or later period; I liken it to the mental state the astronauts experienced when they landed on the moon; it is a feeling of unreality, that your senses are somehow being fooled, as the situation is something so far removed from our usual day-to-day existence. Some people simply accept a shift in time, whereas others border on freaking out, mostly because they fear they will not return to their own time, which is understandable.

Early in 2015 I received two more intriguing accounts of timeslips concerning Bold Street, a thoroughfare which (as regular readers of my books will already know) has developed quite a reputation for the transportation of unsuspecting pedestrians into the past and future. After studying the "Bold Street timeshift phenomenon" for many years, I am convinced that a wormhole – the glib scientific term for a shortcut through spacetime – is active in very close proximity to the Lyceum, that beautiful colonnaded gem built in Georgian times. In January 2015 I received a letter from an eminent historian and biographer, telling me of a very strange incident concerning Birkenhead-born F. E. Smith (1872-1930), legendary barrister, Lord Chancellor, outspoken MP, and close friend to Winston Churchill. In December 1908, Smith was a barrister at the Assizes, St George's Hall, the K.C. in a high-profile defamation case. Around this time, Smith was invited to the Lyceum, which was then a library celebrating its 150th anniversary. At some point during the visit, F. E. Smith went missing, and despite a thorough search of the Lyceum, could not be found. Suspecting foul play to be the cause of Smith's absence, the police were called for, but the barrister suddenly reappeared, apparently looking pale and disoriented. Smith was renowned for his wit and quick tongue, yet he was unable to give an account of where he had been during his absence, but years later he confided to several close friends, including Churchill, that he had "stepped into a future age" at the Lyceum, and told of "futuristic marvels" including people flying about like birds, gigantic buildings of glass, and police armed like soldiers. Britain was at war with some foreign power but all the fighting was being done by machines, and Smith was told this by a man who revealed he was 124 years of age and in his prime. Churchill advised Smith to keep quiet about the incident but in 1930, the year he died, Smith published a book called *The World in 2030* which contained many uncannily accurate predictions. In January 2015 I also interviewed a lady named Kelly, who, in 1994, was sitting on the steps of the Lyceum at 3am one morning, singing at the top of her voice in a drunken state after a night out at a club, when she was waylaid by two very strange men – dressed in top hats and old-fashioned clothes. These outdated men both dragged 18-year-old Kelly backwards up the stairs and down an alleyway which, according to Kelly, 'shouldn't have been there'. One of the men called the other "Birdy" as they debated whether or not they should keep Kelly, and during the hurried discussion the girl saw what seemed to be the gaslit Bold Street of long ago with horse-drawn hansom cabs and cobbled roads. Kelly was eventually taken back to 1997, and "Birdy", who looked about 19 years of age, seemed fascinated by Kelly's clothes, which might have seemed outrageous to him. 'I have observed you on many occasions passing here,' Birdy told Kelly, and seemed besotted by her, but she found him creepy and afterwards avoided going near Bold Street after dark, as she believed the top-hatted men to be ghosts. 'Ghosts' with descriptions matching those of Birdy and his companion have been seen day and night near the Lyceum on many occasions, and I don't think they are the usual phantoms at all – but curious Victorians who have merely stumbled onto the Lyceum time-portal, which gives access to our era, as well as a future Liverpool. Although Bold Street seems to dominate the timeslips phenomenon locally, there are many other parts of this region I will now touch upon, and the following stories have all been reported to me by people I have found to be level-headed and rather down to earth individuals. Take the case of a Bootle-born man named Bob Stewart; at the time of writing he is a 37-year-old accountant who now lives in London, but back in the spring of 1985, when Bob was just seven, he had a number of weird experiences which would give him recurring nightmares for over twenty years. Here's his very strange story.

One sunny but breezy morning in March 1985, a 7-year-old boy named Bobby Stewart was gazing out the bay window of his home when he saw the arrival of his eccentric Uncle Colin in his viridian-coloured Morris Marina. Bobby's dad didn't like his brother Colin because he had made a lot of money down south and disowned his accent, but Bobby loved him. Uncle Colin brought him sweets and told funny and exciting tales. On this day, Colin tried to persuade the Stewart family to have a picnic in Derby Park, and only Bobby took up the unusual offer. Colin gave the boy a real cricket ball of all things, and the boy was throwing this at a tree as Colin sipped his Pimms and clear lemonade and nibbled salmon pate and cucumber sandwiches - when something inexplicable took place. A mist from the Fernhill Road side of the park rolled towards Bobby, and when it cleared, he could not see his uncle, and the sky was now darker, and the sun had changed position in the sky so that it now seemed to be rising. No birds were singing, and this dawn was so silent, it was as if the entire city of Liverpool had died in the night. All about was as silent as the moon, and then Bobby saw it – a towering scarlet figure, moving mechanically – a robot, about 7 feet tall. It was about 100 yards away and headed towards him down a path, and now he could hear its rhythmical thudding feet as it walked with a very peculiar machine-like gait. The frightened boy heard hissing sounds, as if the robot was perhaps partly hydraulic in its workings. Bobby turned and ran, and he suddenly noticed the sun return to its original position in the sky before everything had changed and simultaneously the faint hubbub of the traffic outside the park could be heard. Bobby found his uncle sitting on a gingham tablecloth spread out on the grass near a tree, and the boy excitedly told Colin about the robot but his uncle merely smiled, probably dismissing the far-fetched account as a figment of a feverish young imagination.

Weeks later, several other people saw the robot in the park, and one witness, a 17-year-old boy named Phil, said the mechanical man had the words "Mike" written on his chest in white. It was unfortunately on 1 April when Bobby had another encounter with "Mike" when he saw the weird crimson automaton standing between the gateposts of the park, and this time a stray dog was barking at the robot. Bobby could see that the word on the breast-plate of the entity was "mycop" – not Mike, but then the boy seemed to pass out. When he came to and claimed he had encountered the giant robot, most people thought Bobby was either an April Fool prankster or had been the victim of one, and after a few more alleged sightings of the humanoid machine, it was seen no more. Bobby suffered terrible nightmares about the robot for decades, until he volunteered to be hypnotically regressed by a psychotherapist who wanted to unearth the repressed trauma. First, Bobby was put in a trance by the hypnotist, and asked to read the make of a watch he always wore as a boy. 'Timex,' Bobby correctly replied. This was done as a test to see how effective the hypnotic recall was working. Bobby was also asked to describe the television programmes he had watched that day and his answers were checked against newspaper TV listings for the date concerned – and Bobby was again found to have accurate recall. Then the hypnotist asked him what had happened that day when he saw the robot, and Bobby began to tremble. He said the mist had enveloped him again, and this time he could see dead bodies everywhere, covered in flies. The bodies looked black because there were so many flies coating them, but when the robot picked these rotting corpses of men, women and children up, the flies would scatter and reveal the ghastly decomposing carcasses. Bobby could also see that all of the buildings in the area were in ruins, but he could not identify them all. The red robot and many other ones were picking the corpses up and throwing them into what looked like huge bin wagons, which seemed to pulverise the cadavers to pulp. Seeing and hearing the bodies being crushed and the bodily fluids spraying out made Bobby nauseous. Now and then the robots spoke in slightly distorted, over-amplified voices that sounded Russian. Something terrible had evidently happened to Liverpool; it looked like the aftermath of either a nuclear attack or a natural disaster, such as a massive earthquake, Bobby reasoned, and he woke up in tears – but after the hypnotic regression session he never again had nightmares about "Mike". Incidentally, the word "mycop" Bobby had seen on the robot means "rubbish" in Russian, so perhaps the mechanoid was some futuristic Russian-manufactured refuse collector that had been programmed to 'clean up' the streets of decomposing dead bodies. If so, did Bobby somehow see the aftermath of some future apocalyptic war waged by Russia? It would surely have to be some time in the far-off future as modern robotics technology (as far as I know anyway) does not seem too capable of producing the type of robot Bobby encountered. Hopefully, this is a future that can be avoided if we take this case as a warning.

In the summer of 2014, the brother of an elderly priest who recently passed away told me a very intriguing story which certainly fits in with this chapter on timeslips. Here is what I gleaned from the conversation with the late priest's brother, along with my own research into what was told to me.

On Tuesday March 29, 1960, in the middle of the afternoon, a series of mysterious explosions were heard in the skies over Liverpool. *The Liverpool Echo* and several other newspapers later reported on the mysterious bangs which shook houses at their foundations and sent soot billowing down chimneys. The shockwave from one of these mystery blasts resulted in a huge neon light falling onto two office workers at a building in the city centre. That same afternoon, an Irish Catholic priest we shall call Father Timothy was in Liverpool city centre, walking down Paradise Street, on his way to see a senior priest at the Sailor's Home, when he got the shock of his life. Walking towards him was a couple in their early twenties – and they weren't wearing a stitch of clothing. The woman had dark blue hair and tattooed arms, and the man had what could only be described by the priest as a 'mushroom-shaped hairstyle' with circumferential stripes of brown and green in it. Before the shocked priest averted his gaze he thought the man also had a green-tinted van dyke. And then Father Timothy saw that everyone else around him was nude, and the buildings had changed into futuristic edifices of glass. Flying silently along in this ultra-modern setting were vehicles which resembled buses, only they had three decks, and two of these flying vehicles went through openings, high above street level, in a building, which from descriptions given by Father Timothy, seem very similar to the John Lewis building in today's Liverpool One shopping complex. The priest realised he was attracting the attention of the *au naturel* citizens – probably because he was the only one wearing clothes. The priest ran off and found himself in Manesty's Lane, and now everything looked normal again – they were all wearing clothes!

Most people had not heard of timeslips in 1960, and Father Timothy later told a senior priest about the strange incident and asked him if he thought it was some form of 'temptation of the flesh' by the Devil. After a long thoughtful pause, the wise old priest shook his head and talked of the nature of time, and said: 'We know so little about the workings of time. In Psalm 90 it says a day in heaven would last 1000 years to us.' The wise old holy man also talked of the well-documented case of Honi ha-M'agel, a Jewish 'miracle worker' of the First century BC who fell into some sort of sleep and woke up 70 years later thinking minutes had passed. Over tea and biscuits in the presbytery, the well-read priest also discussed Hindu mythology and the story of King Raivata Kakudmi, who met the creator Lord Brahma and discovered another scale of time. When Kakudmi returned to earth, around 400 million years had passed.

'And Isaiah,' Father Timothy suddenly recalled the story from the Old Testament, 'when the angel took him to heaven for two hours, he later discovered 32 years had passed by on earth.'

'Time dilation, Einstein called it,' said the old priest, and he advised: 'but I'd keep quiet about it if I were you.' And Father Timothy did for fifty years.

A former airline pilot I shall refer to as Philip told me how, one December back in the early 1960s, he was flying a Cambrian Airways Vickers Viscount 701 from Cork to Liverpool, and as the plane passed over the north-western tip of Wirral, Philip and several other members of the aircrew – as well as a few passengers – saw something flying five-hundred feet below the turboprop plane: it looked like a giant prehistoric bird. Philip estimated the creature's wingspan was almost equal to that of the Viscount – around 90 feet! Even the Quetzacoatlus – the biggest prehistoric bird –only possessed a wingspan of 36 feet – but the grey bat-like monster flying eastwards over northern Wirral – towards Liverpool - had a wingspan two and a half times that. Philip lost sight of the backdated reptilian bird as he turned the plane towards Speke, but it would seem that the same terrifying pterosaur was later seen from the ground in several places within a radius of about a hundred miles. On a glacial December morning in 1965, 32-year-old Mrs Stevens visited Jones the Chemists on Heswall's Pensby Road to pick up some cough medicine for her young son, and in the pharmacy she overheard two elderly ladies (who were waiting for their prescriptions to be dispensed) talking about a 'giant bird' that had been seen over the area. Mrs Stevens smiled at the silly gossip, and she purchased the cough syrup, then went to The Rainbow newsagents next door, and once again she heard two customers - this time middle-aged men -

talking about a 'big bird' that had been seen diving down out of the sky over the golf course. When Mrs Stevens was on her way home from the shops, the sun started to break through as a wind from Liverpool Bay cleared the clouds. When she was about 200 yards from her detached house in the suburbs of Heswall, Mrs Steven was startled by the huge flitting shadow that passed over her and the entire street; something as big as a plane had just flown silently across the blue sky like a glider, but something told Mrs Stevens it had not been something manmade at all. With a mounting sense of trepidation she looked up and saw gigantic and fearsome-looking bird of some sort with a pointed head and a massive beak with rows of teeth set in it. It was circling her. Mrs Stevens felt her legs turn to jelly as she tried to walk on, and then she heard an ear-splitting shriek on high as the jaws of the demonic dinosaur opened wide. With legs which now felt numb with terror, Mrs Stevens found herself trotting to her house, and not another soul was anywhere to be seen – not a neighbour or a single passer-by. She reached the front door, fumbled with the key in the lock, and then once she had stepped into the hall, she shut the door and bolted it. She ran into the lounge, panting, and listened. Had the thing gone? Then she heard a clatter on the roof above, and the tell-tale angular shadow of the bird was cast onto the back-garden. The weird quivering shadow covered the lawn, flower beds and the greenhouse. The thing was roosting on the roof. Then the shadow flitted away – but less than a minute later the huge pointed beak of the chilling cretaceous creature tapped at the lounge window, and Mrs Stevens thought the pane was going to come crashing in because of the force with which it was struck. She got on her hands and knees and crawled under the table in the dining room and prayed for the thing to go away. She wondered if she should make a dash from the house but felt certain that the giant bird would swoop down on her, and she recalled the creatures long jaws rimmed with those razor teeth. She recalled the telephone! It had only just been installed and Mrs Stevens decided to alert the police to this bizarre but deadly winged animal. She crawled from under the table and got up, and she could now hear the thing screeching as it beat its wings. She dialled 999 and the operator asked her what service she required. Instead of just saying: 'Police,' Mrs Stevens told the operator of a situation which would have been very far-fetched – and suspiciously implausible to say the least. 'A giant bird is attacking my house!' Mrs Stevens told the bemused emergency services operator.

'A giant bird?' the woman asked with a trace of sarcasm in her voice. 'How big is it?'

'I don't know, but it could be hundreds of feet across, I really can't say,' Mrs Stevens said in a stammering, nervous voice. 'It's got a pointed head and it was peeping through the window at me!'

'A pointed head?' the operator faded for a second and seemed to have placed her hand over the microphone, perhaps to consult a colleague – or to snigger. She came back on and asked, 'And you haven't been drinking or anything?'

'No I have not!' Mrs Stevens recoiled, her fear giving way to anger at the bureaucratic rigmarole. 'It's real! A huge bird!'

'Can I have your name and address please?' the

operator asked, and when Mrs Stevens supplied the requested details, the operator said, 'Wasting police time and abusing the emergency services is a very serious offence Mrs Stevens.'

'Please send someone! Please!' Mrs Stevens yelled as she heard a tremendous crash in the garden. She threw down the telephone and ran to the front door, then tried to open it but recalled that she'd put the bolt on. She took it off, but then decided not to go out in case that thing just picked her up in its beak and flew off with her. She was so confused and afraid. She slammed the door and hid in the cupboard under the stairs. About half an hour later, Mr Stevens came home and found his wife hiding in that cupboard, and got the shock of his life when he found her cowering there in tears. He had come home earlier because his boss had taken a funny turn and had been admitted to hospital. He didn't believe his wife's story, and said she had probably seen a large kite, and that triggered a huge argument. His wife took him to the back garden, and something had produced narrow deep holes in the lawn, and the greenhouse was leaning onto the fence, as if something powerful had nudged it. Even more telling were the missing slates on his roof; they were found in a garden at the end of the street. I have many further reports of what seems to have been the same bird flying around the Great Orme, and even one sighting off Southport. There was also a spate of sightings of the same type of bird over Yorkshire in the 1980s. A timeslip is the only theory that might explain the presence of the prehistoric-looking bird over Heswall that December day in the early 1960s, and there are people in Wirral and other parts of the

North West who can still remember seeing the alarming form of the ancient winged reptilian as it glided through the skies. The spectacle of such a giant terrifying bird in Anglo-Saxon times might have been responsible for the legends of dragons and other monsters which are to be found across the British Isles. A cave once existed on the shores of the Mersey which was said to be the home of the Runcorn Dragon hundreds of years ago, and for all we know, this beast might have been a dinosaur which had strayed through a hole in the fabric of space-time.

If a timeslip is the cause of the reappearance of a winged animal that became extinct millions of years ago, then perhaps our planes can sometimes fly into these openings into the past with the end result being the inexplicable disappearance of aircraft, and there certainly have been many strange cases of planes apparently vanishing into thin air during their flights. Take the case of Flight G-AKBL, a Miles Messenger aircraft piloted by Captain Matthews-Naper of County Meath, one of Ireland's most able and respected airmen. The Miles Messenger plane left Northolt in North-West London at 6.40pm on Wednesday 1 April 1953 and was due to land at Dublin at 10pm, but when the staff at the control tower at Dublin Airport contacted Matthews-Naper ten minutes before his scheduled arrival, he told them he did not know where he was. He did not know his geographical position and seemed confused, and then contact was lost. The fate of Matthews-Naper and his plane are unknown, and nothing more was heard of him again. By November he was presumed dead, and his last will and testament was read out. There were theories that the experienced pilot had crashed into the sea west of the Isle of Man, but not a stick of debris was ever found. This mid-air vanishing act is just one of many in this area, but there have been many other inexplicable disappearances in the skies of the world.

I sincerely believe a timeslip is the only theory that explains the presence of the prehistoric-looking bird. Here's another local case where another time period *seemingly* intrudes into the present, although I'm not entirely sure that this account should be included within this chapter; see what you think.

One afternoon in early December 2014, a 34-year-old Roby man named Brian Greene set out to visit his mother Delia, who lives in the Widnes area. It was typical British December weather, with a strong hail-laden wind buffeting his Nissan Qashqai. He joined the M62 and turned on the radio to listen to Juice FM. He passed through Junction 6 of the M62 in the centre lane, passing beneath the bridge of the M57, heading into the Tarbock interchange when the sun suddenly broke through - and a strange silence filled the car. The radio had gone stone dead, and for a few seconds Brian couldn't even hear the hum of the Nissan's engine or the rhythm of the windscreen wipers. He purposely coughed to see if he'd gone deaf, and suddenly, the nightmare at the back of every driver's mind became reality right before his eyes. Brian's ears popped, and the engine sound returned, and he could now hear the wipers, but still the radio remained dead. An alizarin-red Ford Focus tailgated him and then zipped alongside him in the left lane, scraping the side of the Nissan. The Focus then shot forwards, about to overtake, when the juggernaut in the slow lane suddenly veered into the middle lane, knocking the Focus aside as if it was a toy Dinky car. Brian stared death in the face in that instant because the Focus in his path was now upside down and sliding along trailing sparks, granulated glass and what looked like blood. In a manoeuvre like something out of a Bond film, Brian somehow reflexively swerved the Nissan and avoided the inverted Focus, but he was not out of danger yet, because that thundering juggernaut had tried to move back into the slow lane, and hit another vehicle – it looked like a purplish Volkswagen Golf hatchback, and that car was now rolling along on its sides throwing glass and metal - and its front tyre – into the air. Brian went ice cold as he took his car between the Focus, which had snow slammed into the posts of the central reservation, and the rolling Golf. He looked back as he passed between them and saw that the juggernaut had now toppled onto its left side after the impact and moments later Brian saw the flash in his rear view mirror and actually felt the faint heat as the mammoth of the motorway burst into flames and vomited up billowing black clouds speckled with orange embers. He was not a religious man, but Brian said, 'Oh thank you Lord,' over and over, and he slowed and manoeuvred into the middle lane and kept glancing in the rear view mirror at the carnage behind him.

Juice FM suddenly blasted out of the speakers of the car and he jumped and thumbed the volume button. Hail battered the windscreen again, and became so heavy, Brian could no longer see the flames of the HGV. Brian intended to report the crash and the collision with the red Ford Focus at Widnes Police

Station on Milton Lane, but before he could get there, he pulled over and took a look at the left side of his vehicle – and saw there was not a single scratch there. He looked the Nissan over and there was not a dent or a minor scrape to be seen. Then came the first hint that Brian had seen no ordinary accident on the M62, because a friend he had known since his schooldays – a man named Paul Morley – pulled up alongside him on his way to a roadside café. Paul had just come down the M62, and when Brian asked: 'Haven't they blocked the eastbound yet?' Paul returned a baffled look and asked him why it would be blocked. Brian told him about the two car smash and the overturned juggernaut, and Paul raised his eyebrows and assured him he had not seen the aftermath of any crash when he had come through Junction 6.

'You can't have come through that junction, then,' Paul told him, and when Brian raised his voice and insisted he had narrowly missed death in a horrific three-vehicle incident, Paul enraged him by suggesting that he'd had what is known as a 'microsleep'. 'I've had them myself,' Paul told his red-faced friend, 'you actually drop off for a few seconds and dream up all sorts, and then – '

'I did not drop off,' Brian barked, seeing spots before his eyes from mounting blood pressure now, 'I was wide awake and there *was* a horrible crash! I saw blood! People must have died.'

Paul calmed his agitated friend down and persuaded him to come into the café for a coffee. They sat at a table, and Brian called his wife Lyndsey and asked her if there had been any news about a major accident on the M62. Lyndsey had been listening to the radio and had heard nothing in the past hour, and so she consulted Google and the BBC News website – but there was no news about any incidents on the M62 motorway. Brian did not mention being involved in the crashes as he knew Lyndsey was a real worrier. Paul asked Brian to describe the vehicles involved, and Brian recalled that the juggernaut had been royal blue with a red stripe along it but he had not seen any logo or firm name upon it. He then described the red Ford Focus and the purplish Volkswagen Golf. He also mentioned the strange silence in the car which preceded the motorway carnage and the way the radio went dead – as well as the sudden change in the weather, from heavy hail, to a sunny clear sky, back to a downpour of hail again.

'It doesn't make sense, mate,' Paul said, with a look which suggested he was worried about his friend's mental well-being; Brian could read this in the face of his old chum. 'And there were no marks from the Ford Focus on your vehicle,' Paul added, 'which is odd isn't it?'

'But I saw it; it happened,' Brian said, gripping the coffee mug hard, 'I was wide awake. Why would I make something up like that?'

Reassuringly, Paul slowly nodded and said, 'I've known you for twenty-five years mate, and I know when you're telling the truth, and I don't doubt you saw something, but I can't explain it.'

'What do you think I saw, Paul?' Brian knew his friend was pretty clever, and must have formed a theory about this. 'You think its something a bit "out there" don't you?'

Paul sighed and shrugged. 'Maybe – and this is a big

maybe, pal – maybe it was a premonition. Perhaps the next time you're on that motorway you should take extra care near that junction.'

In late February 2015, Brian Greene was travelling along the M62 with his wife Lyndsey beside him. It was unusually sunny and he was taking her to her sister's home in Widnes. They were chatting when they passed under the bridge at Junction 6 of the M62, when suddenly a red Ford Focus approached from behind, and came a bit too close to Brian's Nissan. He froze, because in the slower lane there was a dark blue juggernaut with a red stripe on. Brian shocked his wife by accelerating like a bat out of hell into the fast lane to get away from the red car. 'Oh my God, Brian, what are you playing at?' Lyndsey screamed, as Brian did eighty. Brian looked into the mirror and saw the Focus far behind swerving recklessly around cars. The strange feeling increasingly grew in Brian - that if he had not got out of that car's way - he and Lyndsey – and the drivers of a few more vehicles would have all been dead by now.

Was this all down to some premonition of a multiple crash on the M62 or did Brian experience a timeslip that wintry afternoon? It really is hard to say.

The aforementioned accounts are just a small fraction of the stories I get about slips in time from readers, and hopefully in the future I will be able to devote an entire book to the subject. You will find a few more timeslips tales further in this book, and you will also find stories which seem to suggest that our timeline of reality has many parallel versions which seem to exist alongside this one, and in a way this optimistically hints that all of the various outcomes of our lives are set in stone, but there are countless stones upon which our destinies are inscribed upon, which means we may really have free will after all, and we *can* choose our predestined fate to a certain extent.

HUGO

The following strange and disturbing story was told to me a few years back, and it's hard to provide a rational explanation for the incidents mentioned in this account. The case to me is a stark reminder that between our current understanding of the workings of the universe and the true nature of reality there is still a gulf as vast as the light years of interstellar space which separate our Solar System from the nearest star. 'Popular science' stars such as Professor Brian Cox paint a smug picture in the mind of the TV viewer which gives the reassuring impression we know everything about the universe, when in fact we know less than 1% of the cosmos and its mind-boggling stretches of time and space. When we take this humbling ignorance into consideration, stories such as the following seem even more frightening, because they hint that there are forces in existence which we know nothing of, and some of these forces are mischievous and like to toy with us mere mortals, while others are positively evil, and the entity in this tale belongs to the latter category. It strikes me as some metaphysical opportunist that derives sadistic pleasure out of assaulting people, namely a particular female. Such person-centred hauntings are more common than you think, and in my experience, is one of the worst types of paranormal persecution.

One sunny May morning in 1974, about a quarter of an hour before noon, a beautiful redhead of nineteen named Julie Colmane left the shop she was working in on Liverpool's Lord Street and went with her 22-year-old co-worker Mary Jones to have an early lunch at the restaurant over Woolworths in nearby Church Street. The shop the girls worked for closed half day today, it being Wednesday, and the boss had let them go earlier than normal because he had to pick his wife up from a clinic at noon.

As the young ladies were about to enter "Woollies" Julie suddenly let out what sounded like a muffled cry – a sort of strangled yelp – and Mary turned to see her fall backwards in a very strange way – almost in slow-motion, as if an invisible man was laying her down in a careful manner. Julie started to scream and kick as she lay on her back on the pavement, and her arms began to windmill as she threw punches randomly. A man of about thirty went to her help and tried to pick her up but she slapped him accidentally as she threw her arms in the air. 'Is she having a fit?' an old man wearing a tweed cap and a dark long coat asked, halting at the scene.

'Julie! What's the matter?' Mary asked, in shock at the strange situation.

'He found me!' Julie said to her concerned workmate, and again something seemed to muffle her voice. Her lips seemed to be pressed against glass, and she couldn't speak or get up.

'She hit me,' the would-be Samaritan who had been accidentally slapped by Julie told the growing circle of bystanders, and he got up. 'Someone should call the police or tell *them* in there,' he said, nodding to the interior of Woolworths.

'Someone help her, she's having a fit,' said an old woman who put down her shopping bags and tried to kneel beside Julie. 'Ooh, I can't get down,' she said, and seemed embarrassed and annoyed.

'I'll go and get an ambulance,' a well-dressed man of fifty announced, and went to a telephone box further up the street.

Julie Colmane was suddenly lifted up from the pavement, even though her body was rigidly straight, and her maxi skirt, which had been down by her ankles, was also being lifted – all on its own. Everyone present could see her brown stockings and garters – and her underwear. Julie screamed and lashed out again, and then she was thrown backwards about six feet and there were exclamations of surprise and horror from the crowd – which was now choking the right entrance to the famous store. At this time, the council had placed huge white-painted concrete tubs along that part of Church Street with flowers in, and these tubs were about five feet in diameter. Julie was thrown into one of these tubs, and as she landed on her back, she shouted out, 'Help! Someone help me please! Get *him* off! Get him off!'

And then she was apparently pinned down by something, and a man who reached out into the tub to grab Julie's hand received a blow to his face which sent his spectacles flying from his head with such force, the glasses broke on the ground about twelve feet away. Some said something unseen had inflicted the blow, whereas others said Julie had kicked him in the face with her platform shoe.

As the crowd looked on, they saw Julie with her legs

wide open, and the concrete tub she was in was rocking in a rhythmical manner – as if something was making love to her.

The ambulance arrived on Church Street, and so did the police, and in the confusion, someone said Julie had attacked a man and he had thrown her into the huge container housing the flowers. The police tried to extricate Julie from the tub and more people got in the way, and one of the policemen was allegedly punched – with quite some force – by someone. Within minutes, Julie was taken to the police bridewell on Cheapside, probably suspected of being drunk and disorderly, even though the girl had not consumed a drop of alcohol. In the cell at Cheapside, Julie screamed and went into convulsions, and received medical attention. The "fit" eventually ceased and the girl was released from custody shortly afterwards. Around 3pm that afternoon, when Julie went to her home in Norris Green, she found her mother, sister and brother waiting there in a terrible state, along with Mary Jones, for the three members of the Colmane family and six of the neighbours present had heard about the strange lunchtime incident from Mary. As soon as she entered her house, Julie said to her mother, 'He found me, mum.'

'Who did, love,' Julie's mum asked, with tears in her eyes, so relieved at seeing her daughter back home.

Everyone circled Julie, who had bruises on her face and neck, and they all hugged her and asked if she was alright. Julie told her 12-year-old brother Michael to leave the room a moment, and the boy refused at first, until his mother gave him some money to get some sweets.

Julie then told the people present that she felt as if she had been raped. Everyone was speechless with shock.

Julie explained how no one human had carried out the despicable act, and no one but her mother knew what she was talking about. Julie's mother took her traumatised daughter upstairs after diplomatically asking every non-family member present if they could leave and give her and her daughter some time together. Eventually the living room emptied and only Julie's mother and 17-year-old sister were left; Julie's father had not yet returned home from work. Julie told her mum that 'that thing – whoever he was' had found her again, and her mother shuddered at the mention of this entity. Since the age of fifteen, a terrifying icy presence - which sometimes manifested itself as a shadow of a tall thin man – had been preying on Julie Colmane. The thing had made its heart-stopping debut one April morning in 1970 at 2.40am in the hallway of the little unremarkable terraced house on Scargreen Avenue. That morning, a fifteen-year-old Julie Colmane had decided to go downstairs for a drink of water, and as she went to cross the hallway from the stairs, something obstructed her. It was like walking into an invisible wall. The hallway was in semi-darkness at that hour and only the faint bluish light from a mercury vapour lamp shining through the window of the front door from the street provided the scantest illumination. Julie had reached out to feel the thing stopping her, and then suddenly, she felt a hand grasp at her pony tail and yank her backwards. Something she could not see dragged her backwards up the stairs, and she tried to scream for help but she was so afraid she couldn't make a sound. She was pulled into her bedroom and thrown about like a rag doll by something – or someone. When Julie jumped up from the bed, something which felt like a huge cold hand pushed her back onto the mattress. This invisible presence then covered her, from her face to her big toes, and it began pressing her down hard into the bed. Julie could not breathe or cry out because of the crushing pressure, and passed out from the pain. On the following morning she awoke around 8.15 am with her mother and father standing over her. They had been trying to wake her up after they had heard her screaming, apparently having some sort of nightmare. Julie began to cry from a sharp pain on the left side of her chest, below her left breast. It turned out to be a cracked rib. It was assumed that the girl had fallen during the night from her bed and passed out, but Julie knew it had been that thing pressing down on her that had broken her rib. She made a long and painful recovery from the injury, and for a few weeks she was not visited by the unseen assailant. Then, one Saturday evening, Julie stayed over at her friend Deborah's home near Spellow Lane in Kirkdale. Deborah's mum and dad had gone out at 7.30pm and were expected back around midnight, and so that evening, the girl had to mind her two younger sisters, Nicola and Lisa, aged 6 and 9. Julie turned up at 7.35pm, and played hide and seek with Nicola and Lisa until almost 8.30pm, when their big sister Deborah told them it was time for bed. The little girls eventually settled down in their beds and then Deborah went downstairs and she and Julie watched TV and around a quarter to ten, Deborah brought a bottle of her father's

Strongbow cider from the fridge and she and Julie drank some and also started on the crisps and chocolate bars Deborah's mother had bought for her daughter and Julie. Around 10.40pm, Julie went to the toilet, which was upstairs in Deborah's terraced home, and seconds after she entered the toilet and closed the door after her, something brushed past the girl, and she knew that it was that invisible attacker. The teen pretended she hadn't noticed the thing was there, and she reached for the door handle – but something turned the circular knob under the handle – which meant that the door was locked. Julie tried to unlock the door but felt a pair of hands slide around her waist and pull her backwards. She was pressed against the wall, and her lower abdomen and thighs were pushed against a hot radiator. What happened next was so shocking I could not put it into print. On this occasion, Julie was able to scream out for help, and as soon as she heard Deborah's feet thumping up the stairs, the thing released Julie – but she had the horrible feeling that it was loitering in the corner of the toilet. Julie opened the door and Deborah saw her in tears with her clothes disarranged. She asked her what had happened, and Julie burst into tears that evening, waking up Deborah's kid sisters.

Julie told Deborah about the thing and it really scared her, and eventually, she stopped hanging around with Julie. The unknown entity continued to assault Julie, almost every week after that attack at her friends house, but after six months there was a hiatus which lasted about two months, but then the thing returned again one afternoon when Julie was in Garston, buying meat from the butchers for her paternal grandmother, who lived nearby in Speke Road. Julie waited in a queue with her mum at the butcher's shop (which was called "Top Cut") when she suddenly felt someone touch her leg, just behind the knee. Julie jumped in fright and looked around but there was only an elderly man, and he was gazing at the cuts of meat in the window. And then, all of a sudden, Julie felt something breathe close to her left ear, and she knew it was *him*, back again. She told her mother, who returned a worried expression, and looked about nervously. This time the paranormal pervert touched the legs of Julie's mother, even though she was wearing slacks – she could still feel large rough hands stroking her. Julie's mother was so scared by the antics of the ghostly groper, she grabbed Julie by the arm and dragged her out of the shop in front of the bemused shoppers standing in the queue.

After the attack in May, 1974, Julie and her mother visited a Catholic priest and told him about the infra-visible violator and the holy man blessed the mother and daughter and told them to attend church regularly if they could. Julie and her mother went to church that Sunday and attended church regularly for about six weeks, and during that time there were no indecent advances from the phantom pest, but around August, Julie's maternal grandmother, who was blind, came to visit, and as she sat at the table, about to have dinner, the old lady began to tremble and asked, 'Who's that?'

'Who's who?' Mrs Colmane asked, puzzled.

The old blind lady let out a terrible shriek and cried: 'he's horrible!', and then she became hysterical. As Julie's grandmother screamed, something picked up the hot roast potatoes off Mrs Colmane's plate and pelted the old distressed lady hard. This shocking unearthly incident was witnessed by eight people present. Julie's grandmother became so upset, she had a funny turn and was taken home to recover. She later said she had received an overwhelming impression of something evil and disfigured in the living room at Julie's house, and she never ventured into the house again. The nerves of the Colmane family were frayed enough, but this incident made the atmosphere in the house even tenser.

The entity then went away for almost a year, and Julie believed the thing – whatever it was – had finally lost interest in her. She began to see a 22-year-old Walton man named David, and in the summer of 1975, he took Julie to North Wales on his motorbike on warm Saturday morning. At this time, Julie had only been seeing David for a fortnight, and had no intentions of telling him about the unearthly thing which had made her life a misery for years. As the couple approached Prestatyn on a busy stretch of motorway, David felt something trying to turn the handlebars of the motorcycle. At first, David thought there was some mechanical fault but then he felt the bike almost tip over, and he instinctively accelerated, and the knees and elbows of David and Julie were inches from the tarmac, and the bike was hurtling along at 60 mph. Julie clung onto David and was so afraid, she couldn't even scream, and thankfully her boyfriend was an experienced motorcyclist; he took the curve of the motorway expertly, accelerating to just the right velocity and calmly adopting the correct posture so the bike didn't topple over. As the bike was brought under control, a juggernaut thundered past in the middle lane, and still David felt something tug at the handlebars. He cruised to a halt on the hard shoulder and Julie's legs were that weak with the brush with death, she literally fell off the motorcycle. David took off her helmet and carried her to a grass verge and laid her down. She told him she was alright, and he went to look at his bike and could not find a thing wrong with it. Julie wanted to tell him there and then about the malevolent entity which had blighted her life, but she just couldn't get her words out. The journey continued without incident, and the couple eventually arrived at Colwyn Bay. By early evening they were back in Liverpool, and David said he'd get a mate named Gareth who worked as a mechanic to have a look at the bike, just to make sure it was roadworthy. It was then almost a week before Julie saw David again, as he worked in a shop for his father and was very busy. The couple met up on a Friday evening and went to The Excelsior pub on Dale Street where David's garage mechanic friend Gareth and his girlfriend Josie joined the couple. The foursome then went on to another pub nearby: Rigbys – and David and Gareth intended to take the girls to the She club later in the evening, but something took place at the Dale Street pub to upset their plans in a shocking and most unexpected way. As Julie stood at the bar with David, she felt her short skirt being lifted up, and Josie actually witnessed the strange spectacle of the skirt lifting up by itself, and couldn't believe her eyes. Then her own skirt, which was a bit longer than Julie's – almost calf-length in fact – also lifted up at the back, all on its own, and Josie let out a yelp and turned around. A young man of about 19 or 20 sat there at a table, grinning, and he said, 'Wasn't me!' and he turned to his friend, a lad of a similar age, and asked, 'Did you see that?'

Gareth asked his girlfriend what had happened, and she said something had lifted her skirt up, but in the noise of the busy bar, Gareth thought Josie said *someone* had lifted her skirt, and when he saw the two young men seated at a table near to his girlfriend, smiling, he put two and two together and got five.

'Outside,' Gareth said to the younger men at the table, and one of them asked, 'Why?'

'Wanna see you outside,' Gareth insisted, banging his pint hard down on the counter.

'Gareth, it wasn't them – ' Josie tried to explain, but her boyfriend was known to be pathologically possessive about his girlfriend and he once again asked the two men to accompany him outside.

'Why? Do you wanna whisper sweet nothings in our ears?' the nearer lad asked, and grinned.

Gareth seized him by the throat with both hands and started to shake him, and Josie screamed, and David, who had been unaware of the unfolding bit of aggro, turned around, startled.

A huge muscular man intervened between Gareth and the youth and broke them up. He was a professional rugby player, and he told Gareth to pick on someone his own age, and David calmed down his friend, and the foursome left the pub. Outside, Josie told Gareth what had happened but he didn't believe her and almost accused her of sticking up for the young men he'd had a go at.

All of a sudden, Josie's eyes widened and bulge and she let out a shriek. She reached out with both hands for Gareth, who pushed her away, thinking she was just messing about to defuse his anger – but Julie could see that the girl's skirt was up – and her underwear was now down by her knees.

'Oh God, no!' Julie said, and David followed the line of her horrified eyes and he could see the girl's skirt up at the back. He swore and asked Josie if she was alright. The girl looked as if she was having a heart attack.

'Oh pack it in!' Gareth said, turning away.

David and his girlfriend saw Josie's skirt fall down, and Josie seemed in shock.

'Josie, are you okay?' Julie said over and over, and Josie walked back to the pub in a strange manner, and Gareth, oblivious to what was going on, warned her he was finishing her if she went back into Rigbys. Josie went in, followed closely by Julie, who was now in tears, for she knew what had happened. *He* had just had his way with her, and Julie felt sick, because she blamed herself for bringing this thing to Josie. She ran after her and went into the ladies with her, and when the girls came out again, Gareth had a bloody nose and David was pushing the rugby player back.

The whole evening was ruined, and Josie could not put into words what had happened to her outside the pub, but she tried to tell Julie what had happened, and Julie told her to go and see a priest. She inwardly prayed that the thing which had cast such a horrible shadow over her life would not also start troubling Josie's life as well.

Gareth hailed a hackney cab and went home on his own, as he blamed poor Josie for 'the barney' that night, and he never saw her again. David took Julie and Josie to a friend's house, and they stayed up all night, drinking coffee and smoking innumerable cigarettes. Julie told David and Josie the whole story, of how something evil had assaulted her for years, and she expected them to leave her, but David said he'd fight the thing, whatever it was, because he loved Julie, and he gave his girlfriend his late grandmother's rosary beads and also gave Josie a St Jude medal. Josie took the assault very badly, and later went off the scene, and Julie later heard that the unfortunate girl had suffered a nervous breakdown. David and his parents and brothers witnessed the attempted attacks by the malign presence on Julie stretching over five years, and David, or one of his family (all Roman Catholics) would cite scripture or say the Lord's Prayer, and the activity would always cease abruptly. Around December, 1980, the last attempted assault took place, and this occurred one morning as Julie (now engaged to David) woke up next to her fiancée and found herself unable to move. She could feel a tremendous weight pushing down on her and had the impression that the would-be rapist had a huge round stomach. She could feel this stomach crushing her and she also felt cold lips pressing on hers. In her mind, Julie began to pray, and eventually the smothering sensation faded away. That was the last time the lecherous being assaulted her. In 1985, Julie and David had been married two years, and in December of that year, just before Christmas, the couple visited a relative of David's in Yorkshire. Just before they returned to Liverpool, they went for a drink in a pub called The Bingley Arms in Bardsey, Leeds; the pub is said to be the oldest one in Britain. As the couple sat by the fire, enjoying their drinks, a woman who professed to be a gypsy entered the premises, and she sat down for a while, and then looked over at Julie with a peculiar expression. Julie became aware she was being observed by the darkhaired lady, and she felt very uneasy. David noticed the woman staring at his wife too. The gypsy came over and to the couple she said, 'I'm so sorry to bother you, and I know you're about to go on a journey home, but I have some information.'

David was already sighing, and reaching for the loose silver in his pocket.

'No, I don't want your money,' the gypsy told him with a look of utter indignation. 'I want to tell your wife something,' she added, and turned to look at Julie, who was now a little worried. The gypsy said, 'There's someone following you round love, and his name's Hugo. He is absolutely infatuated with you, but he's a bad person. He came to you when you were young, didn't he?'

Julie, despite her closeness to the pub's crackling fire, went ice cold inside. She was lost for words.

'And do you know why he er – how can I put it? Latched onto you?' the gypsy asked Julie, who was now squeezing her husband's hand.

'No,' was all she could muster in way of reply.

'You were playing with that glass, and his name came through – and you laughed at his name, didn't you?'

Julie turned to look at David, who was now becoming rather annoyed, and he tried to offer her the money, but she swore and continued.

'He's still around…he is still around, and don't ever mess with a glass again.' The gypsy then went out of the pub.

'Did any of that make any bleedin' sense?' David asked Julie, and she had a strange faraway look in her eyes.

The memories came flooding back. All those years back, at her mate Maureen's house in Page Moss, when she was about fourteen, just before that thing first attacked her, she had played the game of the upturned glass – the Ouija – and it had spelt out HUGO, and she and Maureen, assuming the other one had deliberately pushed the glass around to spell out that name with the cut-out paper letters, had burst into hysterical laughter. She had clean forgotten about that incident. When Julie said the name in her mind, she felt the hairs on the back of her neck go up as if *he* was right beside her in that pub. By even thinking of that name she knew somehow that she was acknowledging him again, and that she must never do that or he would come back into her life.

David told the barman about the gypsy, and received a cold stare in return. The barman said the woman he had described used to come into the pub – until she died in a ghastly road accident a few years back.

David smiled, thinking it was some joke, but the barman was deadly serious, and he went and served another customer.

To this day, Julie says her prayers morning and evening, just in case he – Hugo – or whatever his name is – comes back into her life.

THE LIST

At around 7pm at the Philharmonic pub on Hope Street in March, 1979, a week before St Patrick's Day, a Galway-born Irishman in his late fifties named Reilly Alroy Duggan was deep in thought at the urinal in the pub's exquisite marble gents when the old man standing next to him having a pee suddenly turned to Duggan and remarked: 'I'd say I have two thousand days left.'

'Sorry?' Duggan asked him, baffled at the remark. The man shook himself, zipped up and went to wash his hands in the white enamel sink. He addressed the perplexed Irishman's reflection in the mirror. 'I'm seventy, you see.'

'And by God you bleeding well look it,' joked Duggan.

Unaffected by the jocular jibe, the silvery-haired man continued: 'And I reckon on the law of averages that I'll have another five years, and that's about two thousand days.'

'You morbid sod!' Duggan finished at the urinal and went to the sink, where he looked at himself in the mirror as he pressed the liquid soap dispenser. 'Started going bald in me twenties, still got colour in what's left though, and all me own teeth except for the back-left molar in the bottom lot.'

'Life's half spent before we know what it's about,'

mused the oldster, drying his hands on a conveyor-belt arrangement of a towel as he watched the Irishman's hands working up a lather under the taps.

'You know what your trouble is, don't you?' Duggan addressed him with a steely-blue-eyed stare. 'You need a woman, you old crab! You need to get laid pop!'

The old man, who eventually gave his name as Jim Laurston, laughed and said his amorous days were long gone, but Duggan turned on the old blarney and said: 'No way – I mean I'm not into men but I think you look handsome. Can you still get it up though?'

Jim laughed, 'Oh aye, but it won't stay up.'

'Are you spoken for, like?' Duggan took his turn at the towel on a roll, quickly drying his hands.

'Oh no, was married thirty years, then lost her – I mean, she died like – '

'Oh, sorry to hear that Jim,' Duggan gave such an empathic look of pity at the old man. 'But you're footloose now and on the market.'

'Yeah, but who'd have me?' Jim asked in a self-deprecating manner. 'I've got dentures and cataracts and – '

'Whoa whoa whoa!' Duggan put his index finger to his mouth, gesturing for the pensioner to be quiet and with great authority, he told him: 'Don't start putting yourself down Jimbo! If *you* can't love yourself how can you expect a lady to, eh?'

'Nah, it's over for me, ' Jim said with a smile, and Duggan knew he was secretly fishing for compliments – and he got them.

'Jim, it is only just *starting* for you! Now, we are going to go out there and we are going to survey the local crumpet tonight like two playboys of the Western world, and we are gonna reel in some of the hottest young ladies in Liverpool.'

'What's your name? You never told me,' Jim asked, and Duggan gave his full title. 'Mr Duggan you have really got the gift of the gab,' Jim said, shaking his head as he pushed the door, leaving the toilet with the Irishman.

'What are you having?' Duggan asked him, but Jim held his palm up and refused his offer. 'No, let me get this,' he said, and to the barman he asked, 'Can I have a pint of golden and can you give this man here whatever he normally drinks?'

'You'll have to be more specific,' the barman chortled, 'Duggan has been drinking all sorts.'

'A pint of Guinness please,' Duggan told the barman, gracefully buttoning his jacket.

Duggan introduced an Irish lady named Dympna in her fifties to Jim, and out the corner of his mouth he whispered to her, 'He's well salted – 'kin loaded.'

Dympna stuck to Jim Laurston all night, and the old man was so elated at having female company he bought Duggan shorts and pints for the remainder of that evening. At 10.30pm Duggan was looking a little inebriated. He was trying his best to look sober and trying his utmost to keep still but couldn't help swaying.

'I'd get you another pint, kid but I don't want to get you blotto,' said Jim, noticing Duggan's red glazed eyeballs.

Duggan patted the worried old man on the shoulder. 'Oh, you needn't worry! A pint is like a daisy in the mouth of a bull to me.'

As Jim got in another round, Duggan noticed a very

odd figure standing a few feet to his left at the bar. He was over six feet in height, had white hair in the style of a medieval page boy, a short black cape, and a long black ankle-length coat. Duggan loved reading characters, guessing occupations, and he was determined to find out who this peculiar drinker was.

'You work for the church?' Duggan asked, sensing something priestly and ecclesiastical about the stranger.

Without turning to face Duggan, the man said, 'No,' in a deep voice.

'Well, in that black get-up you've got to work for the undertakers then,' Duggan quipped.

The man smiled but didn't turn to look at him. 'You could say that,' he mumbled. He studied the whiskey in his glass as if there was a fly in it, and he slurped a swig, gulped the rest down, closed his eyes, sighed loudly with pleasure, and left the Philharmonic pub.

To the barman, Duggan remarked: 'Funny fellah that one. Never seen him in here before.'

'He came in here about a week back, when that lot was in here from the funeral,' the barman told him. 'Kept on asking for a double scotch, and he was really relishing it and saying it warmed him.'

'There are saner people locked up in Rainhill, there are,' said Duggan.

'No, but the funny thing is, when I felt his hand – you know, when I was taking money off him or handing him his change – it was really ice cold.'

Duggan then noticed a long envelope on the counter where the weirdo had slurped his whisky, and he slyly distracted the barman by pointing to someone behind him and saying, 'Think your services are required.' And as the barman turned to look, Duggan swiftly picked the envelope up then went to sit in the corner. Jim brought the pint of Guinness over to him then went back to Dympna at the bar.

Duggan looked at the door, and waited a moment in case the caped crank came back in – and then he opened the envelope. Upon a huge piece of parchment that had been folded twice, there was a list of about two hundred names, all written in black ink in a strange wobbly calligraphy – and one of the names on the list was one *Reilly Alroy Duggan*, and next to it were the words 'Heart attack, Saturday 17 March, 11.45am.' On the same page there were two other names Duggan recognised: Teresa Yately, and Jim Laurston – old Jim, who was now laughing at the bar with Dympna. Mrs Yately had died from pneumonia, aged 85, just over a week ago, and the correct date of her death had been written next to her name on the list. According to the morbid list, Jim Laurston's date of death was tomorrow: 11 March! He'd pass away in his sleep, it said. Duggan folded the unnerving list up and put it back in the envelope, then pocketed it. Jim Laurston said he'd meet Duggan tomorrow evening at 7pm in the Philharmonic pub, and just before Duggan left the pub at midnight, he shouted to Dympna: 'Be careful with him, love!' He then hailed a taxi, and intended to have another look at the bizarre list when he got home but once indoors he fell fast asleep as soon as he sat on his sofa.

On the following day, just after 7pm, Duggan breezed into the Philharmonic pub and was greeted with some terrible – and worrying – news. The barman said that Dympna had been in earlier in tears, because the fellah she had started seeing – Jim – had been found dead in his bed.

Duggan swore under his breath and went cold. He had *that* envelope containing the list on him, and was going to show the barman it as a topic of conversation, but now he just wanted to get rid of it. He bought himself a large gin and tonic and sat alone in the corner, trying to fathom out how that eccentric white-haired man had known poor old Jim would pop his clogs today. A dark thought crossed the Irishman's mind and it took him over. Was the stranger in the cape Death himself – some sort of Grim Reaper? Duggan knew deep down that this really was the case. And that meant that he would die on St Patrick's Day, according to that list. Duggan felt sick at this realisation. He became obsessed by the idea that he was going to die on St Patrick's Day, and unlike every other Irishman on earth, Duggan dreaded the arrival of that celebratory day.

On the Friday night of 16th March, he was sitting in a dark corner of the Philharmonic pub, and by now he looked gaunt from all that worry, and his eyes looked sunken from all those sleepless nights.

'You look like death warmed up there Duggan!' came a voice which shattered Duggan's morose dwellings. It was Danny Donovan, a fellow Irish countryman who often visited his relatives in Liverpool. He and Duggan went back to their schooldays.

'Oh, Danny! Nice to see you, lad!' Duggan rose from his seat, so glad to see his old friend (in the light of his unearthly predicament). He ordered a pint of black and tan – Danny's favourite tipple. Danny didn't possess the sharpest of intellects, so Duggan had to carefully explain the provenance of the 'list of the damned'.

'Burn it, Duggan,' Danny said with a look of utter fear in his bulging eyes as he surveyed the columns of handwritten names on the broadsheet. 'It's got to be from the Devil, that.'

The trembling hands of Duggan folded the paper and slid it back into the envelope. 'What good's burning it gonna do? My name's on it, and that means my number's up; what should I do?'

Danny insisted: 'Go and see a *priest*, Duggan – Father Spain or someone, get blessed and well, I think you can request sanctuary in a church so you'll be safe.'

The two friends sat and drank and smoked and talked of the mysteries of life and of weird supernatural incidents they had experienced over the years, and by 9.45pm, Danny seemed really scared, and made his excuses to leave. Duggan pleaded for him to stay till closing time but Danny up and left.

That man in the cape must have literally passed Danny as he walked out that door, because seconds later, the tall hollow-cheeked white-haired figure of fear strolled silently into the Philharmonic pub.

Duggan froze in his chair. It was the eve of St Patrick's Day – possibly the last night Duggan would ever see.

The sinister man approached the counter and Duggan heard him ask the barman if anyone had found a long envelope that he had mislaid here about a week back.

The barman shook his head but Duggan found himself getting up out of the chair. 'Is this it?' he asked the bogeyman of his nightmares, taking the long envelope out of his inside jacket pocket.

The eyes of the snowy-haired man widened and his stark coal-black irises became fixed on the envelope. A long arm shot out and a bony white hand with tapering thin piano-playing fingers snatched the envelope from Duggan. One of those fingers momentarily touched Duggan's palm and it felt as cold as an icicle.

'What can I get you?' the barman asked the tall thin man but he was too concerned with opening the envelope to reply. He unfolded the rectangular parchment and scanned it, then cast a beady eye over the top-left corner of the paper at Duggan.

'Oh please take me off that list!' Duggan clasped his hands together, and before the barman and a few bemused drinkers, he knelt at the long tapering black shoes of the figure he believed to be Death.

'No,' the lanky weirdo replied in a gruff voice.

'Please,' Duggan's eyes were dripping tears now. 'I don't want to die. I'll give you anything!'

The stranger responded by making a bizarre hissing sound, and when he folded the paper to put it away, revealing his face, he was smirking. The hissing sound was his way of laughing.

'Please remove my name, and I'll give you anything in return!' Duggan was now pressing his palms together, as if in prayer.

'I will have a large scotch then,' the man decided, and Duggan leapt to his feet and to the barman he said, 'A *triple* scotch! Two triple scotches!'

The white-haired creep hissed and he unfolded the list again, took out a long black pen, and crossed something out. Duggan was shown the list, and he saw it was *his* name which had been crossed out.

'This had better not be some stupid joke,' the

barman grumbled at Duggan, 'you'd better pay for these,' he added, and rapped down the two triple scotches. Straight away, the tall man seized a glass with each hand, and he drank the first triple scotch in one go and smiled. 'Makes me feel so warm inside,' he sighed. He then drank the other glass, and Duggan offered him another one, but he smiled and shook his head – then left.

Duggan slapped down his money on the counter and took out a hankie to absorb his tears. He survived St Patrick's Day, but never went into the Philharmonic pub again.

THE BLACK ANGEL

The sunken graveyard known as St James's Cemetery adjacent to Hope Street is an infamous example of mass desecration carried out by the authorities. If you or I walked into a cemetery and began to uproot a gravestone we'd be fined and possibly imprisoned, and yet, in the 1960s, Liverpool City Council swept away thousands of gravestones and whole tombs from St James's Cemetery, and in a half-hearted attempt at softening the disgraceful organised clearance of the grave markers, monuments and vaults, they lined parts of the newly landscaped hallowed ground with the uprooted gravestones of men, women and children. Imagine hiring a team of workmen to bulldoze all of the gravestones of Anfield Cemetery in order to turn the cemetery into a park, before lining the new park with all of the grave markers around its perimeter; there would be a huge outcry, but this is exactly what happened to St James's Cemetery in the Sixties. Before this violation, gravestones, tombs and obelisks covered the cemetery next to the Anglican Cathedral, and as any reader of my books knows, some very strange occurrences took place there over the years – and I know for a fact that ghosts and some very sinister entities are still at large in the sanitized version of the cemetery today.

The following story took me years to uncover. Like many people who lived in the vicinity of the Anglican Cathedral as a child, I had heard all sorts of unsettling rumours about the place: Satanists dancing around fires among the gravestones on certain nights of the year that they held to be sacred to Lucifer, occultists breaking into tombs to plunder hair and body parts of the dead to use in arcane sacrilegious rituals, as well as the many spine-chilling stories of ghosts that are said to haunt the place. I had heard about a certain gravestone which was said to glow in the dark, and when I first brought my stories to local radio, I not only received many reports of this luminous headstone, I also had a photograph of it sent to me by an old photographer who lived on Gambier Terrace in the 1950s and 1960s, and he told me how two young students who lived next door to him – John Lennon and Stuart Sutcliffe – often went down into the cemetery to take a look at the glow-in-the-dark grave marker, which might have given off light because it contained some natural radioactive element. Local radio proved to be an incredibly vast source of information from people who had stories to tell about bygone Liverpool, and many of the accounts from the listening public touched upon weird incidents in St James's Cemetery back in the era when it was a true

Victorian and Edwardian graveyard. A lot of accounts from the 1950s and 1960s mentioned the statue of an angel that was said to move after dark – and even spit; yes, you read that right – spit. I had heard a very vague reference to this when I was a child living on Myrtle Street, and I remember asking my mother if the rumours were true and from her unconscious behaviour I knew she wasn't telling the truth when she would say things like, 'Oh, don't be daft; who told you this? Statues can't move.' My mother would glance nervously at my grandmother and their silent expressions and nervous tics told me that there was some grain of truth in the weird stories, and knowing how the supernatural played on my young mind, they'd desperately try to change the subject. Children – especially nowadays – are more perceptive than adults realise, and I certainly was, and always knew when the adults were being evasive when asked about the eternal subject of the paranormal. I mentioned the statue of the angel which became animated after dark – and allegedly spat – on the Billy Butler Show one afternoon, and a woman named Jean, who had a terrible nervous tremor in her voice, called the station. Billy put her on air and she told us how she was now in her seventies, and when she had heard me mention the angel, her heart had skipped a beat. A very scary memory from a lifetime ago came back to her, and Jean calculated that this terrifying incident must have taken place in what would have been the autumn of 1938, when she was ten years of age. Jeans parents ran a newsagents shop on Renshaw Street at the time, and the family lived over this shop. Jean sneaked out of her home one foggy afternoon in November, just after she had come home from school, and she called on her slightly older friend Violet Bates, who lived on Berry Street, and the two of them went wandering off quite a distance in the fog, even though the girls had always promised their parents they wouldn't stray far from home. The girls were drawn to the eerie cemetery next to the 'Proddy Cathedral' (as they called it) and intended to run through the swirling mists and the gravestones and come out the other side on Upper Duke Street. Violet, however, noticed the silhouette of a tall, life-sized angel, standing on a low plinth. She suddenly informed Jean that her Uncle Wilfred had told her that this angel was a man who was just pretending to be an angel. He kept still all the time, and he was pretending to be a statue because he was a murderer who was hiding from the police. Jean called Violet a liar and Violet grabbed Jean by the hand and pulled her to the stone angel saying, 'Very well then, I'll show you he's alive! Come on!'

Jean began to cry, but Violet was a strapping big girl for her age, and Jean was pulled along like a rag doll. The girls halted beneath a statue which looked gigantic to them, but it was probably (from other descriptions I have received) about six feet tall, including the height of the plinth it stood on. The angel had its arms raised at its sides and it was black with the same sooty residue which had coated St George's Hall and the Liver Buildings. Its body and its face – which was turned upwards to heaven - were also streaked with bird droppings and lichen.

'I want to go home,' Jean sobbed, trying to break free of Violet's grip on her wrist. 'You're hurting me.'

'Just shut your gob, and if you promise you won't

run away, I'll let go – alright?' Violet said firmly, clenching her teeth.

Jean nodded.

'If you run off, I'll catch you and drag you back,' Violet promised. 'You called me a liar, and you're supposed to be my best friend.'

'I believe you,' Jean wiped her eyes with her free hand.

'And if I tell Uncle Wilfred you said he was a liar as well, he would give you the strap!' Violet seethed, then slowly released her grip, and once again promised she'd make Jean come back if she ran off.

Jean stayed put, and she began to cough in the thickening fog. 'I can't breathe,' she complained. Jean felt as if the damp thick fog was sticking to her lungs.

'Just be quiet, and keep watching his face.' Violet crossed her arms and looked intently at the face of the stone angel as the foghorns of the Mersey groaned ominously in the grey void. Perhaps because of the way fog dampens sound, or because of the acoustics of a cemetery so far below street level, a peculiar silence then became noticeable by Jean. She *could* hear her heart pounding though, and it thrummed in her eardrums.

Jean looked at the face, and she began to tremble – not just because of the chill of the sodden fog but because she really did think the statue would move.

All of a sudden, Violet turned to her left, and she was saying: 'Don't run now – just wait a bit more – ' when the statue moved – first its head, which now tilted downwards, and then its lips, which opened as it spoke one word. 'Hello!'

Violet screamed and ran into Jean, knocking her to

the ground and actually (but unintentionally) stamping on her face as she ran off in sheer terror into the fog. Jean lay there on her back, and began to wet herself with a fear she would never feel again in her life, even when her home would be explosively demolished with her in it by a German bomb three years later in a World War Two air raid. Jean lay there in the icy soaked grass, paralysed with fear for a moment, and the head of the unearthly creepy angel made a grinding sound as it turned right, and it said something to her. Jean had never heard a single swear-word in those days because of her upbringing, but she later realised that the entity – whatever that thing was masquerading as a religious statue – had used the F-word. With a smiling face it had said, 'You'll fucking burn in Hell!'

Jean somehow got to her feet and ran off screaming in the swirling mists, but she couldn't find the gateway – she was lost and hopelessly disoriented by fear and the fog – and, she soon realised that the salty taste in her mouth was her blood. When Violet had run off, stepping heavily on her face, she had injured Jean's nose, and the heel of Violet's shoe had also grazed Jean's gums near her upper front teeth. Jean ran into gravestones and obelisks which had taken on all sorts of menacing shapes in the fog. She shrieked when she saw the angel again, but realised it was a smaller different statue (minus its hands) than the one that was alive. Jean became so scared she threw up several times and had the feeling that the evil angel was following her. She followed a path through the darkening cemetery which led to a gate – which was typically closed – but she was so afraid, Jean somehow managed – with all of her might - to squeeze through the railings of St James's Cemetery, and when she got home, her mother recoiled in shock at the amount of blood which had trickled down Jean's nose onto her new coat. The girl had also not only wet her knickers, she had also defecated in them. Jean was understandably grounded by her furious parents and never again allowed to associate with Violet Bates, and when Jean repeated the words the statue of the angel had spouted, her mother slapped the girls legs at the mention of the profanity. A listener named Jack Ennis then called me at the radio station off-air and told me how, in 1958, he had been a diligent cocky watchman, and one summer night in August he had been watching roadworks near Windsor Street, Toxteth, just a few hundred yards from St James's Cemetery, when a gang of kids came running up to him. The kids, aged between nine or ten to early teens, all spoke at once in a very excited manner, and the gist of their babbling was that the 'black angel' down in the graveyard had chased them. Jack told the kids they had overactive imaginations and that they'd be seeing little green men next, but the children pleaded with the watchman to go with them to see the moving statue for himself. Jack left his brazier and red oil lamps, and walked across the road with the gang of kids as he put on his coat. He thought the pointless journey would provide him with a little bit of much-needed exercise, but upon crossing 'Upper Parly [Upper Parliament Street]' Jack saw a distinct dark figure with outstretched wings behind the railings of the cemetery. He halted. He didn't like the look of this thing, and he knew that it was not some prankster dressed up or anything.

'See? See?' one of the children said to Jack. 'That's

it!'

'Get home kids, get home,' Jack advised the children, and he saw that the shadowy winged being was still there, standing stock-still behind the railings in the shadows of a tree's overhanging branches.

'Go and see him, mate, he's horrible!' one of the children suggested, but Jack shook his head and shouted at the kids, telling them to get home, but not one of them would move from the spot; they were terrified of the entity across the road yet fascinated by it. Jack then went back to his little red and white striped tent and sat there, feeling very nervous. The children gathered around him and he shared a bag of boiled sweets with them, but then as darkness completely fell, the children left Windsor Street one by one, and Jack Ennis spent one of the most unsettled nights of his life on that job, for he had the unshakeable feeling that the thing in the cemetery was watching him, and he could feel the hairs on the back of his neck standing up continually. 'I can't explain it,' Jack Ennis told me, 'and I was never one to believe in ghosts, because in all the years I worked as a cocky watchman, I never saw or heard anything remotely supernatural on the streets of Liverpool, but that night, I feel I saw something that was not of this world, and I don't know how I sensed it but it gave off what I can only describe as something really evil. I never had much luck after that night either, and lost my brother in the Merchant Navy and a few close friends, all within weeks.'

A week after I mentioned the menacing angelic statue on the radio, I was once again going into the studios of BBC Radio Merseyside when the receptionist, June, told me that a man named Gerry had been patiently waiting for me in reception for about forty minutes. Gerry was, by his own admission a former gangster, now in his seventies, and he had a strange tale to tell me regarding that angel in St James's Cemetery. What follows is based on Gerry's account as well as hours of research by myself, and also the testimony of several other people's stories about the so-called "Black Angel".

Around "Duck Apple Night" (the old name for Halloween in Liverpool) in 1964, a small-time thief from Falkner Street named Rod, broke into a certain theatre in Liverpool one evening, and stole a number of costumes, including that of a policeman's uniform and helmet. Rod decided to dress up as a copper and call upon his mate, Darren, another small-time crook who lived with his mother in a crumbling house on Grove Street. Darren was terrified of the police and Rod intended to hammer on the door with his truncheon and knew he'd scare the life out of his friend. However, as Rod was walking up Bedford Street South in his police costume, he saw an old Bedford van parked outside a house, and he believed the black man at the wheel was an associate of his named Peter, so he waved to him and hurried towards the van, intending to tell Peter about his plan to scare Darren – but the van suddenly tore away from the kerb with a screech, and then the driver tried to do a 180-degree turn, but for some reason – possibly panic – he lost control of the van and it smashed into the huge stone gatepost of a house. The impact threw the driver through the windscreen and he landed unconscious in the garden of a house. The impact also threw one of the rear doors of the van open. Rod then saw that the driver was not his friend Peter, but a man he had never set eyes on before in his life. Being the eternal opportunistic thief, Rod peered into the van and saw what he thought was about thirty-odd shoe boxes, and he jumped into the back of the van and started picking them up. They were too light to contain shoes. When Rod lifted the loose lids of these boxes he saw they contained bottles of pills of various colours, and some he recognised as purple hearts – early antidepressants composed of amobarbital, which was prescribed to lift the mood of a patient and keep him or her up all night as a side-effect. The drug was originally given to "tired housewives" as uppers. The Prime Minister Anthony Eden was put on purple hearts in the late 1950s and became so addicted to them, it is thought that the drugs interfered with his thought processes and impaired his judgement during the Suez Crisis. Many of the groups playing at the Cavern around that time allegedly took purple hearts, which gained their nickname because they were purplish-blue and triangular in shape. The other drugs in the boxes Rod had stumbled onto were "prellies" (Preludin, an appetite suppressant and stimulant), and "Christmas Trees" (green-coloured capsules with white polka dots that contained Tuinal, a rather powerful sedative) and "Black Bombers" (black capsules containing Benzedrine, a euphoric stimulant that was also nicknamed "Bennies"). Rod carried about twelve boxes from the van and looked up and down Bedford Street South. Then came a stroke of luck. A battered-looking hackney cab pulled up, and Rod saw it was driven by his old schoolmate Freddie, and the latter asked him what was going on. 'Freddie, I didn't know you were on the cabs, mate.'

'Been on them for two years, got to make a living haven't I?' Freddie replied, his head protruding from the side window. 'You joined the cops, have you yer turncoat?' he asked, looking Rod up and down with a look of disgust.

'No, this gear was knocked off from a theatre,' Rod told him with a proud grin.

'Is he dead?' Freddie inquired, seeing the driver of the van laying face down in the flower bed of the garden, surrounded by granulated glass.

'Never mind, mate, just wait there a mo,' Rod told his old friend, and he opened the passenger door of the taxi and placed the boxes of stolen drugs on the back seats. And then, as Freddie was saying he didn't want to get involved, Rod went and got the rest of the boxes from the crashed van and he piled them on the cab's back seats. The driver was beginning to move about and groan now.

'Take me to ours Freddie, pronto, mate!' Rod instructed his chum from school, and got into the hackney and slammed the door hard behind him. 'Falkner Street! Go 'head!'

'You've just announced my name you stupid bastard,' Freddie reminded Rod, glaring at him in the rear view mirror.

Rod took off his helmet. 'He won't have heard that, mate, he'll be hearing bells after that crash. Step on it!'

On the way to Falkner Street, Rod promised Freddie he'd give him one of the boxes but the driver said he didn't want anything to do with drugs and he didn't fancy going to jail either.

'Well, I promise you I'll give you a few bob for all this, mate,' Rod assured him, but Freddie vigorously shook his head.

'You're going worse Rod,' Freddie told him, talking to the reflection of his friend in the rear view mirror, 'that gear belongs to some big lads, and they'll find you mate. Have some sense and get shut of it.'

'They won't know who I am, I was dressed as a copper,' Rod laughed.

Freddie dropped Rod off at his dilapidated old house where the latter lived with his mother, father, two older sisters and a younger brother named Marty who was what was then termed as "a bit slow" – he had learning difficulties and was a very innocent and introverted young man. Most days he fed bread to the pigeons at the pier head, and sometimes he would take hazelnuts down to the squirrels in St James's Cemetery who would trustingly descend the trees down there and eat out of Marty's hand.

Rod stashed the bottles of drugs in the attic under the floorboards and when Marty saw him do this, he asked his brother what he was doing. 'Never mind, Marty,' Rod told him, 'you have to cross your heart and hope to die, that you will never tell me Mam or Dad or anyone about those bottles – have you got that?'

Marty nodded, and asked if the bottles had sweets in them; Marty liked sweets, and recalled the ones Rod had stolen from Taverners a few years back.

Rod shook his head. 'No, they are *not* friggin' sweets, Marty, and you are not to try and eat any of the things in the bottles or you will have to go to hospital, got that?'

Marty nodded excitedly. 'I won't even look at them, and I promise I won't tell me Mam or me Dad, or my sisters, or anyone Rod.'

'Good lad,' Rod told his brother, and then he left to go down the Blackburne Arms to have a glass and a scheme; he had to think of a safe way to distribute these goodies he'd found.

Someone might have seen Rod unloading the boxes from the taxi that evening, and that someone must have informed the wronged party who had had their consignment of narcotics hijacked by an amateur crook. Someone paid a visit to Rod's house later in the evening, and Rod's parents had gone out to the cinema, and his sisters had gone to a nightclub with their boyfriends, but poor Marty was in on his own as usual, and so they abducted him and took him to a house in what seems to have been Huskisson Street, and here, Marty was interrogated about the whereabouts of the drugs. He kept his promise to Rod and refused to tell the head of the gang where the bottles of pills were stashed. The attic had been searched by the gang members but they had not examined the floorboards. Marty was repeatedly punched in the stomach until he threw up blood. One of the gang produced a pair of pliers and said he'd pull out Marty's teeth unless he broke his silence.

One of the younger gang members, a man named Richie, often went courting down in St James's Cemetery with his various girlfriends, and on a few occasions he had seen Marty feeding the squirrels until it began to get dark, and Richie had heard the 'backward' Marty tell people in the cemetery to stay well away from the Black Angel, a statue that had generated a lot of local urban legends over the years. Richie told the other gang members they'd do serious time if they wrenched the 'half-wit's' teeth out. He said they should instead play on Marty's superstitious streak to make him talk, and he procured a length of rope. The plan was to tie Marty to that statue he seemed so afraid of, and to leave him there with a gag in his mouth to scare the life out of him for a while. He'd soon talk after he'd been left in the cemetery for a few hours in the dead of night.

'One more chance Marty,' one of his interrogators stipulated, 'or we'll take you down to the big bone yard and tie you to that angel.'

Marty said nothing in reply, but he started to sob and said he wanted his mum.

Richie slapped him hard across the face, then took off his tie and wound it round Marty's head, gagging him. They took the terrified abductee down to St James's Cemetery and they located the uncanny-looking angel, and they bound him to it with the long length of rope. They left the necktie gag on Marty, and said they'd be back in a few hours, and then the gang members walked away, laughing as they heard the frantic muffled cries of Marty as he tried - in vain – to free himself from the statue. All of this was witnessed by two teenagers – Frankie and Maureen, aged sixteen and seventeen respectively. They had been petting against a tree, unseen by the gang, and Maureen had chosen the venue on this night because she found cemeteries romantic. As soon as the gang left, Maureen went to Marty and undid the tie from his mouth.

'You alright?' she asked, and felt so sorry when she

heard Marty sob loudly.

'I want me Mum, I want me Mum!' he cried.

'Be quiet! You'll have them coming back!' Frankie told Marty, and tried to undo the knots, but they were complex and as well-tied as a fisherman's knot.

'Haven't you got your penknife, Frankie?' Maureen asked him, becoming impatient at his failed attempts to untie the knots.

'Would I be trying to undo these if I did?' he yelled.

'Alright narky arse,' Maureen replied, and she wiped the tears from Marty's face. 'What did you do for them to tie you to this thing?' she asked.

'Maureen...' Frankie muttered.

'I didn't do anything,' Marty replied, sniffling. 'I want my mum.'

'Maureen!' Frankie backed away from the statue and grabbed at her arm. 'This thing's just moved!'

'What?' Maureen turned her baffled face to her boyfriend of three weeks.

A blob of brownish thick liquid pelted the girl in the left eye, and she screamed and almost fell backwards.

'Maureen!' Frankie steadied her and then turned and saw that the lips of the stone angel were pursed. Those lips spat at Frankie too, and the phlegm-like glob went into his mouth. As he turned and ran off, abandoning Maureen, Frankie spat out the vile matter from his mouth, and he halted for a moment, looked back at the strange scene, and saw the arms of the statue curl around Marty and embrace him. Frankie then turned away and ran off as fast as his legs could carry him.

Maureen also ran off, but felt her legs going weak at the knees as she ran, and she heard weird deep laughter as well as the awful screams of Marty as she decelerated to a stumble. She cursed Frankie for running off and leaving her, and the teenager ended up on all fours, numb with fear, trying to get away. Frankie suddenly ran back and said: 'Come on you stupid mare!' And he grabbed her hand and dragged her along, but she fell, and scraped her kneecap hard against the gravel and soil path. In shock she continually wiped the ghastly spit from her eye and babbled about the ladder in her tights, and she saw the expressions of unbridled fear on Frankie's face as he dared to glance back at the moving statue. The screams of poor Marty were echoing back and forth across the cemetery, bouncing off the marble and blackened slabs of the graves and the walls of the tombs.

'We can't just leave him there, Frankie!' Maureen suddenly said, and burst into tears.

'We bleedin' can! Come on, get your feet in gear!' Frankie dragged her onto Upper Parliament Street, into the beautiful light from the tall streetlamps. 'I told you I didn't want to go into that place!' Frankie snarled at Maureen. 'You and your lovey-dovey thing about graveyards - you cracked bitch!'

Maureen fell to the floor and sat there crying her eyes out.

'Get up or I'm leaving you!' Frankie yelled down at her. 'Get up!' he roared, more out of fear than anger, and he shouted so loud he began to cough because he'd strained his throat.

Maureen swore hysterically at him, and Frankie took out the dog-eared packet of prophylactics and threw them at her before storming off, but he only got about fifty feet when he suddenly turned around and ran back. He picked his girlfriend up and carried her, fireman's-lift style, to Hope Street, where he put her down and hugged her and apologised for his harsh words. The couple then went to a coffee bar on Bold Street.

Richie and five gang members returned to the cemetery around midnight, and found only a tangled and coiled rope at the foot of the statue.

'Someone must have freed him,' Richie reasoned, and the colleague who had wanted to yank Marty's teeth out with the pliers cast a look of utter hate at him as he patted his palm with the ball of a hammer he'd brought along to hopefully smash Marty's kneecaps in with.

'Hey, look at that – ' another gang member said, nodding at the statue of the angel, 'it wasn't like that before. Look at its head.'

The head of the angel was craned backwards, facing the sky, and its mouth was wide open and the eyes of the statue were closed. The expression on the graven face was almost one of orgasmic delight.

'Let's get out of here, I hate this place,' one of the gang said, when Richie suddenly pointed to something with a bit of white to it, moving slowly in the distance among the gravestones.

'Is that him?' Richie asked.

'Yeah, but what's that he's got on his head?' another said.

The six of them crept through the dormitory of the long-dead, and came upon a queer scene. Marty was stumbling about, whispering gibberish, and the lad's hair had evidently turned white. This was the white thing that the gang had seen from a distance and assumed to be some hat.

'Hey, you!' Richie shouted, and Marty turned slowly to face the gang with a very odd smile which fazed a few of them – but that was nothing compared to his eyes. As Marty walked towards them, the gang saw that his eyeballs were white, as if they had rolled back to hide his irises and pupils.

'Well, well look who's here,' Marty said, and it did not sound like his voice at all.

'Are you going to tell us where our gear is or do we have to do you in?' Richie asked, and his friend with the hammer approached Marty.

'I'm not telling you, and you can't do me in, so what's the third alternative?' Marty asked in a low calm voice.

The hammer man lunged forward and tried to grab Marty by the throat, but the young man seized the thug's hand with amazing rapidity and pulled him forward. The free hand of the would-be assailant raised the ball hammer, intending to bring it down on Marty's white head, but Marty punched him hard in the face with a lightning jab, and all or a sudden, blood and dislodged teeth were hitting Richie and the man standing next to him. The hammer man crumpled to the floor, out cold. The five of them jumped Marty and pinned him against the wall of a tomb, and Richie picked up the hammer dropped by his unconscious confederate and he began smashing it down on Marty's head as the other gang members cried for him to stop.

But with each strike of the hammer against skull and scalp, a grinning Marty shouted out, 'Ow! Ow! Ow!' and laughed.

'Bastard!' Richie shrieked with nerves, and he brought the hammer down so hard, the wooden shaft broke and the hammer head flew into the air.

'Try harder!' Marty said, and gripped Richie by the throat and threw him backwards. Richie landed with a thud and felt the wind being knocked out of his lungs. He lay there in shock, dazed, and everything seemed dreamlike now.

One of the gang ran away, but one of the three remaining lackeys, a muscular Scot, picked up a vandalised fragment of a stone cross, and he lifted it above his head then threw it hard at Marty. The slab of sandstone smashed into Marty's chest and sent him hurtling backwards into a leaning white marble gravestone. Marty slid down the gravestone laughing hysterically, and he sat there, shaking his head wheezing with laughter, and then got to his feet again. Anyone with a modicum of common sense knew that no human being could recover from such an attack, and the three members of the gang ran off, leaving the unconscious hammer man and the winded Richie on the floor. Marty roared with laughter and walked off into the darkness. Rod went to a chippy from the Blackburne Arms that night and got home around half-past twelve to find the house turned over. He checked the floorboards in the attic and found the drugs had not been touched, but he became worried about the whereabouts of Marty, and went looking for him without any success. When Rod returned home his father grabbed him by the lapels of his coat and asked him to explain the bottles of pills in the attic. Rod had not replaced the floorboards properly and had left the attic door wide open. His father had also found the shoeboxes piled in the yard. He had dumped the bottles of pills in an alleyway behind a condemned house a few streets away. He slapped Rod repeatedly across the face as his wife begged him to stop.

He pushed his wife back, and she almost went through a glass cabinet. 'He's brought trouble to our door again! Whoever he robbed those drugs off has turned this house upside down already, and they'll be back! All because of his pilfering! I've got a good mind to turn him over to the police, I have!'

'Dad, I'm sorry!' Rod tried to prise his father's huge fist from his lapel and collar.

'Where's Marty?' his father barked, raising his fist, ready to smash it into his troublesome son's face.

'Dad, I don't know! I've looked for him high and low, but I'll find him!'

'Ruined a great night out, you have!' his father seemed near to tears. 'First night me and your mam have had out for ages and you do this you little rat!'

'I'll find him, Dad!'

His father threw him across the room, towards the door. Rod ran out of the house, and in a daze he tried to collect his thoughts. There had always been a sort of psychic bond - like that between twins - with Marty and Rod, and he kept thinking of the cemetery by the cathedral, and so he felt drawn to the place, and he eventually found Marty sitting in the south-eastern corner of St James's Cemetery. At first he thought it was a grey-haired tramp, but then he recognised Marty's clothes. By now, Marty's eyes had returned to normal, but he had blood splashes all over his clothes, hands and face. He sat there on the grass, smiling inanely, barely visible from the streetlamps high above at street level.

'Marty, what happened to your hair? What's all this blood on you? What happened?' Rod had so many questions, but there no answers were forthcoming from his younger brother. Rod thought he couldn't speak because he was in shock, and when he led him out of the cemetery onto Upper Duke Street, Marty suddenly let out a terrible scream, then hugged his startled brother. Marty said, rather cryptically, that he had 'been dead' and then rambled on about the angel, and the 'bad men' who had tried to kill him. Rod hugged him and patted his back and said, 'You're safe now, our kid.' Rod took his distressed brother home and was relieved to find that his violent, drunken, father was fast asleep in bed, but his mother had waited up, and when Marty saw his mum, he bear-hugged her hard.

'Oh Marty, you're hurting me,' his mother groaned, 'my ribs.'

'Marty, ease off will you? Marty!' Rod restrained him a little, and the three of them stood there as the dying flickering flames of a fire in the grate cast undulating shadows on the tall walls of the parlour.

The years went by, and Rod turned his back on crime and ended up working in a bakery in Everton, and one day, a fellow worker in the bakery named Carl told Rod that he had heard the story about the night Marty had been tied to that angel. Carl said one of his relatives had been one of the gang members who had tied Marty to that angel. Rod said the story about Marty somehow being possessed by that angel must have been nonsense because his brother never had a scratch on him, just blood from someone else. If he had been hit repeatedly with a hammer and struck with a slab of sandstone, he would have been killed. But Carl insisted that his cousin never lied, and had told him exactly what had happened. That cousin was Gerry, the man who had come to the radio station to tell me the story. A married couple also vindicated the story – they were Frankie and Maureen, the couple who had been courting in the cemetery. One man even got in touch to tell me how he was one of the workmen who had been employed to level the cemetery in the 1960s, and he said he recalled the 'Black Angel' clearly, and the strange thing was that it went missing on the day it was due to be uprooted and disposed of. Its present whereabouts are unknown.

The stories about the angel being something evil in disguise may well have some bizarre grain of truth to them. Many of the world's cultures say there was a War in Heaven a long time ago, and that the renegade angels who chose to back dissident angel Lucifer were cast down onto the earth with him. These beings were afterwards referred to as demons, and some hid underground and some were said to have hid in trees, mountains and even the graven idols of primitive races. Perhaps the angel in the cemetery really was a Fallen Angel in disguise.

SOME WEIRD APPARITIONS

The behaviour of ghosts is often very repetitive; some of them do the same thing over and over with a sort of obsessive compulsiveness, and such entities are known as re-enactment ghosts in the world of the supernatural. Merseyside has many of these types of ghost, and here's an account of one of the more bizarre apparitions of this type. In October 2014 a reader named Yasmin told me how she and her friend were walking through Wolstenholme Square in the city centre at 4.30 am on their way home from a party at a relative's when they saw something very strange indeed: an old-fashioned looking bed, around 12 feet in length, standing on the cobbled road near the entrance to the square. Yasmin and her friend both had the intense feeling of being watched by someone, and quickly moved on without looking back. This surreally long bed has been seen since at least the

1960s, always in Wolstenholme Square in the wee small hours, and when I mentioned reports and letters I'd received about it on a local radio programme, I received dozens of more accounts from people who had also seen it. One night in November 1967, a teenaged couple, David and Cathy, left the Cavern after having a row because David had been dancing with two popular go-go girls (Big Yvonne and Little Yvonne) at the club. Cathy stormed off home on her own during the slanging match and ended up taking a short cut through Wolstenholme Square – when she noticed what she initially took to be a long bench, but as she drew nearer she saw that there was a bizarre-looking bed, which looked three times the length of a normal one, standing in the square. The bed was covered with long white sheets and had two pillows at its head. The headboard looked very gothic, possibly mahogany with strange faces carved into it. There wasn't a soul about yet Cathy heard a weird voice from somewhere near call out: 'Where are you going? Come back!'

In 2006, the Cuban sculptor Jorge Pardo installed his huge modern work of art entitled "Penelope" – consisting of multicoloured globes on stalks – in the middle of Wolstenholme Square, and a few days after this, two female art students named Austen and Teegan decided to go and take a look at "Penelope" one night after having a drink in the nearby Pilgrim pub. It began to rain and the students headed back to their flat on Canning Street, and so they walked to the Parr Street exit of the square – and found their way barred by a peculiar elongated bed, and this time there was someone in it. This person had jet black hair in a type of 'basin cut' and his face looked as if he was wearing white clown-make-up. Around this time there were street performers on stilts knocking around the city centre, and the art students thought the man in the bed was one of these, as he looked as if he was abnormally long. The man shouted something rather coarse to the students, and when they ignored him he got out of the bed and walked towards them, but he was not wearing stilts – just an old-fashioned nightshirt, and he had freakishly long thin bare legs. The girls ran off and when they came back in the daytime the bed had gone. The identity of the weird ghost haunting that square in that outlandish long bed is still unknown.

Another bizarre-looking apparition – and one that has almost caused fatalities – is said to haunt an old Victorian era terraced house on Bootle's Hawthorne Road. I first learned of this case after giving a talk on the local ghosts at a retirement home in Bootle many years ago. The old folks there were a font of stories, and what follows is derived from one of these stories coupled with a little research.

In the late 1950s a family with the common surname Smith lived at a redbrick corner house which dated back to Victorian times. This house was on Hawthorne Road at the Marsh Street end. It was quite a draughty dwelling with a damp cellar but it was the home to Mr and Mrs Smith and their four children – two boys, aged 7 and 9, and two girls, Paula, aged 13 and Monica, aged 15. The family had lived at the house for some five years and had never experienced anything remotely supernatural on the premises – until one July afternoon in 1959. It was a Sunday, and

Monica was sitting on her bed, reading her favourite strip in the *Bunty* comic – 'The Four Marys'. She was also looking forward to cutting out the 'paper dolls' on the back pages of the comic and dressing them with the various outfits (which she would have to cut out and fold around the figures). Next door, in her own room, Paula was playing the latest pop records on a record player her grandmother had bought her for her birthday. The boys were playing in the back yard with the kids from next door and Monica's mum and dad were sitting in the kitchen, chatting with Mrs Cairns from next door. The July sun was shining into Monica's room, and the window was partly open, so when Monica heard a rustling sound, she assumed it was the summer breeze blowing the curtains – but it wasn't something that mundane at all. A shadow of something passed over Monica and her bedroom wall, and she looked up to see what was casting it. There, floating about five feet off the ground was a man in an old-fashioned "jack tar" sailor's uniform of some sort, with a wide-brimmed black leathery-looking hat, bushy sideburns, rosy cheeks, and a pair of piercing icy blue eyes. He wore a wide evil grin on his face as he floated down towards Monica, who was paralysed with terror. She saw that he wore a scarlet shirt under a navy-blue jacket with a yellow neckerchief round his throat, and on his legs he sported wide flared white trousers. Upon the frightening levitating ghost's feet he wore a pair of huge black shiny clogs with massive buckles.

Monica tried to run from the bed but in a heartbeat the sailor - who seemed, from his antiquated attire - to date from the 18th century flew down at the girl, and knocked her face down onto the bed. Monica tried to scream but he pushed her face into the mattress to muffle her cries, and then he seized a pillow and put it over the girl's head. Monica's wrists were bound together, and then she felt something – a cord or a rope, being tied around her neck. The girl lost her breath, and tied to stand up but the entity shoved her back onto the bed, and Monica became so convinced she was about to be strangled, she passed out. She awoke to hands feeling her wrists and kicked out with her feet, thinking it was the sailor, but she heard her dad's voice, and suddenly the blue and white striped pillowcase was removed from Monica's head. Her father untied her hands and the girl turned to see her father, crying mother, two young brothers and tearful sister Paula standing there. 'Who did this to you?' Monica's father asked, and the girl described the floating sailor, but her puzzled parents would not accept that she had been tied up by a ghost and almost smothered by it. Monica the learned that she had been unconscious for about half an hour, and that Paula had found a piece of paper tacked to her door which bore the words: 'Suicide Here' scrawled in what looked like black ink. When news of the strange attack reached the ears of the old neighbour – 78-year-old Mrs Morrison – who lived next door, she collapsed after crying out something. When she regained consciousness she told a doctor that the ghostly sailor had done the very same thing to a young girl in the 1930s, and that girl had been in Monica's room when the incident took place. Like Monica, the girl had been around 15 – but Mrs Morrison couldn't recall the girl's exact age – but the old lady recalled that the girl was named Clara and she had almost died from asphyxiation. There were rumours that several suicides in the Hawthorne Road area – all of them involving young females who had died by hanging – had in fact been the work of "Jack Tar" as they called the ghost. A friend of Mrs Morrison named Mrs Molloy claimed that some of the alleged notes left by the so-called suicides bore the very same handwriting style of the latest "Suicide Here" notice.

The family brought out a priest to bless the house and Monica's father moved his daughter into a spare room and nailed her former bedroom door shut after leaving a Bible on the window ledge. Days later in the evening, the family were just about to have their tea when Paula drew their attention to a rhythmical thudding sound which seemed to be coming from upstairs. The family gathered on the stairs and shuddered when they heard the stomping sound – for it sounded like a *clog* being brought down .Then came the uncanny sound of a penny whistle playing a very good rendition of that old nautical melody *The Sailor's Hornpipe.* the stomping gradually speeded up, and so did the penny whistle playing, and the Smiths' little boys seemed upset because they could see the fear in their mother's face. Monica was trembling like a leaf, and eventually ran out of the house, and the psychopathic sailor above began to scream with laughter, perhaps because he might have sensed the distress and panic he was causing. Enough was enough, and the next day, Mr Smith moved the family out of the house and stayed with his brother at his house near Warbreck Park. For man years afterwards, the floating apparition of the backdated sailor was seen looking out the upper windows of the house on

Hawthorne Road, and on some nights his eerie pipe music was often heard as far as the Hawthorne Hotel pub. The identity of the ghost remains a mystery and his murderous intention towards young females is also inexplicable, but perhaps he is re-enacting some murder (or *several* murders) he might have carried out when he was alive…

Another weird apparition that has been reported to me – which also defies any attempts at explanation – is technically a group apparition – and this is (and you won't believe this collective noun) a superfluity of nuns – some accounts say up to a dozen of them – that have been seen kneeling prayer near to an overturned bus full of dead or seriously-injured groaning passengers on a certain stretch of Queen's Drive West Derby, quite close to Holly Lodge Girls' College and the Jolly Miller pub. The nuns and the phantom accident have been seen since about 2005, and in some reports of this bizarre supernatural spectacle, a crashed lorry is also seen near to the toppled double-decker bus. The curious thing is that the phantom accident is usually seen in the late summer, or early autumn, and the illusory carnage has been reported to the emergency services by motorists who believe they are seeing that aftermath of some shocking collision. The nuns seem to appear out of nowhere, just like the overturned bus and the lorry – which appears to be on its side on the central reservation. One couple – Mariel and David – both in their fifties - described to me how they came to a standstill on Queens Drive West Derby one afternoon around 4pm in late August 2006 when the queue of cars in front decelerated and came to a halt. Then

David, who was driving the car, told his wife that there was a bus on its side where the traffic lights of the Mill Bank junction are. Mariel leaned over her husband and saw the bus on its side too, and she then noticed the nuns in a line, kneeling near to the overturned vehicle, apparently in prayer. As the traffic crawled by, David got a good look at the green bus on its side. He could see that the bus was on its left side and David could also see its chassis, suspension and axles – and also streams of scarlet blood that had trickled from the bus along the tarmac (which was covered with granulated glass). Being squeamish, David looked away – and further up Queens Drive he saw a large goods vehicle lying on its side on the central reservation. It was white with three axles and around twelve to sixteen tyres on it. The traffic queue eventually started to move a bit faster, and when the couple reached their home in Walton, David switched on the radio and tuned it to a local station, thinking he would hear the details of the terrible crash – but he heard nothing of the sort – and it was the same when he turned on the teatime telly; he thought that such a horrific collision, between a heavy goods vehicle and a bus, would surely make the news. Under the pretence of going for some cigarettes, David drove to the scene of the crash – and saw no overturned lorry or bus anywhere. There wasn't a piece of glass in the road at the spot where he had seen the nuns praying as the mingled blood of the crash victims had trickled along the macadam. David drove back home and told his wife about the mysterious absence of any trace of the collision, and she was of the opinion that the whole incident had been some paranormal occurrence – perhaps an omen of a future crash – or even a warning for David to take extra care on the roads. David eventually contacted me by email, asking if anyone had seen a phantom crash on Queens Drive West Derby, and in his first email he had not mentioned the nuns, so he was very shocked when I mentioned them, and also informed him that many people had seen what he and his wife had seen that day. Police have seen the phantom accident and the attendant nuns, and so have schoolchildren, and people from all walks of life who drive down Queens Drive West Derby, and perhaps David's wife Mariel is right – perhaps the weird replay of the shocking crash is a warning of some dreadful accident that will one day occur at that spot, at the junction of Mill Bank and Queens Drive West Derby – but I certainly hope it *never* does come to pass. The presence of the nuns in this vision of horror is nevertheless intriguing; where do they come from? I believe there is a Carmelite monastery near Cardinal Heenan Catholic High School on Honey's Green Lane, just a mile away from the site of the spectral smash.

We now move a few miles north into Knowsley to look into another case of a weird - and gruesome - apparition...

One untypical sunny February afternoon in 1994, 15-year-old Huytonian Brian Garrock, and his 14-year-old girlfriend Joanne Jones, of Westvale, Kirkby, boarded a Number 21 bus at the stop near the Johnny Todd pub and headed to the upper deck. The 21, bound for Liverpool city centre, had about half a dozen (mostly senior) passengers on the lower deck, but upstairs there wasn't a soul. Joanne wanted a window seat, but so did Brian, and so they had a bit of a childish tiff and Brian ended up sitting behind his girlfriend. It was ironic because today was Monday, 14 February – Valentine's Day, and the two of them had feigned illness today so they could stay off school and then sneak out for a romantic trip to town when their parents had gone to work. As the bus moved along, the young couple sat in silence – and then, all of a sudden, Joanne called out her boyfriend's name, and it was almost a whisper.

'Brian – ' she seemed to gasp.

Brian ignored her and looked out the window to his left, but then he heard Joanne cry out.

'Oh my God!' she yelled.

Brian turned his attention to her now, and then saw she was looking at someone who was standing at the front right seat on the bus – and this person had no head.

At first, Brian couldn't take in the surreal sight. There was a man in what seemed to be a tuxedo or a three-piece suit with a dickey bow and a pink carnation in his lapel, and he was holding a lit cigarette – but he had no head – just a red stump encircled by a white starched collar.

Brian found himself getting up, ready to run downstairs, but the elegantly-attired headless figure turned and walked a few feet down the aisle and blocked the escape route. Brian and Joanne therefore ran to the back of the bus, and in doing so, Joanne fell over. Brian turned and saw that the headless apparition was feeling its way along the chrome bars that run along the back of the seats, and the boy went back and pulled his girlfriend to her feet. Joanne screamed and jumped over the seats to get to the stairs, and Brian followed her, and the teens made such a racket, the driver halted the bus and looked through his periscope viewer, but he saw no weird figure without a head upstairs.

Brian and Joanne tumbled down the last few steps and fell over one another. They asked the driver to let them off, and when he refused and began to ask them what they'd been doing upstairs, Brian pressed the emergency exit button, which opened the doors, and he and Joanne ran off in a terrible state.

Many years later I interviewed Brian and Joanne – as well as several other people who had witnessed the dapper decapitated ghost on that same bus over the years. A public transport historian told me that the bus in question had been involved in a horrific crash many years before in Manchester; it had gone under a bridge that was too low and had injured a group of passengers and killed one man by decapitating him. That man had been going to a local Valentine's Day wedding, and was dressed in a smart suit and waistcoat. The bus was later repaired and sold to a firm in Knowsley, and no one was aware of its tragic history. Ghosts often 'haunt' vehicles they were in when their earthly lives came to an abrupt end, and there are even cases on record where parts of planes salvaged from air crashes have apparently caused the ghosts of crash victims to haunt the planes which have incorporated the salvaged pieces from airline wreckages. The most famous case of this kind was documented by the writer John G Fuller in a paranormal bestseller called *The Ghosts of Flight 401*. In December 1972 an Eastern Airlines Tri-Star jetliner, Flight 401, crashed into a Florida swamp. The pilot,

Bob Loft, and flight engineer Don Repo, were two of the 101 people who perished in the air crash. Not long afterwards, the ghosts of Loft and Repo were seen on more than twenty occasions by crew members on other Eastern Tri-Stars, especially those planes which had been fitted with parts salvaged from the Flight 401 wreckage. The apparitions of Loft and Repo were invariably described as being extremely lifelike and solid-looking, and were not only reported by people who had known the dead men; the ghosts were also subsequently identified from the photographs of the deceased men by witnesses who had not known Loft and Repo. The strange tales of the ghostly airmen of Flight of 401 circulated in the airline community, and an account of the paranormal goings-on even appeared in a 1974 US Flight Safety Foundation's newsletter, giving the eerie stories great credence. Best-selling author named John G Fuller carried out an exhaustive investigation into the hauntings with the aid of several cautious airline personnel. A mass of compelling testimony was produced as a result, including many controversial claims. It was said that flight log books which had recorded sightings of the apparitions had actually been withdrawn, and that crew members who had encountered the ghosts had been threatened with a visit from the airline company's psychiatrist. A séance was eventually held in the presence of Don Repo's widow, and evidence was produced supernaturally which allegedly convinced Mrs Repo that her deceased husband still existed in the 'hereafter'. Unfortunately, further research into the well-witnessed paranormal incidents was severely hampered by the airline company, which steadfastly refused to co-operate with the ghost investigators.

Here's another haunting involving an odd-looking apparition, and coincidentally, like the headless bus passenger incident – this also took place on Valentine's Day, and it *also* occurred in Knowsley. The incident took place in a certain well-known cabaret club, not far from Kirkby, in 2009. Paul and Jackie Vinter, both 22, went along to the club to celebrate their recent engagement on February 14, and when they got there, the club steward said they'd arrived an hour too early; it was Paul's fault – he had written the opening time down wrong during a telephone conversation with the steward. Rather than turn them away, the steward kindly admitted the couple into the club and served them a drink. He then went to tend to his business and so Paul and Jackie sat in the club facing a low stage. There wasn't a soul about of course, and Jackie saw the funny side and was just about to have a conversation with her mum on her mobile to kill time when suddenly, the lights went out. There was then a blast of brass music – the intro of a karaoke track of a certain song – later identified by Jackie as *Vehicle* by the band Ides of March. Jackie only discovered this 1970 song by Googling parts of the lyrics she could remember involving a 'black sedan' and something about going to 'the nearest star'. During the brass intro, a spotlight appeared on the scarlet satin curtains, and out popped a rather unusual man. He wore a white suit and white gloves, and what looked like a pair of white shoes with black crepe soles. Jackie also noticed that this man wore yellow socks. Stranger still, the stranger had black arrows all over his suit, reminiscent of the archetypal outfit a cartoon convict would wear. He had a short black haircut and wore a little make-up on his face, creating the effect of a pallid face with eyeliner and accentuated arched eyebrows. He began to walk slowly across the stage in a strange fluidic gait as he sung the words to *Vehicle* in a passable American accent. The music faded and the bizarre-looking performer began to crack surreal jokes in an accent that lay somewhere between Wigan and the West Coast of the US. Now and then, this unknown comedian would exclaim "Spook!" after a joke and simultaneously jump back with quite an impressive agility before landing in a comical stance. Most of the jokes were interspersed with the word "Slither", which he would utter as he beckoned his two-person audience with his white-gloved hand gestures. Paul thought the man was funny, and clapped a few times and whistled. Paul assumed the comic was obviously rehearsing his act to the virtually empty club, but Jackie thought there was something eerie about the comedian, and throughout the act, she squeezed Paul's hand on the table. Paul clapped at the end of the routine, which went on for about seven minutes perhaps, and then the unusual comic bowed his head – and did a funny type of backwards walk which took him back behind the curtains. Fifteen minutes afterwards, the lights all came on in the club and five members of a group came onto the stage and began to set up their equipment. The club steward then reappeared, and Paul asked him who the unusual comedian was in the 'escaped convict' suit, and he received a blank stare. The steward had no knowledge of any such comedian in the club, nor had he booked anyone remotely like the man Paul had described. That evening, after the couple left the club at 10pm, they went to their local, and when Paul mentioned the offbeat comedian, the barman, after some quiet contemplation said, 'There used to be a fellah years ago – and I'm going back to the early 1980s – and I can't remember his name, but he used to dress *exactly* as you've just described, with the arrows on his suit, and the white gloves, and he used to say "Spook" and "Slither" and he had a few other catchphrases. I cannot remember his name, but he was on evening entertainment programmes like *The Bob Monkhouse Show* and that type of thing.'

'Well he's come down in the world to be on at that dive,' Paul remarked, and he noticed that Jackie looked worried. 'What's up?'

Jackie ignored the question from her fiancé and with a grave look she asked the barman: 'Do you know if that comedian you mentioned is still *alive?*'

Paul swore and smiled, shaking his head. 'He wasn't a bleedin' ghost, love, but he's probably died a few times on stage though.'

'I couldn't tell you,' the barman admitted, shaking his head slowly. 'Someone in here'll remember him, surely.' The barman asked several of the regulars about the comedian with the arrows on his suit and a few drinkers said they did indeed recall such an act, but none of them could remember the performer's name, although a few said it was some flip made-up stage-name, just like the one the late Dustin Gee used (Dustin's real name was Gerald Harrison).

Paul later discovered that other people had seen the same comedian at that club, even though he had died from an illness a year before in Spain. Jackie's diligent search on Google provided her with the shocking answer; the comedian she and Paul had seen was Roy Jay, and she and Paul went cold when they saw footage of the off-beat comedian on YouTube. He had once appeared at the Knowsley club in question and it is said that for some reason, his ghost is seen there even today from time to time. Paul and Jackie – now married – have not been back to that club since that day in February.

STRANGE ABDUCTORS

Over the years I have received dozens of accounts from readers about sinister abductors, and some of these would-be snatchers are even more menacing because they seem to have a supernatural element to them. Take, for example, the case of a St Helens woman in her late twenties named Betty, who went to Lewis's in Liverpool City Centre one busy Saturday afternoon in June 1969 with her 5-year-old daughter Marie. Betty had only been in the store five minutes when she was approached by a young smart-looking woman of about thirty, who told her she was a store detective, and what's more, this woman knew Betty's surname (which was quite uncommon). She told Betty that she was being arrested for shoplifting and pointed to a debonair man at the perfume counter who had a steely gaze fixed on her. 'That is Mr Keys, a detective – go to him now,' the woman said, and kept hold of little Marie, saying, 'Your mummy is being searched; just wait here with me for a while.'

Betty, who was absolutely outraged by the accusation, stormed off to this Mr Keys, then her feminine intuition kicked in and told her something was not quite right, and she turned and saw the "store detective" dragging a crying Marie to the exit. Betty chased after her and when the apparent child-snatcher crossed Ranelagh Street, she seemed to vanish into thin air. She was there one moment, gone the next, and little Marie later said, 'She disappeared mum.' No one in Lewis's knew of a Mr Keys either, which deepened the mystery, but Betty later heard that a similar weird couple had tried the same deception in other big stores. One of the most sinister attempted abduction cases of this type began to unfold in Wavertree in the early 1970s when an 11-year-old child named Julie was going to school one dark December morning. As Julie passed the Coffee House pub and approached Jenkins the funeral directors, a bluish car (with a left-hand drive) pulled over to the kerb and Julie thought the driver was going to ask for directions, but instead, he threw an envelope at her, then drove on. Julie picked up the letter and opened it. A note said, 'I will get you soon.' The word 'will' was written boldly in red ink – but Julie wasn't sure if it was blood.

Julie kept seeing that same blue car everywhere she went, and it even waited outside her house at night. The girl's father chased the car and saw it had blank registration plates that were not illuminated by any little bulbs, and the spectacled driver was heard to laugh as he tore off. Julie was almost knocked over by a car as she ran from the stalking motorist days later, and by now the police went looking for the vehicle, believed to have been a Vauxhall Viva. Across the city, there were more reports of people receiving menacing letters thrown at them from this car, from Great Crosby to Grassendale, and whenever the police gave chase, the car would perform incredible – and suicidal – manoeuvres down narrow side-streets, and, on one occasion, down an alleyway on Wavertree's Lawrence Road – and finally, the mad motorist literally vanished down a dead-end street in Kensington and was seen no more.

The creepiest would-be abductor I have ever researched has to be the tall thin man in black who picked up a 3-year-old girl on Woolton Road in 1899 and ran backwards at an incredible speed as he was chased by the publican of the Halfway House and several locals. The creepy kidnapper finally dropped the girl and vanished into Woolton woods. Some said he was a freak, and others believed the backwards runner was the Devil. They say he is still occasionally seen.

Certain stories are repeated to me over the years and they smack of the archetypal urban legend, but I have learned not to dismiss all of these tales because they often turn out to be true. A case in point is the "Man in the Washing Machine" – the scenario of this story has been reported to me so many times over, and strangely enough, the intended victims always seem to be females, and young females at that. If all the stories are true, then a pretty sinister entity is at large across the North West, from Chester to Chorley, and he's been up to his uncanny tricks for quite some time. This bogeyman goes under various names given to him by the young of different eras: Mr Twisty, Twister, Charlie, Spinner and the Whirlyman to name a few. In

2010 a 32-year-old Moreton lady named Natasha got in touch with me to tell of a very strange incident she recalled from around the age of three; it was a peculiar memory that had haunted Natasha for almost thirty years, and had surfaced many times in her dreaming mind to trigger recurring nightmares. Around 1981, when Natasha was aged three, she had been dozing on her sofa one wintry day. She recalls that there was heavy rain and winds at the time and a downpour was pattering hard against the windows. She woke up on the sofa and panicked because her mother was not there sitting beside her; she had, in fact, gone upstairs to clean the toilet. Natasha distinctly recalls two programmes being on around this time - *Button Moon* and *Rainbow* - both with distinctive themes which young Natasha associated with lunchtime. Anyway, Natasha shouted for her mum, and getting no reply, she wandered into the kitchen, where the Zanussi washing machine was humming away. All of a sudden that machine began to whine and shudder as it entered its rinse cycle, and this loud and higher-pitched noise frightened Natasha, but before the little girl could hurry out of the kitchen, she saw a golden light shine out of the circular plastic window of the door, and this light changed before Natasha's mesmerised eyes into a face which began as a whirling mass of yellow and orange colours, twisting into the smiling face of a man with huge eyes. The whine of the machine halted instantly and the lips of the strange face moved. A voice from the head in the washing machine said: 'Hello Natasha.'

The little girl recoiled at the thing knowing her name and despite her very young age Natasha knew there was something decidedly odd about the face. She remembers stepping back, and as she did, two short arms came *through* the window as the entity reached out to her and said: 'Please come in here.'

'Mummy!' Natasha yelled, but found she could not turn away from the weird man in the washing machine. His arms were stretching out further now, and although the drum and its washing were spinning at about 1000 revolutions per minute, the weird head and outreaching arms were stock still.

Natasha began to feel a bit drowsy, and the face of the unearthly being smiled, but the girl could tell it was not a sincere one.

'I have a present for you, Natasha, come on,' said the unreal-looking manifestation. After he said this, Natasha saw a long box wrapped in white paper with a green ribbon and bow upon it just above the yellow and orange face, and this made her feel a little more at ease. She somehow knew it was some gift for her. She felt soft hands which were like her Playdoh to the touch, and next thing the girl knew, she was being pulled ever so gently into the washing machine. She found herself in a darkened room with the whirring of the washing machine's motor faintly audible in the background, and when she turned to look back, she saw the circular window, and through it she could make out a slightly distorted view of the kitchen.

Natasha looked back towards the man and now she could not see the gift with the green ribbon and bow, and the face of the man was no longer smiling. He was gazing at the girl with intense hatred in his eyes. Then, as Natasha's eyes adapted to the dark interior of the impossible room, she saw that five boys around her age were crouched against a wall with their hands grasping their knees as they sat there. Their eyes were closed, as if they were asleep – or dead.

Natasha began to cry, and then she asked the man to let her go back to her mum, but he shook his head. He had long arms, a torso that was disproportionately small compared to his head, and even smaller legs. Natasha cannot recall the outlandish figure having any clothes on. After a few tense moments, the girl heard the sounds of pots and pans being clanked about on the gas cooker and she realised her mother had returned. Natasha then heard her mum calling for her.

'Natasha! Where are you?'

The girl turned and saw the image of her mother's legs, warped through the plastic window of the washing machine as they went back and forth.

'Mummy!' Natasha screamed, 'I'm in here!'

The two soft clammy hands of the thing which had slyly persuaded Natasha to come into its strange domain seized her arms and began to pull at her when she walked towards the window.

'I want my Mummy!' Natasha said over and over, and although she cannot recall what the exact words the thing said to her, Natasha can vaguely recall that it swore at her and said something frightening about her dying if she went out through the hole.

Natasha felt complete terror in the pit of her stomach, and somehow she broke free of the sinister would-be abductor and found herself on the tiled floor of the kitchen on her knees. She was sobbing. Her mother came running into the kitchen in a hysterical state and asked her daughter where on earth she had been hiding. Natasha tried to tell her mother about the 'naughty man' in the washing machine but of course, her mum believed that the girl had probably hid somewhere, fallen asleep and had merely experienced a nightmare. I told Natasha the story in the following paragraph – taken from a letter sent to me many years back by a woman who had experienced an almost identical incident in Mossley Hill in 1975. I later introduced the woman to Natasha and they compared notes and realised they had probably both encountered the same child-snatcher.

In 1975, three-year-old Gayle Phillips lived in Grassendale, but almost every Saturday her mother would drop the child off at her grandparents house on Booker Avenue, Mossley Hill. Gayle loved her Nan and Grandad, and looked forward to staying over at their home each weekend (while the girl's parents would enjoy a Saturday night out). This particular Saturday fell on a beautiful sunny summer evening in July of that year, and Gayle helped out at the barbecue in the back garden of her Nan's home, but at one point, George, a little boy of the neighbours who lived next door turned up and he and Gayle played hide and seek. When it was Gayle's turn to hide, George faced a tree at the bottom of the garden with his eyes closed tight as he counted, and a giggling Gayle ran past her grandparents and two of their friends as they chatted and ate at a wooden table beneath a parasol. Gayle dashed through the kitchen, and suddenly noticed a very small young man peeping over the top of the washing machine at her. This washing machine was an old-fashioned top-loader type of washing machine, and the man had to be standing in it as he gazed down at Gayle.

'Hide in here, come on!' he said excitedly, and his voice sounded very childish.

There was a pause, and Gayle heard George's voice far off as he cried: 'Coming ready or not!'

To the man above on the washing machine, Gayle said: 'I can't climb up.'

'Get that chair,' the little man pointed to an upright chair in the hallway next to the phone table, and Gayle did as he suggested. She dragged the chair into the kitchen and got on top of the washing machine, and now she could only hear the man's voice inside the top-loader. She got into the washing machine, and there was no shiny metallic drum in there as there should have been, but a cubic room instead, and Gayle thought she must be under the machine in a cellar. It was confusing. She looked up and saw the disc of light – the sunlight reflecting onto the ceiling of the kitchen, and she began to get a little scared. The man who had told her to come into the washing machine had very small legs, a doll-like body, but a big head. His arms also seemed longer than normal, but by now he had changed colour. Before he had looked normal, Gayle recalled, but now he had a green tinge to his skin.

'Can we be friends?' the weird man asked.

'I want to get out,' Gayle said, ready to cry, and she cried: 'Nanna!'

The room started to slowly spin, and the centrifugal force pushed Gayle back against the wall. When she looked up, she saw that the disc of light was getting smaller and smaller, and this really frightened her.

'Say we can be friends and I'll let you get out,' the man said, and the room spun faster – but he seemed unaffected by its rapid rotation and didn't even sway.

'We can be friends! Nanna!' Gayle burst into tears.

'And cross your heart and hope to die if you are telling me a lie!' the man shouted over her.

'Cross my – ' Gayle couldn't remember the words he had just said because she was so terror-stricken.

The man then slapped Gayle's face as he said each word. 'Cross-your-heart-and-hope-to-die!'

Gayle went hysterical and began to punch and kick out at the weird man, and suddenly the room stopped spinning and she felt something lift her up and out of the machine. She woke to excited but far-off voices somewhere in the garden, and she found herself in a space between the fence and her grandfather's shed. She got up and rubbed her eyes - which were still wet from crying, and there running towards her was her Nanna.

'Gayle!' she cried, and tripped over something. She fell in a manner the child found comical, and then she picked herself up off the grass and shouted: 'I've found her John!' John was Gayle's grandfather, and he came running around from the other end of the shed.

'Where have you been hiding, eh?' Gayle's grandmother asked, picking the girl up. 'You've had half the street out searching for you! Where did you go?'

Gayle didn't know where to begin and it came out as babble. 'Nanna I was hiding from George and went in where you put the washing and there was a naughty little man in there...'

Needless to say, Gayle's story was not taken seriously – only by Natasha – the girl who had also met what was possibly the same freakish entity in her mother's washing machine in 1981.

A reader named Adam wrote to me recently and told me how, in 1988, when he was aged four, he was in the kitchen of his home on Norris Green's Lewisham Road one afternoon, mooching for biscuits while his mother had dozed off on the sofa, when he suddenly had an overwhelming fear that there was something in the washing machine, and that something was watching him. Adam ran out of the kitchen and almost dived onto his mother, startling her from a prized nap. 'Mam, there's something in the washing machine!' her little boy told her, and she thought that perhaps the cat had climbed in there, but when she looked inside the machine it only contained the football kit of her older son and some towels she was due to wash. She went back into the living room and told Adam his joke wasn't funny, and as she was about to settle down on the sofa to read a magazine, she and Adam heard a noise in the kitchen. They both went to see what it was. The door of the washing machine was slightly ajar, and the towels it had contained were strewn across the kitchen floor. The football kit lay in shreds, draped over the back of a dining chair, and looked as if it had been slashed with a knife. This naturally spooked Adam and his mother, and when Adam's father came home earlier than usual, mother and son were so relieved. The father was told about the strange goings-on and said a cat had probably torn the football kit, but his wife said that was ridiculous. From then on, large items of clothing would go missing from that washing machine – not just the odd sock which most of us are accustomed to losing from time to time – but jeans, and more sensitively, the underwear of Adam's mother also vanished during the washes. One day around this time, Adam's older brother - 11-year-old Michael - came into his bedroom and said 'I've just seen Mr Whirly in the washing machine. Adam thought Michael was just trying to scare him but he went into detail about seeing a horrible face looking out the circular window of the washing machine, and Adam, thoroughly scared by the account, went and told his mother what Michael had said. She assured him that his irresponsible brother had made the story up, but years later, Michael stuck to his story and said he had indeed seen a face looking out that washing machine, and when it had broken down in the following year, his father seemed relieved to be getting shut of the machine, and drove it to the dump himself. The new washing machine was installed in another part of the kitchen and did not have any aura of menace about it like the previous machine, Adam recalls. I believe that there are entities about, perhaps from one of the many dimensions scientists now acknowledge in their Quantum and String Theories, and some of these beings may – just like their human counterparts – have murderous or sadistic quirks which lead them to entice what they would see as easy prey – children. These evil beings have the advantage of being dismissed as figments of childish imagination, or the fabrications of fibbers and the superstitious, and so they are able to indulge in their sinister activities.

FEATHERFINGERS

A reader named Sarah recently wrote to me to ask if Old Swan's Doric Park was haunted as she had seen something very strange there during a visit to her mother's house on Wharncliffe Road at the end of May 2015. The house of Sarah's mum backs onto Doric Park, which dates back to 1930, and it was from an upstairs window in the house that Sarah and her two sons and mother saw a very strange figure sitting on one of the benches in the park. Sarah thought the figure sitting on the bench looked like a clown, and her sons, aged 10 and 13, having much superior eyesight, confirmed their mother's suspicion, and said they could see that the man sitting on the bench had on a red shirt, and what seemed to be white gloves, as well as a navy bib and brace overalls, and very large and long orange shoes. Sarah's mother found an old pair of binoculars her late husband used for bird watching, and took a look at the clown – and was rather startled to see him wave at her – even though he was just a speck to the naked eye around 150 yards away. That figure was then seen to run up and down the park at a phenomenal speed in what looked like a speeded up manner reminiscent of the old silent films or a *Benny*

Hill Show routine, and this really creeped out the four observers. When I told Sarah that she and her mum and sons had seen "Featherfingers" – an alleged ghostly clown, the colour drained from her face. She really was under the impression that I was just kidding about the red-nosed apparition, but I showed her the file I have on this weird entity, and as Sarah read the various notes and looked at a few sketches witnesses had made of the clown, I saw the goosebumps rise on her arms as fear gripped her mind. Now Sarah knew beyond a shadow of a doubt that I was not, by any stretch of the imagination, pulling her leg. Merseyside seems to have quite a few ghostly clowns, and at the moment I am researching one that has been seen in the alleyways of Birkenhead, and hopefully I'll be able to document him in a future newspaper column as well as a chapter in the next book – but back to the Doric Park clown ghost. I only learned of Featherfingers from a listener to my spot on the Billy Butler Show back in 2010. A woman named Jean Fairbrother told me how, one sunny afternoon in the 1970s, at the age of 9, she had been standing with her back to the railings of Doric Park when a pair of gloved hands suddenly swung forward around her head and covered her eyes. The thumbs of these hands gripped her head hard and she heard a melodic well-spoken voice ask: "Guess who?'

'Mam!' Jean screamed and tried to prise the gloved hands off her head, but the man behind her laughed and said, 'No, it isn't your Mam. Guess who I am?'

Jean somehow broke free, and glanced back, and saw a man standing behind the park railings. He was dressed as a clown with a tiny bowler hat perched on his head of green hair, and he wore a red polka dot (or possibly striped) shirt of some sort, braces, navy blue baggy trousers and ridiculously long red or orange shoes, protruding through the railings. His head squeezed through the railings as he smiled at the terrified girl, but he did not look real; he looked like some two-dimensional cartoon with no depth to him. Jean heard from an aunt she met on the way home that the clown had grabbed a boy from behind when he had stood with his back to the railings a few weeks ago, only he had tickled the boy's ribs and the lad had suffered a fit as a result. He was later found on the pavement in an unconscious state and when he recovered, he had recurrent nightmares about the tickling clown. It was said that one wintry day in the 1960s, rude drawings of enormous phalluses and nonsensical words were sketched in the snow by someone one morning, and "Featherfingers" the clown was blamed. Around that time, many children – and quite a few adults too - living in the vicinity of the park are alleged to have had vivid nightmares of a clown tickling their ribs and armpits until they were insensible. A girl from nearby Woodgreen Road said the clown had approached her in the park one grey overcast afternoon to show her a bloodstained finger of his white glove. He asked the girl to bandage it but she sensed there was something 'wrong' about the clown and she ran off. That was in 1978, but as recently as 2013, I received a letter from a woman we shall call Lisa, who lives in Dundale Road, less than seventy yards from Doric Park. Lisa told me how, at 9pm on one July evening in 2013, she was on her exercise bank in her front parlour with her headphones (connected to her iPhone) on, listening to music as she did her usual twenty minutes of exercise, when she saw some movement through the partially-closed blinds of the parlour window. There's a wide six-foot-tall hedge in front of the window which prevents any passer-by from looking into the parlour, but Lisa could clearly see someone against the hedge through the parlour blinds. Lisa shares the house on Dundale Road with her partner, Graham, and upon this summer night he was out on his friend's stag night, so Lisa was understandably a bit nervous when she noticed what looked like the figure of someone spying on her. She got off her exercise bike, dabbed her face with a towel, and slowly walked to the dimmer switch to lower the light – and when she did, she saw that the figure outside the window had something red on – either a long-sleeved shirt or jumper – and the face of this person was very pallid indeed. Lisa moved nearer to the parlour window and decided to yank the cord to fully close the blinds, but through nerves she pulled the wrong cord and the blinds opened fully instead. Standing there in front of the hedge was a man, about 5 foot 6 or 7 inches tall, and he had a face painted like a classical circus clown with the red nose and heavy eye make up, as well as a huge smile painted across his chalk white face – while his real mouth seemed to be forming a frown. Lisa let out a scream and assumed the weird Peeping Tom would scarper as a result, but the sinister clown just stood there motionless and po-faced.

Lisa ran to her front door, bolted it, and then phoned her neighbour, a woman she had known for about three years – to tell her about the clown outside.

The neighbour assumed Lisa was joking at first, but soon realised that she had been genuinely spooked by something by the quiver in her voice. The neighbour alerted her husband, and he came out of his house with the family Alsatian (who was due to be taken for his nightly walk anyway), and the dog refused to go near the hedge of Lisa's house, and even when it was pulled along by its collar the animal managed to slip out of the collar before whining and running back indoors. The neighbour and his wife searched the hedge in front of Lisa's house and even looked behind the low walls, but there was no one there. The neighbour's teenaged son later said he had seen the same weird clown on the opposite side of the road looking through a bay window at around half-past midnight. Looking through my older records I have a report for January 2001 of a 35-year-old woman named Louise who almost ran over an oddly-dressed man on Black Horse Lane, close to the row of bollards at the Queens Drive end of this cul-de-sac. Louise was visiting a friend named Leah on Black Horse Lane around 8pm and it was dark at the time – the only lights were from her vehicle's headlamps and a dismal nearby lamp post. A figure rushed out in front of the car and Louise recalled the clothes had red and blue about them and the face of the jay walker was white, but he was almost a blur as he ran from her right to the left, thumping a white gloved hand on the bonnet as he flitted across the road. The figure seemed to vanish upon reaching the kerb, and this really unnerved Louise. She told her friend Leah about the weird figure she had almost ran over and Leah's eyes widened. She said the same figure had been seen by her uncle on the allotments at the back of her house. Leah told Louise she had seen a ghost – that of a clown who had been seen in Doric Park weeks before. I presume the allotments Leah referred to would be the Wharncliffe Allotments, but she did not say exactly what the clown got up to there. A man named Joe who is a goldmine of Old Swan's local history got in touch with me regarding Featherfingers and said he had heard about the ghost in his youth, although he'd never had the misfortune to encounter him, but Joe said his mother told him that the ghost was active when there were military huts on the site now occupied by the allotments and parts of Doric Park. These huts were built as a temporary accommodation for American soldiers serving in the First World War. If the ghost of Featherfingers was active then, he's an older ghost than I initially imagined, but I wonder why he haunts this area of Old Swan? Perhaps someone out there will uncover the back story of this eerie painted phantom. In 1977, an 11-year-old boy named Kevin Murphy climbed a tree in Doric Park, and at one point he decided he'd try and drop from a branch, but changed his mind when he realised how high up he was. He was about to swing and throw his legs up in an effort to climb back onto the branch, when something very alarming happened. Thirty years later, in 2007, Kevin told me what took place. 'I was with another lad named Mick, but he was on the ground, and was shouting up to me, urging me to drop and not be a coward, when all of a sudden, I felt hands tickling my sides. I thought someone else had climbed up at first but when I turned my head to look there was no one there. The hands felt like the hands of an adult, and the fingers dug in hard between my ribs, causing a tickling sensation which made me let go of the branch. I hit the ground and the impact knocked the wind out of me. Mick was laughing as I got to my feet, and in shock I ran home to Acanthus Road, where I started getting my breath back.' There was definitely no one else up that tree, and given the supernatural history of the park, one naturally wonders if the invisible tickler was Featherfingers.

WALLS HAVE EARS

Although the highest point in Liverpool is Woolton Hill, the district of Everton has some of the steepest streets because of its ancient hills, and at a certain house on a street perched on one of these Evertonian hills in the 1960s, a rather eerie incident took place. A very brainy 14-year-old lad named Edward was allowed to use the loft of his home as his laboratory, because the teenager was a wizard with a soldering iron, and his knowledge of electronics was astounding, given his young age. Not only did he build his own radios and TV sets, he also invented various contraptions such as walkie-talkies that used the earth's magnetic field to convey messages and a gas laser made from the tube of a shop's discarded neon sign. In April 1966, Edward constructed an amazing invention – a highly directional microphone which he called a "Sound Telescope". Just as an optical telescope magnified distant images with lenses or curved mirrors, Edward's cylindrical invention boosted distant sounds with a 'sonic-focussing element' (as he called it) so he could hear Sunday hymns being sung in the Anglican Cathedral, dogs barking on Bidston Hill across the river, and surfacing seals barking in Liverpool Bay. Living in proximity to the city's two main football stadiums presented the problem of acoustic overload when the crowds roared during a match, and Edward also had to watch the clock after noon each working day in case the One O'clock Gun at Morpeth Dock deafened him and blew his circuits.

The boy knew it was morally wrong, but he began to eavesdrop on conversations in houses in the evening when the hubbub of traffic and human commotion died down, and the Sound Telescope tuned him into a real nosy parker. He became wrapped up in the overheard details of other people's lives and at first he told no one about his invention's ability to listen through walls and closed windows, but after a few days of electronic eavesdropping he blabbed about some of the scandalous things he'd heard.

'Mrs Byrne's eldest daughter is having a baby to her married neighbour Mr Marshacke,' Edward told his mother one morning at the breakfast table.

'Who told you that nonsense?' his mum replied, and Edward said his Sound Telescope had picked up the hushed conversation and it had sounded as clear as if Mrs Byrne was in the same room as him.

'Well, you shouldn't be listening in to people's business, Edward,' the bright spark's mum told him, and she said Mr Marshacke was a well-respected and very upright member of the community in his fifties, and not the sort to have affairs with teenaged girls - but then Edward's mother later found out that her son's shocking claim was true, and she found out through listening to local gossipers at the laundrette.

Edward began to jot down the hush of secrets his prying electronic ear uncovered in an exercise book, and his mum would avidly read the juicy contents of the book at the fireside each night, gasping with shock, smirking and tutting at each scribbled revelation.

The police received an enormous amount of anonymous tip-off's around this time from someone who seemed to know what every criminal in North Liverpool was up to, from simple robbers of roof-lead to sophisticated embezzlers. Each tip-off was written on lined paper like that from a school exercise book, and all of the correspondence was signed 'Walls have ears'. Edward thought the tip-offs were great fun, but eventually tired of helping the law.

Then one evening Edward trained his Sound Telescope on a house half a mile away, and he looked through the telescopic sight attached to the probe. He saw the distinct silhouette of a man in a flat cap on the blinds of a first-floor window. This man suddenly said, 'I found my beloved wife Doreen at the bottom of the cellar steps with a broken neck. She must have tripped going down to fetch some coal.'

Edward then heard a female voice cry out: 'George, where are you?' and the silhouetted man replied, 'Coming Doreen, my love.' Edward realised that this man was rehearsing the murder of his wife; and that he'd make it look like an accident. He heard the man say the very same lines the following night, and the night after that, so Edward reported him to the police and said he'd been passing his house as he overheard him say his odd words. Edward watched the police turn up at the house to investigate his tip-off, but they couldn't get an answer at the front door. A female neighbour came out of the house next door, and through the Sound Telescope, Edward heard the woman tell the police constables that no one had lived at the house for about five years.

'What a liar you are missus!' Edward gasped, listening to the woman's claim in his headphones. He decided to telephone the police from a call box and the operator put him through to the local constabulary. He told a policeman how he had overheard the man named George apparently rehearsing his wife's murder, but when Edward gave George and Doreen's address the policeman said, 'You must be the joker who sent the police to that address the other day. No one has lived at that house for years. If you continue to play silly buggers son, you'll end up in big trouble for wasting our time.'

'But I heard him sir,' George insisted.

'This is the final warning, lad, alright?' the policeman shouted down the phone, then hung up.

Then one night about a week later, the silhouetted man in the flat cap was again picked up by the Sound Telescope, and this time he said, 'Edward, eavesdroppers never hear well of themselves, and I'm afraid you're going to die soon. You are going to have a horrible death! A horrible, horrible death! Oh, the blood! The Blood!' And the shadowy man took off his cap to reveal a pair of *horns* on the head of his silhouette. He laughed for a while, and Edward went ice cold and shuddered. The silhouette then vanished and the light in the window went out. Edward became ill with worry for weeks, and was too scared to even venture outside. He experienced pounding palpitations and shortness of breath, and he really thought his heart was going to explode at one point, but the days went by, and then weeks elapsed without incident, and then the months went by, and as nothing happened to him, Edward started going to St George's Church in an effort to protect himself from the Devil – for who else could that person with the horns have been? Edward dismantled the Sound Telescope and never eavesdropped on anyone again.

HADLOW NEXT STOP

It was around 5.35pm on a warm summer day in August 2009 when Liverpool accountant Ray Spearman Corliss left his workplace off Old Hall Street and walked to a bookshop on Bold Street where he looked – in vain – for a particular book about accountancy software. Instead he Bought a small book on ornithology, an old interest of Ray which he was trying to rekindle. From the bookshop Ray took a short stroll to Central Station where he boarded a train to take him to his Little Sutton home. He texted his wife as usual, saying he was on his way, and then he sat and browsed the book he'd bought about birds, and when he looked up he saw a beautiful bronzed blonde lady in her twenties with ice-blue eyes sitting across the aisle. She smiled pleasantly at him and he smiled back and nodded, before sticking his nose back into the ornithology book. At Rock Ferry, Ray must have dozed off; he'd only had about three hours of precious sleep last night because of a bout of insomnia. Anyway, in the depths of the lovely sleep on the train, he heard the automated female voice on the tannoy announce: 'Next stop – Green Lane,' and he saw colourful birds from the book taking off silently from a sunlit field as he drifted away, back into the idyllic realm of dreams. In the dream, a blotchy-faced farmer in some brown smock grabbed Ray's arm because he was trying to pick up one of the peacock-like birds. Ray was then roused from the dream by a tug to his upper arm and he opened his bleary eyes to see a uniformed man in black leaning over him.

'Hadlow next stop, sir,' the man said.

Ray Spearman Corliss looked around, and saw he was on another train, for there were no yellow plastic fittings or neon lights – but snugly upholstered leather seats and dark interiors which smelt of cigarette and pipe smoke. Ray looked to the seat on the other side of the aisle where the pretty blonde had sat, and saw no one there now. What is this? He wondered. There wasn't a tracksuit or stylish clothing logo to be seen on any of the passengers – just quality clothes; tweed caps, mackintoshes, trilbies, bowler hats, cloches. The accountant got to his feet and did not recognise the scenery scrolling past beyond the windows. 'Where in heaven's name,' he muttered, and an elderly bespectacled woman smiled at him in the seat facing and slyly looked him up and down. She wore a little quaint brimless Miss Marple hat with a blue flower in it and sat there, tensely clutching the crocodile handbag on her knee.

There were no automatic doors and no robotic voices announcing this stop and Ray stumbled along with the other passengers out of the train onto a platform. A sign said "Hadlow Road", and Mr Corliss asked a railway guard where he was but the man was too involved in a loud disagreement with a lady passenger. Ray suddenly noticed the train he'd left was not electric – but had a funnel with steam rising from it. 'What the – ' he gasped, and was herded - by a lazy ticket inspector – along with a gaggle of commuters through a doorway, and the bewildered accountant soon found himself outside the station on a cobbled road which looked as if it should have been in a museum. The penny still hadn't dropped. Ray's mobile bleeped; it was his wife Jenny, asking him where he was. Ray yawned, rubbed his fuzzy eyes so he could see the screen, and then he texted the reply: 'Hadlow Rd station?' and smiled faintly at the idea of being lost. How long had he been asleep on the train?

He saw what looked like an old T-Model Ford rattling down the road, and only then did his stomach turn over. Had he stepped into a bygone era? His heart pounded. He asked a passing schoolboy: 'What year is this?' The boy looked amused, and rather docile. He made no reply, so Ray asked him the question again, and the boy said: '1931,' then walked on slowly. Corliss felt the little hairs on the back of his neck stand up at the mention of that archaic year. He entered a newsagent, picked up a newspaper from the counter and read the date on it: Saturday 7 March, 1931. There were articles about Ghandi, teenage actor Jackie Coogan's earnings, and atrocities in Russia. 'This isn't a library you know sir,' said the incensed newsagent. Corliss put the paper down and wandered in a daze towards Willaston village, when the mobile rang. Corliss whipped it out of his pocket and answered. 'Yes?'

'Ray, Hadlow Road Station closed yonks ago – in 1956 - according to Wikipedia,' Mrs Corliss chortled, and there was a pause as if she was waiting for the punchline to some long-winded prank her husband was staging.

'Love, I'm in 1931,' Ray told her, and there was another pause. She really did think he was joking. 'I'm serious,' he resumed, looking at the old cottages, 'and it's scaring me.'

'You must have got off at the wrong stop Ray,' his wife assured him. 'Or maybe they are filming some – ' she was saying when the mobile network suddenly vanished along with Jenny's voice.

Ray tried to telephone his wife but the "No Network" message came on the screen, and this happened whenever he attempted to call his wife.

Corliss walked for miles, looking for some sign of 2009; some satellite dish mounted on a house, or the sound of a jet plane flying overhead, but he saw and heard no such things. Night soon fell, and Ray - a man who had been proud to class himself as an ardent atheist - resorted to saying a mental prayer. The thought of being stranded 78 years away from his beloved wife Jenny turned his bowels to water. He stumbled towards a grassy hillside, confused and cold, and kept checking the screen of his phone. Then suddenly, by the light of a waning gibbous moon, Ray sighted the M53 motorway- and he swore and punched the air with joy. The mobile then buzzed; twelve text messages and fifteen missed calls from his frantic wife were listed on the mobile's screen. When Ray got home he gave his wife a blow by blow account of the strange adventure, from when he left the bookshop to the hour or so he spent wandering miles of countryside looking for Little Sutton.

'There has to be a rational explanation, Ray,' Jenny told him, sitting beside him on the sofa squeezing her husband's hand as he sipped a brandy to steady his nerves.

'I somehow went back to 1931,' Ray told her with a furrowed brow. He remained perplexed by the incident.

'No, that's impossible,' Jenny assured him, 'what's gone has gone, but perhaps you dreamt you were there, and had one of those lucid dreams, you know - the ones that feel so real.'

'No, I went back alright love, ' Ray's grip tightened around Jenny's fingers. 'I know I did, but I don't know how it happened.'

The next day, Ray left his workplace, and tried to recreate the same sequence of events which had apparently led to his personal timeslip. He went to the bookstore, browsed there for about a quarter of an hour, then made his way over to Central Station. His train came and he got on it and sat down, and then the very same blonde he had seen the day before got on the train and when she saw Ray, she came over to him and delved into her handbag. 'Excuse me,' she told him, and Ray looked up at her, startled. 'I hoped I'd meet you again,' she said.

'Sorry?' a faint smile broke out on Ray's face.

'This is yours,' she said, producing his book on ornithology.

'Oh, thank you,' Ray took it off her, and listened to the woman – whose name was Payge – tell him something quite intriguing.

'You fell asleep yesterday as you were reading that,' she told him, pointing to the ornithology book.

'Yes, I remember you, you were sitting over there,' Ray interrupted.

The lady nodded. 'Yeah. I saw you reading the bird

book, and I just looked away from you for a few seconds, right?' said Payge, then she paused and continued. 'I then looked back, and you were gone. The book was there on the seat where you'd just been sitting. You vanished.'

'Vanished?' Ray gripped the book as he heard this fascinating bit of information.

Payge nodded and continued as the train moved off. 'The ticket inspector came down and I picked up the book and told him you'd vanished into thin air, and he said you couldn't have got off the train, and that no one had passed him.'

Ray said nothing in reply to this information, which made some sense to him. He felt as if his excursion into the past was now being vindicated.

'Where *did* you go?' Payge asked him with a slight smile, as if she thought he was going to tell her about some amazing fare-dodge trick.

'If I told you, you'd think I was nuts,' Ray told her, and self-consciously flipped through the ornithology book.

'What do you mean?' Payge was so curious to hear an explanation now.

Ray attempted to offer his explanation. 'I woke up, on a steam train, and found myself at a place called Hadlow – '

Payge looked puzzled. 'You woke up on a steam train? How?'

'I haven't a clue, but I give you my word, that is what happened, and here's something even more unbelievable – I found out that this steam train was back in 1931.'

'That's mad,' was all Payge could say in response.

'It happened to *me*,' said an elderly-sounding voice from the seat behind Ray.

Ray turned in his seat and looked over at a man in a flat cap and a chocolate brown jacket sitting there. He wore thick pebble-lensed glasses and he nodded as Ray and Payge looked at him.

'I'm sorry to interrupt, like,' the man – a Mr Walker – apologised, but Ray said, 'No, no, please go on; the same thing happened to you?'

'Aye, around 1999 I think it was. Was going to Eastham Rake – a morning it was – around half-eleven, maybe a little later. Fell asleep reading a newspaper by Green Lane or Rock Ferry. Woke up and found the train I was in had all changed. The guard said "Hadlow next stop" and I remembered Hadlow had closed years ago, but there it was. Everything looked old; horse-drawn carts and that, and I walked as far as Capenhurst, and then I was nearly knocked down by a car – a modern car, like. I swear this happened on my daughter's life. I can't explain it, but it happened, and I tell you what lad, if it happens again I'd like to stay there because I'm sick of so-called modern life.'

Ray still takes the train from Central Station five days a week when he leaves his workplace each day, and he would actually love to have the timeslip experience again, as long as it isn't permanent and he can return to his life today, but so far he has not experienced any further shifts in time.

By the way, Hadlow isn't the only 'ghost station' – there's another one called Swansdown – but that, as they say, is another story…

ZODIUS

When you leave an elevator, don't walk out – jump out. That's what Marie Rodgers always advised after the shocking death of her husband in London in the late 1960s. The Liverpool woman was thirty-eight when the horrific incident happened, in a certain store. She and her husband James had spent the morning shopping in Oxford Street, and had called into the big store to visit the café. After the brunch they entered the elevator to take them to the first floor, but James decided to get out on the second floor to buy his wife some gloves, and as he put his right leg forward to get out, the elevator suddenly plummeted – and catching him by his midriff, cut him in half, although Marie didn't know this at first, because she had hold of his legs, which were still trembling. She thought he had been caught between floors, but then she saw the urine and loose faecal matter drip down from the end of his trousers onto his brogues, and then came the streams of blood from the top of the elevator door.

The spectacled man in his forties standing next to Mrs Rodgers stood there in muted shock, and he simply said, 'Uh Oh!'

Meanwhile on the second floor upstairs, a

traumatised female shopper in her twenties and two female store assistants tried to pull James Rodgers 'free' – and saw that the elevator had smashed through his spinal column. The bisected man regained consciousness and began to drag himself across the floor towards the screaming women. He was gasping for help, and they could see his ripped bowels and ruptured organs trailing along with his shirt tail as he slid along snail-like, leaving widening pools of blood in his wake. 'Get an ambulance…' he murmured, his head lolling about as the horrified witnesses heard Mrs Rodgers muffled screams in the lift that had jammed between floors.

'I can't feel my legs,' Mr Rodgers croaked, and tried to turn to look at legs that were hanging, jammed in the elevator door, below, out of sight.

He died seconds later from shock and loss of blood.

In the elevator, Marie Rodgers hugged the stranger, and pressed her sobbing face into the lapels of his grey jacket. 'He's dead isn't he?' she asked, over and over.

'I'm afraid it looks like that, Marie,' the stranger replied.

Despite the emotional supernova of grief, Mrs Rodgers wondered how the stranger knew her first name, and she pulled away her tear-streaked face from his chest and looked at him. He had reddish-brown hair, salted with a little grey, and a pair of dead slate-blue eyes peered through the lenses of his glasses. 'Do I know you?' she asked him.

'No,' the man replied, and then he told her: 'I used to love you a long time ago.'

There was a pause, and in the silence, Marie heard the urine pitter-pattering on the elevator floor and the rhythmical thud of brown fluid from her dead husband's involuntary bowel movements.

'What?' She pushed away from him.

'I made all those calls to you a long time ago,' the stranger said in a monotone voice which started to ring bells in Marie's echoing mind.

'Calls?' she said, trembling, and looked at the Emergency Alarm button on the wall of the lift, just below the floor buttons.

'All those calls in the middle of the night to tell you that I loved you. I had to let you know, see, and I suppose I overdid it.' He sounded machine-like, and he turned to see the legs that had now stopped shaking.

Marie began to cry again and she said, 'I can't believe this has happened; why did he want to get out on the second floor? It must have been to get me those gloves. I'm sorry I mentioned them, I'm so sorry I mentioned them!'

'Things happen, Marie,' the stranger remarked, and he watched her reach out and press the Emergency Alarm button. Harsh electric bells sounded and made the brushed aluminium ceiling of the elevator vibrate.

'He mightn't be dead,' Marie hoped, gazing through splayed fingers at the dangling legs and the blood and liquefied excrement dripping from the brown brogues and green socks. She turned to her old weird admirer and putting aside the fact that he had stalked her for five years over ten years back, she asked: 'Do you think he might still be alive?'

He shook his head and looked down at the pool of red and brown on the elevator floor.

When the firemen opened the elevator door, almost

forty minutes later, the trousers of her husband containing his shattered pelvis and bloodied legs, fell into the elevator, and Mrs Rodgers leapt back from the legs in horror as they landed on their knees. The elevator shuddered violently and Marie grabbed her former stalker. The elevator was being pulled upwards towards the second floor. A fireman appeared at the opening when the elevator halted. He was about three feet up from the elevator floor. He quickly wiped the blood and slime from the ledge above with a green rag, and then he jumped into the elevator and helped Marie out first, and as she was being passed through the gap, the elevator shook again and she screamed. She was passed safely to two other firemen, and then the remaining lift passenger was helped out, and within minutes this individual managed to vanish into the crowds of morbid shoppers who were being herded away from the covered remains of Mr Rogers.

It took years for Marie to get over the nightmarish event of that day, and in the early 1970s she had finally met someone else - a Prescot man named Phillip - and married him. Then, one evening in 1972 at her Prescot home while her husband was working late at his office, Marie received a telephone call, and the caller said nothing for about thirty seconds, and then in what could only be described as a fierce whisper, the caller stated: 'You shouldn't have married that man, Marie.'

Marie instantly recognised the monotone way of speaking; it was *him* - the stalker from her younger days – the man she had been in that elevator with on that horrific day in London. 'I'm going to tell the police about you!' Marie hissed. She'd had quite enough of this unbalanced crackpot over the years and she wasn't about to let him ruin her new married life with Phillip.

The line went dead. In those days there was no way for a person to trace calls made to their telephone, and when Marie told the police about the call, they advised her to change her number. She told Phillip about the nuisance call and of the caller's history of stalking her, and Phillip had the telephone number changed to a private one. Within days though, always when Marie was alone, the stalker called again. He told Marie she should divorce Phillips and marry him, and she slammed the receiver down. Marie took to drawing the curtains and blinds after dark, as she thought the spectacled weirdo was watching her from somewhere out there.

The calls stopped suddenly after a few weeks, and then months went by and it seemed as if the stalker had given up on Marie. Then, one sunny afternoon, Marie and Phillip went down to Chester for a day out. They shopped, and ended up in a delightful café – where Phillips suddenly slumped forward and fell face down onto the table. Marie screamed and an old man on the next table – a retired doctor – rushed over to see what the matter was with Phillip. He expertly felt for a carotid pulse and also pulled back the lids of the man's closed eyes before telling Marie that Phillip was dead from what might have been a heart attack. At that precise moment, just before Marie tried to shake her beloved husband awake, she saw a familiar face at the window of the café – her stalker was outside, peering in at her.

An ambulance was called but it was found that Phillip had indeed died of a heart attack, and once again, Marie found herself all in black, heartbroken, and facing a lonely future. After the funeral, Marie was comforted by her younger sister Patricia, who lived in Widnes. Patricia persuaded her widowed sister to come and stay with her, and although Marie was reluctant to do this, because she was fiercely independent, she finally accepted the kind invitation and moved into her sister and brother-in-law's home. Marie stayed with her sister in Widnes for almost three years, and then she met a man named Charlie, a widower in his early sixties, at a social club. Marie and Charlie began to date, and one afternoon they went to a cinema in Liverpool, and just before the lights went down in the build up to the start of the film, Marie saw a frighteningly familiar face about ten seats to her left; it was the weird and highly unlucky stalker. Fear of the creepy jinx soon gave way to anger, for Marie thought that something fatal would soon happen to Charlie, now that the stalker was present, so she got up off her seat and stepped on the feet of several ruffled cinemagoers as she shuffled along the row to get to the persecuting weirdo, but the spectacled oddball deftly avoided a confrontation by getting to his feet and stepping over the back of his seat to get away. The lights started to go down and Marie tripped on one of the wide carpeted steps leading to the back of the auditorium. When she got up, she saw Charlie gazing at her with great concern, and he went with her into the lobby to ask her what she was doing. She had not told him about the creepy man who had been fixated with her for years and how he seemed to bring horrendous luck whenever he put in an appearance, but now was the time, and Marie told Charlie everything, and then she burst into tears and hugged him and kept asking him if he felt alright, because she was so afraid of losing him now that she had fallen intensely in love with him.

'I'm fine, I'm fine,' Charlie said, patting her head and holding her tight. 'Come on,' he suddenly said, 'let's go to a restaurant; it's a bit too early for films. Let's go and get something to eat.'

The couple went to a restaurant on Church Street and Marie kept clutching Charlie's hand, expecting him to keel over, but he remained in good health, and a year later the couple were married.

There is a bizarre postscript to this strange story. In 2004, Marie, then aged 75, was once again a widow, having lost her husband Charlie to Parkinson's Disease in the 1990s. One May morning around 9am, Marie was lying in bed at her home in Litherland, feeling quite sick with the flu, when she felt someone stroke her hair. She opened her eyes, and assumed it was her nephew George, who called in each afternoon to look after her, and Marie called out to him as the person swiftly left the bedroom, closing the door behind him. Then Marie realised that it was morning, and George, an inveterate late sleeper, never came around before two in the afternoon. Marie sat up and groggily looked at the door of the bedroom, which was still rather dark because the curtains had not been opened. She then noticed a small envelope on the bedside cabinet, resting against the old alarm clock. Her first name had been written on it in handwriting which looked unfamiliar. Marie opened the drawer in the cabinet and located her spectacles. She put them on, opened the envelope and read the strange short message it contained. That message read: 'Marie, I am sorry about the obsession with you and for all the calls and all the times I followed you. It was just love, that's all.'

And the unsettling letter was signed: 'Zodius'.

With a sense of mounting panic, Marie's trembling hand dialled 999 and she asked for the police. Within fifteen minutes there was a heavy knocking on the front door, and Marie tiptoed downstairs to answer. She told the police about the letter and two constables immediately searched the house, but there was no sign of any intruder. Just how "Zodius" gained access to Marie's home remained a mystery, and Marie thought it odd how the person who had left the note had moved so quickly for someone who had been at least ten years older than her – if it had actually been her stalker. George was ruled out as the writer of the letter because he did not even know about his aunt's stalker, and at the time of the bedroom visitation, George was still in bed.

After that encounter with the eerie fixated admirer, Marie never saw or heard from him again, and she passed away in her sleep after a short illness in 2010. 'Zodius' is apparently a surname that is fairly widespread in Romania, and it's also known in France, Canada and Australia, but beyond this, nothing more is known about the sinister stalker who used the name as his moniker.

BELLE VALE GHOSTS

The district of Belle Vale has quite a variety of ghosts and hauntings, from the mischievous phantom lady of Belle Vale Shopping Centre to the enigmatic but scary 'Man in White' who has been seen running towards people (and *through* them) on the Liverpool Loop Walk (formerly the Gateacre railway line); more of these two entities later in this chapter. Some of the ghosts of Belle Vale are fairly modern, but a few seem to date from the early 18th century to modern times, and this chapter will deal with just a small selection of them. The ghosts that can be seen can be frightening enough, but there are also supernatural entities that choose to be invisible to our limited range of vision, and one of these has been active in Belle Vale for many years. One of this ilk that comes to mind is the thing which causes havoc with cars on the B517 – the official name of Belle Vale Road. This road stretches for almost a mile, spanning the Gateacre Brow/Halewood Road junction in the west and Childwall Valley Road in the east, and it has been the scene of some rather bizarre goings-on in the past. Let us start in chronological order. At around 2.30 am on the Thursday morning of 12 April 1979, a 27-year-old Childwall man named Malcolm was driving his Ford Granada from his Uncle Martin's house on Acrefield Road to his home on Childwall Valley Road, and this journey necessitated taking the Belle Vale Road route. Malcolm had been helping his uncle to decorate his house since 8pm and was now fit to drop with exhaustion after painting three walls of a living room. The Granada curved right, around the mini roundabout on Acrefield Road, and cruised onto Gateacre Brow. Upon reaching Belle Vale Road, Malcolm wound down the side window to admit some fresh air into the vehicle to stop him from nodding off. The road was bathed in the serene pale light of the full moon, and at that time in the morning there were no other cars on Belle Vale Road nor any pedestrians about, which Malcolm found a bit odd because he had made the journey down this road before around this time and he usually saw a taxi or someone walking a dog. The car passed under the railway bridge and when it had covered about fifty yards – just before Belle Vue Road, there was an almighty thump which seemed to come from the roof of the Granada, and simultaneously the windscreen shattered and turned white – and opaque – Malcolm couldn't see a thing, so he put his fist through the screen, sending a few hundred pieces of granulated glass onto the bonnet. He pulled over, got out of the car, and looked around, first wondering if someone with an air rifle had taken a pot-shot at him, but then he recalled the loud bang on the roof of the vehicle, and when he looked at the top of the Ford Granada, he saw a slight dent there – about the size of a fist. Malcolm stood there in the silence, scanning the moonlit bridge, the road, the bushes in the nearby gardens of the houses, as well as the bushes, saplings and tall grass of the embankment leading to the railway bridge, and there was no sign of any mischievous young sniper with a catapult, air pistol or air rifle. Malcolm knocked the rest of the shattered glass out the destroyed windscreen and drove home, wondering what had happened. The next morning, Malcolm's dad told him that a car in front had picked up a piece of grit with its back tyre and slung it at his windshield, but Malcolm recalled that there had been no cars on the road, and certainly no vehicles in front of him, so that explanation did not apply. On the following month – May – again on the twelfth, which happened to be a Saturday, Malcolm was again driving home from his Uncle Martin's house on Acrefield Road, and this time he had left a little later – almost 3.10 am because he had been helping his uncle and a friend with the wiring of the house on Acrefield Road. Like last time (and I have checked this with an almanac) there was a full moon out. Malcolm passed under the railway bridge in his Ford Granada, and he thought about the windscreen-shattering incident last time as he travelled up a moonlit Belle Vale Road. He passed the spot where something had struck his vehicle a month back, and looked around as he slowed down to about 15 mph. Again, like last time, there wasn't a soul about. Malcolm was just about to accelerate slightly when the windshield frosted over as something struck it, and this time he heard no thump on the roof of the vehicle, but he did think he heard a single click before the windscreen was shattered. He stalled the vehicle, put on the handbrake, and got out the car, determined once and for all to get to the bottom of this second attack on his vehicle. 'Bastards!' he whispered fiercely and clenched his teeth as he looked up and down the road. He felt as if someone –

or maybe *something* was watching him and relishing this latest act of vandalism. It had to be a sniper – perhaps someone up on the railway bridge. Malcolm looked up at the bridge and saw no one peeping at him, and not a stir of movement. He heard a dog barking somewhere far off in the distance, and that was the only sound he could hear besides his breathing because he was so livid at this weird occurrence happening to him again. He heard a noise behind him – a slight thumping sound – and he turned quickly and saw his car rock slightly, and this really unnerved him because it was as if something invisible – and something endowed with a lot of strength – had struck the vehicle hard, making it rock on its suspension. He swore loudly, purely out of nerves, and then Malcolm got back in his car after knocking the granulated glass out of the rubber windscreen frame. Of course, when his mum, dad and sisters heard that Malcolm had fallen prey to the windshield-smasher yet again, they thought it was a joke, but Malcolm wasn't laughing, and he had to shell out again for a replacement windshield. From then on, and for many years afterwards, Malcolm refused to travel up Belle Vale Road after dark. Then, around 1981, Malcolm's mother woke him up one morning and told him a bit of news that she had just heard. At around one in the morning, a neighbour – a Mr White – had been travelling along Belle Vale Road on his way back from a school reunion, when his windshield had exploded. Mr White thought someone had taken a shot at him but drove on and reported the matter to the police, and a policeman told him – "off the record" – that there had been dozens of these incidents on that stretch of Belle Vale Road – always after dark – where something had smashed the windshields of taxis, vans and cars – and although the police had patrolled the area, hoping to catch a sniper or someone with a catapult, the culprit was never found. Stranger still, most of the attacks on the windshields took place around the time of a full moon. Mr White said he didn't understand what the policeman was trying to say, and asked if there was something supernatural about the attacks. The police officer shrugged and said he personally believed a juvenile in the area with some air rifle that shot pellets made of something which disintegrated upon impact was probably to blame, but that he must be a master of camouflage because no one ever spotted him before or after the attacks.

A camouflaged sniper who goes by the phases of the moon is a possibility, but what about the thump to the roof of Malcolm's car during the first incident, and what struck his car - making it rock - on the second occasion? And what sniper could do the following on that seemingly accursed stretch of road? One *moonless* Thursday night on 12 December 1985, minutes before midnight, Mr and Mrs Cheeseman, a couple in their thirties were travelling in a car down Belle Vale Road, returning from a Christmas visit to their friend's house in Childwall and bound for their home near Hunts Cross Avenue. As the Cheesemans car was passing the stretch of road between Belle Vale Park and Lee Park Avenue, the headlights went out, and then the sodium lights atop of the concrete lamp posts died. Mr Cheeseman clicked his headlamp switch on and off but they remained out, even though the lamps of the fascia display remained on with a steady greenish glow. The car travelled along an almost pitch-black Belle Vale Road, and Mr Cheeseman checked his mirror and then looked at the road far ahead, and saw that there were no other vehicles on the road. Mrs Cheeseman switched on the car radio to test the vehicle's electrics and immediately heard *Today in Parliament* on the station her husband always had on in that vehicle – BBC Radio 4. Mr Cheeseman thought there must be a logical explanation – and he did not know much about the workings of his car – but he thought that perhaps a fuse had gone which had killed the headlights, and perhaps through some astronomical coincidence, the lights of the highway had also failed through some short circuit somewhere – but deep down he felt that this was not the case. The car passed under the railway bridge – the one Malcolm had passed under just before his windscreen was smashed on those two occasions. The couple heard a shriek which sounded like laughter mingled with a screaming gale, and all of a sudden, Mr Cheeseman felt his car being pushed onto the pavement – towards a concrete lamp standard. He twisted the steering wheel right as his wife screamed – and the car scraped its side against the lamp post, taking the paint off. The brakes were slammed on and Mr Cheeseman asked his wife if she was alright as he applied the handbrake. Her right hand clutched his left hand and she nodded. Then all of a sudden, the headlamps of the car came on all by themselves and so did the lights of the highway. Mr Cheeseman took the handbrake off and drove off, and the car behaved fine. No windscreen was smashed but the electrics of the car seem to have been affected in some paranormal way on Belle Vale Road, and perhaps the blacking out of the highway lamp posts was also connected to the strange goings-on that night.

In February 2015 I investigated a number of reported encounters between members of the public and a man in a white periwig who was dressed in fine 18th century attire on Belle Vale Road. The solid-looking ghost was mostly seen near to a bus stop close to the bridge which crosses the road – and that same bridge which featured in the accounts of the windshield-shattering ghost and the account given by the Cheesemans. This unidentified ghost actually chatted (in what seems to have been some archaic tongue) to two girls at the bus stop by the bridge one night around 10pm. One of the girls – Riley, aged 18, said the ghost addressed her as "fair maiden" but she and her friend Sarah could not understand the rest of his comments. The face of the chatty backdated phantom looked very pale and his eyes were described as two black holes. The girls thought the man – who they estimated to be in his early thirties – was just a joker in fancy dress, until he wandered out into the road and straight into the path of their bus. The driver had not seen a thing but when the bus moved away, the weirdly attired figure reappeared by the bus stop and the girls now refuse to go anywhere near that stop. At the time of writing I have received more reports of this ghost and it seems he has quite a history. One medium I have consulted believes he is one of the illustrious Norris family – possibly Sir William Norris (1658-1702) the second son of Thomas Norris of Speke Hall. William died of dysentery at sea in 1702, and left no issue. If it *is* his ghost haunting Belle Vale Road, I do not know why he has returned from beyond to chat up two teenagers, but from the sheer number of sightings of this ghost, I have no doubt that a bewigged ghost in 18th century clothes is haunting Belle Vale Road. Another ghost – not as old as the aforementioned one – dates back to Victorian times and is known as the Blue Lady. She haunts Belle Vale and Gateacre and has been seen quite a lot of times walking along Runnymede Close and Acrefield Road – and she may be connected to a grand dwelling which once stood on land occupied by those locations: the mysterious Gateacre Hall, a fine listed building – sadly demolished between 1892 and 1904. Standing proudly on Halewood Road, Gateacre Hall dated back to the mid-17th century, and was surrounded by rumours of a very sinister murder which supposedly took place within its walls around 1850. One weird rumour, said to have come from a dismissed servant at Gateacre Hall, maintained that the tenant of the Hall, a broker (and a prominent committee member of the Liverpool Art Union) named Thomas A. Bushby, murdered his wife and buried her body in a shallow grave near to a strange concave depression in a field nicknamed the "Woolton Crater". The murder allegedly took place during a ball, when Mrs Bushby asked to be excused because she felt unwell. Mr Bushby is said to have tried to strangle his wife but was forced to cut her throat when she regained consciousness and attempted to shout for help. By sheer luck – some would say the Devil's Luck, Mr Bushby found a female servant who was his murdered wife's exact double, both in face and figure. This doppelgänger wife was coached to talk just like her. Everything seemed to go to plan until the ghost of the *real* Mrs Bushby turned up, dressed in the beautiful blue dress she had been murdered in – a dress that now had vivid blood stains around the collar where Thomas Bushby had sliced through her jugular. The hauntings became so spectacularly grisly (pools of blood appearing on the tablecloth during dinner and on the sheets of the master's bed) Mr Bushby and his impostor wife up and left, and a Scottish coppersmith from Hope Street named Leishman then took up the tenancy of Gateacre Hall, and he and his wife, two friends and several of the servants, all allegedly saw the "Blue Lady" both roaming the Hall and drifting about the estate's 30,700 square yards. She was seen in the Hall's stables, coach-houses, hothouses, plantations, gardens, the lodge, and the gardeners' and labourers' cottages.

Successive tenants of Gateacre Hall and many locals saw the forlorn figure of the Blue Lady in every corner of the mansion, and she was also seen walking outside, always during the hours of dusk, and when Gateacre Hall was eventually altered (vandalised by developers) into becoming a hotel, the Blue Lady still walked the premises, and by now her appearance was regarded as an omen of death. When Mr Edward Litler-Jones, an owner of the hotel property saw her, he believed his days were numbered, and in June 1937, after suffering a severe nervous breakdown he shot himself in a South African hotel where he had been hoping to recover his sanity.

They say the Blue Lady still walks even today, and I have many reported sightings of the female ghost, but beyond the anecdotal data given, I am not sure of the identity of this Belle Vale phantom. The Grey Lady who haunts the railway bridge over Belle Vale Road is another unidentified apparition. Some say she is the ghost of a suicide that took place on the bridge in the 1920s, but no one can be sure who she was when she lived as a flesh and blood person on earth. That railway bridge is now part of the Liverpool Loopline - a 13-mile path of disused railway line which stretches from Halewood to Aintree (and on to Southport if you're feeling adventurous). The Loopline makes an excellent traffic-free walking and cycling route where you can take in the local wildlife, the woodlands and the wetlands which thrive in the areas where trains once ran – until 1964, when British Rail abandoned the track. Construction of the Loopline began in 1988 with the final stretch of the converted track being finished in the year 2000. The Loopline is like a magical corridor of countryside in the midst of urban Liverpool, and while many people only use it of a weekend for leisurely walking and cycling, some people, such as a 45-year-old Walton man named Robin, utilise the Loopline as a fabulous traffic-bypassing shortcut to get to work; in Robin's case, he cycles from Walton to his workplace in Hunts Cross via the path, but in the late summer of 2010, Robin was cycling home along the Loopline - crossing the railway bridge over Belle Vale Road - around 5.20pm when he saw a figure about a hundred yards ahead, running towards him. Robin surmised it was a jogger because the figure looked like a man in a white tracksuit, but as he got nearer, Robin saw that it was a partially transparent figure giving off a slight glow, and this ghost had no face, just a vaporous smudge. The clothes – jacket, trousers, shirt, shoes – were all of a pale unearthly monochrome colour, and as the thing jogged towards Robin it did not make a sound. He quickly slowed his Genesis Equilibrium bike and swerved to avoid the apparition – but the ghost also changed course and ran at him. When it was about thirty feet away, Robin could hear a faint hissing and rustling sound emanating from the figure, and it suddenly darted at him at quite some speed, much quicker than a normal *living* person could move, and the cyclist reflexively threw up his hands. The running ghost passed right through Robin, and as it did he actually felt some weird ticklish sensation move through his body, from his chest to his back, and he cried out something which he cannot now remember. Robin turned and saw the ghost jog on down the path, and then it suddenly vanished in an instant when it was about twelve feet away. Robin gripped the handlebars of his bike and he pedalled away from the spot as fast as he could. He saw a woman approaching with a dog on a lead, and he slowed and warned her: 'Be careful if you're going down there, love,' he said, 'there's a ghost down there.'

The woman shot a bemused look at Robin and carried on anyway, saying, 'Oh, really?'

Robin continued on his way and when he reached his home in Walton he told his wife about the ghost and she seemed to think the encounter was some omen of tragedy, but no ill luck or bad news befell Robin or his family, and he never saw the running spectre again, although he is always on edge whenever he cycles down the Loopline. There have been many other sightings of the Man in White on the Loopline. A whole family saw him run past them in July 2011, again near the Belle Vale Railway bridge, only on that occasion, the semi-transparent ghost did not purposely run through anybody, but silently ran past the terrified family in a southerly direction. The most recent sighting seems to have taken place in March 2013 when two 17-year-old Broadgreen girls - Lucy and Ella – decided to go on their first run. Both girls believed they were overweight, and thought they should take up running to slim down. Neither of them had ever tried running longer than a few minutes, and aimed – rather unrealistically – at covering seven miles. Someone had told them that if a person ran 7 miles a day they'd keep fat at bay, and filled with this misinformation, Lucy and Ella set out from the point on the Loopline near Thomas Lane Playing Fields in their trainees, shorts and tee shirts with their hair piled up in buns. Lucy had the nous to carry a little 500 ml bottle of Evian spring water, but Ella said she wouldn't need any water during the run. The duo had only covered three quarters of a mile when Ella cried out: 'Stop! Stop! Hang on!' and she came to a halt and bent over and with her hands on her bare knees, she gasped for air, spat, craned her head back to look at the remarkably (for March) clear and blue sky and took in more air. 'You knackered already?' Lucy wheezed, but did a bit of ridiculous running on the spot, making out she could have continued on the run, but she soon stopped the act. Lucy unscrewed the top of the Evian and began to take big gulps of it, and soon Ella's hand was wrenching it from her grasp. The teens decided it would be wiser to just walk for the time being, and this they did, laughing and singing as they strolled along, heading south. When the girls got to the railway bridge which passes over Belle Vale Road, Lucy suddenly shouted: 'Oh my God! Look!' as she tapped Ella hard on her shoulder. Ella turned, thinking Lucy was just messing about, and there, running silently sown the Loopline – in their direction – was a weird-looking figure which to Ella's eyes just looked like a man in a sports jacket and trousers who had been dipped in a vat of white paint. Neither Ella nor Lucy could make out any facial features on the stranger. The bizarre running man was about twenty feet away, and he suddenly performed the same menacing manoeuvre he had when he had approached Robin five years before – he accelerated and flew towards the girls at a phenomenal speed. The girls screamed and Lucy threw herself aside, but the ghostly runner went straight through poor Ella and the girl almost fainted with the shock. She didn't feel the tingle Robin had reported, but the very act of something invading her body, albeit momentarily, gave her nightmares for months.

The figure ran on down the track and this time he did not vanish as he had done after Robin's encounter. Instead, the girls watched as the ghost ran far into the distance until he was a white spot. Lucy and Ella never set foot on the Loopline again after that creepy experience. Lucy maintained that the incident took place just before 4pm that day, but Ella said she was sure it occurred around 4.30pm, and both thought it was odd how they had not seen any walkers or cyclists pass them that day. The faceless ghost of the Loopline remains a mystery, but some diligent researcher into the paranormal may be able to find the back history of the phantom one day.

I've received a lot of emails, letters and telephone calls from people over the years who have told me of their experiences with a ghostly lady (named "Cathy" by some) who is alleged to haunt Belle Vale Shopping Centre. Many years ago a woman who worked at a cake shop in the shopping centre told me how she would sometimes arrange cakes in the glass display counter only for some of them to disappear. At first, when the cakes vanished, suspicion fell on a young woman who had recently started at the confectioners on a work experience scheme, but then the cakes would vanish even when she wasn't around, and some of the cakes would also turn up days – and even weeks – later, sometimes in a stomach turning state of staleness. Eventually, the girls in the cake shop realised they had a ghost on the premises, and even the van driver who brought trays of the cakes to the confectioners told how he would feel hands tapping him on his arm when he drove into the loading bay underneath the shopping complex. The most frightening incident happened when a woman in her fifties named Ena came into the cake shop in the shopping centre one morning and calmly told one of the girls serving: 'There's a woman all in black standing there, to your left. Her name's Cathy and I think she either lived in this area or worked here. She's going mad because I've told you about her.'

The staff went cold when they heard this because one of the security guards had seen a shadowy woman in black drifting along one morning when he came into the shopping centre. The guard was later told that the same eerie entity had even been seen on the security CCTV cameras. Another woman who worked at a certain store in the shopping centre told me how, late one afternoon she was sitting on the toilet in the staff room when she heard a violent rattling of the lock.

'There's someone in here!' the woman shouted, but still the annoying rattling sound continued. The woman got off the toilet, made herself decent, and undid the lock and yanked open the door, and for a brief second she saw that there was a tall woman wearing either a black polo neck sweater or an old-fashioned high collar standing before her. That woman vanished into thin air. Another woman who used that same toilet later said she had felt a presence as she sat there, and had actually heard breathing and what sounded like a chuckle. The female employee was so spooked, she got up, and without flushing the toilet, rushed out of the cubicle as fast as possible. About a week after this, the ghost reverted to its toilet humour when it turned on the taps in the staff washroom in front of several witnesses. Abnormally long black patent leather shoes with small heels were also seen under the gap in a toilet door for almost an hour but when the door was opened the toilet cubicle was found to be empty. In the 1990s, a group of nine friends at a house on Hartsbourne Avenue decided to dabble with the Ouija board one evening, and at one point in the supernatural experiment, the name "Cathy" came through. 'Did you used to live in this house, Cathy?' Steve, the self-appointed head of the Ouija group asked.

The glass slid over the circular dining table's Formica surface and nudged a piece of paper someone had written the word "No" on.

'Then where did you live?' Steve asked. He was not at all flippant in the manner he addressed the possible spirit because Steve believed there was *something* behind the Ouija board's alleged powers of divination, even though he did not know exactly what the thing was.

The glass began to move about, touching the little squares of paper with the letters of the alphabet on. It never once touched the ten squares bearing the numerals zero to nine.

'Chilwall Val Road' the glass spelt out, obviously referring to Childwall Valley Road. Then came another message which read: 'Bel Vale shopin senter' – a badly spelt reference to Belle Vale Shopping Centre.

'Why do you mention the shopping centre?' Steve asked, looking up at the ceiling.

'I died in der' the Ouija glass spelt out as a reply.

Then a chilling message came through. It read: 'Lesleyhobbs hobshobs'.

A few did not know the relevance of this garbled group of letters beyond seeing that it contained the name Lesley, but Steve and a few other people who had grown up in Belle Vale recognised the name: Lesley Hobbs – a 12-year-old schoolgirl who had lost her life by being stabbed and bludgeoned to death - allegedly by a 15-year-old boy - at her home on Childwall Valley Road in December 1962. The murder scene was less than half a mile from the house where the Ouija session was taking place and of course, Belle Vale Shopping Centre is within a stone's throw of Hartsbourne Avenue. The meaning of the message through the upturned glass was typically vague, but some of the sitters at the session were particularly scared because they worked at Belle Vale Shopping Centre and some of them were aware of the ghost that haunts the place. I am informed that there are still ghostly goings-on at the shopping centre, but whether it is at the hands of "Cathy" or some other entity is not known.

Coincidence is a common occurrence in the world of the paranormal, and funnily enough, on the very same night the Belle Vale Ouija session was taking place on Hartsbourne Avenue, another group of people – not as many as the aforementioned one – were gathered in a lounge at a detached house over in Cherry Vale, a pleasant much sought-after residential lane in leafy Woolton. The results of the *this* Ouija session were just as dramatic, because the word 'HANG' kept coming through, and at one point, screams filled the air at the table of the sliding glass when two women said they saw the shadow of a hanging man cast onto a wall. Days later, a neighbour told the man who lived in the house where the Ouija session had taken place that a teacher had hanged himself in one of the houses on Cherry Vale many years ago after suffering from a long bout of depression. That night, Susan, the wife of the man who had arranged the Ouija board session, had a vivid dream in which she was visited by a man with a broken neck. He warned her to never again hold a Ouija board 'party' in her home or he'd come back from the grave and kill her. Susan told her husband about the dream and he assured her it had just been a nightmare, but a month later, Susan came home from work late one evening to find her husband and three friends messing about with the Ouija in the kitchen. Susan had a blazing row with her husband, and during the argument, all Hell broke loose as knives, forks, spoons and knives flew all over the place. Dishes were smashed against walls, and the sitters ran out of the house. The poltergeist activity became worse, and that night, Susan and her husband clung on to one another as the bed they lay in was rocked violenty as something pounded the walls and rapped on the windows. The terrifying activity died down for a week, but when Susan and her husband attended the funeral of a friend at Anfield Cemetery a fortnight later, they were pelted with stones from nowhere. Mourners, pallbearers and the priest witnessed the rain of stones all the way to the gravesite. Every stone that fell was of the same type – a black pebble measuring about half an inch across. Many of these stones bounced off the coffin as they rained down and one struck Susan's leg. To this day a crucifix hangs on the wall in the kitchen where the poltergeist activity took place, and there have been no weird occurrences at the house since.

I'd better wrap up the chapter on Belle Vale Ghosts now, but before I do, let me tell you of a strange supernatural entity which used to haunt one of the "Five Ugly Sisters" of Belle Vale; these were the five 14-storey blocks named after the Prime Ministers Eden, Chamberlain, Churchill, Atlee and Macmillan – all built by Wimpey between 1963 and 1965 on the Lee Park Estate. A few of these eyesores had ghosts, but the paranormal thing which frequented Chamberlain House seems to have been in a terrifying class of its own. Around 1971, a family of three - mother, father and a 10-year-old girl we shall call Laura, moved into Chamberlain House after leaving a condemned property in Everton. The family settled into their brand new 3-bedroom home in the tower block. About a week after the family moved in, a cousin of Laura – two-year-old Danny – came to stay because his large family had unexpectedly received a number of guests at their crumbling already overcrowded house in Kirkdale. Danny was only due to stay for a week until something was sorted out, and the boy loved Laura and his aunt and uncle.

Danny slept "top-tail" – at the bottom of the bed, and Laura slept at the other end, and on the third night at the new flat, Danny lay sleeping one morning at around 2am, while Laura was having enormous difficulty in getting to sleep for some odd reason. She sat up and looked towards the bedroom door, and she saw it steadily open. At first she thought it was her mother or father coming in, but then she realised that the door had opened by itself, and she could see no one in the dark hallway. Then what Laura could only describe as a small blue flame – just like the flame of a typical candle – only blue in colour – came floating into the bedroom. The girl froze at the unnatural spectacle as the flame drifted towards the bed. It hovered over the head of her sleeping cousin, and the spectral pale blue light cast by the flame fell on Danny's serene face.

The boy suddenly made a strange sound as if he was choking. He opened his eyes, and those eyes rolled back, and then closed, and the boy's little mouth opened slightly. That blue flame then moved away from the bed much faster than it had moved before, and as it went into the hallway, the bedroom door closed behind it with a loud bang. Laura knew something was wrong with her cousin and she sprung out of the bed, switched on the light, and tried to wake him by gently shaking him, but he wouldn't react.

Laura had a very bad feeling about this and ran crying into the bedroom of her parents. They too tried to wake little Danny, but he remained unconscious and Laura heard her father say he wasn't breathing. He then ran out to go to a public telephone box, and he dialled for an ambulance. The ambulance men soon turned up, and after trying to resuscitate Danny for about half an hour, they told Laura's mother and father that the boy was dead.

Laura fainted.

The coroner said that Daniel had died from a rare disorder known as 'Ondine's Curse' - a central nervous system failure by which a person stops breathing when they fall asleep. They then suffer a respiratory arrest and die without regaining consciousness. Laura told her parents – and her auntie and uncle – Danny's parents – about the weird blue flame which had come into the room and hovered over Danny before he died, but of course, Laura was accused of having a vivid imagination and of dreaming of the blue flame. Then, a few months later, Laura's Auntie Bernadette moved into Chamberlain House, along with her new baby girl Sarah and her other three children, aged three to six. Bernadette's husband was in hospital being treated for jaundice at the time. Three days after moving into her new home, Bernadette woke up one morning and found to her horror that little baby Sarah had turned blue. Bernadette tried to walk to the nearest hospital with her baby – who was unconscious and apparently not breathing – and a neighbour spotted the distressed lady and called for an ambulance. The ambulance men performed nothing short of a miracle when they somehow resuscitated the baby and got her breathing. At first the doctors who treated Sarah thought she had choked on her own sick but that was not the case. The baby had been in the best of health, so the doctors never really determined what had left her unconscious and close to death. Today, a little more is known about Sudden Infant Death Syndrome, but this was 1971, and medical knowledge of babies' health was woefully inadequate. Bernadette wept when she saw Sarah smile at her and she kept checking on the baby in her cot all the time when she got back home. Then Bernadette's six-year-old son said a strange thing, but like Laura his story was met with doubt. The boy said he had got out of bed to get a drink of water on the morning Sarah had been ill, and "a blue light, like a fairy-light off a Christmas tree" had floated past him in the hallway. The boy had not heard of the blue flame that Laura had talked of seeing the morning Danny died. Bernadette told her son he'd been half asleep, but all the same she would watch over Sarah each night for as long a she could until she fell asleep exhausted.

When Laura was 13, her mother gave birth to a baby boy named Michael, and when the baby was 9 months old, that sinister blue flame was seen again. On this occasion, Laura was on her way to the toilet at 3am, when she saw the blue flame come through the solid front door of the flat – and this time the flame was a bit brighter, and Laura felt a shudder travel down her spine when she saw that the flame was being carried in the hands of some ghostly woman in a hood. The ghost was very faint, but Laura could make out the outline, and realising that the entity was heading for the room of her mother and father – where her baby brother Michael was sleeping in his cot – the girl let out a scream and swore at the creepy baleful entity. 'Leave us alone!' Laura shrieked and became hysterical, and the ghost halted and looked at her, and she saw the face in the hood contort into an expression of hate. 'Stay away from us in the name of Jesus!' Laura screamed, and the mouth of the phantom woman opened wide and she closed her eyes by screwing them up into a ghastly expression. The light went out and Laura felt a slight breeze which went towards the front door.

The door of her parents' room opened and Laura's bleary-eyed father asked her what she was screaming at, and when she told him, he said: 'Get to bed! What on earth are you up for anyway, nighthawk?'

He let Laura go to the toilet and then he told her to get to bed and to be quiet. After that morning, Laura never saw the weird flame and that menacing woman ever again.

Chamberlain House and the other "Ugly Sisters of Belle Vale" were demolished in September 1992 to make way for a new housing development, and one wonders what became of that malevolent blue flame and its attendant keeper; will it still haunt the spot where the tower block stood? Hopefully its light will never be seen by anyone living again.

WINSLOW STREET GHOSTS

Winslow Street runs east-west from Goodison Road, the home of the Blues, to Walton's County Road, and the street comprises about 87 terraced houses in its 233 yards, and several of these houses are haunted. One of the dwellings has now been divided into flats, but still the ghost – that of a girl who, from her sober black attire, seems to date back to the Victorian or Edwardian era – still occasionally walks from the hallway to the topmost flat in the early evenings. Why she haunts the property and her identity are mysteries lost in the fog of time, but whoever she is, she seems happy enough, for those who have encountered her say the long-haired girl always has a big smile on her freckly face. One lady – Valerie – had a particularly close encounter with the phantom child one evening around 8pm in the summer of 2007. Valerie was coming down the stairs from her flat at the time, on her way to a shop to buy cigarettes, when she was startled to see a girl of about ten years of age hurrying up the stairs with her hand on the stair-rail. The girl didn't make the slightest sound as she ascended the steps, and Valerie stepped aside and asked: 'Where are you going, love?' She asked this because the girl was heading for Val's flat. The girl did not give a word of reply or even acknowledge her elder's question, but dashed straight though Valerie, her head passing through her abdomen. Valerie let out a yelp and turned, and saw the girl rush to the landing above and dart through the closed door of the flat. Valerie was so shocked at this eerie encounter, she refused to return home alone that evening and her sister Janet, who lives in Norris Green, had to stay over with her for a few days. Valerie had never heard anything ghostly in that house on Winslow Street in the three years she had lived there, but when she told a few of the other tenants in the adjoining flats, they all told her that they had either seen the girl or heard her singing somewhere, always in the evening around nine.

About a hundred yards from that haunted house, there is another abode on Winslow Street which has a paranormal presence. In 2011, a couple – David and Lisa – both in their thirties - rented a flat in this haunted house, quite unaware of its history, but Lisa was curious as to why the rent was rather low compared to the other flats she had viewed in Walton. The couple had only been living at the flat for just under a week when Lisa heard something as she lay in bed around 2.40am. 'Listen,' she whispered to David, who was just about to drop off after a busy day at a certain well known electrical goods store in the city centre. 'What?' he murmured; he heard nothing.

'Shhh!' Lisa dug her hand gently into his side. 'There! Can you hear it?'

This time David could hear what sounded like a radio somewhere, and he told Lisa what he thought. 'It's a car radio somewhere; what about it?'

'No, it's a song on a CD or something, and it goes back to the beginning,' Lisa told her boyfriend, and sat up in the bed.

'Go to sleep,' David advised, then added: 'You're always like this when you've had coffee.'

'I know that song,' said Lisa. 'Ah, what's it called?'

'Lisa just get to sleep will you? I'm knackered.' David turned and lay there face down. He yawned.

The bedroom door clicked, and opened a few inches, and now that far-off music sounded much closer.

Lisa shrieked at the opening of the door, and gripped David hard by his arm. 'There's someone coming in the room!' she yelled.

David swore and got up. 'It's the wind! I've got the bleedin' window open,' he shouted, and turned on the bedside lamp. 'It's a draught, that's all,' he said, but he hesitated, because he could now plainly hear that the music he and Lisa had listened to before was now much louder – and it seemed to be coming from the living room.

'The Thompson Twins,' Lisa said, looking at the door, all wide-eyed and afraid.

'What?'

'That song,' Lisa explained, 'it's by the Thompson Twins - *Doctor! Doctor!* it was called.' She recalled her mother turning the song up whenever it came on the radio years ago.

'That dickhead next door must be playing it,' David reasoned, blaming the young man in his twenties who lived in the second-floor flat next door. He had an annoying habit of playing his latest Ministry of Sound album after 10pm.

'No, that's coming from the living room,' Lisa opined, tilting her head to get a fix on the location of the faint music, and then she suddenly said, 'David, don't go out – close the door and stay in here.'

David was already peering into the hallway, but it was too black to see anything.

'David!' Lisa leaped out of bed and grabbed her boyfriend's elbow. 'I've got a really bad feeling about this,' she said and closed the door as she yanked him back into the room. David could see the raised goosebumps on Lisa's arms; something really was spooking her. The music and vocals ceased abruptly as if a radio or CD player had been switched off.

The couple returned to bed and hugged one another with the bedside lamp left on. At a quarter to eight they both got up and showered together, and each noticed that the other seemed on edge because of the weird door-opening incident of the night before. David dropped Lisa off on Hope Street, and she made her way to the small sandwich shop in the city centre on the university campus where she had worked now for nearly two years. David drove to a multi storey car park on Mount Pleasant then walked to the store where he worked seven days a week. He returned home a little after six and found Lisa in high spirits. She hadn't been in the mood to cook anything though, and from the chippy she had ordered a Thai Red Curry Special for herself and some barbeque spare ribs for David. David smirked when he sat down to eat because instead of the usual bottle of San Miguel beer Lisa usually plonked down next to his plate, there was a glass of wine – and it was neon blue in colour. 'Is that an energy drink?' David enquired.

'Blue Hawaiian apple wine,' Lisa indicated the bottle David had overlooked in the middle of the table with her index finger. He picked the glass of oddly coloured wine up and sniffed it. 'Smells like coconut sunscreen; what does it taste like I wonder?' He took a little sip.

'Thought we'd try something different instead of

beer or lager all the time,' Lisa told him and seemed hurt, and he felt sorry for her seeing her like that, so he pretended the electric blue wine tasted great, but she knew it wasn't to his taste, and went to the kitchen and opened a bottle of San Miguel.

'No, this is okay,' David grimaced at the sweet taste, and Lisa grinned, shook her head and took the glass out of his hand. 'Hey, I appreciate you trying something different Lee [as he called her for short when he was being affectionate].'

'Shurrup,' she replied, dismissively but grinning, and got stuck into the curry.

After tea, the couple watched telly for a while, and finding the news depressing, Lisa curled up like a cat at the end of the sofa with her iPad and surfed Etsy to see if anything took her fancy. David went upstairs and played Fifa online with Eric, his mate from work. Night soon fell, and they got in bed at 11pm and David was soon snoring. Lisa lay there, thinking about the creepy sounds of that song she had heard the night before and the way the bedroom door had opened, when all of a sudden, she heard someone close by inhale loudly – it sounded as if someone was entering the room as they were taking a sharp intake of breath – and all of a sudden, the bedroom door steadily opened as this sound filled the room, and Lisa let out a scream, because this was no breeze opening the door – it was being steadily pushed open as someone entered. David flew upwards into a sitting position, and Lisa could see his head silhouetted against the drawn curtains which were filtering the light of a streetlamp. She could see his mouth open in shock as he looked at the opening door. He got out the bed swearing and turned on the bedside lamp, and he clenched his fist and stood there, ready to have a go at the intruder.

But there was no one there.

David and Lisa looked at the black upright rectangle of shadow – the doorway which led into the dark hall. David swore again and advanced to the hallway, and although it was comical in hindsight, it was not funny at the time when he picked up Lisa's red and white polka dot umbrella from the corner as he advanced to the hallway. There was no intruder in the hallway, and no one to be seen in the living room, spare room, kitchen or toilet. Lisa was afraid of staying behind in the bed so she followed David everywhere, and kept asking him what he thought had opened the door, but he kept saying, 'It wasn't the wind.'

The couple eventually returned to bed and sat up, holding hands, and then, around one o'clock, the two of them jumped when they distinctly heard:

Doctor, Doctor, can't you see I'm burning…

About a minute later, the music and singing voices suddenly faded, and an uneasy tense silence filled the bedroom. Lisa kept looking at the door handle, expecting it to turn and for the door to burst open, but it didn't. Eventually the pale bluish light of dawn came bleeding through the curtains, and a drowsy David reached out to switch off the lamp on the bedside cabinet.

Lisa fell asleep in his arms and he nodded off not long afterwards.

He awoke to Lisa shaking him, and now the room had been fully infiltrated by daylight.

'What?' he asked, seeing her face all screwed up as if she was mad at him for something.

'Don't do that again,' she said, 'it was horrible,' and she turned away from him in the bed.

'Don't do *what?*' David was baffled at her behaviour.

'What you just did, okay?' came the muffled reply from beneath the sheets.

'Lisa, I have just woken up – what am I have supposed to have done?'

She swore at him.

'Lisa – ' he tried to put his arm around her but she slapped his hand away under the covers.

When they both rose at 7.45 am, he asked her once again what he was supposed to have done. 'Why are you narked at me?'

'You know why,' she said, stepping into her slippers without turning to look at him.

'Will you please be civil and stop talking to me as if I'm crap?' he bawled. 'I have done eff all to you! I was asleep for Christ's sake!'

Only then did the realisation dawn on Lisa that he had not stuck his finger in her, and she felt cold inside and sick, and she told him what she had felt as she lay there.

'Lisa, I swear on my Mum's life, I wouldn't do something like that to you...' David assured her and his voice trailed off as he too suddenly wondered if something paranormal had been responsible.

'Maybe we should move from here,' Lisa suggested, and wiped a tear from her eye and hugged David.

They had breakfast and were soon on their way to their workplaces, and that evening, when twilight fell and they went into the bedroom, Lisa put an old upright chair against the door.

'Ghosts go through objects,' joked David, 'that won't stop it.' He realised it was a stupid and inconsiderate thing to say, and he back-pedalled and told Lisa that he had been looking at the website of a reputable estate agent earlier and had seen some really modern flats with a slightly dearer rent down in Fazakerley – close to the home of Lisa's parents. He lay there in bed as the hour wore on, listening to music from his mobile on his headphones, while Lisa kept alternating her attention between the screen of her iPad and the bedroom door.

The two of them soon fell asleep, and at 3am, Lisa was awakened by David getting out the bed to go to the toilet. He moved the chair out the way and left the bedroom, leaving the door wide open. Lisa peered over the top of the duvet at the dark hallway and saw the thin line of light shining under the toilet door. She could hear David urinating. Then she heard that familiar song again, *Doctor! Doctor!*

She froze. Lisa saw the living room door open, and this time a strange orange lamp went on in that room – and the couple had no such lamp in their living room. And then she saw a tall thin naked man with a head of curly hair walking out of the room into the hallway, and Lisa tried to scream but she couldn't. She had heard about this condition before – of people being too afraid to scream – and she had always thought it was nonsense – but now she knew that in some people, the throat closes up with sheer fear. The naked man was walking towards the bedroom, and he had a rope tied around his neck, and the other end of it trailed about three feet behind him. All of a sudden, as the nude apparition reached the doorway of the bedroom, the curly head fell forward as if it was hanging by a string from the neck. The head rolled left and right, and now Lisa suddenly regained the power to scream. She emitted a loud shriek and almost instantaneously the bathroom door opened and out ran David, staring in horror at the bedroom.

The ghost had vanished, but Lisa continued to scream hysterically. She got out the bed in her pyjama bottoms and vest, and ran out of the bedroom, through the hallway, to the front door.

'Lisa! What happened?' David asked, trying to hold on to her, but she threw open the front door and ran onto the landing in her bare feet. David somehow managed to stop her from opening the door onto the street downstairs.

Enough was enough. That day, Lisa went to stay at her parent's house and said she would never return to that house on Winslow Street. David hired his friend Eric to move all of the furniture and personal items from the flat in Walton in a transit van to the house of David's auntie in Netherley. Eric was terrified of anything remotely supernatural, and so David did not tell him why he and Lisa were moving out the flat in such a hurry, and when Eric asked what had facilitated the need to relocate in such a hurry, David said Lisa had seen mice in the kitchen. Some strange things then took place which did not make sense at the time. Eric was asked to go back to the flat a few days later to pick up some mail (a final demand from Santander and a copy of a gaming magazine David had delivered). Eric returned to David in a terrible state. He said he had picked up the mail in the hallway (and this would have been around 7pm) when he heard a loud thud on the stairs. Eric had then been startled to see a pair of bare legs descend between the handrails of the staircase. He had stumbled forward in shock to see that a naked man had evidently hanged himself from the banister, and as Eric looked on, the dangling body began to pee everywhere. Eric ran out onto the street, and told a man and a woman in their forties what he had seen, but when they went into the hallway, there was no hanged man there. Eric began to swear at David. 'That's why you and Lisa got out there, isn't it? Cos its haunted isn't it?'

David was stuck for words as Eric almost came to blows with him.

The couple moved to a house in Huyton, and I visited the haunted house on Winslow Street. I was told by an old woman who lived a few doors down from the house in question that at some time in the 1980s, a young man had lived at the house with his widowed mother – and this was years before the dwelling was subdivided into flats. The young man had a nervous breakdown after he had been rejected by a girl he had been obsessed with. The young man stripped himself naked and hanged himself on the staircase. His mother became so grief-stricken at her son's ghastly suicide, she died from a heart attack not long after. Then, about six months later, the new tenants of the house reported all sorts of strange goings-on night and day. Music would be heard, and the naked ghost of the man who took his life would be seen hanging on the stairs. He also often opened the bedroom door of the couple all hours in the morning. I made a few more enquiries about the haunted house, but no one else recalled the suicide, as most people I talked to where too young to remember something that had taken place around 27 years before, but then I received an anonymous email from someone who knew an awful lot about the house. This person signed the email Mrs W and the hotmail email address was just a jumble of meaningless numbers and letters to ensure anonymity. The author of the email gave specific dates which allowed me to vindicate the claims, as well as the full name of the man who hanged himself. The man, it seems, used to sit in his bedroom playing records, and he was a fan of the Thompson Twins. A song of theirs called *Doctor! Doctor!* hadn't been released long when the young man began to write love letters to a certain girl who lived in nearby Barlow Lane. The girl in question thought the letters were weird and openly laughed at their author when she finally met him. He then went home and played the record which seemed to sum up the way he was feeling, for he was suffering from the cruel fever of unrequited love, for which there is no remedy. He hanged himself as the record played, and days later, his ghost was seen by many, stalking the girl on Barlow's Lane, and it is said that the girl died in a car crash one evening near Anfield Cemetery – where the suicide was laid to rest – and some maintained that the ghost of the lovelorn youth had flitted out into the path of the car carrying the girl he had loved in life, and that she had died from a broken neck when the vehicle smashed into a wall. The driver, her sister-in-law, survived, and swore that someone had dashed out in front of the car waving their hands before the accident. Other witnesses also saw the crash and told police that the body of a pedestrian must also be under the smashed vehicle, but no such body was ever found. They say that the ghost of the suicide still haunts the house on Winslow Street, and David and Lisa know this to be a fact…

THE SEVENTH STEP

The universe isn't as strange as we imagine; it is probably stranger than we can *ever* imagine, whether we are looking at the weird logic-defying behaviour of quarks, photons, fermions and bosons or, at the other scale of existence – the mind-bending properties of black holes and the mystery of dark matter. We must admit that we really know so little, and stories like the following may only be inexplicable because we have not yet discovered certain laws and forces which cause things like multiple coincidences, miracles and other seemingly supernatural occurrences.

A terraced house at the Green Lane end of Guernsey Road in Liverpool's Stoneycroft district was the home of two brothers in 1974. They were John, aged 21, and 37-year-old Derek, who had inherited the Edwardian house from his mother upon her passing two years before. John – a lecherous, self-centred divorcé – currently seeing two girlfriends in different parts of Liverpool – was studying Industrial Sociology and Marxism at the Polytechnic, and had just packed in a summer job working at Tate & Lyle because he claimed to have 'tired blood'. 'Layabout blood, more like,' Derek had told him. Derek was bald, rather conservative in his ways, the antithesis of his younger brother. Derek sold world stamp collections for a living. On this morning at breakfast, Derek read *The Spectator* while John munched marmalade on toast over the *New Musical Express*. He smelt of cheap aftershave and Cossack hairspray.

John's eyes suddenly rose up from the NME, and he gazed up at his brother and asked him why he never let his hair grow.

'Because I don't want to look like a girl, and I'm going a bit thin on top,' Derek told him, and plopped a sugar cube in his teacup.

'Not thin – shiny,' John thoughtlessly remarked, but added, 'although if you grew the remaining hair around the back and the sides long you'd look a bit younger.'

'I'm the age I am, and proud to be mature,' sulked Derek, and he left to go the toilet – to secretly inspect the top of his head with a shaving mirror, and as he was halfway up the stairs he said: 'I wish you'd get a job, John.' And seconds later the phone rang. It was Patrick, the uncle of the brothers, and he was phoning because he wanted John to work part-time in the antiques shop he'd just opened. It was good pay, and only four and a half days a week so John eagerly accepted the offer.

On the following morning over breakfast, John told his brother a strange thing. 'Derek, do you remember that superstition mum had, about the seventh step?'

Derek returned a blank look.

'Think back;' said John, 'she said the seventh stair was broken when she moved in here and a travelling man called, a gypsy, and he mended it, and after she paid him he said she could make three wishes a year when she stepped on that seventh stair; just recalled it now.'

'Oh that? Yes I remember that story now. What an absolute load of rubbish,' Derek chuckled, but John said: 'You wished for me to get a job as you walked up the stairs yesterday.'

'Just a bloody coincidence!' Derek assured his brother as he sat at the table and read *The Times*, but John went to the seventh step and announced: 'I wish my bachelor brother Derek had some female admirers!'

Derek shook his head, smirked and yawned, but that afternoon he paid a visit to the library, and he was searching for a copy of *Wisden Cricketers' Almanac* among the shelves when the shapely librarian Miss Peel suddenly remarked on the blueness of his eyes and asked if he was married.

'Sorry?' Derek replied, thinking he'd misheard Miss Peel's rummy question.

'Are you spoken for?' the librarian asked with a grin, and her bluish-green eyes seemed to sparkle like living jewels.

'Me? Ha! No, no no; who'd have me?' Derek said, fishing for compliments with his fake self-deprecating patter.

'I'd *have* you,' Miss Peel told him firmly, running the tip of her tongue along her top lip, and now her lids seemed heavy and her eyes looked rather sleepily at him.

Derek coughed and asked Miss Peel if she could possibly steer him to a copy of the cricketing almanac, and she placed her hand in the small of his back and gently pushed him to the Reference section.

Upon his way home, two young female neighbours, Michelle and Donna, both in their mid-twenties, stopped chatting outside the butchers and both simultaneously said hello to him. They normally never even acknowledged Derek. That evening Derek went to his local for his usual quiet drink, and Miss Peel, a female friend of hers, and those two neighbours, Michelle and Donna, who'd let on to him earlier, all put in an appearance, each of them dressed in a style that Derek found sexually provocative. Many of the predatory males in the bar closed in on Derek's 'fans' but the girls only had eyes for Derek, who was sitting cross-legged at his table with a red face and tiny beads of sweat on his pate as he was overcome with the stifling, intoxicating perfumes of the overeager ladies.

The four admirers closed in and they all sat near his table in the corner. The glamorous barmaid Lorraine also began to dote on Derek and virtually ignored her regulars, and by 9pm an argument between Lorraine and the librarian broke out because the latter had taken it upon herself to sit at at Derek's table with her friend.

'Derek has come here for a quiet drink, so leave him alone,' Lorraine told the librarian and her friend.

'I'm a friend of Derek,' said Miss Peel, looking Lorraine up and down with an expression of disgust, 'so do *not* tell me to leave him alone – alright?'

'Derek,' said Michelle, the neighbour from next door but one on Guernsey Road, 'is it okay if me and Donna sit at your table as well?'

'Er, yes, but er – ' Derek answered, feeling very claustrophobic and confused.

'No, he's come here for a quiet drink,' Lorraine's voice grated at Michelle through gritted teeth. 'And if anyone is supposed to be sitting at his table, it's *me* actually.'

By 9.15pm each of the five women claimed to have known Derek for some time and warned the others off. Fearing a riot, Derek ended up going to the toilets before he sneaked out of the pub and ran home. He told John what had happened, and put the front door bolts on.

'That's fantastic, Derek,' said John, excitedly, 'I told you that seventh step grants wishes!'

'No! No! I don't want anyone in my life – especially not *five* women!' cried Derek, and he switched off the hallway light. 'I just want my boring quiet life back! I've been single too long!'

'You told me not so long ago you'd like to settle down with a lady,' John reminded him.

'Yes, a quiet bookworm of a woman who loves cricket and cooking maybe,' Derek told him as he walked to the stairs. He went up to the seventh step. 'I *wish* those women would forget me!' he cried, and Lorraine couldn't even remember his name when he next ventured into the pub, and the four other admirers never looked at him in a romantic way again.

When I mentioned this story on the radio, a man named Bob called the station and said he lived in the house were John and Derek had once lived in, and he said that when he moved in he had the carpet removed from the stairs and had them cleaned and varnished. Bob confirmed that the seventh step *had* been patched up with dark long strips of what seemed to be walnut. I went to the house on Guernsey Road and saw this for myself, but neither I nor Bob made any wishes on the step. Perhaps the 'wishes' John and Derek made were all the products of coincidence – but those five women *were* awfully keen on Derek. The strange thing is that since I first recorded this strange story, I have found an old reference to a forgotten Lancashire superstition which says that if you stand on the seventh step while ascending and make a wish, it will come true, but if you stand on the seventh step as you are coming downstairs, you can curse a person, so maybe there was a grain of truth in that gypsy journeyman carpenter's claim...

WHAT ARE THEY?

This chapter concerns unidentified entities of the stranger kind; peculiar beings that do not fit in comfortably with the routine, widely-accepted notions and concepts of ghosts, apparitions or poltergeists. The examples cited here suggest that this world of ours can be easily accessed by intelligences (many of them sinister and eccentric) from 'elsewhere' – a loose term which might involve higher dimensions or undiscovered worlds of the type mooted in quantum physics (and String Theory) which could theoretically overlap ours. We seem to be vulnerable prey to these intruders who not only come and go as they please – they are sometimes unknowingly aided and abetted in the continued persecution and abuse of their victims because the victim speaks out and is not believed, either because the victim is young and is accused of having a vivid, childish imagination, or the victim is an adult and not believed because the assailant he or she describes seems simply too far-fetched to be believable. Let us start with the latter scenario – that of the adult who is not believed because the entity he encounters is simply too ridiculously surreal. In 1985 a 21-year-old medical student from Liverpool named Robert picked up a book on Welsh archaeology in William Brown Street library and read of the many fascinating archaeological finds in the caves of Wales; the hoard of Roman coins found by schoolboys in the Ogorf cave, South Wales in 1965, and of the remains of Neanderthal children found in a cave at Pontnewydd, near Rhyl in 1983. The book mentioned that there were many treasures still undiscovered in the countless caves of Wales, and so Robert and his friend Rachelle - another 21-year-old medical student – decided to have a day out looking around the many caves that are to be found within the 519 square miles of the Brecon Beacons, a rugged place in South Wales where the SAS do their most arduous training; a place of lofty moorlands grazed by sheep, of rocky gorges dotted with ancient trees with spectacularly gnarled and tentacled roots in an immense diverse terrain of cascading rivers, lakes with motionless looking-glass surfaces, and steep mountainsides. Among all of this natural varied beauty, there are ruins and reminders of human occupation from Neolithic times to the 19th century; vestiges such as the gothic-looking Tretower Castle, which was last garrisoned in 1403, and Y Gaer Fawr –an Iron Age fort atop the ancient hill of Y Garn Goch.

Robert and Rachelle set out from Liverpool by train as early as possible, and around 10am they reached the Brecon Beacons after an arduous hike from a youth centre, they passed a memorial granite obelisk, dedicated to the memory of a five-year-old local child who died there alone of exposure in mysterious circumstances in August 1900. They began to climb the peaks of Pen Y Fan, the summit of the Brecon Beacons, which soar 2,906 feet above sea level. Half way up the windswept peak, Rachelle noticed a hole, just wide enough for a person to climb through on all fours, and after inspecting the opening, she decided to crawl in, and she was astounded to see that the tunnel ahead led to a cave where Rachelle was able to stand up. Robert followed her, and finding that the lighting was bad, as the only illumination in the cave was daylight filtering down the tunnel, he struck two matches and looked about. Veins of white marble ran across the walls of the cave, and there was another opening about six feet in diameter, and oval in shape, and it was fringed with stalagmites and stalactites. The matches burnt out and Robert Struck two more, and this time, Rachelle produced an old notebook from her haversack and ripped out several pages to use as a makeshift torch. By the flames of this ad hoc torch, Rachelle spotted something in the darkness of the adjoining cave; at first she thought it was a statue of some sort. She told Robert to pull out more pages of the notebook and he did this and screwed them into a taper which he lit and thrust into the mouth of the cave. What Robert and Rachelle saw by the flame-light of the torch would become etched into their memories for years to come. There was a block of limestone in the centre of the adjoining cave, and upon it there was a very weird statue of a huge scaly snake, bent into an S-shape, and the serpentine sculpture had the life-size head of a woman with a mass of curly hair. This head, like the rest of the statue, was of a dull matt grey finish. The body of the snake-woman, in Robert's estimation, was about 18-20 feet in length, and about as thick as his waist, which was 36 inches. Robert leaned forward slightly with the torch, but did not enter the cave of the eerie statue, when all of a sudden, the head of the snake-woman *turned* quickly to face the burning torch, and Rachelle let out a shriek.

The bulging eyeballs of the animated entity were jet black, and the mouth fluttered as her voice said something which sounded like: 'It's serene.'

Rachelle would later maintain that the frightening snake-human hybrid had said something which sounded Welsh to her ears, but just what it was she was not sure. Rachelle ran out of the cave and of course, had to get down on her hands and knees to crawl down the narrow passage to the outside world. She felt Robert's head bump against her bottom several times as he also got out of the cave rather quickly. The students risked falling to their deaths on the steep slopes of Pen Y Fan, and both heard something making a loud hissing sound behind them as they scrambled downwards, away from the unearthly creature. Once they were sure that the python-like entity was not following them, the medical students made a more careful descent of the peak until they were out of danger. They headed back to the hostel they had set out from and compared notes. They had both seen the same thing, which ruled out some hallucination, but they could not agree on what the entity had said. In May of the following year, Robert suggested returning to the cave, this time with a camera in the hope of capturing the bizarre creature on film, but Rachelle was too afraid to venture back, so Robert went with his older brother Barry and another student who had brought along a cine camera fitted with a light to hopefully record the snake-bodied female, but Robert could not find the entrance to the cave. After a search lasting two hours, the trio gave up and returned to Liverpool. Robert went on to become a prominent surgeon, and he is not the type to imagine some being which looked like something which would not be out of place in the pantheon of Greek mythological creatures, but just *what* was that thing in the cave? It is just one of the many unidentifiable creatures and entities which people seem to encounter from time to time, and some of them have been quite scary, as the following account suggests.

Ivan Kettil-Marriott was a senior store detective in Liverpool from 1964 to 1990, and began his career on a contract basis, but proved to be so efficient at preventing theft, he was employed permanently by a certain well-known department store in Liverpool (which sadly no longer exists). Ivan had seen every type of shoplifter and pickpocket in action during the decades at his unusual job, from the organised shoplifting families and law-savvy professional who knew every legal loophole through which he or she could wriggle out of an arrest, to the habitual petty criminal, the kleptomaniac who stole out of an obsessive-compulsive desire, to the fetishist who stole female underwear. Ivan was an expert in apprehension techniques and was fully aware of the legal boundaries he was allowed to operate within in his job as a 'Loss Prevention Agent'.

One afternoon in 1974, a smart-looking man in a pin-striped suit entered the store where Ivan was employed, and he looked to be in his mid-thirties and had a very debonair air about him. The stranger had short slicked-back dark hair and a thinly-trimmed moustache. The visitor to the store stood out because in that day and age, most men his age wore their hair long, except for the occasional shopper who had a military background. Ivan was in the CCTV room when the man in the pin-striped suit entered and right away he thought there was something suspicious about him, for he knew he was being watched by the way he glanced up at the CCTV camera peering at him in the black inverted dome mounted on the ceiling near to the entrance of the store. The man held his gaze at the camera for a while, then walked to the escalator and rode it to the first floor – up to the menswear section. Ivan left the CCTV room, telling his two colleagues, Paul and Stephen, he was going to check the stranger out, as he had a gut feeling about him, and such intuition about a potential shoplifter often proved to be correct in Ivan's long years of experience. The suave stranger wandered to a corner of the menswear section, and began to constantly glance at the grey nondescript door as he browsed through a rack of ties. This door which seemingly interested the slick customer was the door to a room where shoplifters were interviewed and searched. The window in the top half of the door had inch-wide strips of half-silvered mirror glass so the people in the room could see out but anyone looking at the window saw nothing but their reflection. Why was this man interested in the room? Ivan wondered, and closed in on him as he pretended to look through the tweed jackets hanging up nearby. Ivan knew his two friends, Paul and Stephen in the CCTV room were monitoring the situation via the ceiling cameras.

The man being observed did a rather strange thing. He left the tie rack and walked to the door with the one-way mirror and held his palms out. He gently placed his palms against the door but did not seem to exert any pressure. He then turned – and looked directly at Ivan, and Ivan had the unsettling impression that the odd individual knew he was being watched. The stranger turned and marched towards the escalator, but stopped at one point and began to look at the Ben Sherman shirt on a mannequin. The black dome on the ceiling turned silently and trained its electronic eye on the person of interest.

'IRA?' said a low voice behind Ivan. He turned to see it was Paul; he'd come down to join in the surveillance.

'Nah, just a nut, maybe?' Ivan whispered as he watched the sharp-suited shopper.

Paul walked towards the centre of the group observation and brushed past him as he went to the shoe section. The man then walked back to the corner where the door was located, and this time he tried the handle. It was locked, but he tried turning it several times and began to shake the door by the handle.

'That's out of bounds, sir!' Ivan startled him with his sudden appearance beside him.

The man said nothing, but looked down and walked away. He went down to the ground floor via the escalator and out of the department store – but he came back in after about forty minutes, and this time Paul saw his entrance on the monitor in the CCTV room. 'He's back,' he said to Ivan, who was watching another person of interest – an old woman who was apparently stealing several pairs of gloves.

'I'll deal with her,' Stephen told Ivan, nodding at the monochrome image of the elderly shoplifter on the monitor.

Ivan watched the pin-striped oddball hurry to the escalator on the ground floor. 'What *is* his game?' he murmured, and left the room with Stephen, who was on his way to have words with the old glove-pincher.

Ivan and Stephen parted ways when they left the

surveillance room, and when Ivan reached menswear, he saw that the stranger was once again trying to gain entry to the room which was off limits to the public.

'Sir! What are you playing at?' Ivan asked, placing his hand on the man's right shoulder.

The unidentified customer turned and shoved Ivan hard into the wall, where he hit a fire extinguisher which fell from its mounting.

As Ivan got to his feet, he saw Paul already hurrying from the direction of the surveillance room with his eyes fixed on the troublesome visitor. He and Paul cornered the man, and he tried to make a dash for it, but Paul grabbed his arm and restrained him as Ivan produced a key and opened the door to the room which the stranger had repeatedly tried to gain access to for reasons presently unknown.

Paul shoved him into this room and the neon strip in the ceiling was still flickering after Ivan had switched it on when the man began to threaten legal action against the store detectives in a rather cultured voice.

'How dare you manhandle me like this! You'll both be hearing from my solicitor, you – you thugs!'

'Sit down,' Ivan pulled one of the two chairs from the small table in the centre of the room away, then added: 'mister?'

The man reluctantly sat down and gazed down at the tabletop without giving his name.

Ivan pulled out the chair opposite the man while Paul stood with his back to the door, guarding the exit.

'Why were you trying to get into this room?' Paul asked in an officious voice.

'Look, if I give you my name and address will you let me go?' the man suddenly said, closing his eyes as if it was painful for him to speak.

'If you can supply us with some form of identity, perhaps,' was Ivan's reply. 'Something with your name and address on.'

The man opened his eyes, nodded in a way to acknowledge the request, and said: 'My name is Philip Hughes, and I live in Ormskirk.'

'And do you have any documents to prove who you are Mr Hughes?' Ivan queried.

Mr Hughes reached into the inside pocket of his pin-striped jacket and Ivan and Paul froze for a moment, both wondering if he was reaching for a gun or knife.

He produced something Ivan had not seen since his childhood – a pale blue Ministry of Food ration book from World War Two, dated July 1943.

'Where on earth did you get this from?' Ivan asked with a crooked smirk, and Paul leaned over his shoulder to look at the vintage booklet.

'That's all I have on me for identification purposes,' Mr Hughes told him, then stared straight ahead as if he was looking through Ivan.

'You can't go round with something from 1943 as a form of identification,' Ivan handed the ration book back to him. 'You got a driving licence?'

Mr Hughes continued to stare right through him, and didn't even take the ration book from him, so Ivan placed it on the desk.

At this point, Ivan turned to say something to Paul, who was standing to his left, just behind him, when he saw that his colleague's face bore an expression of shock. His eyes were bulging and his mouth was wide open, and he was gazing at Mr Hughes. Ivan quickly turned to see why Hughes was exerting such an effect on his friend, when he saw something truly terrifying. Mr Hughes was changing shape, apparently turning inside out. His flesh and clothes now seemed to be almost plastic, with a slight sheen to them, and the head of the man resembled some grotesque plasticine model which looked as if it was being turned inside out by an invisible pair of hands. The nose and upper face curled outwards, like a duck's beak at first, while the chin and lower jaw bent downwards, revealing an unsightly mix of scarlet and white shapes – where bone and gum and muscle were being exposed and impossibly stretched, and yet not a drop of blood was shed by this mind-boggling metamorphosis. The store detective Paul was a former soldier who had served in Northern Ireland, and had seen some gruesome sights during his military life, and yet he fled from that room in terror at the sight of something violently turning Mr Hughes' insides into his outsides. It was something far removed from everyday experience, and Paul's mind, unable to take in what he was witnessing, ran off. Within seconds, the thing that had been a seated human had become a melting mass of colours: the red of the man's blood, the pinkish hue of skin, lines of black from his hair, and white swirls of what had been bone. All spiralling now as the melting mass went steadily downwards into the seat of the chair. Ivan got to his feet in a very unsteady fashion, and he felt his heart pounding hard in his chest. He thought he heard something fall to the floor, but he didn't look, and he slowly turned as if he was in a nightmare, and stumbled out of the room. He saw an excited Paul talking loud to Stephen, the other store detective, on the far side of the floor, near to the elevator. Stephen came running over, but Paul deliberately took his time following.

'What the devil's going on?' Stephen asked, seeing that Ivan was plainly in a state of shock.

Ivan was lost for an answer of course, and when Stephen tried to get past him to take a look in the 'interrogation chamber' as the store detectives often nicknamed the room, Ivan gripped his colleague's forearm hard and prevented him from going anywhere near that room.

'Where's he gone?' Stephen asked, looking over Ivan's shoulder as he was walked backwards.

'I couldn't tell you, I couldn't tell you,' Ivan said, over and over.

'What's going on, Ivan?' Stephen demanded to know and seemed so irritated at being pushed back from doing his duty.

'Stephen!' Ivan yelled, attracting the attention of a few shoppers, 'all will be explained, now lets get back to HQ [the CCTV room].'

Fifteen minutes later, Stephen could not take in what his colleagues had told him. 'I'm not questioning what you're saying, but it does not make sense.'

'Of course it doesn't!' Ivan almost screamed, his patience well and truly frayed by Stephen's scepticism. He apologised, exhaled with his face in his hands, and shook his head. 'If I had not seen – with my own eyes – what I saw today, I'd be the same as you, Stephen,' Ivan seemed breathless now. 'I can't explain it, and I'm not going to mention it to the head of this store, and I hope you won't either, because I do not want to be committed.'

'Perhaps,' Stephen said, almost afraid to speak in

case Ivan bit his head off again, 'just perhaps, Mr Hughes slipped you and Paul some sort of LSD? It sounds like something people who take drugs see – '

'I give up,' Ivan fixed his steely eyes on Stephen, then looked at Paul, 'LSD? Ever heard of anything as stupid?'

'Well I'm just trying to explain it – ' Stephen began.

'Look, just let's drop this now, please,' Ivan advised his sceptical friend. 'You've seen the CCTV footage. Three people went in that room – me, him and Mr Hughes, and two people came out.'

'Are we wiping that tape?' Paul asked.

Ivan nodded. 'We'll have to, won't we? Or we're going end up in a psychiatric hospital, and could you blame them for thinking we've lost our minds - or as Stephen has suggested here – tripping on drugs while on duty?'

'What was he?' Paul asked.

There was a long pause. Stephen wanted to give an opinion but was afraid of upsetting Ivan.

'God knows what's knocking around,' Ivan finally committed a bit of his secret opinion on the weird matter. 'You hear of people seeing ghosts and having strange experiences and you pooh-pooh it, and then it happens to you. I am never going into that room downstairs on my own again.'

About a month after this inexplicable incident, Ivan's heart missed a beat when he happened to be in the CCTV room looking at the monitors, when on screen #1, which showed people coming and going through one of the department store's entrances, a man in a pin-striped suit appeared. This time it was a false alarm, the man had his hair slicked back, but his face bore no resemblance to the thing – whatever it was – which had apparently masqueraded as a 'Philip Hughes' that afternoon. Just what the thing was, why it was attempting to get into a room at the department store, and why it was carrying a 1943 ration book are questions that will probably never be answered. The way the man in the pin-striped suit morphed and melted as he seemed to turn inside out reminds me of another local case which was reported to me some years ago. In 2009, a 12-year-old boy named Toby was on Hilbre Island with a few friends when he foolishly decided to go swimming as the tide came in. As anyone who has been to Hilbre Island knows, there are only certain times when you can visit or leave the island because of tidal conditions, as the tides cut off the island from the mainland for up to five hours around every twelve hours. When high tide comes, the island is surrounded by the sea, and some visitors had disregarded the tide warnings over the years with fatal results. Toby and his friends visited the island, and the sun was blazing down and they were more interested in looking for crabs and generally messing about to notice the incoming tide. Toby stripped to his swimming trunks and paddled out into the sea, thinking he'd be alright. He'd swum off the coast on holiday with his parents in Spain after all. He found himself swimming against a powerful current, and he could see his two friends in the distance and could hear their faint cries for him to come back.

'Hey!'

Toby looked to his left to the source of the cry and saw a round face with closely-cropped blonde hair about six feet away. 'I'm trying to get back to the shore!' Toby shouted, trying his utmost to swim against the current.

'I'm made up!' the blonde lad shouted. 'Me mam got me new pumps!'

Toby began to panic, and wondered why the other swimmer wasn't bothered by the nasty undercurrent which now seemed to be pulling him down. 'Help!' Toby shouted and tried to talk but his words sounded as if he was gargling as the water rushed into his mouth.

'Alright!' the blonde kid said, and he said something else, but because of the water in his ears, Toby couldn't make out what it was, but he could feel the boy pushing him towards the shore, and was so grateful because of it.

'Toby! You idiot! Get back here!' Toby's friend Kyle shouted from the shoreline.

Toby now felt the sand and silt beneath his feet and was so relieved he was walking towards the beach. He turned to thank the blonde lad, but saw that he had stopped about six feet away. 'Come on!' Toby invited him with a tilt of the head, 'Come and play footy with us!'

'Nah,' the boy said, then started saying something about his new pumps again.

As Toby walked up the beach to his friends Kyle and Adam, he told them: 'He saved me from drownding!'

'Drowning, not drownding,' Adam laughed.

Toby then looked back, and saw the boy with the blonde hair wave, and suddenly, he was not there – just a pale blossoming liquid just below the water. It was as if someone had opened a carton of milk and let it mingle with the seawater.

'What's that?' Kyle asked, because he saw the strange occurrence as clear as Toby. Toby turned and waded into the water, and at first he recoiled in horror because he thought he could see a huge jellyfish floating towards him, about six inches under the waves. But it was a milky cloudy something, and in that amorphous, shapeless pale object, he saw the face of the blonde boy with his mouth wide open and his eyes screwed shut. Toby turned and tried to hurry away in absolute terror, and almost butted Kyle, who had waded out to see what the thing was in the sea. Both boys fought with one another to get to the shore first. They told Adam what they had seen and he, being a year younger than them, became scared and thought they were just making it all up to frighten him. Then Kyle said, 'Hey, look!'

Further up the beach they saw footprints – the impressions of feet around the same size as their feet, and they originated from a point in the sand where they found a pair of shoes of some sort; they looked similar to the Converse brand of footwear except they were completely black and bore no logo – in other words – pumps, for that was what people of the 1950s-1980s used to call such cheap lightweight shoes. That blonde boy, who had seemingly dissolved into the waters, had told Toby that he was 'made-up' because his mother had bought him a new pair of pumps. The tracks of the footprints led from those pumps into the sea. As soon as low tide came, the three boys made their way back to the mainland and each told their parents what had happened, and no one believed the story of the dissolving boy, but he has been seen a few times over the years, although no one seems to know why he haunts the waters around Hilbre Island. A few children have drowned around Hilbre over the decades, and perhaps he is one of the ghosts of these minors who have perished, but why the 'dissolving act'? This ghost – if that is what the entity is – is a real puzzler.

An enigmatic nocturnal phenomenon that has had virtually no coverage in the Fortean press is the mysterious case of the "probes" – minute pin-points of light that were seen in homes and workplaces across Britain and other countries in the early 1970s – usually (but not always) in the wake of UFO activity. I have collected scores of accounts from people who noticed these laser-like points of light which always appeared in pairs. Dozens of night-workers first reported them crawling along walls at a certain well-known factory in Runcorn, Cheshire in 1972, but then the phenomenon spread to Liverpool, where a night-watchman in the Philharmonic Hall noticed a tiny point of light moving along the wall of the green room. There was a corresponding light on the other side of the room. Every now and then a needle-thin beam would flash between these lights as if they were scanning objects in the room as they moved about. Weeks later, a Liverpool University security guard saw the same "crawling lights" in a building on Mount Pleasant, and at first he thought they were fireflies, but soon saw that they were tiny orbs, millimetres in diameter. These lights moved in pairs, and two of them crawled onto the guard's hand and seemed to exhibit curiosity as they followed the contours of his palm. A few nights later, two other guards saw points of light floating around a luminous diamond-shaped object hovering in a car park near the Metropolitan Cathedral. As the guards looked on, the diamond and its attendant orbs vanished. The diamond was also seen by cleaners arriving early for work one dark wintry morning at Liverpool's old museum on William Brown Street. The diamond hid behind objects in the Egyptian section of the museum, and was able to pass through window panes and float back into the building again. When I mentioned this uncanny geometrical entity on a local radio show, I received many phone calls, emails and letters from members of the public who believed they had seen the same mysterious object. Most reports agreed on the colour of the diamond – a sort of pale greenish-blue – and its shape – a four-sided kite-shaped polygon (described as a quadrilateral figure by one mathematically-minded witness), and many of those who encountered the thing said the it seemed to 'know' when it was being observed by them. One security guard was looking out of a third floor window of a store he'd been patrolling with the lights out as he enjoyed a smoke during his break one morning at 3am. He had a clear view of Church Street, and saw that there wasn't a soul about; a *human* soul anyway. Then he noticed a ghostly greenish blue light floating along Church Alley from the direction of the Bluecoat Chambers. The guard had a small pair of 10 x 25 binoculars, and he grabbed them and had a look at the light moving about below. He was amazed to see that the radiant object was a diamond-shaped object reminiscent of the computer wire-frame geometrical objects that later featured on the early computer screens. The diamond flitted through one of the windows of Burtons and emerged via another window after about two minutes. The diamond then seemed to inspect the windows of a few other stores, and when the security guard lowered the binoculars from his eyes and stepped nearer to the window, the diamond halted, hovering about three feet off the ground, then quickly retreated to Church Alley, where it vanished as mysteriously as it had first appeared. I have the feeling that the roaming diamond entity and the strange 'probes' may be projections of some higher intelligence, perhaps to gather information, mostly at night, when there are few witnesses about, although the probing points of light may be active of a day but invisible because of ambient lighting conditions. On the cosmic scale, humans are very young newcomers, and yet we have sent probes to all of the planets in our Solar System, so its entirely possible that beings who have been around far longer than us might also be sending probes to our world as part of some interstellar information-gathering programme. It's equally possible that the probes may originate from another time period – maybe the future. We'll hopefully know more about them one day. One sceptic called me on air when I discussed the diamond-shaped apparition and thought the whole thing was ridiculous. 'It doesn't make sense, mate,' he said, 'a diamond shape? How would it be alive if it was that shape, not even humanoid; sounds more like a robot.' In reply I told the caller to either Google "bacteriophage" or look it up on Wikipedia. The bacteriophage is a virus which looks like some futuristic spacecraft with a *diamond*-shaped head and six landing legs. It cannot be seen with the naked eye and it's probably being inhaled by you now as it floats around in the atmosphere...

Here's another mystery about entities that are hard to classify, told to me by a number of people who have contacted me over the years or chatted to me after book-signing or talks I have given. In the 1950s a little toyshop opened on West Derby Road. The shop literally appeared overnight and had no sign above its premises, which were rather shabby and dusty. The shop was run by a man named Mr Boleyn (the same pronunciation and spelling as the ill-fated Anne Boleyn, Queen Consort of England (1533 to 1536) as the second wife of King Henry VIII until he had her beheaded on trumped-up charges of adultery, incest and treason. The surname is an English one but of French origin. The Boleyn in this story was very well-spoken and did not possess a local Liverpudlian or Lancashire accent. He was bald, but the remaining hair at the back of his head had been grown long and was of a reddish colour. The most noticeable feature about Mr Boleyn was his long nose, which was shaped like a hook. Around 1954, in the early summer, 7-year-old Bethany Wilkins and her grandmother Gracie were shopping on West Derby Road, when Bethany noticed the new shop. She saw little dolls in the window and a sign that said 'Doll Hospital'. The girl asked her Nan what that meant, and Gracie reasoned that it meant some repair service for dolls. 'Susie's broke, Nanna, maybe they can fox her!' said Bethany excitedly, and her Nan took her into the shop, triggering a bell as she opened the door.

Mr Boleyn came out the back room of the gloomy shop, smiling, and right away, Gracie noticed his prominent hook nose.

'Hello,' said Mr Boleyn, and then he leaned forward

over the counter and peeped over the rim of his bifocal spectacles and said to Bethany, 'Hello down there.'

'Can you fix dolls?' asked Gracie.

'Yes, of course,' said Mr Boleyn, and he crouched over Bethany and asked: 'why, what's wrong with your dolly?'

'She dropped her out of a window, didn't you Bethany?' the child's grandmother said, patting Bethany's had of golden curls.

'Oh dear,' Mr Boleyn said, and his mouth became o-shaped as he feigned shock.

'Its got a crack across its face – ' Gracie was saying.

'Oh, never call Susie "it",' Mr Boleyn said, and he tutted.

'Shall we bring Susie in for Mr – ' Gracie said, pausing for the man to give his name and the toyshop dealer duly coughed and said: 'Mr Boleyn – like Anne, but I still have my head!'

'Will it cost much, Mr Boleyn?' Gracie queried.

The toyman shook his head and closed his eyes, 'Don't you worry about that,' he said softly, 'pay whatever you can afford, love.'

Bethany gazed through the green-edged glass pane at the dolls in boxes and saw they were each only sixpence – quite a low price, much cheaper than the plastic dolls on sale down the road in Woolworths. These dolls seemed to be better made than the ones in Woollies. Before the girl could have a proper look at these colourful little figures, Gracie gently pulled Bethany away by her forearm and said, 'We'll bring Susie in then Mr Boleyn; bye.'

'Bye Bye!' he replied, then added, 'Bye Bye Bethany.'

The next day around 2pm, Bethany handed Susie to Mr Boleyn, and he examined the doll's face with a huge magnifying glass, then smiled and said: 'I'll soon have her face fixed. You can pick her up tomorrow.'

'That soon?' asked Gracie, eyebrows rising.

'Yes, very straightforward procedure, love,' Boleyn answered, and he carefully placed Susie down behind the counter.

Bethany was squinting at the row of dolls in pink and blue boxes. She could hardly see their faces through the windows of transparent plastic on the boxes, but thought she could make out the doll of a sailor, and she wanted it.

That day, after teatime, Bethany asked her Nan if she could have the sailor doll, as he was only sixpence. Gracie said she'd get her the doll if Mr Boleyn didn't charge too much for fixing Susie, and Bethany became quite excited at not only the prospect of Susie being repaired but also of having a new doll, and she could hardly sleep. Susie's face had been fixed, and Mr Boleyn charged two shillings and also gave Bethany - free of charge - a little baby 'Sailor Boy' in a pale blue box. This was the doll Bethany had been gazing at most in the glass case under the counter. As Gracie paid Mr Boleyn and thanked him for the free doll, she felt her grand-daughter tugging at the hem of her skirt.

'Hang on Bethany,' Gracie said, closing her purse and nodding and smiling at the toy dealer. She moved away from the counter and headed for the door, and still Bethany was tugging at her skirt and sleeve.

'Bye now, Bethany, Bye Bye Nanna!' Boleyn said, lifting the counter flap. He walked to the door with them, and as soon as Bethany and Gracie were outside he closed the door behind them, locked it, and twisted the hanging sign in the middle of the glass door so it read: 'Closed'.

'Nanna, that's not Susie's face!' Bethany seemed near to tears as she thrust the repaired doll up to her Nan, and Gracie took hold of it as she muttered, 'You're never satisfied, Beth – '

Gracie couldn't believe her eyes. She recoiled at the sight of the doll's new face and she went cold inside. The doll had the exact same face as Mr Boleyn; same beady set-back eyes, same pointed chin, and the very same hooked nose. Only the curly black nylon hair of Susie and the doll's royal blue dress with the white and yellow daisy pattern remained untouched. From the neck downwards she was Susie, but that ghastly face was Boleyn's.

Gracie saw the 'Closed' sign on the door and rapped on the window with her wedding and engagement ring. She cupped her hands around the side of her head as she peered through the grimy window and saw no movement, so she knocked on the glass door and waited – but there was no answer.

Gracie patted Bethany's head and reassuringly told her: 'He must have made a mistake, Bethany – don't cry love; I'll see if he's open later. We'll get Susie's face back.'

Then came the second shock of that day. The baby Sailor Boy doll was taken out of the box, and he wore a little white sailor hat, a sailor suit and black boots with silver buckles – but his face was not that of the cherub Bethany had seen gazing at her through the cellophane window in the box yesterday – it was the face of Mr Boleyn again. What on earth was going on?

Gracie went back to the toyshop about an hour later, and again got no answer. When she went home and told Bethany the place was still closed, the little girl cried. 'I want Susie back,' she sobbed.

'I'll go and sort this nonsense out,' Gracie's husband Charlie announced as he rose from his armchair. He had been trying to watch the TV but had continually heard Bethany crying about her doll, and so he'd had enough. When Charlie reached the toyshop he found five other people standing there. They were dissatisfied customers who had also found Boleyn's ugly gob on the dolls they had either bought at the shop or had repaired there. There was a clown doll with a red-painted hooked nose in the hands of one girl, and a crying girl of about five with a baby doll with a petal bonnet, and it featured the ghastly face of Mr Boleyn with a dummy in its mouth.

Charlie backed away from the front door of the shop as if he was about to charge at it, but he halted on the pavement and looked up at the window above the shop and shouted, 'If you don't open up, I'm going to the police!'

The curtains moved slightly up there.

'He's in! See the curtain move, then?' one of the parents said, looking up at the window.

'Open up or I'll kick the bloody door in!' Charlie bawled.

'Don't do that, mate,' said a nervous man standing next to his grieving daughter. 'You'll get done for breaking an entry.'

'I'm just bluffin', that's all,' Charlie whispered.

Mr Boleyn never showed and the yelled threats of legal action from Charlie and the other people standing in front of the shop came to nothing. The next day, Charlie called with Gracie at ten in the morning, and the window was empty. They peered through the mucky panes and saw that the shop had been entirely emptied of its wares. Mr Boleyn had done a moonlight flit, a runner!

Strange rumours circulated about the dolls with the sinister face of Mr Boleyn; many maintained that their houses had been broken into days after Boleyn had shut shop, and some swore that the eyes of the dolls seemed to move sometimes. One woman was convinced that Boleyn was some witch and that he could see through the eyes of the dolls that bore his unsightly features. A child named Christine, who lived on Molyneux Road, was another recipient of the weird doll. She had chosen one named Sally, and Boleyn sold it to the girl's mother in a box, but when the box was quickly opened by Christine once she got home, she immediately noticed the masculine and quite repugnant wry face of Sally. Christine's mother saw at once that the doll had the face of the old man who had sold it to her, and took it back, but found the shop had closed. The girl's mother took it to the Tuebrook police station and a sergeant there said he'd look into it and suggested that someone was playing a prank. Not long after that, Boleyn closed down his shop and vanished into obscurity. A listener who had tuned into my spot on the local radio station talking about this creepy mystery said she had also received one of the dolls, and what's more, she still had it. The woman's name was Barbara Murphy-Ellis, and she brought the doll down to the radio station. Its clothes were a bit tatty by now but the face was exactly how I had imagined.

There were no seams visible on the hard plastic of the doll's head, so how the face was attached I do not know. It did have quite a sinister look in its eyes, which seemed to be made of blue beads, and the hook nose was thin and pointy. The mouth was turned up on one side, producing the effect of a lopsided grin. Barbara said her mother was convinced that the doll was alive and claimed that she had once locked it in a cupboard – only to find the doll sitting on the kitchen table shortly afterwards. Why would an elderly toy dealer put his face on children's dolls? Was he simply a vain narcissist who was somewhat unbalanced or was there a more sinister reason? Could he see through the eyes of these dolls? Witchcraft is full of such tales – of witches looking through the eyes of effigies and poppet dolls strategically left on the doorsteps of enemies they wish to spy on.

Where was Boleyn's shop? No one who recalls the premises seems to agree on this question; Barbara Murphy-Ellis believes the shop was near the Music Box record store, while Bethany thinks it was located between Martin's Bank and Sayers' cake shop. Maybe someone out there will have more accurate recollections of the whereabouts of Boleyn's shop.

Another mystery of the unclassifiable kind is the case of the "thing" which haunts a well-known supermarket in Liverpool. I was first to invited to investigate this strange entity in 2013. The thing was first seen on CCTV screens at a room in the supermarket where two guards scan a number of monitors for shoplifters and general troublemakers. The time was just before 9pm, and one of the guards – Ryan, thought his eyes were playing tricks on him at first. A man in a black coat which went down to his shoes was in an impossible sitting position in the middle of an aisle, and it just looked as if he was sitting on an invisible chair. The stranger had close-cropped black hair and was very pale. As Ryan looked at his image on the monitor, the man moved along as if he was sitting in a wheelchair – but a wheelchair which couldn't be seen. 'It was quite bizarre,' Ryan recalls, 'and I called the other guard over – Jamie – and he saw him too.'

The guards watched the man in the non-existent wheelchair scoot along the aisle in a sitting position, and his feet were rocking up and down by their heels as he did this. 'And then all of a sudden, he moved into a standing position, like that – ' Jamie clicked his fingers, 'and started walking in what I can only describe as slow motion.'

The weird figure then walked into the out of bounds area by pushing open two doors leading to the supermarket's vast stockroom. Jamie and Ryan were able to continue watching the bizarre trespasser as he headed for the staffroom. A security guard was contacted in another part of the building and directed by Jamie to go to the staffroom to intercept the weird intruder, but the guard found no one in the staffroom. On the following night, this time around 11.40pm, the man in black was seen again walking into a cloakroom by a guard at the store, but when he went into the cloakroom about fifteen seconds after the unknown man, the guard was startled to find no one there. All he saw was a single black coat hanging up in the cloakroom and he reported back to Jamie. Jamie and Ryan went to take a look at the cloakroom themselves, as they thought that the man in black was hiding in there, but when they entered, they saw nobody, and Ryan noticed that the black coat the security guard had reported minutes before was *absent* and yet no member of the skeleton staff had been in the cloakroom in the past half an hour. The guards told no one about the strange antics of something that was obviously a ghost of some sort, but on the following morning two female cleaners entered the cloakroom around 7.30 am and saw something which sent them running out of the room. The cleaners saw a long black coat hanging up in an open locker, and when one of the women went to close the locker door, she saw the four fingers of a hand emerge from the coat and grip a lapel. The cleaner let out a shriek and backed away from the strange spectacle and the other cleaner saw the hand too. The women left their cleaning equipment behind in panic and refused to go near the cloakroom for days. A member of staff later contacted me and told me in confidence that three employees at the supermarket had been bored on nights, and one morning around 2am these three people decided to 'play the Ouija board' with an upturned glass on a counter with letters and numbers scrawled on pieces of paper. The name "Lonnie" kept coming through, and then the dabbling trio began to get scared and swept the little paper squares of numbers and letters into a bin. That bin started to move about, and the sounds of someone laughing somewhere in the supermarket could be heard, but no matter how they tried, the three staff members could not find the source of the echoing laughter. I researched the history of the site the supermarket had been built in and tried to find out who "Lonnie" was, without any success.

Equipment I brought to the supermarket for vigils would malfunction, and brand new batteries would become drained within minutes. A reputable medium was brought in and almost fainted when she went into the staffroom. She said that the thing in there was laying some sort of trap, and intended to drive a young female worker in the store insane, all for its own weird agenda. What was this entity, and where was it from? Questions I posed to the medium, and she said she had never encountered anything like it before and that it was preventing her from picking up on its origins. The medium then broke out in what looked like heat blisters on her face and hands. We took her outside and she refused to go back into the supermarket. The entity then seemed to vanish as mysteriously as it had first arrived, but in March 2015, new reports of strange goings-on at the supermarket were reported to me again, so it looks as if the thing has resumed its sinister agenda, and it has started to leave weird text messages on the mobile of the girl it seems to be targeting. Just what the thing is – a ghost, something from another dimension, another time, perhaps even another planet – is still unknown. Did the impromptu Ouija session invite this mysterious menace into the store? I'd say it's highly possible.

These are just a few of the weird entities which come into our world from God knows where, and you will find many more of them in this book

THE GOLDEN TYPEWRITER

One clammy hot afternoon during the summer school holidays of 1983, 15-year-old Nigel Aspen had painstakingly typed half of a three-page machine-code listing from a home computer magazine into his Sinclair Spectrum when there was a power failure at his home on Green Lane in the Allerton area of Liverpool. Cowboy workmen excavating a hole for a goldfish pond in the neighbour's garden had accidentally severed a power cable. Nigel hadn't saved a copy of the lost hexadecimal data, but instead of dwelling on his predicament he took a break and decided to go up into the loft with a torch to have a mooch about until the power returned. He found an old gold-coloured manual typewriter in the loft, and he brought it down to his room, fed a sheet of A4 paper into the roller and began to type. The machine still worked, and the words were surprisingly clear. His parents had no idea who the typewriter had belonged to – possibly the previous occupier, Mrs Fairhurst, who put the house on the market in 1970. There was no brand name on the machine, but Mrs Aspen thought it looked like a Vintage Royal model – the type she had used in the 1960s as a student.

Nigel placed the typewriter on his desk in his room, next to his model of the Space Shuttle. He wondered what to write for a moment, then idly typed: 'Keith Aspen and his partner Sam are expecting a baby, and the couple are elated.' This was a private joke; Keith was Nigel's 20-year-old brother, and he lived in mortal fear of getting his girlfriend Sam pregnant because he had no intention of settling down – ever.

Ten minutes later, Nigel was downstairs getting a choc ice from the freezer when his brother Keith and his partner Sam called at the house. As soon as he came through the front doorway he announced to his parents: 'I'm going to be a dad.' Then, hugging Sam, he said: 'We're over the moon; it's about time I settled down. We're getting married.'

As a tearful Mrs Aspen hugged Keith and Sam, Nigel recalled the words he had typed on that machine upstairs concerning his brother; they'd come true! He went back to the typewriter and hammered out: 'Nigel came into a lot of money.' He then waited...and waited – but nothing! However, the next day, the old neighbour *Nigel* McMuldren was one of the fifty people who received £5,000 when their premium bond number was chosen in the July draw. Nigel wondered if this windfall – and Keith's shocking acceptance of parenthood - was all just down to coincidence, and to test the possible supernatural influence of the golden typewriter, he sat in front of it and typed the full name of the school bully, Masher, followed by the words: 'was knocked down by a car.'

Nigel trembled after typing this and his mouth dried up. He looked at the stark black words on the white paper. Would he be a murderer if Masher was knocked down and killed? That evening, Nigel's father gave him a lift to his friend Russell's house in Grassendale, and as the car was travelling down Brodie Avenue, a familiar figure stepped off the kerb about thirty yards ahead – it was Masher! Nigel grabbed the steering wheel of the car and tugged it hard, and the vehicle swerved, just missing the bully by inches. The car skidded to a halt and Mr Aspen yelled at his son for taking control of the car, and he also shouted out the window of the vehicle at a shocked Masher: 'Look where you're going you moron!'

Half an hour later, Nigel was telling Russell about the weird golden typewriter's apparent power.

'Rubbish Nige; just coincidences, that's all.'

Nigel shook his head, 'Look, I'll prove it,' he said. 'That girl – the gymnast you fancy – what's her name?'

Russell blushed and in a low faltering voice he said: 'Lauren Garvin.'

'Right, Russ, come to ours tomorrow and I'll *make* her fall in love with you!'

The next day, a sceptical Russell watched Nigel at the typewriter as he murmured: 'Lauren Garvin will fall in love with Russell Tibbs'. But the keys got stuck, so all Nigel could type was "Lauren Garvin will fall". And that day Lauren Garvin fell off the balance beam during her gymnastic exercises and broke her leg. The keys remained jammed and Nigel's superstitious father later binned the uncanny machine when he heard about its spooky reputation from Russell Tibbs.

A TRICK OF TIME

Most discoveries are re-discoveries. Today, there's a lot of talk about "wormholes" – scientifically valid shortcuts through time and space – but when the German mathematician Hermann Weyl first proposed the wormhole theory back in 1921, most scientists either ridiculed him or failed to understand what he was driving at: the means of travelling through time – something which is more common than you might imagine, but I know for a fact that there is much more to time than the psychological time we measure on watches and clocks. When a timeslip does occur, it is often interpreted as something supernatural, especially if someone from a period in the past is inadvertently ushered into our era, and the following story is a case in point. The story was well-known to me but finding witnesses to it presented a great difficulty – until one day, one of the people who were present during the bizarre incident contacted me during a radio programme on the paranormal in 2002. Because of this witness – a retired policeman – I was able to document this intriguing story as factually as possible, and I also undertook other research to try and establish the background of the 'ghost'. I have had to alter a few of the names in this story, but the name of the paranormal character at the centre of the account is unchanged.

It was an April night in the early 1970s at a certain

Liverpool police station, and the region was being visited by heavy fog from the Irish Sea, the price to pay for an unusually hot sunny day. As the foghorns of the Mersey moaned outside, Sergeant Allen stood at the desk of the police station tackling the last clue of a formidable crossword. 'Eleven letters,' he said to Constable Connor, who was sipping a mug of sweet tea, 'and the second letter's b and it ends in n. Clue is: "The falling asleep of a limb".'

After a thoughtful pause, Connor put the mug on the counter and said: 'Obdormition – that's when your arm goes numb, when you sleep on it like.'

'You sure?' the sergeant asked, discomfited at not knowing the word.

'Yeah Sarge,' PC Connor nodded eagerly, 'it's not a word you'll find in your average dictionary like, but I've got every volume of *The Oxford English Dictionary* and these jawbreakers just stick to my brain like flies to flypaper.'

'There's no bore like a clever bore,' Sergeant Allen whispered back, penning in the letters, but misspelling the word. 'Ah, frig it,' he tossed the pen down onto the paper, and as he did the doors facing burst open, and in came Constable Terry Richards with a grazed forehead, with blood over his right eyebrow, and he was energetically shoving a man of about fifty forwards, and this man wore a top hat and a long black coat. The stranger had a huge red nose and immense bushy sideburns.

'He belted me with this!' Richards held up a black walking cane with a gleaming brass ferrule, then slammed it on the counter.

'What in God's name – ' the Sergeant smirked at the

man in the costume.

'I'll get you a plaster, Tel!' PC Connor told Richards, and he rushed to the first aid cupboard in the backroom as Richards continued: 'He was smashing a Cortina's headlamps in outside the boozer round the corner – and threatening people. He's definitely top twenty Sarge!'

'I dunno,' replied the sergeant, and he sarcastically continued, 'top hats and those ankle-length coats are coming back again you know?'

'So!' announced the oddly-dressed inebriate in a loud slurred but well-spoken voice, 'I am to be charged with being drunk and riotous and haranguing the mob! I'll pay my forty shillings – '

'You will be charged with assaulting a policeman in the execution of his duty,' snarled Richards through gritted, grinding teeth as he felt the lump on his forehead, 'criminal damage, and being drunk and disorderly!'

'Name?' Sergeant Allen opened the log book on the counter and noted the time.

The drunkard's reply was: 'Doctor Francis Pritchard Month of 64, Roscommon Street. May I see your superior, sir?'

'A doctor eh?' Sergeant Allen grinned and squinted at the top hat, 'And have you been to a fancy dress ball – doctor?'

PC Connor dabbed his colleague's forehead with iodine as the drunk began thumping his fist on the counter, and he roared: 'What blockhead policeman are you? I am a doctor! Here!' the alleged physician dipped into his inside pocket and produced a small white card which he threw onto the counter. 'What I say is true in substance and in fact!'

The 5-inch-long card bore the printed name and address of a Dr. F Pritchard Month of 64 Roscommon Street, confirming the verbal details supplied by the eccentric in custody.

'I know Roscommon Street well Sarge,' said Richards, 'and there's no quack of that name within a mile of the place!'

The top-hatted man's face turned as ruddy as his nose and he bawled: 'Quack? You insolent soil-brained Puncheous Pilate!' And as Sergeant Allen laughed at the quaint outburst, the outraged doctor quickly picked up the cane from the counter and in a flash, he brought it down hard on the head of Richards, knocking him clean out. The doctor then bolted out of the station with PC Connor very close behind.

Sergeant Allen left the counter and went to the aid of PC Richards. Another policeman from the back room came out and Allen told him to call an ambulance.

The entrance doors of the station opened, and in came Connor, wide-eyed, and his face looked pale.

'Where is he?' Sergeant Allen yelled as he knelt at the side of the unconscious constable.

PC Connor's lips fluttered for a moment as if he was having difficulty forming words. 'He – he vanished. He's a ghost,' he said.

'What?' Allen shot an expression back at the constable that was a mixture of anger and bewilderment.

'I was that close to grabbing him,' Connor pinched the air with his finger and thumb, 'and he just went. There one moment and then gone.'

Sergeant Allen couldn't believe his ears. 'You lost

him? We're going to be the frigging laughing stock of Liverpool if this gets out! The Keystone cops will have nothing on us! *How* did you let an alky outrun you?'

The police constable from the backroom returned, told Sergeant Allen the ambulance was on its way, and then he knelt at the side of PC Richards. Allen got to his feet and walked to the counter. 'Ghosts don't harm the living and they don't leave cards,' he said, but when the Sergeant looked down at the counter, there was no card to be seen. He asked the constable attending Richards if he had removed the card from the counter, and received a 'No, sir.'

'I – I *told* you, sir,' PC Connor said, upon seeing his superior's continued fruitless search for the little white card.

Sergeant Allen strode to the doors. He pushed them open and immediately the vapours of the fog drifted towards him through the little carpeted hallway from the open door. He went into the street, and saw a few faint ghostly figures of people in the distance, just visible in the thick fog. The sergeant had a strange feeling that something inexplicable had happened tonight, and perhaps it was just his imagination, but he felt as if some bygone era was infiltrating the foggy present, and so, he went back inside. About five minutes later, he and PC Connor jumped when the doors burst open and in came two ambulance men. The official story was that some violent drunk had clobbered Richards with a stick, but there was no mention of the top hat or of doctors on Roscommon Street. The real facts of the incident leaked out and passed into the annals of local police lore – another strange tale of the blue lamp, of which there are many.

I researched the name given by the weird outdated doctor: Francis Pritchard Month, and was intrigued to discover that he *had* indeed lived at 64 Roscommon Street – back in the 1880s. Was the doctor a ghost, or did he – in a drunken state back in Victorian times – somehow walk into the 1970s? Perhaps he lashed out at the headlights of the Cortina because a man from the age of the horse-drawn hansom cab would have been understandably scared of such a contraption as a modern car with electric lamps resembling demonic eyes. If the latter was the case, then our ghost was merely the product of a trick of time.

AINTREE'S GHOSTLY CHILD

There is a ghostly girl haunting Aintree, and she appears to be an omen of death and tragedy. She has also followed people for miles to their homes, which is unusual but not unheard of in the world of ghosts. The first reported sightings I have of the little girl in black date back to the 1950s, but she was probably seen long before that because she looks Victorian, or maybe Edwardian, in her black high-collared dress, dark grey stockings and buckled shoes. I have scoured microfilmed newspaper archives and enlisted the help of some of the regions greatest local historians, but we cannot find her identity and we do not know why she always seems to come from Aintree Railway Station when she latches onto certain people. I had heard of the ominous apparition being active in the 1980s and mentioned her on a local radio programme in 2012, only to receive a deluge of calls and emails from listeners who had encountered the eerie entity, but now it would seem that the ghost is active again, and she has allegedly even caused one person to die from shock.

On the gloomy Monday afternoon of January 5 2015, a 23-year-old student named Niall got off the train at Aintree station and made his way to his flat, chatting on his smartphone to his girlfriend Gemma as he walked along. As he left the station and came onto the main road outside, Gemma's voice became garbled on the phone, and then communication was lost altogether. Niall stopped, dialled her back, and he continued the conversation as he headed homewards to Park Lane. Again there was interference on the mobile, and this time it sounded like a child's single scream.

'What was that?' Gemma asked. Niall said he didn't know, but then he happened to look over his shoulder, and out the corner of his eye he noticed something black behind him. He halted and turned fully to face whatever it was – and got the shock of his life. About twelve feet away, a strange outdated-looking girl of about ten or eleven in a black calf-length dress stood, her arms hanging straight at her sides, and her fists clenched. Her eyes were just two black holes and her mouth was wide open as if she was about to cry out. The girl's shoulder length hair was coal-black, and she wore a blue Alice band in her hair. The face of the odd-looking child was a pallid grey, as were her fists. Niall went cold when he saw her looking at him, and somehow knowing that the girl was dead, he turned away and walked faster. He noticed there was not another soul to be seen, even though this was usually a road busy with traffic and people coming and going to Aintree station. The full moon looming on the horizon only heightened the creepy atmosphere as Niall started to jog along. He glanced back a few minutes later – and saw to his horror that the girl in black was hurrying along after him, her arms still hanging straight at her sides – and that unsettling mouth was still wide open.

When Niall got to the door of his flat, he looked back and saw to his relief that the weird minor was nowhere to be seen. He went into the hallway, and as he recalled the stark image of that weird figure of the girl in his mind, he felt the hairs rising on the nape of his neck as he closed the door. He reached for the hallway light switch – and out the corner of his eye, he saw something black again. The girl was standing at the dark end of the hallway, and as the student looked at her in sheer terror, he heard a peculiar low moaning sound come from the ghost. Next thing Niall knew, he was running out of the place. He was so scared to go home, he stayed in his girlfriend's house on Oriel Drive for three days before he would venture back to the flat (with a friend) in broad daylight. Niall later discovered that his mother – who lives in Manchester – had suffered a stroke the day he had seen the little girl in black. Niall's mum – who was in her fifties – has since passed away, and the student believes the ghost was some omen of her death. I have noticed that the ghost seems more active around the time of the full moon, and she seems to originate from Aintree Railway Station, but why is a mystery. Was she the victim of some long-forgotten railway accident or is she the restless victim of some child murderer?

A lady named Margy told me that in the 1990s, she often saw the ghost standing on a platform at Aintree station, but not everyone could see her. Margy was in her thirties when she saw her the first time, and when she told her mother about the ghost, she told Margy to never acknowledge her or make eye-contact with her, for she knew of a man who had tried to get rid of the ghost by attempting to perform an exorcism, and she had followed him home to Netherton, where she chased him round his house. The man told neighbours about the menacing ghostly minor but they didn't believe him. That night they heard his terrible screams and the man was found dead the next morning from a massive heart attack, and his face was twisted with fear and his eyes were bulging out of their sockets. Margy's mother said that the ghost was knocking about when she was only a girl herself, and had a reputation for bringing bad luck to those who saw her. One woman who wishes to remain anonymous tells me that her sister was plagued by visits from the ghostly girl, and was heard by neighbours screaming one night. When the neighbours responded and couldn't get an answer, one of them looked through the letterbox of the house and saw the woman dead in the hallway. Footsteps were heard going up the stairs of the house, but when police broke in they found no one on the premises. An Aintree man named Robert who used to walk his dog along Ormskirk Road told me how the enigmatic ghostly girl would often follow him as far as Warbreck Moor, and on one occasion, Rob and a friend followed the ghost, keeping quite a distance away from her as they shadowed her, and she was seen to go into Kirkdale Cemetery off Longmoor Lane, Fazakerley. This may be the place where the ghost's mortal remains lay, and might provide me with some clue to her identity. In the meantime, if you're in the vicinity of Aintree Station, watch out for the girl in black...

HUYTON'S FACELESS CHILD

Huyton teen Melissa describes herself as an emo, but takes pains to add that she is not the stereotypical emo (if he or she ever existed); she is not hyper-emotional, painfully introverted or ridden with angst, but she does have the long-swept bang of indigo, slate blue and vermillion hair, purple eyebrows, emerald lips, and panda eyes with spidery eyelashes. Melissa also has skin-tight jeans which make it almost impossible to bend down to tie the laces of her Converse shoes.

Monday 12 May 2014 was Melissa's 17th birthday and she went on Skype that day to show her friend Marielle the tee shirt her older brother Davis had bought her. It featured her favourite band of the moment, Grouplove. Marielle, a 16-year-old who lives over in Southdene, Kirkby, was too busy looking at herself in the little screen below the one showing Melissa on her laptop, and she pouted and played with her blonde and green hair until Melissa swore at her and told her to stop being narcissistic. Marielle smiled and snapped out of admiring herself, and with a bored expression listened to her friend bragging about the other presents she'd received: a Stratocaster guitar and 100-watt amplifier, a Captain America baseball hat, a smartphone, a huge Lush Happy Bathday box, and £200 off her father to get an elaborate butterfly and stars tattoo on her neck.

'Mel,' a wide-eyed Marielle suddenly interrupted her friend, but still Melissa babbled on about her birthday haul until Marielle let out a yelp and shouted: 'Something's behind you!'

Melissa smirked, thinking Marielle was just joking, but her friend looked genuinely scared, and so Melissa turned, and she saw no one in her bedroom.

'There was a little girl sitting on your bed!' Marielle told her in a high-pitched voice, and her hand flew to her mouth as she gasped, 'Oh my God! There was a ghost behind you!'

Melissa swore and told her she was just being 'jelly' (jealous) but secretly felt a little unnerved. Marielle said the ghostly girl had no face and was dressed in old-fashioned clothes. Melissa shook her head and said, 'I've had enough of this shit, peace out,' and disconnected from Skype. She ignored the texts from an angry Marielle and left the bedroom in a hurry. Melissa went down to the kitchen and told her mother Angela about Marielle's supposed sighting of a ghost with no face, but Angela just shook her head and said Marielle was 'a certified attention-seeker' and asked Melissa if she was still a vegetarian as she was making chicken lasagne. 'I'll get back to you on that,' Melissa replied.

That night, Melissa lay in bed, and just after she switched off the row of fairy lights which festooned the bamboo head-rail of her bed, she felt the mattress go in at the end of the bed – as if someone had just sat on it. Then she heard a faint whisper by her right ear.

'Hello,' the eerie voice said, and it sounded just like the voice of a young girl. Melissa jumped out the bed, switched the main ceiling light on, and stood there looking at the bed with her heart pounding. What was going on? First Marielle had said she had seen a faceless girl on the bed and now she had heard a girl's voice. Melissa eventually convinced herself that she had hallucinated the voice because she was overtired and around 2 am she went back to sleep – with her fairy lights on, and she had drifted off wearing her earphones as she listened to the eclectic mix of songs on her miniscule MP3 player – just to prevent any more ghostly whispers being heard. The next day Melissa's grandfather turned up with a belated birthday present – a vintage BMX bike, and Melissa couldn't wait to get on it, and she planned to ride the bike down Dinas Lane, where her latest crush – Adam Lambert look-alike Jason – lived. She left the bike in the front parlour as her grandfather chatted to the window cleaner, and then went upstairs to put on her make-up. She Tweeted Marielle, cryptically telling her she was going out on a bike, and then got on the BMX and pedalled off to Dinas Lane, but at the Charnwood Road junction, the front wheel of the bike came off, and the frame collapsed and threw Melissa forward. She reflexively threw out her hands, and landed hard, spraining a wrist and grazing her palms. As she lay there, groaning in the road, Melissa heard the distinctive sound of a child giggling – a female child. When she returned home her mother took Melissa – against her will – to the hospital, to get checked over, and while she was at the hospital, the girl's grandfather said he had thoroughly examined the bike that morning as he cleaned it, and assured Melissa's father that the wheels had not been loose. The mystery then deepened when the window cleaner said he had seen a little girl inspecting the bike through the front parlour window. Melissa's father said there was no little girl in the house, and this creeped out the window cleaner, who had only seen the girl – who had seemed to be about 7 years of age – from behind. That evening, Melissa was on Skype again, showing Marielle the splint on her wrist when the girl appeared once again, sitting on Melissa's bed, and this time, when Marielle yelled: 'She's back! She's back!' Melissa turned – and saw the faceless child, who seemed to be dressed in Victorian clothes. She had no eyes, no mouth or nose, just a vague pale oval of a face. The child hopped off the bed and ran towards her with her hands reaching out, and Melissa screamed and ran out of the bedroom with the sinister child following close behind. This time, Melissa's parents, her older brother Davis, and her grandfather – all saw the ghost as it came after Melissa down the stairs, and they all saw how the entity was leaning forward at around forty-five degrees, at a gravity-defying angle as it quickly descended the stairs, but it faded away upon reaching the bottom step. Melissa's mother and Davis had to run out of the house to tell the fleeing girl that the ghost had gone. Melissa was now in tears, and it took some effort for Davis to persuade his sister to return to the house.

'They can't harm you, you know?' grandfather said, gazing at the bottom step where the girl had quickly faded into nothingness. 'They just need prayers, ghosts do,' he added.

'We've lived in this house for nearly twenty years,' Melissa's father suddenly said, 'and we have never once seen anything supernatural.' He seemed in shock.

'I think I should stay over in Marielle's tonight, I really do!' Melissa brushed the tears from her eyes. She had black streaks where the mascara had run down her cheeks.

'How do you get rid of them, Dad?' Davis asked his father, who slowly shook his head and admitted: 'I don't know.'

'A priest, that's who,' grandfather said, and he turned to Melissa and asked, 'You alright love? Ghosties won't harm you.'

'That one did!' Melissa suddenly snapped, 'It took the wheel off the bike! It tried to kill me. There were cars on that road!'

The family visited a priest, and expected him to say the ghost was all in the mind and that there was nothing he could do, but he said a strange thing. He told Melissa's parents that he had only just blessed the house next door to their one two days ago, after a group of teenagers decided to dabble with a Ouija board. They had also been visited by the faceless child, and after being banished from that house, she had evidently started visiting Melissa's house. Bibles were left in each room, Holy water was sprinkled about, and prayers were recited, and the unidentified little phantom stopped appearing, but shortly afterwards the faceless girl started putting in an appearance in the house next door but one to Melissa's home. The services of the priest were enlisted again, and at the time of writing (May 2015), the ghost seems to have stopped haunting – but for how long is anyone's guess…

TAXI IN THE RAIN

It was in the Autumn of 1994 when two female students in their early twenties – Karla and Lyndsey – moved into a flat on Wavertree's Sandown Lane. The flat was on the second floor of a creaky old Victorian house and the young ladies finally finished unpacking their belongings nigh on 8pm. They sat and drank cider and chilled out listening to the radio as they looked through curtainless windows at the full moon rising in the east, above trees of burnt gold. Clouds sailed past the lunar disk on a sudden cold scathing wind, and then the moon was completely obscured by rain clouds. As the first patter of raindrops sounded on the windows of the flat, Lyndsey hummed along to the radio, which was playing *Right Beside You* by Sophie B. Hawkins, while Karla, sinking into the huge old soft armchair, closed her burning eyes and began to drift into the surreal realms of hypnogogia with a gradual loosening of the smug smile on her waxy clean foundation-free face.

When the song started to fade upon the approach of the 8pm news, Lyndsey suddenly said, 'What's that?'

Karla opened her slightly bloodshot eyes, startled, halfway between this world and the sphere of the unconscious. 'What?' she asked, annoyed at being recalled from her well-earned slumber.

Lyndsey turned the volume of the radio down and angled her head as she listened intently. 'I thought I heard someone knocking downstairs,' she murmured.

Both girls listened. They heard a low-pitched thrumming noise mingled with a rhythmical tick-tick-tick sound, reminiscent of a diesel engine – a taxi engine. Lyndsey went to the window and looked out. Down in the street, on the penumbral fringe of a lamp post's patch of light, there was a black hackney cab at the kerb, about twelve feet from the front door of the house. Rain slanted down through the lamplight as Lyndsey looked on at the taxi. It was there with its engine ticking over for some time, and as its 'for hire' lamp was out, the student surmised that the passenger must still be in the vehicle, perhaps rabbiting with the cabby, but no one got out in half an hour. Karla yawned and got up from the armchair and had a look at the taxi. A woman of about fifty was standing by it, continually yanking the leash of her terrier as it attempted to cock its leg on the doorstep. Karla tried to quietly lift the sash window open but it squeaked and the woman in the street looked up, startled. 'I think he's on drugs,' she told Karla.

'Sorry?' Karla popped her head out the window. The rain had lessened to a drizzle now.

The woman spoke up. 'He's been sitting there for about half an hour and I asked him if he was waiting for someone and he never said a word. Ignorant get.'

Now Lyndsey joined her friend at the window and asked Karla what the matter was.

'This lady said she asked the cabby if he was waiting for someone and he just sat there and didn't even reply. He's been there for ages,' Karla explained and looked back to the woman with the terrier – which had now managed to urinate on the step and was rearing to continue on his walkies, but he made a coughing, choking sound as his owner pulled him back.

'Are you sure he's not dead?' Lyndsey asked, all tongue in cheek, elbowing Karla and stifling a grin.

The woman on the pavement shook her head. 'No! He's sitting there, alive and kicking, just very ignorant.'

'Let's go down,' Lyndsey whispered, and moved away from the window.

'What for?' Karla moved away from the window too and followed her to the door. 'You're as stir crazy as her, Linz,' she said, smirking. The students went down to the street and saw that the woman looked much older at close quarters – more like sixty-something. She nodded at the silhouette of the driver in the hackney, and said, 'See?'

'Well, you're right,' Karla told the woman, 'he's definitely alive.'

'Go and ask him why he's waiting,' Lyndsey told her friend with a mischievous gleam in her eye.

'No!' Karla protested with a harsh whisper, and under her breath she said, 'he might be a rapist.'

The old woman yanked her Yorkshire terrier and said to him, 'Teddy! Come here!' Then she leaned towards the students and in a barely audible voice she slowly mouthed the word: 'Drugs.'

'What? You mean he's on them or pushing them?' Lyndsey queried, feigning innocence.

'Pushing them, probably. Nothing surprises me nowadays,' the woman wheezed in an asthmatic voice.

'Young man flashed me in the park over there last week – broad daylight too. You never see any police on the beat round here.'

Lyndsey turned to grin to Karla and saw she wasn't there. She was on the other side of the taxi, talking to the driver. 'Karla, what are you doing?' she asked, and went to see her friend was alright.

'Are you waiting for someone mate?' Karla asked, arms folded. The rain was getting heavy again.

The hackney driver sat there. He had a sad pale face and dark twinkly eyes which seemed – to Karla anyway – to be full of sadness.

'Come on Karla, we're going to get drenched,' Lyndsey pulled her friend by her upper arm, and she looked past the silent cabby to see the talkative woman with the terrier stooping to look in at the driver from the other side of the vehicle.

The cabby suddenly sounded his horn three times, and the woman with the dog, and the students, all jumped.

He spoke.

'Come on, love, let's go home,' he said, and these words came as he gazed at the door of the house where Karla and Lyndsey were staying. As far as the students knew, the only other tenants in the house were a very old woman named Mrs Drury and a male student of about 25 who was somewhere out on the town tonight.

'Come on, Karla!' Lyndsey tried to pull her friend away from the cab by her arm but the heavy rain made her fingers slip.

Karla turned and walked with Lyndsey to the flat, nodding and smiling to the nosy dog-walker as they went into the house. They had only reached the staircase when the students heard a loud female scream. It came from outside. They ran to the door, opened it, and saw that lady with the terrier standing there with her hands resting on each cheek of her face. The taxi had gone, and the dog Teddy was trotting away down Sandown Lane with his leash trailing along with him.

Karla ran to the dog and seized the lead and pulled Teddy back to his owner, who seemed to be in a state of mild shock.

'It vanished – the cab,' Teddy's stunned owner said, and coughed.

Lyndsey looked both ways, up and down the road, and saw there was no hackney cab to be seen.

The woman said the cab and its driver had 'just disappeared' right in front of her, and then she told the students, 'He must have been a ghost.'

'Maybe he drove off and you didn't see him,' Karla suggested, trying to calm the woman down, but she took hold of her dog's leash and walked away without saying another word.

'This is creeping me out,' Lyndsey told her friend, grimacing at the raindrops as they flicked her eyelashes. 'Come on, let's get in before he comes back.'

'That's not funny,' Karla hurried indoors with her friend and they raced up the stairs to their flat. They talked about the vanishing hackney cab and both agreed that the cabby had been some ghost, and they recalled the words of the phantom taxi driver: 'Come on, love, let's go home.' What was he referring to?

'Can I sleep with you tonight, Linz?' Karla asked; two things scared her in this world – insane people and ghosts – and tonight's paranormal occurrence was really playing on the young woman's mind.

'Ooh, I didn't know you cared,' Lyndsey joked, then seeing how afraid Karla had become, she tried to reassure her that they would not see that cab again and most ghosts were harmless.

The girls slept together that night in the little single bed from Bensons which Lyndsey had only just bought. Lyndsey was soon snoring, and around 2.30am, Karla was still awake, but she had her eyes closed in case she saw something in the darkened bedroom. She hard the click-clack of a woman's heels pass by and the faint, indistinct voices of a couple talking – probably two clubgoers returning from a night out. The sound of the heels receded into the distance, and then Karla heard that distinctive sound she had heard earlier – the ticking over of the hackney cab's diesel engine.

'Oh God,' Karla whispered, and she was about to shake Lyndsey awake but wondered if the sound might be coming from a real taxi that had pulled up to let out some local late-night revellers. She heard a thump, and a female voice say, 'Keep the change, mate,' followed by a male voice which replied: 'Ah, cheers love.'

Karla breathed a sigh of relief as she heard the faint padding of feet walk away and then the sound of the taxi engine revving up and moving off into the night.

Rain drummed its goblin fingertips on the window panes again not long after, and Karla dared herself to go and look out the window. She sneaked across the room, her size-6 bare foot stepping on a creaky floorboard at one point, and she found herself at the window. 'Must put some nets up on this window tomorrow,' she whispered to herself to steady her nerves – and then she peered out the rain-speckled window.

There was a taxi on the other side of the road with its lights off.

The flow of time in her head came to a sudden standstill and she felt her heart jolt in her chest, wobbling her bosom. Was it the same taxi as the one that vanished earlier? Oh my God, it was – because there was that pale thin face gazing out the driver's side window, and he was looking over at her. Karla ran back to the bed and shook Lyndsey awake, and her friend moaned, 'I'm tired Jack.' thinking she was back with her ex for a moment.

'That taxi is back!' Karla told her, and Lyndsey could plainly hear the tremor in her voice.

'You sure?' Lyndsey asked, and she sat up and looked at the luminous green points and arrow tips of the alarm clock on an upright chair which served as a bedside table. 'Twenny to three?'

'He was looking right over here,' Karla said, unconsciously grabbing Lyndsey's arm hard. 'His face is horrible, all white and his eyes were like black spots.'

Lyndsey levered herself up off the bed, yawned, and then walked over to the window with Karla following right behind her. She cupped her hand against the pane and squinted through the drizzled glass dotted with constellations of out of focus stars, and said, 'Mightn't be him.' And then she opened the window, much to the protestations of Karla. She could see it *was* the same cabby now; he had his side-window wound down and he was gazing intently up at the frightened girls.

'Call the police, Linz,' Karla suggested. Mobile

phones were not available to most people at this time – especially impoverished students – and the only telephone in the building was the payphone down in the hall.

'Oh as if we can report a ghost to the police,' Lyndsey snapped, more out of nerves than anything, 'we'd get done for wasting police time. Maybe we should just spew this flat and get a place somewhere else.'

'I knew there was something weird about this flat, 'Karla recalled, and you said it was my imagination. I should have gone with my gut instincts.'

'If he gets out of that taxi I'm going to make a hole through that wall, I'm telling you,' Lyndsey suddenly said, and this really creeped out Karla, who seemed near to tears now.

'You don't think he will, do you?' Karla asked, and glanced back at her jeans, bra, tee-shirt and trainers strewn on her bed. Would she be able to get dressed in time if the ghost did come for her? She wondered.

'What does it want?' Lyndsey mused, 'Why is it haunting this place?'

'We could go out the back way and stay with Claudia,' Karla suggested. Claudia was an art and design student who attended their college.

'Claudia lives in Crosby – that's miles away,' Lyndsey punctured her friend's proposal.

The taxi headlights came on, and they did not give off the usual light that headlamps generated, but an eerie soft milky-white light. The engine revved and the taxi lurched forward, and for a moment the girls thought it was heading towards Wavertree's High Street, but the hackney swung around and parked in the exact same location as it had earlier in the evening.

Lyndsey walked away from the window and went to a rucksack lying among a mound of plastic bags containing folders, coursework and books.

'What are you doing? Are we going?' Karla wanted to know.

'Going to get his registration,' Lyndsey told her panicky pal, and she found a green Ball Pentel pen and a writing pad full of doodles. She hurried back to the window and began to jot down the registration: 'XJD…'

'Listen! He's talking!' Karla said, her mouth forming an 'O' and her eyes bulging.

'Come on, love, let's go home,' the phantom taxi driver said a number of times, and Lyndsey suddenly said, 'There's something sad about it, isn't there?'

'No, its creepy,' Karla replied, 'very creepy!'

The diesel engine noise stopped as the cab disappeared, along with the shadow it had cast on the pavement. The students looked at the spot where the vehicle had stood a heartbeat ago, and then they turned to one another with expressions of utter wonder on their faces. They turned the light on, turned on the radio, and Lyndsey said they should stay up and get the deposit they had paid on the flat back in the morning. Morning came, and Lyndsey telephoned the lettings office and was told by a docile secretary that the landlord was on holiday and wouldn't be back for a week. The girls telephoned Claudia and asked if they could stay with her, but Claudia said she was living in her parents' house and it was already overcrowded. Claudia came and visited Karla and Lyndsey, bringing a six-pack of beer, a bottle of wine, and a multipack bag of crisps. She said she was fascinated by ghosts and wanted to see the spooky cab. 'You won't be saying that if it appears,' Karla told the art student. The girls had a drink, and talked of boys, of ambitions and of clothes, and Lyndsey asked Claudia where she'd had her hair done – it had been dyed red and was long and straight as a laser beam.

At 9pm, Claudia asked if she could stay over, and the girls eagerly nodded because she was great company and also, they felt safer with her about because of the recent ghostly incidents. Claudia went round the corner to get some more wine and snacks from Threshers and Karla and Lyndsey accompanied her. As the girls were returning from the off-licence, they passed the filling station just before Sandown Lane, and a group of four lads who – from their white shirts and gelled hairstyles – were probably out for the night, emitted wolf whistles and hurled sexist comments at the female trio. The students just returned condescending looks at the pathetic youths and one of the lads yelled, 'Hey redhead, get your lips – ' but before he could finish the lewd remark, a taxi came hurtling towards them like a giant bowling ball launched at four skittles. The right front side of the taxi hit one young man and the impact threw him hard against a brick wall, and the vehicle then narrowly missed hitting or killing the other three, who all screamed abuse at the driver. That taxi swerved silently and left the forecourt of the filling station – and headed towards the three students. Karla happened to glance back – and at once she saw that it *was* that hackney cab – the one which had been paying night visits from some world beyond the living. She let out a sort of strangled cry and Lyndsey turned to see what the matter was – and then she too recognised the sinister cab. Karla ran ahead of Lyndsey, and the latter grabbed a startled Claudia by her elbow and almost dragged her along as she started to run up the street. Claudia was baffled as to what her friends were fleeing from for a moment, and then Lyndsey turned to her with a look of fear which seemed to transfigure her face. 'It's that taxi!' Lyndsey gasped, barely getting the words out. The eerie cab turned onto Sandown Lane and accelerated past the students and waited at the very same spot it had gone to the night before – just outside the house where Karla and Lyndsey were living. Claudia wanted to go and have a look at the taxi, but Karla and Lyndsey would not venture anywhere near it and therefore couldn't get into their flat. They walked to the KFC on the High Street and sat there at a table for half an hour, then returned to Sandown Lane, and, to the relief of Karla and Lyndsey, they saw that the unearthly vehicle was nowhere to be seen. The three girls went into the flat, and Claudia lingered at the entrance, hoping the cab would return, but Karla dragged her to the stairs.

'That was no ghostly cab,' Claudia remarked with one raised eyebrow as Lyndsey poured the wine into three mugs. 'I'm not *totally* stupid you know?'

'We are not winding you up or anything,' Karla told her sceptical friend. 'That taxi vanishes and reappears with him – whoever he is – in it.'

'How can you have a ghost of an inanimate object, though?' Claudia asked with a suspicious look in her huge eyes.

'Claudia, I swear on my baby brother's life that we

are not winding you up,' Lyndsey told her, solemnly, and clumsily angled the neck of the wine bottle wrongly so the rosé gushed onto Claudia's hand, which was wrapped firmly around the waiting mug.

'Say when,' Karla joked, as Claudia cussed. It was a bit of comic relief in the midst of such stressed nerves.

At 3am, the girls were wrecked by the effects of the beer and wine, and Karla was dozing in the armchair, while Claudia and Lyndsey were at the open window giggling and making mocking comments at any passing males out at that hour.

Then the taxi showed up again, moving silently from the north of Sandown Lane. It came to a halt under the window of the flat and only Claudia was still smiling and singing. Lyndsey went to wake Karla and alerted her to the ethereal vehicle's return.

'Claudia, come on, get away from the window,' Lyndsey said, but Claudia refused to budge and she leaned out of the window and in a loud voice, asked: 'That the haunted taxi?'

'Claudia!' Karla grabbed her arm and led her backwards as her tipsy friend laughed.

Lyndsey pulled the sash window down, and then killed the lights. She remained at the side of the window, peeping out at the uncanny hackney cab.

'I'll go down and tell you if it's a ghost,' Claudia announced, swinging her arms backwards and forwards as she marched to the door, but Karla stood in her way with her back pressed against the door.

'Claudia, sit down, please!' Karla told her, and Claudia noticed how her friend's eyebrow was twitching with nerves and though it was funny.

'Claudia, please - you're acting like a tit,' Lyndsey

whispered, her eyes wide and her eyebrows at the top of her forehead somewhere.

The taxi stayed at the same spot as usual outside, and the sound of its diesel engine could be plainly heard. As Lyndsey looked out, she saw a curtain in the window of the house opposite part and the face of a woman look out; she had obviously had her sleep disturbed by the taxi's throbbing engine sound.

Claudia went the toilet, saying she felt sick, but a few minutes later Karla and Lyndsey heard the door being opened downstairs. Karla went straight to the toilet and found it empty; Claudia had sneaked downstairs to see the taxi at closer quarters. Lyndsey went down first and Karla followed her gingerly. The front door was open, and they could hear Claudia flippantly asking: 'Are you a ghost?'

Lyndsey bravely ventured out while Karla – feeling ashamed of her lack of pluck – stayed in the hallway, peeping out from the imagined safety of the front door.

'Claudia, come here now!' Lyndsey called to her, and at that moment a downpour began. The taxi seemed solid enough, because Lyndsey could hear the rain pattering on its black shiny beetle-shell body.

Claudia turned to Lyndsey, swaying slightly, and said, 'Some ghost,' then smirked and pulled a tongue at the unresponsive cabby, who was looking straight ahead - through the rain-streaked windscreen - down Sandown Lane.

As Lyndsey inched forward and gestured with a curling hand for Claudia to come indoors, the intoxicated redhead suddenly reached out – and touched the door handle of the driver's door, and a moment later, something terrifying took place. The cabby's mouth opened wide, and so did two dark holes where his eyes had been, and Claudia was near enough to him to see that these holes revealed a hollow head with some greyness inside, and this really frightened her, for now she knew that this was no human sitting in the taxi. The mouth became larger and through the yawning aperture Claudia saw that same grey curvature of the inside of the head, and she stumbled backwards. The cabby opened the door and as Claudia turned to run, he darted at her with an unnatural movement, and she felt icy long fingers which seemed to squirm like worms around her upper arms. The ghost said something which sounded like a string of swear-words, but spoken in a raspy voice, and Karla and Lyndsey distinctly heard the apparition utter the word: 'Bitch!'

'Help! Lyndsey!' Claudia shouted, but the figure seemed to float backwards with her and pulled her into the vehicle as its interior became dark and vaporous, as if it contained thick black smoke, and as Karla exclaimed, 'Oh God, no!' the taxi's engine sound faded and the vehicle moved off – and faded away.

Lyndsey kept saying 'Jesus' over and over as she held her hands over her mouth and she looked up and saw that woman gazing through the parted curtain again – so she must have just witnessed the weird and terrifying incident, Lyndsey reasoned. Karla came slowly out from the cover of the door and looked at the spot in the road where Claudia had somehow been taken away by something which was not of this world.

Lyndsey looked at Karla and saw that her face was a mass of twitches and nervous tics now, and the girl was also hyperventilating with shock.

'What are we going to do, Lyndsey, what are we going to do?' Karla asked her bewildered friend, and Lyndsey replied: 'The police, the police,' and she staggered into the hallway and went to the payphone, then hesitated.

'What are you waiting for?' Karla asked, questioning her sudden reticence.

'They are not going to believe us,' Lyndsey realised. 'They'll think we're on drugs or just wasting police time.'

'It doesn't matter! Claudia's been taken!' Karla told her sternly, and tears were streaming from her eyes now.

'Karla, a woman opposite saw what happened before,' Lyndsey recalled, 'and she could back us up when we tell the police.'

'Just call them, they'll have to believe us!' Karla was so angry at the way Lyndsey was worrying about not being believed.

'No, listen, Karla, we're going to get that woman to back us up!' Lyndsey left the house and went across the street. She looked up at the window and then her gaze fell on a door with two white buttons. She pressed the two of them. About a minute later, a dim light was visible through the oval of frosted glass in the centre of the door, and then the students heard a chain being removed and a catch being taken off. A woman of about fifty popped her head around the door. Lyndsey thought the lady was the spitting image of Frances de la Tour, the actress who played the character of "Miss Jones" in the television comedy *Rising Damp*.

'Did you see what happened before?' Lyndsey wiped

rain and tears from her eyes as she asked the lady.

'The taxi you mean, yeah but – ' the lady replied in a soft southern Irish accent.

With a sigh of relief Lyndsey continued: 'We're going to the police, but they won't believe us, so would you tell them what you saw?'

'I can't get involved, I'm in bad health,' the woman replied and seemed to hide her mouth behind her hand.

'You've got to – no one will believe us,' Lyndsey insisted.

'You did see what happened?' Karla chipped in over her friend's shoulder.

'It's bad luck, that thing,' the woman replied cryptically, 'I think he needs prayers. But look, I can't go, my heart's in a terrible state, and my doctor has ordered me to stay away from any excitement.'

'I'm begging you please,' Lyndsey put her foot in the door, 'just back us up because we don't know what to do.'

'Alright, hang on, just get your foot out the door a sec and wait there,' the lady said, and then she closed the door.

And then the girls heard the chain go back on, and then came the sound of the catch being clicked on the Yale lock.

Lyndsey pushed the flap of the brass letterbox forward and shouted: 'Hello? Are you coming with us? Hello?'

There was no reply, despite Lyndsey's constant knocking and ringing of the two doorbells. In the end the girls gave up and decided they would walk to Wavertree Road Police Station and attempt to make an official statement about an incident which would seem impossible by the laws of this world. Lyndsey and Karla were soaked as they turned the corner of Sandown Lane onto the High Street. Then, as they passed a tiny cul de sac known as Pearson Street, they heard an eerie wailing sound barely audible through the white noise of the rain.

'Hear that?' Lyndsey asked Karla, and she nodded.

Then there was an echoing scream.

'That came from the park!' Karla opined.

'No, it came from over there!' Lyndsey pointed to the upper windows of a derelict house visible at the back of the filling station.

Karla shook her head of wet stringy hair. 'No, Lyn, its echoing off there, but it's coming from the park!'

'Help!'

Now the girls could clearly gauge that the screams were indeed coming from the direction of Wavertree Park, and that scream had been a female one. They went down Pearson Street and came to an alleyway which led onto an adjacent street, and at the end of this street were the ominous Gothic gateposts of the park, topped with dark spheres of blackened sandstone. The girls thought they would have to climb the gates to get into the park but saw there was a smaller gate at a right angle to the closed ones which was still open. The students crept into the darkness and straight ahead, in a park which was only illuminated by the lights of the lamp posts of Prince Alfred Road and Grant Avenue, there stretched a creepy path into the blackness lined with enormous thick oaks, all leaning to the left at a weird 45-degree angle. To the right was the deserted Wavertree

Athletics Centre with its running track, and to the left was the vast spread of grassy parkland dotted with the occasional tree. A heavy oppressive otherworldly presence greeted the students as they ventured into the park in the dead of night, and it was suddenly pierced by another scream which seemed to come from straight ahead. Then they both saw her – a silhouette of a woman staggering down the long path, and they somehow knew it was Claudia. Karla walked a little ahead of her friend and she recognised the pale face first, and the red hair all ropey with the rain, some of it clinging to Claudia's face.

'Claudia!' Karla yelled and she and Lyndsey ran to her aid.

Claudia was shaking violently and could not get her words out. The nearer they got to the gateposts and the sodium lamp post, the more Karla and Lyndsey could see how scared Claudia looked. She tried to speak and her eyes rolled back into her head as if she was having a seizure. They eventually managed to get her back to the flat, and there, Karla and Lyndsey put on the gas fire and sat Claudia in front of it while they gently dabbed her face with towels while Lyndsey squeezed her hand.

The art student talked incoherently, but after about twenty minutes she began to cry and said the man – the thing – had taken her into the park and *had his way* with her. But as shocking as Claudia's account was, it did not make sense, because she had described the appalling attack as taking place in daylight - even though it would have been well after three in the morning. Claudia also said the outrage upon her had been so brutal, it had left her bleeding and bruised, and yet, in the morning she could see no evidence of any harm at all. She suffered horrific and weird nightmares for many years and even today she still has occasional bad recurrent dreams about the 'attack'. Karla and Lyndsey moved that day their friend was abducted by the entity and its ghostly cab, and they were intrigued to hear that many other people had seen that phantom taxi in Wavertree over the years, and some of the reports go back to the late 1970s. The strange thing is that the hackney is always seen when its raining, and always on Sandown Lane near to that a particular house. In the 1990s the house was subdivided into flats but it is now a private dwelling and a family have lived there for years. They have heard the sound of the diesel engine on several occasions at all hours in the morning but have not seen the hackney cab itself. Some ghosts – both of people and of vehicles – often fade away over time, but sometimes return to our range of vision with a vengeance. There are several phantom buses and an a tram which haunt the roads of Liverpool, and they are usually heard more than they are seen, but the vehicles sometimes appear very solid and they have been seen by people from all walks of life. As recent as 2014, a phantom tram was seen gliding along Smithdown Road near the Oxfam shop, and I am told that long ago, there were tram sheds at this location. But can a ghost rape someone? Sadly, the answer to this question is that yes, certain entities can, although the assault may seem real as a physical one, it often leaves no physical after-effects. Ghosts that sexually assault women are known as *incubi,* and I have interviewed many level-headed people who have been assaulted by an incubus in Liverpool over the years.

Sometimes the ghostly rapist is described as very handsome and resembling the archetypal Adonis, while some attacks have been perpetrated by ghastly disfigured-looking beings, and some are not even humanlike at all. There was a case of a teenage boy in the 1930s that was attacked almost every night at his home in West Derby by something which resembled a *tree trunk* with long tentacles for arms. Whenever this creature appeared in the boy's bedroom he would feel violently sick, and on some occasions the weird bedroom invader would squirt some type of oily substance at him and make a gurgling sound. On one occasion the entity cornered the boy and pressed him into a corner, almost smothering him, and his screams brought his parents barging into his room. They saw the thing immediately vanish, and detected the foul odour it left behind. The late actor Jon Pertwee, probably most famous for his role as Doctor Who (in his third incarnation) in the 1970s, once related a very strange and scary tale which has many parallels with the West Derby case. In the 1920s, the young Jon Pertwee, aged about 9, often stayed with a schoolfriend during the summer holidays at an Elizabethan manor house in Sussex. On this particular occasion, all of the rooms in both wings of the old house were full, so Jon was put in a room at the end of the minstrels' gallery. Jon awoke in the wee small hours in his room and felt a sensation of overpowering nausea which caused him to throw up all over the bedcovers. Jon had to sneak downstairs, get a jug of water and clean the bedcovers, and on the following day, his hosts did not notice anything out the ordinary in Jon's room, but on the following night, Jon's sleep was disturbed again with the feelings of intense nausea, and this time he realised what was making him sick: the potent smell of what seemed to be putrefying flesh, like fish or meat going off, only ten times worse. Jon associated the smell with a dead sheep he had seen once which had been left to rot on a farm. The boy leaped out the bed, fearing he'd vomit again, but this time he saw something very peculiar and unfamiliar to his eyes, and it was standing about four feet from the end of his bed. To young Pertwee this thing resembled a tree trunk and it was light green in colour. As Jon squinted at this bizarre thing in the darkened room, he saw that it 'undulated' – it quivered, and then began to emit what looked like bubbles from the side of its trunk-like body. The unearthly thing then moved ever so slowly towards Jon, and he was that scared, he wet himself. The boy ran around the weird creature, opened the door and his screams woke the entire household as he flew along the minstrels' gallery. The host and hostess were standing at the end of the gallery, and Jon ran straight to the latter, hysterical and in tears, and she hugged him and calmed him down. When Jon blabbed out his account of the thing that had appeared in his room, the husband of the hostess suddenly said to her, 'Didn't I tell you we should never have put him in there?'

Jon later learned from his schoolfriend and other people that the entity he had seen in that room had been making visits for many years, but no one knew what the thing was or where it came from. But the mere memory of the awful odour the creature gave off haunted Jon Pertwee to his dying day.

There is probably a 'back-story' – a history – behind

the ghostly hackney of Sandown Lane. I have researched the registration jotted down by Lyndsey when she saw it during one of its materialisations and it appears the cab belonged to a man who lived near Smithdown Road in the 1970s. He died in a car crash in the 1980s and I have a photograph of him, but none of the students have identified him as the ghost they saw in the wraithlike taxi, but hopefully, the sordid story behind the haunting will come to light one day.

SPOOKED CROOKS

Some of the weirdest ghost stories have been told to me by people who work during that eerie time which commences with the hours of dusk and ends just before cock-crow sunrise. I have told you tales from the blue lamp: things that patrolling policemen and policewomen have seen during the lonely watches of the night, and we have read of sinister tales from prostitutes, who often ply their trade after dark; many of them have met entities such as the likes of Lantern Jaw and Mr McKenzie, two Victorian shades who prefer to roam the world of the living when Liverpool is asleep; I even know of several women of the night who swear they have been stalked by the Devil himself in his black Rolls Royce, which curiously always seems to originate at the bottom of Mount Pleasant. Security guards, milkmen (who are becoming an endangered species) and taxi drivers, are all the more likely to encounter beings from the supernatural sphere than the diurnal worker who toils in the light of day. It seems that when our half of the planet is plunged into night, *they* awake, and the uncanny, the evil and unearthly have free reign in the ensuing hours of darkness. Of course, the night provides the welcoming backdrop to another type of worker, and this is the criminal, and over the years, many crooks and self-employed people working on the reverse coin of the law have written to me – many of them from 68 Hornby Road – to tell me of their brushes with the paranormal. What follows are just three tales of Spooked Crooks, and of course, you will understand that I have had to change the names in these accounts for obvious reasons, but this in no way detracts from the uncanny element of these stories.

How many times have you heard the phrase 'There's no justice in the world' whenever a criminal escapes a long jail sentence or is spared punishment altogether by some loophole in the law or the actions of an over-lenient judge? Well, maybe there isn't much justice in *this* world, but there are other worlds, and I'm not talking about the planets of the universe, but the inner worlds of dreams which we visit in the depths of sleep – and in those worlds, a strange type of justice is often dished out. In the 1970s at a certain Liverpool tenement block, a 30-year-old unemployed man named Rob embarked on a series of burglaries, and all of the victims were pensioners. Rob was investigated by the police after an anonymous tip-off from a frightened member of the public, but despite a search of the suspected burglar's flat, none of the stolen money from the recent robberies – around £200 – could be found. Rob had rolled up the money, which was in one, five and ten pound notes, and he had put them in the end of his curtain pole. Rob then intended to suspend his criminal career until the heat died down, and during this hiatus he was walking along Church Street when an old woman raised her walking stick and took a swipe at him. She said she had seen him running from her flat, the night it was burgled, and she was telling the truth. Rob had stolen £30 the woman had been saving to buy her niece a present.

'Calm down you stupid old fool,' Rob told her as a crowd circled him outside C&A, and he added: 'I could sue you for accusing me of being a house robber!'

A suspicious stocky-looking man looked Rob up and down and asked: 'Why is she saying you're a robber then, mate? No smoke without fire. Did you rob her house, eh?'

'No! She's nuts. She said I exposed meself to her last time!' Rob claimed.

'Ooh, you bleedin' liar!' the poor old lady said, shocked at the accusation.

Rob got more creative with his lies. 'I've just come out the Army, served Queen and country, and I'm getting all this off her!'

'I curse you, you robbing bastard!' the old woman yelled, and she had a funny turn and collapsed. A crowd huddled around her and a woman who said she was a nurse put the old lady in the recovery position and removed her dentures.

Rob sneaked away, cursing under his breath in the confusion. He sneaked down Church Alley by the Bluecoat Chambers and ran off up School Lane.

That night, Rob dozed off in his bed, and he found himself in a grey dismal prison cell. Three concrete walls were behind him and to the sides of him, and there was no window in any of the walls, and in front of him steel bars ran from the ceiling to the floor, and he shook these bars, and cried, 'Let me out!' But no one came. He then realised with relief that he was dreaming – but he couldn't wake himself up. That lucid dream of being behind bars seemed to go on for days, and Rob felt his mouth dry up and the thirst became intense. When he finally woke up he went to his kitchen and drank from the tap for a few minutes and was so glad to be awake. But the next night he had the very same dream. He once again found himself in that prison cell, only this time it felt as if he was there for a week, as the time went by so slowly, and he ended up on his knees, praying for God to let him wake up. The corridor beyond the bars had a flagged floor and ancient sandstone walls, as if it was part of a castle. Rob tried to shout for help, but his throat had dried up because of all of those long hours – dream-time hours in reality, but they had felt just like waking hours to him – and he had thirsted for water throughout them. He clutched his throat and fell to his knees, and he even licked the cold steel bars, but that did not slake his thirst. He unzipped his trousers and tried to urinate into his cupped palms, because he was even eager to drink his own bodily fluids now – but he could not produce a single drop of pee. When would this nightmare end? He searched the walls of his cell in desperation, hoping to find some way out, but found only rough grey concrete walls with not even a hairline crack in them. He wondered if he had died and was now in Hell.

Then he saw a glass of water in the middle of the flagged corridor. He rushed to the bars and thrust his arm through – but his middle finger could only reach within a few inches of the glass. He took off his shoe and he tried to use it to bring the glass nearer, but he knocked the glass over, and he watched, heartbroken as the water from the rolling overturned glass moved away from him in little rivulets into the cracks of the floor.

Then he awoke. He stumbled out of the bed and went to the nearest source of water – the wash basin in the toilet. Rob put his mouth to the tap and turned it, and he drank until his belly was full, and then he looked up into the shaving mirror, and he saw how ghastly he looked; the dark circles of his eye sockets, his pale furred tongue. He knew that tonight, he would go through the same ordeal as soon as his head hit that pillow; he would enter a nightmare where the hours lasted for days, and it would be impossible to wake up.

That night he kept drinking strong black coffee, and if he had been able to get hold of cocaine he would have taken it, just to stay awake a little longer, but by 2am he had dropped off. He was back in that cell. He swore and shouted at the top of his voice. 'Who's doing this to me? Who's the jailer?' he cried.

Then he spotted the tap in the wall. He couldn't believe it. His tormentor had a heart after all. He reached out for the gleaming silvery chromium-plated tap, and he turned it as he stooped forward.

Dry sand fell from it.

He came out with every profanity he knew and turned the tap off. 'Why are you doing this to me? Show yourself you yellow arsehole!'

He then heard the sound of water trickling into water. It was as if a tap had been turned and its water was filling a bath. This sound drove Rob mad. He put his fingers in his ears, and the hours ground past. He tried the tap a few more times just in case the unseen tormentor had had a change of heart. Sand fell each time the tap was turned on, and even the spit in his mouth dried up so he couldn't swallow it when his uvula made him cough with its dryness.

These realistic dreams of water-deprivation and imprisonment went on for over a week, and for some reason known only to his subconscious, Rob recalled the old woman cursing him on Church Street. He felt that this curse was the reason for these cruel, realistic dreams in which he was tortured each night. He returned her money in person and told her to stop the dreams, because he was afraid to go asleep. She looked at him as if she knew what he was talking about, and she said, 'Don't you ever steal off anyone again.' And then she slammed the door in his face.

The dreams still continued - for three days - then stopped for good, and Rob never stole again. A psychiatrist would no doubt say that Rob had some guilt or persecution complex, and perhaps that alone was the cause of the dreams, but as far as Rob was concerned, they were some type of supernatural punishment, and I have heard of similar cases where wrongdoers have been punished in their dreams.

A former mugger named Ryan clearly remembers the time he went looking for victims in Mossley Hill one night in the early 1990s. It was Friday night going into Saturday morning – a time when there would be drunken students ripe for a good 'knocking over' – and Ryan had on his black woollen hat, black padded jacket, dark jeans and black Doc Martens – 'best boots to give someone a good kicking' he told me. The 19-year-old thug had left his home near Durning Road around 11.45pm, and he thought he had found his first victim when he saw a student – a girl dressed in the style of a Goth – staggering down Picton Road. She'd clearly had too much to drink, but as Ryan moved in on her, a taxi driver who knew him halted the cab and took the girl in after asking her where she lived. Ryan gave the Good Samaritan the middle finger gesture and fled down a side street. He reached Allerton Road twenty minutes later, but cursed when he saw the flashing lights of the police and ambulances there. There'd been some fight between boozers from a nearby wine lodge, so once again Ryan's evil plans were thwarted, and this only served to make him more determined to grab a wallet or purse. He stepped back into the shadows, and roamed in search of prey, and at two in the morning he spotted a man of about twenty-five, urinating in a quiet street off Green Lane. He was actually peeing on the gatepost of a terraced house as he swayed side to side. Around this time, there was a hush over the area, a dead period when hardly any traffic was passing, and in Ryan's experience, these periods were the best time to strike. No witnesses. He was just ready to move in when someone opened a door in the street where the young man was relieving himself. A middle-aged woman had opened the door to let a cat out, and the light from the hallway shone on to the urinating man revealing his shameless disregard for people's property. He said 'Shit,' and he gave himself a shake then began to swear and zip up.

'Oi! Go and do that on your own doorstep!' the woman shouted as her cat ran off.

'No, I prefer your doorstep you old bag!' the man shouted and ran off, passing less than three feet of a Ryan and his knife. By the time the woman had closed the door, the man was on the brightly-lit thoroughfare of Menlove Avenue.

Ryan was feeling sorry for himself by now, thinking

it wasn't going to be his night, when all of a sudden, a tall man in silhouette silently passed by him. He was walking from Menlove Avenue down Green Lane, towards Allerton Road, a rather long and poorly illuminated lane at that time. Ryan couldn't believe his luck, and he tip-toed after the man, being as quiet as he could, because his prey was very quiet indeed.

'Now,' the intended victim was heard to whisper, 'who should it be tonight?'

And as he said this, Ryan noticed something that really shocked him; what seemed to be a long pointed blade suddenly descended from the man's right hand. Its uniform motion reminded Ryan of something electric – like the old car aerials which used to come steadily up out of the wing of a car when a button was pressed, only this one was coming downwards, and it continued to come down until it showed about three feet of blade – it was a sword. The man started to swipe at the hedges with this blade as he walked along, shearing off leaves and branches.

Ryan slowed down, realising that this victim was not only armed, but obviously unbalanced. He looked to be about six feet tall, perhaps a few inches more, and the odd thing was that he was in silhouette all the time, even though there were lights shining onto him from the other side of Green Lane.

He stopped dead.

Ryan stopped too, ready to turn around and get away from this sword-carrying lunatic. The mugger was just about to turn when he noticed something that chilled him to the bone. That tall shadowy weirdo had not turned yet – his feet still pointed in the direction he'd been travelling – and yet it was now clear that he was facing Ryan – as if his head had turned – owl like – to face him. This is impossible of course, but that is exactly what Ryan saw, and that face was in shadow, like the rest of the man, and yet Ryan could see he was looking at him with wide, almost round bulging eyes, and a wide peculiar and very unsettling grin. In a flash, Ryan turned and ran, and now the tables were turned; the victim was now coming after him, and what chance would Ryan have against a sword? All he carried was a pathetic 5-inch flick-knife. Ryan thought that if he could make it to Menlove Avenue, where there was better lighting from the sodium streetlamps, perhaps he could attract the attention of a passing car – even if it was a police car – then the maniac chasing would be scared off. But something incredible happened; that silent sword-wielding silhouette flew ahead of Ryan, passing him on his right, and he crossed Green Lane – but then he ran in a bizarre curve, and he came heading back towards the mugger. It was as if he was trying to show Ryan how easily he could outrun him and overtake him. Ryan hid behind a bus shelter for a moment, trying to think fast; should he run back down Green Lane or down one of the streets which run off from the lane? He took out his flick knife, pressed the silver button on it and felt the handle jolt as the blade flew out. He then bolted across Green Lane, between parked cars, and ran for his life down the first street he came to – Greenhill Avenue. As Ryan ran down this suburban road, he kept thinking of how the man chasing him had turned his head through 180 degrees. He looked back – and saw that the figure of shadow was now casually walking along about fifteen yards behind him, swinging the sword up and down. Two hundred yards later, Ryan reached Calderstones Road, one of the quietest roads in the city, especially at this time in the morning, and there was not a person or a vehicle about. To make matters worse, a five-foot sandstone wall runs along most of Calderstones Road, and there were no roads to turn off on that side of the road where Ryan found himself running blindly. He turned around at one point as he headed towards Allerton Road and found, to his great relief, that he was alone – there was no sign of the weird pursuer. Ironically, Ryan found himself out of breath on a road with Rose Lane Police Station on the left and the Allerton Library building on his right. He went to a grid – literally right outside the police station – and dropped his flick-knife through its bars, then hurried along towards Allerton Road. He looked back again, making sure there was no sign of that creepy figure, and he walked up Allerton Road on the left side, passing closed shops such as Ethel Austin. It had been a disaster of a night, and a very strange night indeed, and for the first time in his life, Ryan thought a life of crime might not be his thing. He crossed over the road by the building on the corner of Allerton Road and Queens Drive Mossley Hill, which is now a bank, and he crossed the silent highways there, intending to go towards Penny Lane and Smithdown Place, when, for some strange reason, Ryan had the burning sensation that he was being watched. He looked around nervously and saw no one and nothing except a hackney coming along Allerton Road. He reached the corner of Plattsville Road and Allerton Road, where Woolworths stood for many years, when he suddenly saw the shadow of a man's head and shoulder on the pavement to his left. Right then, Ryan knew it had to be *him* because he never heard a single padding sound of feet. He turned left, and there was that figure, still in silhouette despite the well-lit area it was walking through. Ryan reached into his inside coat pocket, and felt nothing but the lining. He recalled how he had dropped the flick-knife down the grid. He took his hand out of his pocket and he ran as fast as his legs could carry him, and there, in one of the two bus shelters to his left, he saw a stocky young man, perhaps around 22 years of age, leaning heavily against the plate glass, obviously drunk, and perhaps believing in his intoxicated mind that the buses would still be running at this unearthly hour. This drunk was the type of person Ryan usually targeted, but he found himself shaking him by the arm. 'Hey mate, help me! Help!' Ryan yelled at the inebriate, gripping him by the lapels of his jacket, shaking him as the menacing silhouette closed in.

Ryan swung the man to his left, placing him between himself and the figure – which, Ryan had now decided, was not human. The blade descended from the sleeve of the humanoid, which was now pitch black, and the drunk screamed when he saw the appearance of the sword-like weapon. Ryan was just going to throw the drunk at the shadow when there was a burst of bright blue light which dazzled him.

The burst of light came from the flashing roof lights of a police car. The vehicle screeched to a halt at the bus shelter, and before the two policemen could even get out of the car, the silhouetted figure ran off at an incredible speed and flew around the corner of Woolworths onto Plattsville Road. As the policeman chased after him, Ryan shouted: 'You'll never catch him!'

Then there was a loud thud and a brief pain to the side of Ryan's head, and he found himself on his knees. The drunk, believing (correctly) that he was a mugger, had punched him, making knuckle-contact at the right side of his jaw. The drunk was still kicking his ribs and kidneys in when the police seized him.

Ryan did not press charges against the drunk and said it had all been a misunderstanding. He also said he did not know who the man was with the sword who ran off. The police told him they had lost the man on Plattsville Road; he had literally gone to ground within seconds, they said, and were sure he had to be a local man who lived close by. But Ryan knew the truth – or part of the truth. He knew that the man with the sword was some sort of supernatural being, and looked at the whole incident as some omen – some warning from spirits to prevent him from pursuing a life of crime and violence. Ryan *was* a mugger but he was not taking any drugs at the time and did not even drink. He knows he did not hallucinate the shadow man, and the police and the drunk at the bus stop all saw him as well. Not long after that night, Ryan began to look for a job and eventually found one, settled down, and went straight. He still has the occasional nightmare about the entity which chased him that night, and has asked me if I had any idea what the thing was. I don't really have enough data to go on, but I do know that there has been a huge rise in reports of encounters with 'shadow people' in recent years; these are beings which, as their name suggests, manifest themselves as silhouettes, and many of them do not make any sound as they move about – and I recall how Ryan said that he could not hear the tramp of the shadow being's feet when it walked close by. Shadow people often appear in two-dimensional form on walls and then gradually become three dimensional. They are often reported by people who experience paralysis whilst lying in bed at the time, and while some psychologists dismiss the phenomenon as a product of a half-asleep mind, most of the accounts of shadow beings take place while the witness is wide awake and not even in the environment of a bedroom. I saw these beings myself as a child and was not taken seriously when I told adults about them. Many believe the silhouetted entities are evil and there have been cases where people have allegedly 'exorcised' the figures by invoking the name of Jesus. No one knows where the shadow beings originate or whether there is any motive behind the visitation, but one thing does seem clear – the reports of shadow people are definitely on the increase.

Another criminal who had a very strange encounter with the unknown is a Dingle man named Gene, who in the early 2000s, at the age of 18, turned to burglary to supplement his income, along with his 19-year-old friend (also from the Dingle) Daffy – derived from his real name, Dafyd. Daffy had an old H-reg Vauxhall Corsa as his first-ever car, and he and Gene would go "house-hunting" in it – casing neighbourhoods by day for joints to rob at night. The two teens heard from a drunk in the Rose and Crown in Huyton that there was a 'massive mansion' not far from Holly Lodge Girls' College, near the 'back of the Jolly Miller' – and the old woman who lived there on her own was said to be 'well brewstered' – a millionairess in fact. She was practically deaf and screwing that house would be a doddle because there wasn't even an alarm installed – and that was on good authority. Gene and Daffy were young and gullible and went looking for this gold nugget of a job. They drove around looking for this promising mansion during one of the thickest fogs to ever visit the city, and somewhere along Queens Drive in West Derby, Daffy took a turning which led him and his partner in crime to the secluded grounds where a ghostly silhouette of a towering building rose out of the fog. Gene said the place reminded him of the Bates Motel in *Psycho* - and Daffy agreed that the residence did look Gothic and very old indeed. The teenagers carefully closed the door of the Corsa and crept to the dwelling through a fog that was kicking off Gene's chest.

'Look,' Daffy pointed to the faint yellowish square of light which now seemed to be suspended in mid air, because the fog had now become so opaque, the mansion's structure was no longer visible.

'She must be in bed,' said Gene, and he lifted the zipped collar of his tracksuit top and coughed inside it in an attempt to muffle his spluttering.

'Well it is nearly one in the morning,' Daffy said. In his mind he had plans. If there was almost a million in this mansion, he was opening a nightclub in Spain. The front door of the mansion looked solid, so the lads went to one of the five large windows at the side of the grand dwelling, but they were situated rather high up, so the window ledge was about five feet off the floor. Daffy was a bit portly, so he cupped his hands and let the wiry Gene climb up. Gene was a wizard at opening windows, and he used nothing more fancy than an old blunt butter knife to slide into the bottom of the frame and levered it until he could swipe the blade and manipulate the catch. It worked like a dream and as soon as the sash window was lifted, Daffy froze, and expected to hear an alarm.

'Am I a genius or what, lad?' Gene asked, smirking down at Daffy.

'You might have triggered a silent alarm that goes to the cop shop,' Daffy gloomily conjectured.

'No way,' Gene said, and he reached down and tried to pull Daffy up, and almost dislocated his shoulder. He swore at Daffy as his friend huffed and puffed in his ascent to the window ledge.

'I am out of shape,' Daffy said, sitting on the sandstone window ledge, gasping for air.

'You're just fat,' Gene said, almost in tears as he clutched his shoulder.

'Don't start or I'll throw you off this ledge,' Daffy said, ruffled by the insensitive comment. He took out a tiny flashlight pen and swept its feeble but adequate beam across the room. The place looked very old, all dark brown walls and gas brackets on those walls. It looked like a dining room with a very long table. The full moon suddenly shone through a break in the clouds – lighting up the silver Corsa.

'Shit, you can see the motor,' Gene said, still holding his shoulder, 'the moon's a twa – '

'Shh! Listen!' Daffy said, standing by the table.

Gene landed with a slight thump as he dropped onto the floor from the window sill.

'You noisy bastard!' whispered Daffy harshly through gritted teeth.

'What's that noise?' Gene asked. It sounded loud, but distant.

'Shut up a sec,' Daffy told him, and looked at the disc of light from the pen on the carpeted floor as he listened. It sounded rhythmical.

'She's snoring,' Gene said, and beamed a wide grin. 'God, that is loud.'

The burglars searched the dining room but there was nothing of any value except for an old oil portrait of some man with a big nose in a gilded frame. They went into the hall, and saw a suit of armour, various armorial shields and crossed swords on the wood-panelled walls, and Daffy was observant enough to notice that there were no light switches or any lightbulbs or neon strips to be seen on any of the ceilings downstairs.

'Jesus Christ,' that old biddy snores like a dinosaur,' Gene remarked. The snoring was very loud and was echoing down the stairs.

'It's the acoustics in here – ' Daffy was explaining but Gene cut short the scientific explanation.

'Come on lets find this money, lad,' he told Daffy, trying to grab the penlight off him, but Daffy kept hold of it. He had a terrible phobia of the dark.

All they found in the various rooms was old furniture – big expensive wardrobes and writing bureaux, whole walls lined with shelves full of leather-bound encyclopaedias, Chippendale chests and grandfather clocks – all things that were too big to carry out the place, and nothing that could fit in a Corsa without arousing the suspicion of the bizzies.

'If it turns out there're no savings in here I'm gonna

kneecap that drunk,' Gene promised.

'Yeah, I think he's put us on a bum steer,' Daffy said with a rather glum expression. Moonlight was flooding in through a window now as the fog started to lift outside.

The snoring suddenly stopped upstairs.

There came a loud disgusting sound of someone breaking wind, and it was so loud, it really startled Gene, who said, 'Have they got an elephant up there?'

'Do you reckon we should go now?' Daffy asked, casting nervous glances to the dark stairs.

'No, let's have one last look around and then we'll spew it,' Gene said, and he moaned about Daffy having the torch all the while. 'Shine that thing over here will you? Can't see a friggin' thing here.'

There was a succession of loud thumps upstairs.

'What's that?' Daffy asked, his eyes swivelling up to the ceiling. 'I think she's coming down.'

'Through the bleeding ceiling by the sounds of it,' Gene said, and he was calmer than Daffy because he'd had more experience of burgling places and was not as easy to scare.

'Shit, let's get out of here!' Daffy suggested, and looked through the doorway at the open window in the other room.

'Switch that thing off and just cool it, a sec, lad,' Gene told his friend. 'She's probably going the toilet or something; she won't be coming down here.'

'I'm not switching this off, I hate the dark,' Daffy said. 'I'm going if your not.'

A voice that sounded as if it was being broadcast through a 200-watt amplifier suddenly boomed down the stairs. 'Who is that?'

Both teenagers swore simultaneously and held their hands to their ears.

Then Gene noticed something in the moonlit corner. This time he swiped the penlight off Daffy and said, 'Give me that!'

'Giz that back!' Daffy made grabs at the little torch but Gene was too quick and he walked over to the corner and shone the light down at the biggest pair of shoes he had ever seen. They were black flat leather shoes with buckles on – but they were about three feet in length.

'Bleedin' size of them - they're like dodgem cars,' Gene remarked, and thought they were just ornaments of some sort. Then he heard Daffy scream the f-word as he looked to the top of the stairs.

'Look! Daffy cried out, gazing in utter horror to the top of the stairs.

Gene flashed the penlight up those stairs, and saw something out of a nightmare – a surreal nightmare. A giant woman was crouched on the landing. She couldn't straighten up because she must have been about fifteen to twenty feet in height. She had her black hair scraped up into a bun, and a pair of penetrating black eyes, and a prominent sharp nose. Her mouth was turned down into a scowl, and she was looking at the intruders. Gene recalled that she had on some sort of pale nightdress with a high collar. She was leaning with her huge left hand on the steps, and when she opened her mouth, Gene and Daffy heard her utter a deafening unintelligible word. The booming voice made their bodies vibrate. Daffy ran through the doorway, tripped over something in the darkness, screamed, and then jumped out of the window. Gene saw the woman come down the stairs on all fours, and he felt the floor shake as the giantess descended. He was soon jumping out the window too. He ran towards the Corsa and saw its headlight blaze on. He got into the vehicle and as soon as Gene's backside touched the seat, the Corsa's diesel engine thrummed and the car lurched forward, stalled, and then restarted. The vehicle moved off slowly, swung around, and then stalled again. 'What's up with you, you stupid arsehole?' Gene yelled at Daffy, who rambled on about the Corsa having engine trouble lately.

Gene opened the door of the vehicle and ran off, but he could not find the road which they had driven along to gain access to the grounds of the mansion. All Gene could see was thick ground fog, trees and hedges. He heard a loud thumping sound in the depths of the fog, and the moon went back into the clouds as the fog worsened again. Then came the sounds of someone panting, and suddenly Daffy came out of the mists with a look of terror on his agonized face. He was out of breath after just a short run from the Corsa because he was of course, out of shape.

'Where's the car?' Gene asked him, but Daffy was too out of breath to give a reply, and he ran straight past Gene.

Gene ran after him. 'Daffy, you can't leave the motor here, lad, they'll trace it to us!'

Then the two teens heard the sound of something being smashed.

Gene halted and looked back and thought he saw a flash of light and sparks, but then he ran to his friend and easily caught up with him. 'Slow down now, you idiot,' Gene told him, but Gene shook his head and gasped, 'She threw the car – '

The two teens came to a dirt track that took them onto Queens Drive, and they found themselves shaking as they looked back. They could just about see the mansion, and they could hear distant thuds. The teens wandered the streets for well over an hour, going over what they had seen and heard in the mansion until they were back home in the Dingle. On the next morning they returned to the house were that abnormally tall woman had attacked the Corsa, and they were baffled, for the mansion, which is set back quite a distance from the road, was now a crumbling rat-infested ruin, and with the fog now completely gone, the teenagers were shocked to find the Corsa upside down in the grounds, covered with dents and a door was missing from it. Moreover, most of the vehicle's windows were smashed. The vehicle was a write-off, and of course, no one would believe the story of the teenagers, especially two teenaged burglars. The mansion they had met the giantess in was Sandfield Tower - a Grade II listed building dating back to 1851 that had once been the villa of a successful and very rich South American merchant named Joseph Edwards. The villa was a famous landmark in the 19th century, set in what was then a highly private residential estate of many acres of unspoilt countryside. Mr Edwards despised wheeled vehicles coming through his estate, and any carts or carriages that encroached upon his land were charged a penny a wheel for the privilege. The identity of the gigantic woman is a mystery, and the two teenagers had not been taking drugs or drinking that night when they encountered the stuff of nightmares. Perhaps some local historian out there who is well versed in the history of Sandfield Tower will be able to cast some light on this strange incident.

HILLFOOT ROAD HAUNTING

One April morning in 1992 at around 4.30am, Sid and Wesley, both in their early twenties, were travelling down Woolton's Hillfoot Road in a Volkswagen Camper van. To the left of Sid's van was the ancient Iron Age fort of Camp Hill (from which the road derives its name) a place of pleasant strolls and summer picnics, and to the right was the Simpson playing fields, where many of the inner city schools play their football. The two men were headed through this stretch of Woolton to their homes in Speke after a long drive from Lancaster, where Sid had a girlfriend (of two months) named Dinah.

As Sid drove down Hillfoot Road, he was arguing with Wesley over the 'hidden messages' in the music video to the Guns N' Roses power-ballad *November Rain* when Wesley suddenly cried out and pointed to the road ahead. There was a woman in black lying down in the middle of the road at a right angle to the oncoming van so her head and feet were pointing to the kerbs. Sid performed an emergency stop, but it was too late – the camper van went straight over the woman.

'I killed her,' Sid said over and over in shock, gripping the wheel, and Wesley undid his seatbelt, jumped out the Volkswagen and ran back to the spot where he was sure he'd find a mangled body – but there was nothing there but the drifting vapour of the burnt tyre rubber from the skid. Wesley looked under the van – no mutilated and broken body stuck under the chassis – nothing – not a drop of blood. Sensing something very spooky had just taken place, Wesley got back in the van and told Sid there was no sign of the woman. Sid didn't believe him and went to look, and as he was looking, the woman who had been lying in the road approached, walking towards the front of the van from about forty feet away. She obviously hadn't sustained any injuries and was walking normally, but with her arms outstretched. Wesley couldn't believe his eyes. She looked like a nun at first in her black robes and wimple type of head-covering – but as she came nearer, Wesley could see she had pointy-toed shoes, and looked rather medieval. Her face was white as chalk, her eyes were black holes and her grinning mouth was huge and crimson – and devoid of any teeth. Wesley frantically beeped the van's horn, and Sid promptly returned – and he saw the unearthly jaywalker. Wesley urged him to drive off, and Sid tried to do just that; there was a screech of tyres and the vehicle lurched forward as Sid attempted to drive around the woman in black but she somehow jumped onto the front of the van and clung on as it sped down the road. The terrifying apparition looked solid enough and yet she was able to reach through the glass of the windshield and make menacing grabbing motions at Wesley and Sid, and her hand and her fingers looked like bones with a very thin covering of bluish flesh which seemed almost as transparent as tracing paper, and the nails were yellowish and very reminiscent of nicotine staining. Sid tried to throw the evil-looking lady off the front of the van by swerving, all over the road, but instead he attracted the attention of two policemen who had been parked up in their patrol car near Springwood Avenue. The lads were actually relieved to see the flashing blue light of the police car closing in on them, but as the vehicle cut in front of them, the woman in black vanished instantly – leaving a scent of violets in the van.

Sid thought the police wouldn't believe his story but he noticed that in response to his account, the officers glanced at one another with knowing looks, as if the policemen had seen the ghost or heard of her before. One of the constables told Sid to get home immediately, which he duly did in a very nervous state. The ghostly woman has been reported to me many times over the years. She haunts Hillfoot Road and Woodend Avenue near Speke, but her identity, and why she haunts these locations, is still currently unknown. The clothing of the ghost suggests that she could date back to medieval times, and something tells me that there is an element of witchcraft behind this ghost, and I will continue to research the history of the areas she haunts in the hope of finding out more about her.

SAMARITAN SUPERHERO

In *Haunted Liverpool 24* I touched on several intriguing reports and accounts of local "Superheroes" – mysterious individuals who could have come straight out of the pages of Marvel and DC Comics, and the chapter provoked many readers to get in touch with their own stories of caped crusaders and masked crimefighters. I am still researching many of the reports and stories forwarded to me, but here's one fascinating account of a real-life costumed vigilante which some of my more mature readers might even recall. The weird tale begins in Kirkby...

A 30-year-old Northwood woman named Jean was walking down Old Hall Lane, which runs alongside the cemetery wall of St Chads. It was a sunny Sunday November afternoon in 1966, and Jean was on her way to see her pregnant sister Mary, who lived off Whitefield Drive. As Jean walked down the secluded lane, she could see the grave stones of the cemetery over the low sandstone wall, but she wasn't nervous at such a setting as she had come this way down the lane many times – but on this day the housewife had a feeling she was being watched. Some people undoubtedly have this sense – of knowing they are being watched – and Jean was one of them, and had possessed the talent since she was a child. She therefore began to walk a little faster, taking nervous glances around her, and then suddenly, a tall man of about thirty-five to forty, in a black leather jacket and jeans, emerged from behind a bush in the cemetery and leaped over the wall. He stood in front of Jean with a penknife in his hand and he growled: 'Just give me your purse and rings and you can go on your way.'

Jean felt her legs turn to jelly, and she took her purse out of her coat pocket, and even though it only contained ten shillings and a few coppers, she intended to hand it to the robber. Then she saw the criminal look over her right shoulder, as if he had seen someone, and suddenly Jean heard a rustling sound to her right. A man in a black cloak and a bizarre tight-fitting costume which looked like something out of the *Batman* telly series landed in front of her. He had jumped clean over the cemetery wall. This strange masked figure raised his leg high and kicked the mugger in the face, stunning him with a black boot not unlike a workingman's boot, only the top of the boot was bound with long black straps around the man's calf. The caped attacker then threw countless punches at the robber which floored him, and Jean noticed that the man wore gauntlets which had metal caps where the knuckles would be. The man seemed to have some pugilistic skill because Jean recalled the rapidity of the punches – they were thrown in very quick succession and accurately hit the same spot on the would-be mugger's jaw.

Jean staggered back against the cemetery wall, unable to scream as the weirdly-attired figure held the knifeman in a headlock. 'Thou shalt not steal!' the cloaked defender said (and his accent was not a local one) with a chuckle in his voice, and Jean said, 'Thanks,' to the unknown man and then managed to regain the use of her legs. She ran off up Old Hall Lane as she heard terrible thumps and manic laughter as the eerie man in black punched and kicked the cowardly crook about. Jean's husband and brothers visited the spot where this weird incident had taken place half an hour later and saw a penknife lying on the floor, bloodstains on the ground and on the cemetery wall, and a freshly-knocked out front tooth.

Then there came more and more sightings of this real-life 'superhero'. Three days after the incident by St Chad's, a sobbing girl of eighteen was dragged onto Kirkby Golf Course one evening at 10pm by two men with evil intentions on their minds. By the light of the full moon hanging in the sky, the potential rapists were startled to see the silhouette of a cloaked figure running towards them across the green. The first man thought the stranger was some joker until he was knocked clean out by a tremendous punch, and the second man, an amateur boxer, adopted a defensive stance, and mockingly asked, 'Who are you?' to which the masked action-hero replied: 'Fire and brimstone!' he then dived at the baffled crook and grabbed his throat in a hold so tight, his opponent was soon unconscious.

'Why were you here with those men?' the masked man asked the girl, who was speechless with fear. 'Go! And sin no more!' the caped interloper said in a well-spoken voice as he held out his gloved hand and pointed into the distance. At this point the girl saw that the costumed stranger had a symbol – possibly in red - resembling the Maltese cross on his chest, and she ran off, crying and bewildered. There were other reports of the Scripture-spouting vigilante in Huyton, Whiston, the Clock Face area, and possibly even Maghull. And then the sightings and encounters died down and the real-life caped crusader was seen no more. There were rumours that the self-appointed punisher of criminals was a certain young priest who had been influenced by the superheroes of the American comic books that were flooding the country at that time. The police allegedly investigated a young cleric who had quite a collection of Marvel and DC comics and discovered he was also a boxer of some repute as well as an athlete – though nothing could be proved. All the same, once the young man of the cloth had been interviewed by the law, the black-clad hero with the Maltese cross emblem suddenly went into retirement. The questions remain though; was the ecclesiastic Knowsley's only superhero, or were the police wrong – and will someone else perhaps take on the mantle of this intriguing figure of mystery one day?

HELPERS FROM BEYOND

Isla Mason is in her forties now, but she clearly remembers the very strange incident which unfolded on the icy Tuesday night of January 6, 1981 as if it was only yesterday. Isla, an 11-year-old girl from Southdene, Kirkby, had been doing the rounds, visiting her grandmother in Huyton and two aunts in North Liverpool to receive some presents she hadn't been able to pick up from them at Christmas because she had been ill with the flu. Isla's parents, Sue and Geoff, and their 7-year-old son Jack, had gone along with the girl to pick up the presents (dolls, postal orders and record tokens), and the Masons had all enjoyed a slice of cake or two and a glass of 'pop' (as one auntie quaintly called it), but now - with the time fast approaching midnight - the family were heading back to Kirkby from the last port of call, the house of Isla's Auntie Val in Everton. As the family's Hillman Hunter car travelled in a north-eastern direction along a very foggy Utting Avenue, Geoff Mason switched on the radio for some music to listen to on the return trip to Southdene. Isla, in the back of the car, leaned forward and told her father: 'Dad, there's someone standing in the middle of the road.'

'Isla, sit back!' her mother Susan chided her, 'What have I told you about bothering your father when he's driving?'

'Jesus – ' Mr Mason muttered, his eyes fixed on the very pale figure his daughter had spotted, standing in the middle of Utting Avenue, about thirty feet before the railway bridge which spans the road. The figure wore long ankle-length robes and he had shoulder-length hair. 'What's he doing?' Sue Mason asked, seeing the figure raise his arms into the air, gesturing for the car to stop.

'Get out the way, you bloody crank,' Geoff said through gritted teeth. He was tired and just wanted to get home for a good night's sleep.

'Slow down, Geoff!' Mrs Mason told her husband, as the man was stubbornly staying put in the path of the car.

Geoff flashed his headlamps at the weirdly-dressed man, signalling for him to get out the way, and all of a sudden, the figure with outstretched arms lit up and emitted a blinding burst of white light. Geoff, unable to see, braked hard, and Isla flew forward and hit her forehead on the back of her father's seat. Her younger brother Jack, who had been dozing off in the back seat, was thrown against the back of his mother's seat. Fortunately, both children were not injured, just a little shook-up. Mrs Mason tried to look through the windshield but the light was too powerful, and even with her eyes closed she could feel some warmth being given off by the unearthly laser-like glare.

A few seconds later the light went out, and when Geoff and Sue's eyes adapted to the darker setting, they could see that the glowing man had gone. They then saw blue flashing lights through the fog, coming from the tunnel under the railway bridge straight ahead. It was the police attending a tanker that had skidded on black ice and smashed into a concrete lamp post. The tanker had ruptured and inflammable chemicals were flooding the road. Mr Mason would not have seen the lights of the tanker because they had stopped working after the crash for some reason. Geoff and Sue gradually came to realise that the glowing figure had saved their lives, for had they continued along that road in the fog, they would have hit the chemical tanker head on and probably been burned alive by the ignition of the leaking inflammable liquid. Was the shining figure an angel, sent to save the Mason family's lives? We'll probably never know, but such beings have been reported to me so many times over the years and my books are full of them. I have a feeling that the radiant robed being which saved the family on a foggy Utting Avenue was the fabled "Angel of Twelfth Night" – a heavenly messenger I have written about before who has allegedly been encountered many times on that date – January 6 – Twelfth Night. There have been other luminous life-savers from beyond who do not keep a calendar – they appear anytime, anywhere, and there have been quite a few manifestations of these entities across the North West. Here's an intriguing account of one of these incidents. In February 1979, a frail old woman in her seventies named Joan lived on Fairclough Road in Huyton. Joan had recently lost her husband after a short illness and was feeling very depressed and lonely on this wintry evening. She felt as if God had abandoned her, and she no longer attended church because of her crisis of faith. She went to bed around 8pm, a lot earlier than normal, because she was feeling so down, and around 9.10pm, she was startled from her sleep by a rattling sound. Joan sat up in bed without switching on her bedside lamp, and she listened intently, trying to fathom what the sound was. At first she thought the sound was from trapped air in the radiator, but then she heard the front door open, and she realised with a mounting sense of horror that someone had just opened her door – perhaps with a skeleton key or a jemmy. The elderly lady trembled as she heard the soft pad of footsteps coming towards her along the carpeted hall. She got to her feet, feeling dizzy with fear, and she did something she hadn't done for a while – she prayed to God with all her might. Never before had she needed His help than right now. The bedroom door burst open, and there stood a huge man with square broad shoulders, and he was that tall, the top of his head was almost touching the top of the doorframe. He had the nastiest, most hateful expression Joan had ever seen on a human face. 'Where's your savings?' he said in a low menacing voice.

All of a sudden, Joan felt the floor beneath her bare feet shake twice – as if something heavy had just stomped into the room, and then, a bluish light shone onto the burglar from a point somewhere behind Joan, and the stocky intruder's face was now full of fear. His eyes bulged, his mouth opened, and he backed away towards the doorway, and then he turned and ran – straight out of the house. The eerie light in the room then rapidly faded, and Joan went to the hallway and closed – and bolted – the front door. She went back into the bedroom, and prayed again, thanking God for sending some sort of Guardian Angel down to save her – at least that's what Joan believed. Just what the burglar saw behind the old lady remains a mystery, but it seems it put the fear of God into him.

What seems to have been a similar luminous angel-like protector was allegedly seen on Mount Pleasant in the summer of 2014. Around 2am, two female students in their early twenties - Riley and Aislynn - were walking up Mount Pleasant after a night out at a club in the city centre and were scanning the road for a hackney cab to take them home to the flat they shared in Wavertree. Both girls were not drunk because they had only had a few drinks and had spent most of the night dancing. Neither of the students had touched any drugs or pills of any kind either, both being very clean-living girls. As Riley and Aislynn were about to pass the Liverpool John Moores International Study Centre – an old red brick building at 70 Mount Pleasant, the girls were intrigued to see a bright intense red light shining from a tree branch. When the students first reported this incident to me I could not place this tree, as Mount Pleasant is a typical urban thoroughfare which is not known for its verdancy, but when I visited the spot, there was the tree which I must have passed and missed so many times whenever I have walked up Mount Pleasant; it is set back from the street in the railed-off area of the International Study Centre and its branches almost overhang the railings. Upon this tree in the early hours of that June morning in 2014, Riley and Aislynn noticed a bright vivid red light shining, and its intensity reminded them of a laser. 'What's that?' Riley wondered, and as she and her friend strolled nearer, the light dimmed somewhat and in its place the students now saw what looked like a humanoid figure, perhaps the size of an

Action Man doll, sitting on a branch, and it was luminous and of an orange-red colour. This diminutive figure suddenly lifted its arms and made a gesture – a waving of the hands towards them – as if to gesticulate a 'turn back' message to them. This little figure struck the girls as being male, and Aislynn was very unnerved by it because of its doll-like size, and she instantly stopped and swore out of fright. Riley walked on a little, fascinated by the little man, but Aislynn called her back: 'Rye! Come here! Don't go near it!' she cried. The glowing figure now stood up in one swift movement, startling the students, and waved for them to go back in an even more pronounced manner, and this did scare Riley a little; she stopped advancing, walked backwards, and Aislynn gripped her arm and pulled at her as she walked in the other direction. As the students were crossing Roscoe Street, a car coming down Mount Pleasant from the direction of Hope Street, suddenly screeched out of control, and mounted the pavement exactly where the girls would have been had they not walked back because of the weird little glowing figure. The driver of the car, who looked underage, regained control of the car, and swerved back into the road, headed in the direction of the Adelphi Hotel. When the students looked back at the tree, it was in darkness. They stood on the corner of Mount Pleasant and Roscoe Street for about five minutes, realising that the miniature glowing man had probably saved their lives, and so the girls went back to the tree and had a good look at it as they held onto one another, and saw nothing unearthly within its branches. They were so engrossed in searching for the little life-saver, the students missed a hackney cab which passed them with its amber 'for hire' light on, but they later managed to flag down another cab when they reached Hope Street. Neither of the students had been able to make out the face of the strange little entity, and each could not recall if there were any distinguishing marks on the glowing body. Both girls were not particularly interested in the paranormal and neither of them had experienced anything remotely supernatural before. It will be interesting to see if there are any further sightings of the miniature glowing man in that tree on Mount Pleasant.

NOT OURS TO SEE

In 2014, Tucker, a 27-year-old Bootle man, decided to quit his job working at a call centre. He was single and free, and his friends thought he was mad chucking the job in without any plans to find better employment, but Tucker said he wanted to have a go at being a security guard. The positions he'd seen advertised on a jobs website told him that the pay could be as high as £10 per hour, that security officers get the usual eight bank holidays a year off, as well as nearly a month's annual leave.

'Come into the real world,' said Jimmy, the barman in Tucker's local when he overheard his regular client's utopian claims about security guards. 'They throw in a few weeks in Benidorm as well, and a few escorts,' Jimmy said in a silly voice.

'Its hard work, security work,' said Tucker's best mate Mike, shaking his head as he headed for the door of the pub to have a smoke.

To Mike's back, Tucker said: 'Well I'm not going back to the call centre; all the insults and that, I'll emigrate if push comes to shove.'

A few days later, Tucker came into the pub with a smirk. He told Jimmy he had an interview with a private security firm based down at the docks. 'It's for a static security guard,' Tucker told the barman.

'Should be easy; think static means you sit watching CCTV monitors all night.'

Jimmy sighed and shook his head. 'Bloody semantics; it's just a term, static; doesn't mean that at all mate; it means you'll *probably* stick to one site, that's all. You'll still have to patrol the site, check the place is secure and that, and some of those places at the docks are like a miniature city.'

'Well, its seven quid an hour, ten at night till six in the morning,' Tucker told Jimmy, and counted the pound coins in his hand. The money was getting low.

'And do they give you a month's leave and all the bank holidays off, then?' Jimmy asked, cupping his hand to his ear in a mocking gesture.

Unconsciously, Tucker placed the exact amount of a pint of lager and his usual tip in Jimmy's waiting palm. 'Ah, well, they don't give you a month, but you get twenty days annual leave, and there's like a company sick pay scheme thingy and a contributory pension scheme. And no, I have to work the bank holidays, which is a bit harsh, but well, I have to graft or I'll starve.'

Tucker went for the interview, and brought along all of the documents pertaining to his previous employment. They told him they needed to see a five-year checkable employment history and a clean driving licence. They took all of his documents and asked for the phone numbers of employers stretching back yonks, and then they told him if he got the job he would be guaranteed forty-two hours per week.

The next day he got a call; he'd got the job and they wanted to see him. They told him all about the rota, strict timetables, shift handovers and gave him a light legal education about tackling criminals. They took him around the complex: a building he had never even noticed before overlooking the river, and he was introduced to two older guards – Trevor and Rod – both in their early forties. Tucker soon got into the routine and the first day he went to work, he called in at the pub and showed Jimmy his uniform and endured a few laughs from him and his friends. Then something strange happened one Monday morning, around 3am, and this was about a month into the job. Tucker was on with Trevor on this occasion and it was pouring with rain beyond the plate glass double-glazed window of the third floor, where Tucker was munching a breakfast bar and sipping from a plastic cup of black coffee. Trevor came in and chatted to him, then five minutes after this, Tucker left the station and went on his rounds with his MagLite torch. As he walked down the silent long corridor of a bridge between the station and an annex, he saw someone moving down below. The person was a silhouette, and he or she was walking slowly down an old cobbled and disused road that had once belonged to the old dock building. A chain-link security fence topped with a helix of barbed wire ran parallel to the cobbled road – and that road led to a sensitive area of the complex where HGVs would be arriving to pick up their freight. Tucker alerted Trevor with his walkie-talkie and told him he was going down to see who it is. Trevor went to the window and then quickly called Tucker back on the radio transceiver. 'Let it go mate, she's harmless, over.'

'Who is she? Over.' Tucker wanted to know, and went down the stairs anyway.

'She's harmless, mate, that's all you have to know – over.'

'She an alky?' Tucker asked, and he got no reply to his question, but Trevor told him again to come back. Tucker ignored his request, thinking it was shoddy security practice to do so, and for all Trevor knew, this might be someone else; some scally, perhaps.

Tucker disabled the alarm with a quick stab at the key panel and then he unlocked the door and stepped out into the heavy downpour with his MagLite throwing a sweeping sparkling beam through the raindrops like a light sabre. The spotlight fell on the woman and Tucker could see she was a down and out, and possibly homeless. He felt sorry for her already, and she hadn't even turned to see who was shining the torch at her yet.

'Scuse me love!' Tucker's voice seemed to be swallowed up by the wide open space devoid of any reflective surface and the torrent of slanting rain which glittered like tinsel in the hard beam.

She turned and he could see she looked like his old Nan, but when he got close up he saw something which made him feel very unsettled: her eyes – they seemed to be almost fluorescent and of a pale baby blue colour.

She stood there without a trace of emotion on her lined face, and did not even grimace in the pelting rain which spattered her straw eyebrows, her eyelashes, and the faint fuzz above her lips.

'It's dangerous here, love,' Tucker said, so full of irrational fear because of those faintly glowing eyes, 'lorries are coming and going here, girl – 'heeyar; come with me love.' And Tucker nodded to his left and gestured with his hand for her to follow him, and she slowly acquiesced – and never said a word, even though he fired many questions at her. The final question: 'Fancy coming in to get dry and have some coffee – or tea – and biscuits, eh?' was not answered. The woman seemed to purse her lips and then she walked off the way she had came, and Tucker watched her go through a gateway and on towards the dockside road, where she was lost in the shadows.

'I told you to leave her, over!' Trevor's voice crackled from the walkie-talkie, startling Tucker.

'They told me to go by the rule book in this job, Trevor, no cutting corners or – '

'Piss off and get on with your rounds,' Trevor told him with irritability in his amplified voice, and then he added: 'I've been here fifteen years, not fifteen minutes – over.'

Tucker couldn't wait to finish his rounds so he could get back to Trevor and quiz him about that strange woman and her peculiar eyes. Trevor said the woman was 'bad news' and did not go into any detail. Tucker pressed for more info about her, and Trevor finally told him: 'They think she's one of them Romany people or something, but when she turned up here last time one of the lads had a bit of trouble.'

'Eh?' Tucker was curious now. 'What do mean, "trouble"?'

'Mental stuff – psychy stuff – breakdowns,' Trevor replied, and behind his spectacles his eyes seemed afraid.

'Breakdowns?' Tucker was baffled at the reply. 'You mean you think she's unlucky? Where was she going, anyway?'

'Look mate, the next time I tell you to do something, just do it, alright?' Trevor told him and shook his head as he looked away – and gazed out through the rain-speckled panes at the lights of Wirral.

Tucker wouldn't let it go. 'Is it like a curse thing – '

'Just shut up and forget the whole thing!' Trevor roared and turned to present a flushed face. 'I've had enough lumber recently, so just talk about footy or birds or anything but don't go near this again.'

'Alright, alright, narky!' Tucker told him, and sulkily asked where the carton of milk was that he had put down a few minutes ago.

'I don't know,' Trevor replied, averting his gaze.

'The carton of milk that I had before, where is it?' Tucker asked again.

'Up Ben's hole on the second shelf!' was Trevor's surreal reply, and Tucker smiled and said, 'Haven't heard that in years.'

Trevor was seen to shake from behind. He was laughing and didn't want to ruin his tough guy image, but Tucker walked around him and laughed with him, and soon the strange episode about the "gypsy" woman was forgotten.

Then the dreams started. Each night, Tucker had graphic nightmares – always about something bad happening; plane crashes, fires, horrific deaths, motorway crashes, and even a bus smash – and these dreams would always come to pass. Tucker never connected the nightmare premonitions to the old woman with the strange eyes at first, but one night when he told Trevor about the dreams, his colleague returned a knowing look, as if he had heard it before – and it turned out that he had. The last person who had encountered that woman with the unearthly eyes had started to have premonitions in his dreams, and then he had visions of approaching death while he was awake, and it eventually led to him being certified insane. Trevor told Tucker to start saying his prayers of a night, and to attend church for either the mid week Mass or the Sunday service. Tucker thought he was joking at first, but then he saw that Trevor was not in the least amused.

'I'm a lapsed Catholic,' Tucker recalled with a forced grin, 'haven't been to church since my brother's marriage three years back.'

'Go back, Tucker,' Trevor told him earnestly, 'go back and those dreams and all that might go away.'

'I feel as if something passed between me and that woman that morning,' Tucker rambled, 'when our eyes met. Felt it. Something happened.'

'And you'll have to put all that out your mind, ' said Trevor, and he noticed the day of stubble on his friend's face, 'and start looking after yourself – like getting a shave and showering mate.'

'Trevor, I swear I won't mention that woman again after this, but – well – what's she doing walking round all hours in the morning down at the docks?'

'She's lost her mind,' Trevor replied, 'brother-in-law works in the social services, and he said she has psychiatric problems, and they don't think she has anyone – no relatives or anything to look after her. Think she's living somewhere up by the cathedral down the Tocky end.'

'Oh, ' Tucker said faintly, and gazed at the controls on the walkie-talkie. 'I can guess what turned her mind – '

'No more now, mate,' Trevor nipped further speculation and talk in the bud, 'don't let it take over, because that happened with the last fellah and it wasn't a pretty sight, and do not – repeat – do not – ever talk about this to Rod, because the fellah who had the breakdown was a good mate of his – got that?'

'Yeah, and not another word, Trevor, I promise. God, if I had listened to you in the first – '

'Tucker, hadn't you better go on your walkies lad?' Trevor intervened.

Three days after this, Tucker was on patrol, and on this occasion Rod was on duty with him. Rod was not as sociable as Trevor, and had no sense of humour whatsoever. He contacted Tucker by walkie-talkie and told him there were two suspicious characters down by the gate, in-between the perimeter fence and an old dilapidated shed. Tucker went to see who the men were, and when he reached the spot as directed by Rod, he saw that they were two young men, perhaps aged about twenty, and they were locked in an embrace as they kissed in the shadows. The faint light from the sodium streetlamps of the dock road about a hundred yards away was giving their presence away to Tucker, and he was about to train his blazing beam of light on the youths when something bizarre happened. He saw one of the men with his head completely devoid of hair, and he was lying in a hospital bed, and the other man – the one who was kissing him now – was holding his hand and sobbing. Tucker could see the specialists in white coats talking about scans and metastasis and that terrifying word – cancer. It was in his testicle. Tucker heard the echoing words: 'They could have saved him if he had been diagnosed earlier'.

He could smell the antiseptic scent of the ward. He saw the mother of the cancer-stricken man, and she was saying: 'He had lovely hair, sort of red with bits of blonde in it...'

'You wanna join in do you?' One of the men said, noticing Tucker standing there on the other side of the chain-link fence.

'No, it's not what you think,' Tucker mumbled, and then he came out with it, 'look, which one of you has red hair, eh?'

The men started to walk away but then the dazzling beam of the high-powered torch fell upon them and they froze. Tucker could now clearly see that the one with the red hair was the one who would die of testicular cancer...unless...

'Hey you, with the red hair!' Tucker bawled, 'You need to go and get checked out down below!'

'I could report you for saying that, mate,' the redhead told him, squinting at the retina-searing light.

'No, you soft thing, I don't mean that! Jesus! Look, please go to your doctor, and ask him to check your balls mate, because you have – ' Tucker could hardly say the word, because he felt so sad and choked up.

'You've got problems, you arsehole!' the other man shouted, and the two men hurried away into the night, and Tucker was left clinging to the fence, sobbing, feeling such a failure. 'What is wrong with me?' he said over and over as the voice on the walkie-talkie asked him to respond. In the end, Rod came down and saw him in tears.

'What in God's name happened? Did they attack you?' he asked Tucker, who shook his head, unwilling to say anything, and unable anyway because he had promised Trevor not to bring up the subject of the premonitions to Rod. Tucker just said: 'Think it's the male menopause Rod,' then grinned, and took a deep breath, and returned with the older guard to the complex.

On the following Saturday afternoon, when Tucker should have been in bed, he found himself on the upper deck of a bus, headed to town to do a bit of shopping. He didn't risk driving into town because he thought he'd fall asleep at the wheel with the fatigue. He thought about sleeping pills but then he knew he'd be trapped in those horrible dreams of death and disaster, unable to awake. He yawned and looked at the buildings of Liverpool scrolling by, and nothing seemed real. He glanced up at the clear blue sky and saw a constellation of floaters gliding down because of the tiredness. He saw a jet high in that serene azure sky, and smiled, wishing he was on it, bound for Spain or somewhere in the Med – but then he suddenly knew that one day that jet was going to crash. He went cold as he saw the people in it praying, and some running towards the back of the aircraft, thinking they might have a better chance of survival; children's faces streaked with tears, burying their heads into the bosoms of their terrified parents. 'Oh stop it, please!' Tucker cried out to the vision, and threw his face into his hands as he swore. When he looked up, some of the passengers were looking at him as if he was mad, and some giggled and grinned, while others seemed a bit scared.

The security guard looked out the window – and saw black smoke – lots of black smoke – billowing in the sky over the city centre. 'Oh what is it now?' he said, but this time he just mouthed the words. And then the bus turned, and he saw that Beetham's West Tower was on fire! People were jumping from thirty floors up! Some of the bodies were black, featureless, sexless, and indistinguishable from burnt shop window dummies... Oh, the fear and desperation of those trapped up there!

'I've had enough! I've had enough!' Tucker hauled himself out of his seat and amidst the giggles and murmurs of the passengers, he barged down the aisle to the stairs, and on his way he saw a young couple at the front – they must have been in their late teens, early twenties – and they were holding hands, but then Tucker saw them upside down, their seat belts trapping them in a car that was in water – yes – a canal. They were drowning and fighting with bulging eyes to get out. 'Stick to buses, mate!' Tucker told the puzzled lad, 'Forget your driving test! Hear? You'll die otherwise!' He saw the grinning faces of the couple sink below the handrail of the stairs as he descended, and heard the laughter of the damned above.

'There a fire in town, mate?' Tucker asked the driver, who didn't hear what he said the first time so the disturbed guard asked him again, and the driver said, 'Not as far as I'm aware, why?'

'Nothing, must have misheard – cheers mate,' Tucker said, a bit overeager to get off.

His mind started turning towards the tragic future of that driver, but somehow he blocked it out by humming a tune as loud as he could.

He walked through the town, and a policeman and a policewoman passed him and he nodded and smiled at them, and then saw the two of them machine-gunned to death by a deranged man with an automatic weapon on Dale Street. 'Ah well, nothing I can do about it,' Tucker said to himself, and he looked up, and saw the Dobermans – about a dozen of them – running down Paradise Street towards Liverpool One. Tucker usually only saw the dogs – which always represented terrorists – in his dreams – but now they had crashed through into his waking life. 'Why are they going to Liverpool One?' he asked himself, and already he could hear the rat-tat-tat of automatic gunfire, and by the time he reached Debenhams he saw the bodies of shoppers lying about in widening pools of blood. A woman in her fifties was reaching out to him. She was laying on her front with a brown coat and there was a huge bloodstain on the back of the coat. As Tucker said, 'You haven't happened yet,' he saw the back of her head explode before the bang of a gun somewhere, and she fell face down. He closed his eyes, and he heard the Dobermans running towards him now, and they were passing him as he opened his eyes. Tucker kept saying the C word over and over and two women who passed him gave him looks of disgust. He was swearing at that old woman – the one who had given him this ghastly ability.

Tucker looked up to the clouds, scared of seeing some other disaster – a mushroom cloud or a falling asteroid – for he sensed that these would come upon the city one day – but instead he saw only blue sky. He prayed, and he pleaded with God for help, and in the depths of his mind he saw Christine, a girl he should have married years ago. He had no idea why he saw her in his turbulent mind's eye, but there she was, walking along with her pretty head bowed, self conscious and so humble. He turned around and decided he would call on her. She lived over the river in Bromborough. He walked to James Street and happened to look towards the Mersey before he entered the train station – a big mistake – because in its place he saw the expanse of the Irish Sea instead, and there was the *Queen Mary 2* sliding under the waves. A bomb! Oh should I tell the authorities? He wondered, and knew it would be fruitless. He entered the station and whistled as he paid for his ticket to what would hopefully be some form of salvation.

'Now, Tucker!' came a familiar voice behind him as he descended the stairs to his platform. The security guard looked over his shoulder and saw it was an old friend from his schooldays – Phil. He'd lost most of his hair but he had retained the boyish face from all those years ago in the seniors. He was smartly dressed in a dark blue suit.

'God, you alright, lad?' Phil asked, his face full of concern. 'Your eyes are all red.'

'Yeah, I'm fine, Phil,' Tucker told him, and tried to divert his probing eyes of doom to the posters on the stairway walls. 'How are you mate? Long time no see. Looking smart there.'

'Just going to see me future wife mate, over in Port Sunlight,' Phil said with a proud look. 'You married yet?'

'Me? No, no, no - married to my freedom, mate.' Tucker replied, and he thought that the words felt so hollow and faux as they came out of his mouth.

'Sure you're a cyborg, lad - no heart or any feelings,' Phil told him straight. 'You were always a cold fish though, weren't you?'

The two men reached the platform, where the electronic noticeboard told Tucker that his train would be arriving in less than three minutes. Phil was talking about Amanda, a girl he had met at a club last year, and how they were going to get married in Wales at a place overlooking the River Usk.

Then *why* is he sawing her up in a bath then? Tucker wondered, becoming desensitised to these horrific visions. The torso with floppy breasts was in the bath and the knife the future Phil was using to cut her head off had got stuck, and the dismembered arms were bound up with what looked like electrical cord.

'You're in a world of your own, Tucker,' the voice of Phil reached him at last, and then his friend looked around, and slyly asked: 'You doing skunk?'

'Phil, this girl Amanda,' Tucker said shaking his head as he tried to get the awful crimson image out of his flypaper mind.

'Yeah?'

'Would you ever harm her?' Tucker faced him now with his laser stare.

'What are you on about?' The smile on Phil's face morphed to a look of disgust.

'Listen mate, remember this: whatever Amanda does to you, cheats or whatever, its just life, got that? Don't end up going to prison for it, alright?'

'You're definitely tripped out, lad,' Phil reasoned, stepping away with flaring nostrils from his morbid friend.

'Remember what I said,' Tucker said, watching Phil walk away down the platform, and he heard him swear.

'Forgive her!' Tucker shouted after him and Phil gave him the finger.

The train arrived and Tucker sat in a separate carriage from the friend he had upset, and as the train rattled through the tunnel beneath the Mersey, he saw the carriage fill with smoke from a future fire, but he gently placed his palms over his face, blocking out his vision, and thought of Christine. Tucker felt the train climbing the slight gradient now as it trundled along beneath the ancient bedrock of the Mersey, and at Green Lane, he watched a young female Goth get on board. She was about sixteen years of age, and she sat in a corner. She was going to take the world of popular music by storm one day, but she was also going to die from a drug overdose; it looked like heroin, but it was a different colour, possibly some designer narcotic not in circulation yet.

'Excuse me,' Tucker said to the girl.

Huge black moth-wing eyelashes fluttered as she turned to look at him.

'You're into music – ' he began.

'Huh?'

'You're into music, and you write songs, don't you?'

Her eyebrows dipped and pointed to her nose as she thinned her eyes with a sarcastic response.

'Keep at it, you are going to be massive, but the drugs will kill you, especially the one you inject, alright?'

The girl got up as she muttered, 'Oh-kay dude.' She went to the next carriage, and then she glanced through the window of the separating door at Tucker as he raised his eyebrows and looked at his reflection in the train window. 'I tried,' he told himself.

'Tickets!' the ticket inspector shouted, and Tucker dug into his inside jacket pocket and produced the little laminated card. As the inspector glanced at it, Tucker told him in a preachy manner to get his mouth checked out and to stop smoking, and the inspector, accustomed to meeting every oddball who travels with Merseyrail, simply replied, 'Will do,' and moved on to the next carriage.

After witnessing a future derailment and a suicide to come (by a youth who laid his head down on the rail) Tucker eventually reached Bromborough and as he made his way to Christine's home, he saw a passenger jet approaching at rooftop level, coming from the east, and it was tilting right with an engine on fire, trailing sparks and smoke as it moaned. It was heading towards him in slow motion, passing over Wirral Metropolitan College and now Leverhulme Sports Ground where the tiny red and blue specks – teens playing football – were scattering as the ominous shadow of the leviathan of the skies passed over them. The queue of traffic on New Chester Road would be obliterated soon, and already, Tucker could see the white reverse tail lights of some of the vehicles come on as they backed up in panic and smashed into the cars behind them. A young lady fell out of her car and was that scared, she looked as if she had lost the power to move her legs. Other motorists were abandoning their cars, making a futile dash for it, and an old woman about fifty yards in front of Tucker was trying to run, but she fell flat on her face. People were climbing over the hedge of the playing field and running for their lives and all the time that incapacitated airliner was getting nearer and nearer.

Tucker shook his head, knowing that the plane had taken off from John Lennon Airport minutes before and a bomb had gone off onboard the plane in its cargo hold. He could feel the sheer terror of the men, women and children on the stricken jet, and knew not one of them would escape the ensuing inferno, and not one person on this road would survive – only a mongrel which was bolting past him now, and that would suffer serious burns. Ninety tons of aviation fuel... Jesus Christ...

Tucker squeezed his eyes and said, 'Hasn't happened yet! Not yet!' but he could still hear the apocalyptic devastation – the deafening roar of the exploding jet, the screams cut short by the ruthless blast furnace of superheated gas...

'Dickhead!'

Tucker opened his eyes, and saw that the New Chester Road and the adjacent playing fields were still there, and a mischievous kid had just shouted a profanity from a passing car after seeing Tucker standing there at the kerbside with his eyes squeezed shut. Tucker smiled at the kid, who was now waving at him. He was glad the boy was still alive, but before his mind began to delve into the ultimate fate of that boy, he looked away and made his way to Christine's house. She wasn't in so he sat on her doorstep, and when she arrived with three carrier bags of shopping he ran to her aid and she was naturally stunned to see him.

'How are you?' she asked, stuck for words as usual.

She looked as lovely as ever to Tucker, and he saw her notice his eyes, and he said: 'I need to have a word with you over something.'

She opened the door and a cat ran to her but halted when it saw Tucker.

'It's alright, Henry, its only Tucker,' Christine told

the feline.

Tucker certainly didn't want to know about the future demise of Henry and looked away. He put the bags down on the Formica worktop in the little kitchen and then began to tell her of the seemingly outlandish predicament as she unpacked her groceries. A few times he became annoyed because he thought she wasn't paying attention, but she would tell him she *was* listening.

They ended up sitting on a sofa, and Tucker had held his head in his hands by that point, and started to unashamedly sob. 'You've got to help me, Christine, before I go insane.'

'Perhaps the woman you met that morning;' Christine told him, stroking his hair. She held his other hand and squeezed it, 'if you could meet her again and tell her to take back this gift or whatever you call it.'

'It's no gift,' Tucker sniffled, and lifted his red tear-sodden face to look at Christine, 'a curse is what it is. And I do not want to see that – that old hag – ever again.'

'Well, you can stay here for as long as you want,' Christine reassured him, 'and I'll help you in whatever way I can.'

'Thanks love,' Tucker was so grateful for her being there. Then he realised something – he had not had a single premonition about Christine. He thought about this, and then he deliberately look ed at her face – and she blushed, not knowing he was testing his macabre faculty. 'Christine; guess what?'

'What?' she asked, blinking and fidgeting with her fingers.

'I can't see *any* of your future; how odd.'

'Does that mean I don't have any?' she asked, and now the colour drained from her face and she looked so concerned – in light of what he had told her about his grim power.

'No, if you were going to die – even years from now – I'd probably see it all in glorious Technicolor! This is so odd, but lovely.'

Tucker gave up his security guard job at the docks over in Liverpool, and he stayed with Christine, and they rekindled the love they had, and she was his rock when the visions of death came upon him, but he noticed how those horrible glimpses were becoming less frequent, and then one day, he was standing in the kitchen with Christine as she was stirring a soup she had put on the stove for him, when he stuck his neck out and said, 'I love you.'

She stopped stirring and turned; she seemed a bit stunned. 'I love you too,' she told him.

There was never another vision of a forthcoming tragedy after that day. Tucker felt he had committed himself to loving someone – and for so many years he had always sneered at the idea of love – but now he felt that love had somehow been the key to locking away that awful ability of seeing life end in all of the distressing ways of this world. Something equally mysterious told him deep down that now that he had a life to live, he did not need to look into the lives of others, and he felt as if that poor lady with those radiant sad eyes had been someone who had never possessed a life – had never had anyone to love – but he could not explain how she had come to possess the nightmarish capacity to foretell every calamity, great and small. In the many years I have spent investigating the vast sphere of the supernatural, I have learned that almost anyone can cultivate psychic talents, from healing to telepathy and clairvoyance, but to become fully endowed with the ability of precognition – to see into the future – requires a very disciplined mind, and I have noticed that many Romany fortune tellers will block out knowledge of their own future so that they will not even know if they are going to come down with the flu in a few days' time. The old joke about the sign on the fortune-teller's door which says 'Closed due to unforeseen circumstances' is often a reality to those with psychic gifts. There was an item in the news recently where a couple from Scunthorpe won the Lottery twice, and if you could look into the future you'd be able to see six numbers that were due to be drawn; but would you use your gift to make money, or would you warn people of forthcoming brushes with death? Some of the most sceptical people have had glimpses of future Lottery numbers. In 2009 a sceptic on the Continent is said to have asked a psychic for future winning lottery numbers and he was told to pick numbers that meant something to him. The sceptic noted the time on the clock: 04:15, and then the date – the 23rd – of that month, plus the sceptic's age (24), the age of his wife (35) and the age of the medium (43) – and all of those numbers came up. The sceptic said this was pure coincidence – and then the unbelievable happened: four days later, the lottery numbers were drawn again, and they were the exact same numbers the sceptic had previously picked 'at random'. The people of Bulgaria thought the whole draw had been staged and demanded an inquiry into draw fixing. An official of the Bulgarian lottery said any manipulation of the random number generator was impossible, and the odds of the same six numbers coming up within four days were one in four million.

Whenever I have given talks on precognition and mentioned ways to forecast the lottery numbers, I have seen people's eyes bulge with greed, and there *are* ways to forecast such results, although some systems go into the world of quantum physics, but one person who could foresee supposedly random numbers was Charles Wells, that legendary personage they wrote a music hall song about - *The Man Who Broke the Bank at Monte Carlo* in Victorian times. In my book *Strange Mysteries* I have devoted an entire chapter to this fascinating man, dismissed as some confidence trickster by historians, but the facts remain: Wells *did* have some system which allowed him to foresee where the little ball would land on the roulette wheel. Most people are not aware of the enormous power that lies within even a humble dictionary of mathematics. There are formulae contained in such books which could make a person a billionaire, but the unambitious and the robotic-minded fail to see the explosive potential of them. Benford's Law, for example, eerily predicts patterns in raw natural data and is even used to detect fraud, and the Laws of Large Numbers has been seriously mooted by mathematicians as a way of predicting numbers in twenty lottery systems around the world. Card games such as blackjack and poker are also subject to the laws of mathematics, and the American mathematics professor Edward Thorp, wrote a fascinating book about the use of his wearable computer to overcome the house advantage of a casino. Thorp's 1962 book, *Beat the Dealer* is heartily recommended to illustrate what I am saying about the unrealised powers of mathematics in the sphere of money-making.

NORRIS GREEN HAUNTINGS

For me there's nothing quite as tantalizing as an unidentified ghost; there is a faceless phantom which haunts the top deck of a certain bus in Liverpool, but I eventually identified it through research helped along by the human internet of readers who regularly email me with queries and answers. The unidentified ghost of the kind I am referring to often possesses a face, but seems to have no reason or back story for haunting a place or neighbourhood, and a case in point is the 'Man in White' currently haunting Wavertree as I write this chapter; he is a short-haired spectacled middle-aged man in a red tie, but every other item of clothing – from his suit to his slip-on shoes is white - shades of Marty Hopkirk! Early in 2015 a doctor driving home at 6.45pm slammed on his brakes on Rathbone Road when the Man in White stepped out in front of him. The vehicle skidded *through* the ghost and he continued nonchalantly on his way to Picton Road. Several taxi drivers have also reported the ivory-attired phantom to me, and one cabby told me how he saw the man in white go into a building on the corner of an alleyway of the Wavertree High Street which used to be the local post office. When the taxi driver drove to the spot out of curiosity, he saw that the man in white must have passed through a locked door, and he promptly drove off soon afterwards.

Another unidentified ghost has wound me up for many years, and he's a lot more sinister – and baffling - than Wavertree's Man in White. He often puts in an appearance in the winter months, and is seen from the late afternoon to around 10pm, and as far as I know, he was first reported one January afternoon in 1933, when 59-year-old Mrs Rita Haynes left Sayers on Muirhead Avenue East with a box of custards and blackcurrant tarts for her two grand-children, Marie and Jimmy, both off school with the flu. Rita was looking after the children at her home on Scargreen Avenue, and no sooner had she got back home and put the shopping down on the kitchen table when there was a knock at the door. She thought it was the "clubman" calling early, but instead, she got the shock of her life, because there on the doorstep stood a man in a long black coat with his head swathed in bandages. 'Oh!' Rita yelped, and the bandaged stranger said, 'Well, aren't you going to let me in?'

'Sorry?' Rita gasped, still in shock. The man said, 'It's *me* – have you forgotten me?' to which Rita replied, 'Who *are* you?'

The man slowly shook his head, then barged into the house, and as he passed Rita she felt an icy coldness in the air move past her with the strange caller – who hurried upstairs – where Marie and Jimmy were recovering from the flu in bed. 'Hey you! What do you think you're doing?' Rita chased after the weird intruder – but when she reached the landing, there was no sign of him. She searched every room, but he was nowhere to be seen, and she asked the sick children but they had seen no one. The next day, Rita was in a fruit shop called Tunney's when a neighbour, Gladys, asked her who the man with the white hair was who had been knocking at her door yesterday afternoon. Rita realised Gladys was referring to the stranger's white bandaged head, and was relieved Gladys had also seen him. That phantom swathed in cotton bandages has been seen many times since then at houses across Norris Green and West Derby, and usually says the same line: 'It's *me* – have you forgotten me?'

There was a theory that he was the ghost of a WWI soldier, who had sustained horrific facial injuries, but this is pure speculation and no one knows who the bandaged entity is and why he calls at houses, only to go into them to vanish. He allegedly called at a house on Utting Avenue as recently as January 2011, where he vanished on the stairs after inviting himself in. Such ghosts that roam around are rather rare in the world of the paranormal, as most phantoms usually haunt one specific house or locality. Hopefully someone out there reading this might know whose cagey ghost is calling on the people of Norris Green with a head swathed in bandages.

We move now eastwards just a few hundred yards from Scargreen Avenue to Wellesbourne Road where a certain house was once the scene of a dramatic haunting in the 1970s. This Norris Green incident unfolded on the Thursday evening of 21 August 1975. That nearest world in space, the moon, hung low and full over the rooftops and chimneypots of Norris Green. The time was half-past eight and a chill hung in the air. Inside a terraced house on Wellesbourne Road, a mother of three in her early forties named Sheila was dozing off as she watched the end of the comedy *It Ain't Half Hot Mum* in her fireside armchair. Sheila's husband Bob was sitting at the table, reading a newspaper and periodically eyeing the clock, thinking of an excuse to go down the pub to see his mates. The couple's two older kids were playing with their neighbour's children next door but one, and the youngest of Sheila and Bob – three-year-old Michelle – was staying at her Nan's over in Fazakerley tonight where she was being doted upon because she had a sore throat.

'Go and have a lie down, love,' Bob suggested, and his words of advice startled Sheila from her nap.

'No, I'll be alright, love,' she said, rubbing her bloodshot eyes. 'Listen, you go down the pub if you want. Seen you looking at the clock by the minute.'

'You sure?' Bob asked, getting up off his chair.

'That finished now?' Sheila squinted at the credits rolling up on the telly screen.

'Yeah,' Bob told her and switched over to ITV. 'Ha! *Barnaby Jones* - you like him don't you love? Jed Clampett – '

Sheila shook her head and waved her hand dismissively at the screen. 'Oh I've seen that one, where Frank Cannon comes into it and helps him to find out who shot his son – turn it off!'

Bob didn't even bother getting a shave, and within minutes he was out of the house and walking eagerly to the Western Approaches pub on Lower House Lane, just four-hundred yards away, while Sheila was climbing the stairs to the bedroom, overcome with fatigue. She'd been up since five in the morning, tending to little Michelle with her sore throat, and now she was fit to drop. She couldn't find her nightdresses, and realised that they were still hanging on the line in the yard, and so she remembered the old one her older sister Maureen had given her a few years ago. It was folded up on the top ledge of the wardrobe, and Sheila stripped to her underwear - then closed the curtains over a bit because she thought she saw someone gawping up at her from the street – and then she put on the nightdress, and although she thought it had an aroma of lavender upon it, she switched off the light and got into bed. Sheila had a smug smile on her face as she closed her eyes. Her head sunk into the new pillows she'd recently bought from Woollies, and soon she was floating off into the comforting world of sleep.

'Get it off! Get it off!'

Sheila awoke to the screaming female voice and the feel of hands with sharp hard nails digging into her arm as she was dragged out the bed.

Utterly confused and stunned, Sheila lost her balance and fell off the bed and landed on her back on the carpeted floor. She saw a shadowy tall figure of a woman with white hair, and she was dressed in old-fashioned loose bloomer type knickers and a bra.

'Aye Aye! Get off!' Sheila screamed back, and a wrestling match ensued as the lanky old woman ragged Sheila by her curly hair all around the room. The crazed stranger somehow yanked the nightdress off Sheila, then seemed to fade away near to the bed.

Realising she had just been attacked by a ghost, Sheila let out a scream and ran down to the hallway. She found Bob's old slippers, and she put her feet in them, then took her long coat off the hook in the hallway and quickly got out of that house in a right state. She thoroughly embarrassed her husband Bob when she turned up at the Western Approaches pub wearing only that coat to cover her knickers and bra. She babbled incoherently to Bob at first as his mates grinned at the way Sheila was dressed.

'God! You've had a nightmare!' Bob told her, and ushered her to the door of the pub. He went home with her, complaining about the way she had made a show of him by turning up like that, but he knew Sheila had encountered something that had caused her to take to the cold night streets dressed like that, and when he reached his home with his trembling wife, he told her to wait in the hallway as he went up to the bedroom to confront the ghost. Bob found the bedroom trashed. Someone had scattered everything from the dresser and they had even ripped down one of the curtains, and yet, on the overturned mattress of the bed, the old nightdress that had been torn off Sheila was folded perfectly.

Sheila later discovered that Maureen had taken that nightdress from a woman who lived less than a hundred yards from Wellesbourne Road several years ago, and this woman had taken the nightdress off the body of her aunt, who had requested to be buried in it. 'Nah, that's a decent nightdress, that; brand new; I got it for her – too good to be buried in that; what's wrong with a normal shroud?' the penny-pinching niece had said, and had the nightdress taken off her aunt as she lay in the undertakers. Sheila was so angry at Maureen for giving her this haunted piece of apparel. Sheila later saw a photograph of the woman's aunt and felt faint. Although the picture was of the woman twenty years before she had died, Sheila saw it was unmistakably her; she was well above normal height, quite slim, and although her hair was black in the photo, the face was the same as the ghost that had wrestled with her that August night. Maureen maintained that her sister had just had a nightmare that evening and yet she was not keen on keeping the nightdress and gave it to Oxfam.

From Wellesbourne Road we move but a short distance to Broad Lane, where, in the 1980s, another ghost of sorts was encountered, and a very unusual 'ghost' it was, too. The strange story comes by way of Joan Fisher, a lifelong Norris Green resident who passed the story on from her grandfather Bert Johnson, a bricklayer who, back in 1925, was working with a gang of men on the construction of houses at the end of Broad Lane not far from St Christopher's Church. Unlike many of the tower blocks that have come and gone across the city, the terraced houses Bert and a gang of labourers built are still standing and still lived-in today, which is a testimony to the architectural and building skills of our forefathers. During housing construction in the 1920s, children often played on the building sites, and one hot summer day in 1925, a very peculiar-looking child of about five years of age turned up on the building site on Broad Lane where Bert Johnson and his colleagues were hard at work. The boy had long blonde hair in a type of bob, and wore a one-piece blue suit with *three white lines* running down the outside of each arm. The boy also had white shoes on similar to tennis shoes. He gave his name as Michael and when the foreman of the site told the lad to go home, Michael started to cry and said he could not find his house. Bert Johnson asked the boy what his address was and he said he lived at a certain number on Broad Lane, but the brickie thought the child was mistaken because the address given was the number of the very house he was currently building! In that day and age, timeslips were unheard of, and the workmen thought Michael was either lying or was mixed up about his address. Bert offered the boy one of his corned-beef sandwiches from his parcel of "turning out" but Michael screwed his face up in disgust and shook his head. Bert therefore wondered if Michael's parents were well-to-do, because most kids in those hard times would not have turned down the offer of a sandwich. Bert asked Michael what he normally ate and the boy said 'pizza' which was something Bert had never heard of.

Michael was seen to enter the house that was under construction and run up the stairs, and when the foreman gave chase, fearing an accident, he discovered to his horror that he could not find the boy anywhere. Michael reappeared two more times on the building site and told Bert that he had found his home, and again gave the address of the house that was being built. Two superstitious men who worked with Bert on the building site believed the boy was some ghost and were very nervous when the boy put in an appearance. Michael apparently described going for rides in his dad's car, and said he was getting a bike for his birthday soon – and then at one point as the chatty child talked of his home life, Bert turned away to look for one of his tools, and when he looked back, Michael was nowhere to be seem. One of the men Bert worked with was staring at the space where the boy had been standing seconds before, and he seemed in shock. This man told Bert that he had seen the boy literally vanish before his eyes. The man who saw Michael vanish into thin air took to wearing rosary beads, believing the incident was the supernatural work of the Devil. Bert often told his daughter the story of the strange 'ghostly' boy over the years, but in light of the many timeslip incidents reported locally (as well as across the world), it's possible that Michael was simply a boy from the future who had somehow walked – via a timewarp – back to 1925. The three stripes of his one-piece suit sounds suspiciously like a modern-day Adidas tracksuit, and the long blonde hair also sounds modern. When the child gave his address as the very house Bert was working on, he may very well have been telling the truth – if he was from a future age when that house had been built. Perhaps there is some resident of Broad Lane named Michael who recalls talking to some old-fashioned-looking men on a building site when he was a child...

From possible timeslips on Broad Lane we move next just six hundred yards north to Fairmead Road, the scene of not one but *two* strange hauntings. The first one is at a terraced house on the east side of this street, and it took place in July 1970. A woman named Rita left her three children, whose ages ranged from six to ten, in the care of a 15-year-old babysitter named Sue, from nearby Strawberry Road. Rita went to town to get a pair of shoes for her husband and also a few items of clothing for herself and her children, and none of the latter had an idea what shops their mother would be visiting; all they cared about was their mum remembering to bring them back sweets, as she usually did when she went to town. Rita assured Susan she would be back no later than 5pm and that she would give her ten bob (50p) for minding the kids. As soon as Rita had left the house, Tony, her youngest child, aged six, suggested a game of hide and seek, and so

Sue the babysitter closed her eyes with a smile on her face and counted down from twenty as the excited children fled to their ad hoc hiding places. Tony ran upstairs to hide in the wardrobe in the spare bedroom. Susan soon caught the other two children: Judy, aged ten, and Alan, aged eight. The babysitter was just going to search upstairs for Tony when the boy came running down in an excited state. 'Susie, come and look at this! Quick!' he yelled at her and then turned and ran back up the stairs. The babysitter and Tony's brother and sister followed close behind, curious as to what Tony had found. Up in the spare bedroom, the curtains had been opened and so the place was in semi-darkness. 'What?' Susie said to the animated boy, and he said, 'Look! Look! Me Mam!' and pointed to the wall facing the window, to a space between the side of an old wardrobe and the wall which divided the house from next door. There, faintly visible, was a scene on the wall, as if it was being thrown there by a movie projector. Susan instinctively waved her hand in front of the image, expecting to trace the beam of the projected scene, and the shadow of her hand, but there was no beam and no shadow.

'Mam,' Judy said, and smiled as she pointed to a woman in the scene on the wall, which showed a row of shops. Susan had a good memory, and later recalled the names of some of the shops she saw in that weird rectangle of light on the faded wallpaper; the names were 'Sterling Shoes', 'Du Barry' and something called 'Golden Griddle'. The scene showed the windows of these stores and the latter, which, Susan later discovered, was a restaurant. There was Rita, the mother of the three spellbound children, walking past the fronts of the shops with other people milling by, and she was going into Sterling Shoes.

And then the scene faded and the babysitter and the three children went to the wall and Susan felt the wallpaper and looked about, thinking someone might be playing a trick on her.

'Who did that, Susie?' Alan asked the babysitter, and Susan shrugged and said, 'I don't know.' She felt a little unnerved, and suddenly had the feeling she was being watched by someone – or something. Susan still recalls that unsettling sensation today. Anyway, a few minutes later, the teenaged babysitter and the children were about to leave the spare room when they heard a woman's voice cry out. 'Oh!' the voice exclaimed, and it came from that space between the wardrobe and the wall where the inexplicable street scene had been shown. Susan and the children gingerly went and looked at the wall where the sound seemed to originate, and this time they saw an alarming scene. They saw what looked like the interior of a shoe shop, with all the shelves of shoeboxes and various footwear on display – and there was a group of people standing around someone on the floor, and a few of these people stooped as the babysitter and the kids looked on in awe. Then Susie and the children she was minding saw to their horror that the person on the floor was unmistakably Rita. She had collapsed.

'Mam!' Judy yelped, and as the child did this, the scene faded, and it never did return. Tony began to sniffle and asked Susan why his mum had fallen down, and Judy started to cry. Susan led the children downstairs and told them to sit on the sofa, and then she went next door to tell a neighbour – a woman named Jean – what had happened. The distressed children left the house and came round to Jean's crying, and Jean thought the babysitter was just being silly with her story of the eerie scene on the wall of the spare bedroom. However, Rita did not return by 5pm – even though she had told Susan that she would. Rita's husband John arrived home at ten to six, and asked where his wife was. Susan was just going to tell him the seemingly far-fetched story about the mysterious projected vision when there was a knock at the door. It was Mr Jones, a friend of the family who lived around the corner on Lorenzo Drive – and the only friend of the family who had a telephone in his home. Mr Jones told John that he had received a call from a nurse in the Royal hospital saying that Rita had collapsed in town and was currently being operated on for appendicitis.

Rita made a full recovery from the operation and later told an astonished Susan that she had collapsed in agony in the Sterling Shoes shop on Lime Street. Susan told her about the 'live coverage' of this incident and Rita thought the teen was just telling some wild story but the three children backed up Susan's story, and Susan recalled the names she had seen on the signs above the windows in the strange scene on that wall: Du Barry, Sterling Shoes and the Golden Griddle – and Rita then realised that these *were* places on Lime Street, but she could not understand how Susan and the children had seen that uncanny view on the wall of the spare bedroom, although Rita did later say that she had always had the feeling of being watched in that back room, and guests who stayed there always said the same too – that they felt a presence in that room.

The second paranormal occurrence at Fairmead Road took place over a fortnight in 2011. I have had to change a few details to this story at the request of the couple who still live in the house, because they are scared their children will find out about the hauntings and fear it might play on their minds. One warm August night in 2011, a 32-year-old man named Lee woke up in a sweat next to his wife of five years, Tricia. She asked him if he was alright and he said he'd had a very realistic nightmare of a man in black – black suit, black polo neck and black shiny shoes – who kept telling Lee to kiss his wife. Tricia went cold when she heard about the nightmare. Lee said the man's face was white as snow and he had a pair of beady bloodshot eyes. He spoke in an upper class voice and kept saying: 'Go to the drawer in the kitchen and get one of those steak knives and stick it through her. Do it now.'

In the dream, when Lee said he wouldn't and that he loved his wife, the man would laugh and shake his head and urge him again to get a steak knife.

'Ooh, isn't that a horrible dream?' Tricia said, gripping Lee's hand. She noticed his hand was sweaty and clammy, and he sat up in bed and turned the bedside lamp on to see the time on the wall clock: a little after 3am.

'Why would I dream of knifing you?' Lee asked, 'I know nightmares can be weird, but it was as if this was real – it was horrible.'

'I know you wouldn't harm me love,' Tricia said, smiling, trying to reassure her husband. 'Maybe you had the dream because you've seen someone getting stabbed in a film?' She surmised, but Lee shook his head and said he hadn't. All he had watched earlier was sport on the TV.

Lee got up and went to go to the toilet.

Tricia yawned and settled down to sleep, lying on her tum with her face turned to the left, towards the window. She heard a terrible scream which gave her a real jolt and set the two young children next door crying. The scream was from Lee.

'He's in the toilet!' Lee said, as he barged into the bedroom. He looked terrified and confused.

'What?' Tricia jumped out the bed and went to him, and they both stood near the bedroom doorway.

'That man in the dream!' Lee yelped, and sounded as if he was losing his voice. He coughed. 'He was standing in the shower cubicle, and he said "Go and get that knife!"'

'Lee, calm down, that was a nightmare, he doesn't exist,' Tricia told her husband and held his trembling hand as he looked in horror through the doorway down the landing at the door to the toilet.

The toilet flushed.

Lee jumped and Tricia let out a shriek.

'I told you! He's in there!' Lee's eyes were bulging in terror.

Tricia ran to the room next door to get her crying children – 3-year-old Liam and 5-year-old Alice, and she and Lee took them downstairs. Tricia and her husband then heard footsteps which went from the toilet to the stairs, but they saw nothing and did not hear anyone come down those stairs.

The children slept on the sofa with their mother for the remainder of that morning, and at sunrise, Lee dared to go upstairs and saw nothing amiss. He began to wonder if the fear from the nightmare had somehow spilled over into his waking life, but he found it hard to rationalise the way the toilet had flushed itself and how could he explain the distinct sounds of footsteps upstairs? And of course the hardest thing to explain away was the presence of the man in black in the shower cubicle. Lee had seen him through the frosted glass of the cubicle, but he was in no doubt that it was the same creepy man he had seen in his dream, and he had definitely heard him say "Go and get the knife!"

On the following day, Lee – a plumber by trade – went to work, and Tricia went to work at 10am; she worked as a school dinners lady. Tricia's mother took Liam to her home in Broadgreen after dropping Alice off at the infants school. Tricia returned home at 4pm and Lee came home around six and they talked about the ghost, and Lee said he'd had a word about the incident with Graham, a born-again Christian who worked with his firm, and he had told Lee to confront the ghost if he saw it again saying: 'In the name of Jesus the Christ, I tell thee to go.'

'And you think that might work?' Tricia asked, sceptical of the advice.

'I don't know anything about ghosts,' Lee admitted his ignorance. 'Just hope we don't ever see it again. I believe a lot of ghosts are seen once and then they are never heard from again.'

When bedtime came, the couple lay under the duvet, hugging one another, but there were no strange goings-on, and when Tricia had to go to the toilet, Lee went with her. Then Lee fell asleep, and soon afterwards so did his wife. Lee dreamt he was sitting on the bed, and of course, he was not aware he was dreaming; if he had been aware that it was a dream, that would be what is known as a lucid dream – a dream in which the person dreaming realises he or she is still asleep. Lee got up off the bed and found himself walking along the landing, on his way to the kitchen. He went down the carpeted stairs slowly, so as to not awake his wife, and upon reaching the hallway, he waited a moment then walked into the kitchen. He searched through the cutlery drawer, and a familiar, chilling voice behind him said, 'That's it, get the steak knife.'

Lee turned in the dream, and there was the man in the funereal black attire and bloodshot eyes. He grinned, and nodded. 'That's it,' he said softly, 'don't be afraid. Go and finish her off.' Lee seemed in a trance. He was not scared now of the weird stranger, and felt as if he *had* to kill Tricia. He saw the moonlight streaming through the gaps in the partially opened vertical blinds, and then he looked at the blade of the long sharp knife and saw the lunar light glint of it.

'She has to die,' the man told Lee, 'so go and put it through her.'

Lee walked into the hallway and climbed the stairs in a careful manner. He reached the landing upstairs and headed for the bedroom door, but as he walked through the door there was an almighty scream which not only woke the neighbours – it also woke Lee – who was sleepwalking with a steak knife in his hand.

Lee felt his heart somersault as the scream brought him back into the world of the waking, and he saw Tricia pressed into the far corner with her hands to her trembling mouth. She looked absolutely terrified. Next door, the children were crying again after hearing their mum scream.

Lee realised that he had walked all the way down to the kitchen to get the knife, and – God forbid – if he had not awakened in time – he would have plunged the knife into Tricia as she slept. He put the knife down on his bedside cabinet and rushed to Tricia, and she seemed scared of him; that really hurt Lee – the idea of the woman he loved being afraid of him. He wanted to kill the mysterious entity in black, but then realised he – or it – must already be dead.

'We can't stay here any more!' Lee embraced his shaking, sobbing wife. 'We've got to get out of here love!' he told Tricia, eyeing the knife as he stroked her head.

'We need a priest or something,' Tricia told him between sobs and sniffles, and she went to comfort the children.

A priest was consulted and he said he believed a psychiatrist would be of more help in this situation, which really annoyed Lee and Tricia. Tricia went to see her cousin, a woman in her late thirties named Dawn, who was a practising white witch. Dawn visited the house on Fairmead Road and said that there was definitely a presence, and she enlisted the services of a friend named Fleur, who is very psychic. Fleur asked to left alone in the bedroom upstairs for a while, and later came down and said that the ghost was completely fixated with Tricia, and had been for some time. He wanted her to join him for some arcane reason. The ghost was very confident, sinister and had successfully prevented Fleur from obtaining even his first name. The psychic said that she felt that the menacing ghost had a thing for Tricia possibly because she reminded him of someone he had loved a long time ago, and that person had moved on to the life beyond this – a place where this ghost was not able to go, for some reason.

'When you say he's been fixated for some time,' a worried Tricia asked Fleur, 'how long are you talking about?'

'A good few years. Time where the ghost is does not pass at the same rate it does here, but I'd say a few years – maybe three.'

'So he wanted me to do away with Tricia so she'd be with him?' Lee asked, and seemed disgusted at the idea.

'Yes, which is ridiculous really, because Tricia would not stay on the same plane of existence as him – she'd move onto the next plane, the next life.'

'What are we going to do, then?' Tricia asked, 'how can we get rid of him?'

'I've had a bit of a think about that, and I could try and get my guide to tackle him,' said Fleur, matter of fact.

'Guide?' Lee was baffled at her words.

'I have a guide,' said Fleur, 'a spirit guide they call them, and he's always helped me, even since I was a child.'

'What's his name?' Lee asked, intrigued.

'I don't really want to say, because *he's* listening in now,' Fleur replied.

'The guide?' asked Lee, his eyes sliding left and then right.

Fleur shook her head gently. 'No, *him* - the one we

want to get shut of.'

The idea of the ghost who wanted to kill her eavesdropping on the conversation really chilled the blood of Tricia.

'Can you take the children to a relative tonight?' Fleur asked Tricia, who nodded and said, 'Yes, of course. I'll take them to me mum's.'

'Good,' Fleur told Tricia. 'They sometimes resort to some dirty tricks when they're cornered, you see, and even children aren't safe.'

'We've never had any trouble in this house in all the years we've lived here,' said Lee, 'so why is all this happening now?'

Fleur shrugged. 'I really can't say, but its very common with ghosts; they can just become active all of a sudden. Some things just seem to kick them off – anniversaries, redecorating a place – all sorts.' The medium then looked to a corner of the ceiling as if she was focussing on something, and then she stood up and said: 'So, is tonight, say about seven, alright?'

Lee and Tricia nodded in unison.

That evening at around five minutes to seven, Dawn and Fleur arrived at the house on Fairmead Road and Lee and Tricia were told to stay in the kitchen. In the living room of the house, a number of candles were arranged in a pattern on the coffee table and lit. Lee strained his ears and heard Fleur murmuring something over and over for what seemed like an irritatingly long time, and then Tricia said, 'Listen, hear that?'

Lee listened intently. They could hear a man's voice. To Lee's ears, it sounded a bit higher in pitch than the voice of the weird ghost he had heard.

The couple heard the living room door open, and footsteps came to the kitchen door – and halted. Lee and Tricia stood near the table, holding hands tightly as they gazed at the door with a look of fear on their faces.

The door opened, and a man of about fifty-five to sixty popped his head around the door. He wore a black bowler hat, and had a moustache that looked slightly waxed at the end. His face was very friendly, and in the voice that the couple had heard earlier, which bore no trace of any regional accent, the man said, 'Don't worry – just stay there and we'll soon get rid of this deadbeat.'

He then withdrew from the kitchen, closing the door softly behind him.

Lee and Tricia looked at one another and didn't know whether to laugh or continue to be afraid. It was so surreal and unexpected. Was *he* the spirit guide or was he some friend of Fleur's who had turned up to tackle the ghost?

The couple then heard thumps upstairs and the noises became so loud, the neighbours on one side of the house began to rap on the wall and there were faint shouts of 'Hey! Pack that in, will you?'

Then there was an almighty crash, as if an elephant had fallen through the roof.

Fleur came into the kitchen and gestured with an outstretched palm as she said: 'It's working, just stay there though; he hasn't finished.'

'Yeah, alright,' Tricia said, nodding, but Lee said, 'What's going on up there? World War Three?'

'Be right back,' Fleur said, backing out of the kitchen, closing the door behind her.

There was a single loud – male – scream – and then silence fell. Then came the sound of a heavy ran tan on the door. The couple from next door asked what was going on and wanted to see Tricia and Lee, but Dawn said: 'They're not available; sorry about the noise.'

'Not available?' asked the middle aged woman from next door with a sarcastic look, and she turned to her husband and said, 'they'll be available when we take them to court for anti social behaviour!'

Dawn did her best to calm down the couple at the door, and they eventually went away. Fleur then went into the kitchen and said: 'I think he's gone.' The medium's hair looked as if it had stood up from an electric shock.

'Can we go up?' Lee asked, wondering if all this talk about guides had been a huge con trick. He took Tricia by the hand and led her up the stairs and expected to find the bed, wardrobe and dresser upside down, but everything was in its place – but there was a strong sweet smell reminiscent of roses.

Fleur gave a lengthy explanation about her guide – Mr Ajax – and Lee couldn't follow the narrative at all; all he said afterwards was that the name Ajax reminded him of the old bleach brand, to which an indignant Fleur said: 'It's Welsh actually, and probably descended from the French Huguenots.'

When the medium and Dawn had gone, Lee asked his wife if she really believed Mr Ajax had been a guide. When Tricia said she believed he had been, Lee said, 'I don't know, he seemed very real to me, and he was determined to keep us in the kitchen.'

Tricia seemed offended at the suggestion. 'You think he was just a normal flesh and blood person, and that my friend Dawn is a conwoman in other words?'

'I'm not saying that,' Lee tried to back-pedal, realising he had upset his wife with his voiced suspicions.

'You are, Lee, and you're really paranoid,' Tricia told him straight, 'and I don't see what that medium would get out of it because it wasn't as if we paid them or anything.'

'Let's just agree to differ,' Lee said, grabbing his wife's hand as they sat on the sofa, but she wrestled her hand loose from his grip.

'I'd better go and pick the kids up from me Mum's,' Tricia said with a distant look.

That night, around half-past midnight, the couple lay in bed. Tricia was browsing the web on her tablet and Lee was lying on his back and starting to snore. Tricia looked at him and shook her head. She whispered, 'Will you shut up?' to her noisy husband. She then heard a faint thud. It sounded like something falling over, like a chair, next door. Tricia yawned. She was feeling a little sleepy now, and she reflected on the eventful day.

All of a sudden, Lee threw his arms up into the air and made boxing movements with his clenched fists. His hands then went to his throat and he held his neck and made a wheezing noise – as if he was choking.

'Oh my God!' Tricia dropped the tablet and leaned over Lee and shook him until he awoke. He shot up into a sitting position, trying to get his breath back.

'What happened? You alright?' Tricia asked, so afraid. She thought he was having a heart attack.

'He was back! He came back!' Lee gasped, and started to breathe a little more normal. 'The man all in black came into my dream, he came in through the front door – went through the door – and then when he got into the hallway I tried to fight him, but that man in the bowler appeared, and pushed him back towards the door.'

'Mr Ajax?' Tricia asked, intrigued, but also a little scared of what she was hearing.

'Yeah, and he started throwing the man in black all around the hallway, and he knocked over that thing you hang your coat on – '

'The coat and hat stand?' Tricia asked.

Lee nodded and rubbed his bleary eyes. 'Yeah, and then the fellah in the bowler pushed him straight through the door, and he went through the door with him. It was so real, and the funny thing was that the hallway was in darkness, and you could only see things by the light coming through the window in the door from outside.'

Tricia suddenly recalled that sound she had heard just before Lee had awakened; she had dismissed it as coming from her neighbour's house. She told Lee what she had heard, and he also guessed that it had been the sound of the coat and hat stand being knocked over. The two of them went onto the landing, where Tricia switched the hallway lights on. She and Lee then went down the stairs ever so slowly, and when Tricia saw the long black coat and hat stand lying on its side on the floor of the hallway, her heart jumped. This meant that the dream Lee had had must have really happened. Lee righted the stand and then looked about the hallway. He soon rejoined his wife, who remained on the stairs, and went with her back to bed. They hugged all through the night and when they finally did sleep, they did not have any nightmares about the ghosts or Mr Ajax.

The ghost did not make any further appearances – in dreams or in waking life - after that night. The identity of the ghost remains unknown, and I have a feeling he has moved on to someone else – perhaps some lady who reminds him of a lost love, but hopefully, if you're female, that person won't be *you*...

SOME HAUNTED CHURCHES

As I stated in the very first *Haunted Liverpool* book, it is a myth that ghosts, and the Devil for that matter, cannot set foot inside of a church, and even our two Cathedrals in Liverpool are haunted by a number of apparitions and presences. This chapter details just a few of the many churches in our neck of the woods which are either haunted by ghosts or have been the scene of supernatural goings on. I can't always name these places of worship because the Church largely frowns on anyone being even remotely interested in the paranormal, and a few vicars and priests do not want undue publicity derived from spectres and phantoms roaming the aisles of their churches. On a more democratic note, some open-minded ministers and men of the cloth have granted me permission to name their churches, and I am very grateful for their gracious openness. I think the presence of some supernatural entity in a church, past or present, does not in any way detract from the sanctity of the place of worship, for ghosts and demons (and of course, Satan) are all documented in the Bible.

The winter of December 1962 to February 1963 is often cited as one of the most severe in history, but the briefer nationwide blizzards of March 1970 were also as relentless and quite unexpected. As usual, the authorities were unprepared and the heavy snowfall from Caithness to Kent brought Biblical chaos to road, rail and air transport; towns and villages were also cut off, power lines were brought down, and sporting events were wiped out. One of the many power failures resulted in 688 miners being trapped 3,000 feet down a mine in Kent – the appropriately named Snowdown colliery, but British Rail attempted to get passengers from Liverpool to Euston Station, and they somehow did – eight hours late. Liverpool was buried under record snow-drifts in these arctic conditions, but a novice (and some would say naive) priest decided to keep the doors of a well-known Catholic church unlocked for confession. In a duffle coat and scarf he sat patiently in the confession box for almost an hour without a single visit, and then decided to close the church – but as he stood up he heard a voice through the grille: 'Bless me father, for I have sinned. It has been *one hundred years* since my last confession.'

There was a pause. 'Did you say a hundred years?' the priest thought the well-spoken penitent was drunk, unbalanced or joking.

'Yes, father,' said the man behind the grille, 'a long time I know, but I am ready to face my maker now.'

'Recite your sins,' the priest told him, and in response heard something shocking. The man had murdered his wife and seventeen other people, and had started the killings after a head injury in an abattoir. The confessor went into all of the gory details, and after the priest had given absolution, he heard the man sobbing as he left the confessional. The holy man opened the door and tried to catch a glimpse of the self-confessed mass murderer as he walked off, but all the priest heard was footsteps receding down the aisle. The oaken door was thrown open, and a howling wind brought a vortex of snowflakes into the church. The door then closed itself, and outside, the priest eventually traced the footprints of the tormented ghost in the snow - to a certain 19th century grave in the churchyard.

Another supernatural mystery took place in Scotland Road's St Anthony's years earlier when a young priest was appointed to conduct a marriage service instead of an older priest who had contracted a bad dose of influenza. The young priest had not met the couple he was scheduled to marry, and when he saw the bride and groom, he was utterly stunned. The bride was a lady he had long loved from afar, and the groom was the exact double of the priest – a doppelgänger in fact who even sounded just like him when he spoke. The priest was heartbroken as he married the couple, and he conducted the service in a broken voice. He regretted choosing a life as a celibate priest and wished he had courted the young woman before him, and from the looks the bride gave she knew he was tormented as he married her and the priest's rival. Then the priest remembered how he had found great consolation in the teachings of Jesus – and at that moment, the groom's face changed to that of a man who bore no resemblance to him. When the priest told an older colleague about this incident, the elderly priest said: 'That's been the fellah down below; he plays some sneaky tricks to undermine our faith.'

In the 1970s, a rumour spread that the Devil had appeared in St Michael's Church in Huyton, and that he had been wearing a scarlet velvet suit. Just what the Devil would be doing attending church, and St

Michael's Church in particular, was not explained in the rumours, but the weird tale was given currency by a number of priests, including two I interviewed. I mentioned the visitation of His Satanic Majesty to the church on the *Billy Butler Show* one afternoon, but did not give details of the alleged visitation that had been supplied by the priests. I was therefore intrigued when a cleaning lady called and told me those same details that had come my way from the men of the cloth. The cleaner, named Jan, told me how, one midweek morning about 7.20 am, she was mopping up in the church, and went to have a smoke at one point, leaving the mop bucket in the middle aisle of the church. She stood near the front door of the church, having a 'few drags' when she heard laughter, followed by gibberish — words she just couldn't understand: 'Not in a language I'd ever heard before,' was how she described this. Jan turned, and got the shock of her life, a man, about six feet in height or more, was running down the aisle from the direction of the altar, and he looked very odd indeed. His jet black hair seemed to be combed up at the sides of his head into two points, resembling the ears of a cat, and this strange individual had a bluish face. He also had a turned up moustache, a van dyke beard, and he wore what looked like a white shirt and a yellow or possibly golden coloured tie, and a dark red suit of what seemed to be velvet. He wore red pointed shoes which matched his suit, black leather gloves and he twirled a walking cane. As Jan looked on he stopped running and began to move forward in incredible bounds, seeming to defy gravity as he leapt high into the air. Jan screamed, sensing the figure was evil, and the creepy visitor to the church yelled something unintelligible, then kicked the mop bucket with quite some force, sending it sailing about ten feet into the air, and showering the cleaner with dirty water in the process. Jan did not see where the Mephistophelian character went, but she didn't bother looking – she ran out of that church and refused to return for a week. Jan later heard that the same figure had been seen years before in the 1960s by a priest just before a morning service. Just what the thing was that was seen in St Michael's Church is unknown, and I can't hazard a guess as I don't really have enough eyewitness testimony to go on. One caller to BBC Radio Merseyside said he was going to tell me stories of Satanism that had gone on near St Michael's Church which accounted for the visits of the Devil, but he never called back.

Similar rumours of Devil-worship in the vicinity of the Anglican parish church of St Chad's in Kirkby have been reported for years, not just to me but to other investigators of the supernatural in the 1950s and 1960s. There were reports of eerie silhouettes dancing in what looked like a mass of blue flames at around 3am in the churchyard of St Chads as recently as October 2011. These reports were made by quite a few locals, and two people who saw the strange spectacle – two students named Trin (short for Trinity) and Abi – saw the blue flames as they were returning from a visit to a friend's house in Northwood. Abi was driving her car up Old Hall Lane on her way to the flat she shares with Trin in Westvale, when Trin noticed the blue glow among the gravestones of the churchyard that are visible over a low wall. Abi slowed the car then halted on Old Hall Lane, and wound down her window. She could see that the blue glow was a mass of what looked like flames of a light blue colour, and there were shadowy figures performing strange movements and apparently dancing within these flames. Trin got out the car, against the wishes of her friend, and tried to get a better look, but then the silhouetted people all suddenly stopped moving, and stood in a row, as if they knew they were now being observed and were now looking in the direction of the students. Trin rushed back to the car, and Abi tried to drive off but stalled the vehicle. Trin became hysterical and claimed that the figures were getting nearer and Abi started the car and tore off. Abi said she saw some movement near the sandstone churchyard wall, as she looked in her rear view mirror but could not say with certainty that it was those figures she had seen silhouetted against the weird blue fire. All the same, Abi now refuses to drive past the churchyard of St Chads after nightfall, and instead she takes the long way round if she pays a visit to her friend in Northwood. Many people saw the 'blue flames' of St Chads in 2011, and regular bonfires have also been seen in the churchyard years before, but it seems that whenever the site of the bonfire is examined on the following day in broad daylight, there is rarely any signs of the fire on the ground – no charred wood or blackened gravestones. Some think the blue flames may just be an atmospheric phenomenon similar to St Elmo's Fire or the Will-O'-the-Wisp, caused by nothing more mysterious than escaping marsh or methane gas and static electricity which creates an ionised glow. The site St Chad's Church is built on is very ancient, and was revered by the pre-Christian people of the area for some reason. A chapel – a plain red brick affair – dedicated to St Chad, was first built on this sacred spot back in 870 AD. The present church was built in 1871 when it was surrounded by vast unspoilt tracts of countryside – earning St Chad's Church the nickname of the Cathedral of the Fields. Just *what* the early settlers worshipped at the site of St Chad's is unknown, but it may have been some deity or force of nature linked to Druidism, which was widespread in those days.

And finally, here's another case of a haunting which took place in an ecclesiastical setting, and it was related to me many years ago by Barbara, a woman who grew up In Walton but who now lives with her husband and family in Scotland. The story concerns Barbara's grandmother, 78-year-old Sadie, a woman who, in December 1970, was still quite ill after recovering from pneumonia. Sadie had always gone to the Midnight Mass at Christmas Eve, and upon this snowy Christmas Eve, she had her sights on attending such a mass being held at St Mary's Church, Walton (or Walton-on-the-Hill to give the place its official title). Sadie's daughter had made her mum promise she would not be venturing out in her state to go to church on such a wintry night with gales and more snow forecast, but when 11.30pm came around on the big old clock on the mantelpiece, Sadie began to put on her fur-lined ankle-length boots, her coat, and her headscarf. She could not find her mitts anywhere. She had lost her husband a few years back and missed him on nights like this, because he would have accompanied her hand in hand to the church. Sadie's daughter was living over in Litherland at the time, probably preparing to leave her children's presents under the Christmas tree, and had she known her mother was going to church, she would have been furious. Sadie felt a little guilty for two reasons; firstly because she decided to take a sip of Lamb's Navy Rum from the old bottle her husband had left untouched before he died, and secondly, the old woman felt that it was wrong risking a fall on the icy and snowy streets, and what that would entail for her daughter – and she knew she was being a bit selfish but she felt she just *had* to go to Midnight Mass; to stay in on Christmas Eve and to forego that service would only make her even more depressed. She switched off the television which was showing the story of the Magi.

And so, out Sadie went into the night to be greeted by a knifing wind from the river. Above her on this moonless Thursday night, the stars twinkled like jewels as she embarked on the 600-yard journey to St Mary's Church. She could see the stained-glass windows of the church at the end of her street – Bedford Road. As Sadie inched along, being careful not to slip on the icy layer concealed by a few inches of frozen snow, she thought she heard someone walking behind her. When she stopped, the footsteps behind her stopped, so she paused, took a sly look over her shoulder, and out of the tail of her eye she could definitely see a shadowy figure, and although she didn't turn her head further, she knew it was a man. She naturally felt a little scared because there had been a mugging in the area a few weeks ago (and in those days the term "mugging" was virtually unknown, a sad reflection on life today when the term is so commonplace). A woman in her sixties had been attacked and robbed near County Road by a youth, and he had not been caught – so was this him lurking behind her now?

Sadie reached the junction where Stuart Road cuts across Bedford Road, and here, close to the Stuart Hotel pub on the corner, a hand grabbed Sadie's right elbow and the woman yelped and recoiled in terror. But when she turned she saw it was her old neighbour Thelma Jeffries. She had lived next door but one to Sadie many years ago in Hawthorne Road. 'Oh! Hello there!' Sadie said to her old mate and felt so relieved at meeting her.

Thelma had a strange story to tell. She said she had been in her daughter's house on Westminster Road, literally just around the corner, when she had received 'a strong impression' in her mind to go to Bedford Road to see Sadie. Thelma's daughter had told her mother (who was 73) to stay put, and that she was in no state to go out. 'But I couldn't help it, I had to go and see if you needed help,' Thelma told her, and she then added, 'I take it you're going to Midnight Mass.'

Sadie nodded. 'Yes, are you coming with me?' And she had a suggestion: We can have some supper and a drop of Guinness afterwards if you like,' she said.

Thelma laughed. 'You're a case, you. I'll have to get back to my daughter afterwards love, or she'll have the police out looking for me.'

Sadie halted and looked around. The man had gone. 'There was a fellah, up to no good by the looks of it, following me before.'

Thelma looked down the silent street. 'Well, he's gone now,' she said, and gently moved on up Bedford Road with her old friend. They chatted and talked of old times, of lost loves and funny episodes and dramas in their lives around Walton, and they got to the church, and sat next to one another, and when the service was done, Sadie felt so incredibly happy – it was a case of those mystical peak experiences people report from time to time when they suddenly feel as high as a kite without any drugs – just the drug of friendship and the lovely setting of the church with all of the beautiful candles and incense. Sadie turned and said, 'Well, I suppose we'd – '

Thelma was not there.

Sadie looked up and down the aisle, at the people leaving the church, and Thelma was not among them. She waited at the church door and people passed her, smiling, saying 'Merry Christmas' to her even though they didn't know her, but Sadie could not even raise a false smile, because she could not see Thelma anywhere. The Reverend came to the door and shook hands with the last person out of the place – an old man with snow-white hair. Then the Reverend turned to Sadie and he could see she looked distressed, and he said, 'Hello Sadie, are you alright?'

'Yes, Reverend, it's just that er – '

'You didn't come here on your own did you?' he asked, looking about for Sadie's daughter.

'I came here with Thelma, an old friend of mine, and I seem to have lost her,' Sadie told him, feeling a bit embarrassed.

'Not Thelma Jeffries?' the Reverend queried with a peculiar expression of puzzlement.

'Yes, do you know her?' Sadie asked.

'A friend of mine knows the family. Thelma is very ill, do you know that?'

'Ill? Thelma?' said Sadie, and shook her head slightly.

'She *was* ill recently, I recall her saying, and her daughter was looking after her, but she accompanied me to the church tonight.'

'But she's in a terrible state, Sadie, she has cancer. Didn't you know? I'm so sorry if you didn't.' The Reverend took hold of the old woman's trembling cold hands and clasped them, and Sadie immediately felt warmth spread to her heart.

'But she came here with me tonight,' Sadie told the Reverend with such a grave look in her eyes.

After a pause, the Reverend said: 'Sadie, I think I should give you a lift home. Come on,' the Reverend led her to his living quarters. His wife made her a cup of tea and gave her sweet biscuits because she seemed to be in shock over the news of Thelma having a life-threatening illness.

The Reverend took her home and he lit the gas fire and told her to try and get some sleep once the house had warmed up. The next day, Sadie went to the house of Thelma's daughter on Westminster Road, and she discovered to her horror that Thelma had died the night before at around 11.15pm. What's more, just before she died she had been rambling about going to see her old friend Sadie and had even tried to get out the bed, but she had been too weak and Thelma's daughter and son-in-law had been near to tears watching her in a delirious state.

Sadie began to cry, but was soon comforted by her late friend's daughter and her husband. They would never believe Sadie's story, but Sadie knew for a fact that her close friend had somehow left her deathbed to be with her and to attend that Midnight Mass at St Mary's.

THE DRUID BOY

At teatime on Saturday 1 November 1969, a 14-year-old girl named Kathleen left her home on Lynholme Road in Anfield and walked around 800 yards to the terraced house of a family we shall call the Johnsons, on Skerries Road, which is located quite near to LFC's football ground. Kathleen arrived at the Johnsons around 6.20pm, and one of her favourite telly programmes was on, featuring Simon Dee, a radio DJ who now hosted a TV chat show. Kathleen had come to babysit Mrs Johnson's 2-year-old son Celéstin – a name the boy's stepfather would not accept (and Mr Johnson called the boy Stan). Mrs Johnson had the child to a modern-day self-appointed Druid in France during the Summer of Love. Celéstin loved Kathleen, and would always ask her to tell him stories, but then he'd interrupt her and take over the narrative. Kathleen found him a very strange child with large dark lively eyes. The Johnsons left their Anfield home at 7pm as *Please Sir!* was starting on the telly, and Kathleen watched this comedy with Celéstin sat on her knee until 8pm when she took him up to bed. She told him about the Three Bears but he butted in and said, 'No, wait, I'll tell the rest,' and he picked up a little torch, clicked it on, placed it on the bedside cabinet, and then he put his hands together, and by sticking fingers and a thumb out in the torchbeam he projected the shadow of what looked like a rabbit on the wall, but then it changed. 'That's a devil,' Celéstin said, and Kathleen went cold. 'He goes and eats Goldilocks all up!'

The silhouette looked like a horned grinning face in profile. 'Stop that, Stan!' Kathleen told him. 'Celéstin, not Stan!' the boy said, and he placed his hands on the bedclothes – but the shadow-devil on the wall stayed there for a moment. 'How did you do that?' Kathleen was stunned and a little scared. The boy told her a story: 'There was this girl named Kathleen and she had a boyfriend named Steven, but he got sick and died.'

Kathleen's boyfriend was named Steven and she'd told no one about him yet. Celéstin then said, 'When Kathleen went home down a dark alley, these big hands strangled her and – '

'Pack this in, Stan! I'll tell your dad otherwise,' the girl threatened, 'now get to bed.' But the boy said, 'He's not my real dad! And I don't want you going with that Steven, you're *my* friend!'

When the boy eventually settled down in his bed, Kathleen went downstairs to watch a film, and throughout the evening she felt tiny hands on her arm, foot and head, and this freaked her out. She also heard Stan laughing upstairs. She was only too glad when the child's parents returned at 11.30pm, but as she walked down an alley that evening on her way home, she felt something cold on the back of her neck, and she turned to see a huge pair of disembodied hands, floating in mid-air – and they tried to grab her throat!

The girl ran screaming all the way home, and never babysat for the Johnsons again, and recalling what Stan predicted about Steven becoming ill and dying, she thought she'd lose her boyfriend, but he never came to any harm. The Johnsons moved to Wales and I don't know what became of the 'Druid's Boy'.

FORD CEMETERY'S REAPER

One grey and dismal morning in March 1983, three men - John, aged 35, Peter, aged fifty, and 22-year-old David, arrived at the house of a man named Terry near Octavia Hill Road, Litherland. John and David had been hired to lay down crazy paving and Peter had been enlisted to render the external walls of the glorified outhouse he'd erected last summer with a Tyrolean finish. Peter began the job immediately, while John and David decided to have coffee and biscuits for their elevenses first and the kettle went on as soon as Terry had left for work.

'I've got this weird feeling that we are being watched,' John told David as they waited for the kettle to boil. His comment made David nervous.

'You mean snoopers from the DHSS?' David asked, and his eyes darted to the kitchen window, where they could see Peter hard at work.

'Nah, nothing like that,' John replied, 'just some weird feeling of being observed. I've had this thing since I was a kid; I know when someone's looking at me, honest, no word of a lie; I can actually feel a person's eyes on me when I'm being blimped.'

'Well I can't see anyone watching us, mate.' David peered out through the window again and could see no one except white-haired Peter.

John made the coffees then turned – and recoiled in fright because David had positioned his face inches from the back of John's head, to test his supposed sense of being watched.

'I've been gawping at you like that for ages and you said you knew when you were being watched,' David laughed, but John just shook his head, annoyed at being tested – and feeling discredited, he swore at David.

There was then a knock at the window and the two men jumped. It was Peter. 'Here!' he said, beckoning them outside. They went out and Peter said, 'You should have seen this thing before; something went past the fence out there, and I could see it through the gaps. I had a look and it was like a black mist.'

John and David rushed down the back garden and climbed the fence and had a look, but there was nothing there. David said it had been smoke from some barbecue somewhere but Peter was certain the mist was something supernatural. It had been very dark – black almost – and too well-defined and cohesive to have been smoke from any barbecue he'd ever seen.

On the following day, John had the same unsettling feeling of being watched, and then shortly afterwards all three men saw the black mist go by, and David and John climbed the fence and followed it.

'Its smoke, isn't it?' David asked, nervously, *wanting* a rational explanation, because he knew deep down this vapour seemed to be under intelligent control.

John shook his head, 'That's not smoke, mate,' he replied – and the two men followed it down Octavia Hill Road – to the railings of Ford Cemetery, where the dark nebulous thing snaked through a gap in the railings and went into the forest of gravestones.

At the exact same time on the following day, the black mist appeared again, and John and David urged Peter to follow it with them, but he refused and made the sign of the cross. 'Leave it well alone, lads,' was Peter's advice, and David and John noticed the plasterer's right eyebrow twitching away with nerves.

David and John pursued the weird smoky entity out of sheer curiosity, even though they sensed that it was unwise to follow the thing.

This time the mist halted near the railings of the cemetery – and condensed into an abnormally tall and very sinister figure – a woman all in black with a flour-white face and eerie huge staring eyes. She pointed at the graves beyond the railings, and then she faded as she floated through the railings as if they weren't there.

When David and John got back to Peter, he told them they shouldn't have gone after that unearthly being, for he sensed that thing had something to do with death, and in his opinion, he believed it was a bad omen of some sort.

'Nah,' David dismissed the older man's words with a bogus smile. 'Just some sort of ghost – don't believe in all that omen crap.'

A week later, David was driving to a toy shop on Walton's County Road to get a birthday present for his niece, when he lost control of the vehicle and hit a wall. He died instantly. He was buried in Ford Cemetery, less than twelve feet from those railings the vaporous 'reaper' had passed through.

The Reaper of Ford Cemetery has quite a history stretching back to at least the 1920s. In the 1950s there was a flasher at large in Ford, and he exposed himself to several women in the cemetery, mostly at weekends when working people were more likely to pay respects to the graves of loved ones. A woman in her fifties and her 20-year-old daughter were approached by the flasher one Saturday afternoon, and he did his usual thing and then ran off, but the story goes that he was found dead, leaning against a large memorial stone – still holding his manhood – with a look of utter horror on his face. His eyes were bulging and his mouth was wide open. That afternoon, in broad daylight, several people - including the woman and her daughter who had been 'flashed' – reported seeing a very tall figure, possibly a woman, in a long black robe and a covering on her head that was reminiscent of the headdress nuns wear. Was this the eerie reaper? And if it was, did it scare to death the pervert who'd been exposing himself? I mentioned the reaper-like entity on the radio once and a well-respected occultist got in touch and told me that the figure in the long black robe is the 'Keeper' of the cemetery – one of the first people to have been buried at Ford, and that she was assigned to look after the dead. I recently mentioned the weird figure in my column in the *Liverpool Echo* and received many reports of recent sightings of the figure. Most of those reports were from people who believed the entity was female.

A GATEACRE MYSTERY

Mysteries surround us; they are to be found in the sky, whether it's in the form of UFOs or planes (such as Malaysia Airlines Flight 370) which vanish without a trace – and there are also a welter of mysteries in the sea, from unidentified submarine objects, to fabled submerged islands such as Kilgrimol (which once existed off the coast of Blackpool) and even lost continents such as Mu and Atlantis. A growing body of ufologists are now even claiming that there is an underwater UFO base close to Puffin Island off the coast of Anglesey. But there are just as many enigmas lying beneath our feet, below ground, from unidentified tunnels (and there are many below the North West, especially beneath Liverpool) to mysterious subterranean humming noises – and also inexplicable fossils. In the 1950s, an amateur geologist named Mike Quinn was breaking open loose stones in Woolton quarry – where much of the stone that went into the building of the Anglican Cathedral (Europe's largest cathedral) was quarried. Mr Quinn split open a piece of sandstone, hoping to find a fossil, but instead he found an object which resembled a tiny gun similar to a flintlock, and this gun must have been a charm of some sort, Quinn reasoned, because it was too small to be a working model as it was about an inch in length!

The mystery deepened when it was established that the tiny gun had been encased in sandstone formed in the Triassic period – two million years ago – when Britain was tropical and Liverpool was a desert. Quinn sent the out-of-place fossilized firearm to Liverpool University, and nothing more was heard of it. Was it genuinely mislaid and lost – or did some worried academic confiscate such an ancient manufactured object (which would have required machine tools for its construction) because it plainly made a mockery of scientific dating techniques? In late Victorian times on a piece of land in Gateacre where Siskin Green now joins Cuckoo Lane, a farmer's plough uprooted a sinister black-wood coffin which was found to contain a wooden effigy of a male about seven inches in length, and this little 'doll' had pins through its eyes and torso. Three more of these eerie miniature coffins were found, and instead of donating them to a museum, the farmer and a few superstitious locals had the boxes burned. It was said that four local people who had been suffering from long-term mysterious illnesses made sudden miraculous recoveries when the "witch coffins" were burned.

One of the most intriguing stories concerning an excavated object has to be the cluster of clear crystals unearthed at a site near a slate quarry in Corris in the Welsh county of Gwynedd in March 1985. The man who found the geode-like cluster of quartz crystals was a 24-year-old Gateacre man named Kevin who lived with his mum Jane and dad John off Hartsbourne Avenue. Kevin was an electrician by trade and when he brought the coconut-sized clump of crystals home, he decided to test them for piezoelectricity – this is a small voltage which is generated when quartz is subjected to pressure, and you will find a tiny crystal of quartz in most electric lighters which generate an ignition spark through pressure being exerted upon the tiny crystal. Kevin got the shock of his life when he tested the Welsh quartz with his multimeter because it was giving off enough kilowatts to power up the entire house. Kevin raved about this to his mother on the Saturday night of 23 March 1985, but Jane was more interested in watching Leslie ("Come on down!") Crowther on *The Price is Right* TV show. Kevin told Jane he had made a major discovery and that they could kiss electricity bills goodbye with this new geological battery. That night around midnight, Kevin went to bed, and his mother specifically recalls watching an old black and white Diana Dors film which ended around 1am. She then went to bed. Her husband John was working nights and not due home till 7am. At 2am, Jane awoke to a weird humming sound which rose and fell in pitch in a hypnotic fashion. She turned over and went back to sleep, but at 4am awoke, and feeling parched, Jane went to get a glass of water from the kitchen. Before she even entered the kitchen, the Gateacre housewife could see red light shining from under the kitchen door, and naturally wondered what it was. What happened next was to give Jane nightmares for months. Jane went into the kitchen and heard that humming sound she had noticed earlier, and she saw that bright crimson light was shining through the kitchen window from outside. That light came from two discs the size of dinner plates, and these discs had dark circles in them, so that Jane got the impression that a huge pair of red luminous eyes was looking in at her from the back garden. What's more, on the aluminium drain board, next to the sink, that chunk of quartz Kevin had brought from Wales was slowly moving along towards the window – as if some invisible force was tugging at it. 'Oh God!' Jane yelped, and as she did, the humming sound jumped up an octave and the 'eyes' beyond the window blazed even brighter – as if she had startled the thing outside. She screamed and turned – and distinctly felt something dragging her back, but she managed to run up the stairs to alert her son. When she and Kevin eventually tiptoed down to the kitchen, the place was in darkness – and that prized chunk of crystals was nowhere to be seen. Kevin never found the quartz again. He returned to the place where he originally found it and he dug with a few friends but there was not a trace of quartz to be found there. That same week when Jane saw the unearthly glowing eyes gazing in at her through the kitchen window, strange lights were seen over Gateacre, Netherley, and Halewood, where a row of red glowing spheres were seen hovering over the New Hutte School by several witnesses at 2.30am. Perhaps the 'crystal generator' Kevin unearthed in Wales was either of great interest to passing UFO occupants, or the stone was originally one of theirs, perhaps the source of their craft's propulsion, and they had lost it in Gwynedd centuries ago. The whole case is yet another local mystery which may be unravelled one day

PUNCH

It was 10.30am on the sunny Monday morning of 25 May 1964 – the Spring Bank Holiday – the day the McCulloch family of Wavertree were due to go to Blackpool – and 9-year-old Terry McCulloch decided to play a catastrophic game of "Chicken". He stood in the backyard of his home on Eastdale Road with his barmy friend Billy, who had a large empty lemonade bottle in his hands. Billy was supposed to do three upward launch motions before letting go of the bottle but he just hurled it skywards with quite some force. Now Terry had to decide: catch it or chicken out. He ran. The explosive smash sent Mr McCulloch, who had been packing Primula cheese-spread sandwiches with his wife, running to the kitchen window. He heard his son swearing at a laughing Billy as the two of them ran down the alleyway.

'That's it! Terry's not going!' Archie McCulloch bawled, and his wife knew he meant it. Terry had already had three warnings, and this was the final straw – no Blackpool day out for him - he was staying with his Gran instead, and she was a right old nuisance who was always sending her grandchildren on errands. Terry sobbed when he came home and found the door locked and everyone gone – and his Gran wasn't in either when he called at her house on Penny Lane. The forlorn boy wandered over to Wavertree Park and saw that a fairground had appeared overnight for the holiday, but he was skint. Terry figured he could still rob some candy floss from a younger kid and perhaps ingratiate himself with one of his schoolmates to cadge some sweets. He mingled with the kids and adults watching a weird Punch and Judy Show which was quite violent. When Punch whacked the policeman, blood squirted out his ears; obviously too red to be real blood, but shocking all the same. The kids screamed with laughter and the adults complained about it. 'That's the way to do it!' Punch lifted a sword and lunged forwards, impaling the policeman's chest, and thick red poster-paint blood spilled out the wound. Children laughed hysterically at the gory slapstick. That sword looked awfully real, and its blade was catching the sun, dazzling a morbidly curious Terry. The baby cried and Punch grabbed him and screamed: 'Go to sleep!' before hurling him through the backdrop curtain. Then Judy found herself on the receiving end of the first antihero of theatre when she said, 'You killed the baby!'

'Oh no I never!' Punch screeched back.

'Oh yes you did!' Judy lifted a little rolling pin, but before she could belt her husband he took her head off with the sword and a spurt of blood shot out of her neck stump and a little of this crimson spotted the dollop of ice cream in the cone of a 4-year-old girl standing too close to the show. Her bottom lip protruded and she started to whinge.

'This isn't funny at all, its rude and disgraceful,' complained a woman watching the tragic-comedy. Punch left the stage and the crocodile appeared – with the baby in its clacking jaws…

Terry did something no kid would normally do: he went 'backstage' - behind the red and white striped canvas theatre and had a look at the puppeteer – a Mr Rinstead - with his schwazzle contraption in his mouth, operating a footpump (to propel the cheap-looking blood) while his hands manipulated the crocodile and the baby – and there was Punch, sitting offstage on a ledge – smoking a ciggie! His beady eyes met Terry's, and he seemed to mouth the words 'Eff off,' and Terry went cold inside on such a hot day. This Punch wasn't a puppet, he was some incredibly small man – some 'freak of nature' as they termed such people in those days - with a weirdly unreal face. Terry backed away, afraid of the diminutive man in the red velvet gold-braided coat and candy-striped breeches. The confused boy fell backwards over a tent peg where a fortune teller had set up her business. He got to his feet, and everything felt like a dream; the swirling waltzy carnival music, a dizzy amalgam of carousel noises, the salty aroma of hot-dogs mingling with the sweet-smelling suffusion of pink spun candy floss, and distant screams of children spiralling down the helter skelter. Terry had moments of unreality like this, always when he was under stress, and he stumbled across the grass, back to the crowds watching the show. Punch appeared in a scene where he tricked Jack Ketch the hangman into hanging himself. 'Those are real hands! Look!' said an adult, eyeing the realistic hands of Punch as he wielded his ruler-sized sword. Terry caused a stir when he shouted: 'He's a real little man, not a puppet! Punch is a bleedin' midget! It's all fake!'

'Stop shouting child!' an appalled vicar told Terry in

a camp-sounding nasal tone. He looked a bit like Kenneth Williams to the boy with his flared nostrils, gaping mouth and outraged facial distortion.

But a few in the audience agreed with Terry about the way some midget was being passed off as Punch; it was wrong, and people moved away, a little scared, because that dwarf dressed as Punch seemed too small to be, well – human.

A rowdy girl of about twelve threw a half-eaten apple at Punch, knocking his cap off, revealing he was bald. Punch swore at her, using the c-word, and in a panic put the cap back on – but back to front. Terry clapped to the audacious apple-thrower and she smiled back at him and looked for something else to chuck.

It was now obvious that Mr Punch had to be one of the smallest people in the world, less than two feet tall.

'Short arse!' Terry shouted at the fuming puppet-imitator. The lad was showing off to that girl with the gawky grin who had thrown the apple, and she still hadn't found anything to throw at the elevated 'stage' in the booth.

'Language!' the vicar bellowed at Terry.

'Knickers!' Terry cried back, and ran off. The Punch and Judy show was packed up, and the critical crowds drifted to the other fairground attractions. Terry mixed with the crowds again and went looking for dropped coins, and when twilight fell, he headed for the park gates with the princely sum of three pence, hoping that his grandmother would be back home by now. As the lad passed between the enormous blackened sandstone gateposts he had the weird feeling he was being watched – and followed. He saw something moving out the corner of his eye, and he quickly turned his head – and saw him – Punch – minus his costume and make-up, peering through the bushes, watching him through the railings of Wavertree Park, and he held that little sword.

Terry ran as fast as he could but the doll-like man slipped through the railings, and for a diminutive person he had powerful lungs, and he shouted: 'I'll slit your gizzard! I'll dice you like a piece of pork!'

Terry shouted for help, but not a single car coming up Smithdown Road even slowed, and the drivers were probably ignorant of the surreal menace of a little man with a long-bladed prop sword.

'I'll cut your head off you little bastard!' the pint-sized psychopath promised, and Terry thought of Judy's head being lopped off and that spurt of theatrical blood from the wooden neck stump.

He was gaining on him, and Terry began to cry. He was developing an agonising stitch in his side, and it slowed him down. He would have to face the nightmare killer and try and fend off his thrusts with that blade.

There was a scream behind Terry. A huge Labrador had attacked Punch, and the little man had taken swipes at the dog, but its owner – a huge stocky man – was running towards his pet. 'What's that, Alby?' the man asked the growling hound. 'Is it a moggy, eh?' the man asked.

Punch, under the cover of the falling darkness, went into the retreat and slipped through the railings of the park, cursing the Labrador.

Terry called at his grandmother's house on Penny Lane and was so relieved when she opened the door.

'What have you been doing now, eh?' she asked,

seeing her grandson's eyes were red from crying. He told her about the weird little man masquerading as a puppet and she told him it had just been a midget. 'What do you expect, giving cheek to a dwarf like that, eh?' she told Terry, who tried to get a word in edgeways to explain the situation in more detail but his Gran talked over him. 'You're getting worse, and it's ever since you started knocking round with that Billy what's his name from Piggymuck Square [a derogatory slang name for a very undesirable area of Wavertree near Spekeland Road].'

No one believed Terry's story and he had nightmares about Punch for years. Then, in the 1978, when Terry was an adult, he was drinking in the Brook House on Smithdown Road on a date with a girl named Cherie McKenzie when he overheard two middle-aged men named George and Peter talking about the fairgrounds and shows that had been put on locally over the years, and one of these men – George - said: 'Hey, do you remember the Punch and Judy show with the little fellah who was done up to look like Punch?'

Terry literally felt his stomach go into freefall at these words, and then he heard the other man – Peter reply: 'Oh yeah, and do you remember the funeral they gave him? He was from Warrington wasn't he? I was working up there and we saw the horse-drawn hearse go by with a coffin which looked as big as a shoebox. Think he's buried in Warrington Cemetery in an unmarked grave though, so he won't be at rest, poor little fellah.'

This mention of the little deceased actor caused Terry to have some realistic and terrifying nightmares which he occasionally has even today.

STRANGE CALLER

One blustery March evening around 9.15pm in 2009, a 32-year-old bachelor named Leigh Jones was watching the TV over a pizza at his semi-detached home on Childwall Valley when he heard a heavy knocking at his front door. Thinking it was one of his mates calling for a beer, Leigh answered the door. Despite it being pretty dark out on this windy March evening, the smartly-attired caller stood there wearing sunglasses. Leigh had never seen him before, and said, 'Whatever you're selling I'm not interested.'

The man was about six feet in height, black suit, white shirt, black tie, black slip-ons, and a black trilby on his head. His complexion looked very smooth – almost feminine in fact. 'I'm not selling anything – I've just been in a bad car crash; oh Jesus, help me,' he said, in a curious accent which Leigh could not place, and the caller said these words calmly. Leigh felt there was just something *wrong* about the whole thing; people in shock have staggered from car wrecks in a calm manner, but this person just didn't seem at all distressed in any way.

'A car crash?' Leigh queried the claim. 'Where?'

'Over there,' the stranger lifted a very pale hand and

pointed in the direction of Score Lane.

All of a sudden, Leigh's best friend, Ethan, swung his car into the drive, and the sweeping headlamp beams from this vehicle shone momentarily through the sunglasses – to reveal the caller's eyes; they were huge and oval – almond-shaped, and in that quick penetrating flash of the headlights the eyes had seemed blood-red. This really unnerved Leigh, and he was glad his friend had turned up. As Ethan was getting out of his car, Leigh said, 'Well, shall I call an ambulance, mate?' and the man shook his head and said: 'Can I come in a moment? I'm really hurt.' The caller stepped forward.

Leigh stood his ground in the centre of the doorway and told him sternly: 'No, stay there, I'll phone for an ambulance – and the police.'

The caller in black with the creepy eyes literally turned 180 degrees and without saying a word, he walked off down the drive, bowing his head as he passed Ethan. The studs on his shoes made a metallic rapping sound as he strode away.

'Who's that?' Ethan asked his friend, 'one of the Blues Brothers?' and Leigh replied, 'Someone very odd, mate, hang on a sec,' and he followed the caller in black onto Childwall Valley Road. Leigh heard the sound of the man's taps come to an immediate halt – as if he had stopped walking – but when Leigh looked up Childwall Valley Road, he saw not another soul except for a young couple about 300 yards away. Wondering if the weird caller had hidden behind the neighbours' hedge, Leigh peeped behind it but saw the evening caller was not hiding there. Leigh turned and was startled by Ethan who was right behind him walking silently in his Converse. 'Where's he gone?' Ethan asked, as baffled by the man's vanishing act as Leigh.

'You've just come up Score Lane – ' Leigh remarked, his eyes still searching the locality for the vanished man.

Ethan nodded.

Leigh looked back to his friend with suspicion strong in his eyes. 'He said he'd been in a crash over there; did you see anything like that when you came up the lane?'

'Nothin',' Ethan replied, 'no crash – clear all the way.'

About a quarter of an hour later, Leigh and Ethan were sat in the lounge, watching TV at the Childwall house. The only light in the lounge came from the telly and some stray light filtering through the kitchen hatch, where the little doors were ajar. Ethan was eating the last slice of his mate's pizza, when he suddenly stopped munching and looked at the window with a puzzled expression. 'He's back.'

Outside, that same man in the trilby who had called earlier was peeping at Leigh and Ethan from behind a hedge. Leigh couldn't believe his eyes, and thought the stranger had to be crazy to think he wouldn't be noticed. Both men could plainly see the silhouetted form of his trilby, head and his shoulders because the sodium streetlamp was shining behind him, casting a shadow.

'Who is this guy?' Leigh said, glancing at his mobile, because he felt a bit nervous by the oddball's antics. Not many things scared Leigh, but people who were insane unnerved him; he knew that someone with serious mental problems could put a knife through him and then simply be ushered away into psychiatric care, while he'd spend eternity in the grave or in an ash urn. He had a bad feeling about this nut, and wondered if he should call the police, but he didn't want to appear afraid in front of Ethan.

'Go and have it out with him, mate,' Ethan suggested, his jaws chewing the pizza again. 'Might be one of those Peeping Toms.'

'Hey, have you noticed the security light hasn't come on?' Leigh realised. That halogen light, mounted on the wall over the front door, was supposed to come on when its motion detector sensed people walking by – but it hadn't come on and here was that loony lurking at the bottom of the drive.

All of a sudden that silhouetted figure darted at a phenomenal speed to the left – flitting up Childwall Valley Road. Both men swore at the way the man zipped away so fast that he appeared as a blur. Then a youth of about seventeen, who lived a few doors away, suddenly walked past, and Leigh realised that the sinister stalker had moved off because of this young lad's approach, and as soon as the teenager had passed, the shadowy figure reappeared at the hedge again.

'What the hell is going on?' Ethan asked, standing to the left of the window, peeping through the gaps in the blinds at the uncanny spy. 'He's back, Leigh,' he shouted, and from the darkened hallway, Leigh whispered: 'I know, I'm watching him now.' Leigh was peering at the suspicious figure through a stained-glass pane in the front door. The behaviour of the eerie stranger was really creeping him out now.

'Hey, he's not by my car, is he?' Ethan asked, losing

sight of the figure. 'Where's he gone?'

'He's just moved to the hedge on the left,' said Leigh, still in the hallway. 'I have never seen anyone move that fast.'

'What does he want?' Ethan asked, his nose nudging the blind has he squinted at the nightscape outside. Everything had that orange-amber colour to it now because of the light from those dreary streetlamps.

'Fuckin' hell!' Leigh yelled, and there was a simultaneous thud at the front door.

Ethan's heart skipped a beat. 'What? What?' he shouted towards the open door of the lounge, to the darkness of the hallway.

Leigh came shuffling in, his face white. 'That's not a human being, mate,' he informed Ethan. 'It shot from behind the hedge, and went up the drive towards me, whacked the door, and then went back to his original position by the hedge. Like a flash he was - unbelievable.'

Ethan let out a scream. In all the years Leigh had known him, he had never heard his friend scream. Ethan was screaming at something behind Leigh, and Leigh could hear a soft pad of feet in the doorway, and was so afraid, he would not turn around, because he knew that thing had now entered the lounge.

'Leigh! It's in! It's in here!' Ethan yelled, and he lunged through the blinds, opened the window catch, and threw the window open. All in one swift movement! He almost took the blinds with him as he jumped outside and ran to his car. Leigh felt the hairs on the back of his neck rise up as the figure in black walked towards him, and so he too got out the window and shouted every profanity he knew as he abandoned his home. He reached the car, and already, Ethan was sitting in the driver's seat. Leigh got in the car and it peeled rubber as it reversed onto Childwall Valley Road, narrowly missing a man on a bicycle who swore at Ethan and waved his fist. Leigh expected to see the man in the trilby emerge from behind the hedge of his garden and chase after the car, but he saw no one. Ethan drove off, intending to go to his home in Garston, but Leigh told him to go back to Childwall Valley Road.

'Why?' Ethan asked, and his cheek was twitching now – something it always did when he was really stressed out.

'Someone could screw me house, that's why?' Leigh replied, and he was taking big gulps of air between words. 'You can stay in the car, I'll face that thing or whatever it is,' he said, knowing very well he was acting the martyr.

'Tell the fellah next door – Bob, whatever his name is – you've got an intruder,' Ethan suggested, and he turned the car around and headed back to Childwall Valley Road.

'What's going on, eh mate?' Leigh asked, and seemed as confused as Ethan.

When the men arrived at the deserted house, they found the window still open and the March wind rattling the blinds. Leigh felt annoyed now by the unhinged intruder; if he was still on the premises he'd give him a good hiding or die attempting it. Leigh stormed the lounge through the window, getting tangled in the blinds and losing his temper as he thrashed at the blinds he turned the air blue. He was followed by Ethan, who had brought a lug wrench from the boot of his car to clobber the hyper-agile weirdo. The two men went together through every room in the house, and found no one, nor did they find anything missing or any signs of a disturbance. Ethan left at nearly 2am, and Leigh decided to try and sleep on the sofa with a carving knife by his side, but he only managed about an hour of sleep and nothing untoward happened for the remainder of that morning. Ethan texted his friend a few times then called on him around 8.30am. He then gave Leigh a lift to his workplace – Dale Street – where he served behind the counter of his cousin's newsagents. Three days later, Leigh was sitting in his lounge, this time with the blinds drawn and the main light on the ceiling blazing and the floor lamp switched on as well. Although he was playing Fifa with Ethan online on his Play Station, he still had the TV on in the corner – just to make him feel less lonely.

At around 9.30pm there was a knock at the door; a heavy knock. Leigh froze, he crept into the hallway and peeped through that stained-glass window in the front door – and there was his on-off girlfriend of four years, Emma. Leigh was glad to see her and quickly opened the door. She said she'd had a blazing row with her father; he had called her a layabout because she couldn't find a job and she'd been signing on now for nearly six months. Leigh told her to calm down and to sit in the lounge while he got her a drink but she went with him to the kitchen, talking incessantly about how she was headed for a breakdown if she stayed at home any longer.

'Stay here then,' Leigh told her, silencing her with the unexpected suggestion. 'I won't try any funny stuff either, honest,' he said, and looked as if he meant it.

'What? Stay here?' Emma asked, 'Isn't that cohabiting though? These nosey sods round here'll probably report me.'

'Oh come into the real world,' Leigh found a clean half-pint glass and poured foaming, fizzing Kronenbourg lager into it. 'No one's interested in anyone's arrangements these days,' Leigh assured her, 'we're all busy trying to survive ourselves.'

'How come you're being all nice to me, anyway?' Emma asked. She was nobody's fool and quite a perceptive person.

'I'm just being civil, that's all,' Leigh told her, a bit offended by her question. 'You're not used to civility in your house.' He went to tell Ethan he was ending the game. He then sat with Emma and thought about the strange incident of three nights ago but thought it wise to say nothing. He needed company now, and he knew Emma was terrified of anything remotely supernatural.

She moved all of her stuff into his place, and took over the bathroom with her Lush soaps, sulphate-free shampoos and conditioners, Japanese mud masks, hand creams, waterjet flosser, leg razors and Disney towels among other things. Most of Leigh's wardrobe now contained Emma's vast shoe collection and all of her dresses, tops and coats. All Leigh had in that wardrobe was three tee shirts, two white 'going out' long-sleeved shirts and some jeans and shoes. She hijacked his laptop and was forever on YouTube, browsing the 'make-up haul' videos and since she had arrived, she had made him change the bed-sheets and pillowcases after saying they were minty. It was a real upheaval for Leigh but worth it, and already he had forgotten about that creepy visitor.

Then a week later, Leigh was awakened by Emma shaking him as he lay next to her in bed. 'What?' he asked, drifting into harsh reality.

'There's someone in the room!' she gasped into his ear.

He sat bolt upright and squinted into the darkness. The walls of the room were pale, and so anything dark stood out, even though the only light filtering into the bedroom was coming from the streetlamp outside. There was a dark shape next to the wardrobe.

'That's your coat, isn't it?' Leigh asked, then rubbed his eyes and answered his own question: 'Yeah, that's your coat hanging up.'

But that coat moved.

'That's not my coat it's some man, ooer!' said Emma, and Leigh could feel her little hands trembling as they held his forearm.

Leigh reached out and switched on the bedside lamp – and there was that man in the black suit and trilby again, standing next to the wardrobe with his shades on. He did not react in the slightest as Emma screamed and covered her bare breasts with the duvet. The figure simply stood there, motionless, its head tilted downwards slightly as it beheld the couple on the bed.

'What do you want?' Leigh asked, getting out the bed. He looked for something to hit the weird and enigmatic intruder with, but he heard Emma let out a shriek, and when he turned to look back at the figure, it was gone. Emma was convinced she had seen a ghost of some sort, and Leigh still didn't tell her about his previous encounter with the mysterious entity, but his girlfriend was that afraid of seeing the figure again, she said she wanted to sleep in the car. Leigh told her the apparition wouldn't return but she persuaded him to kip in the car with her, and they hardly got a wink of sleep. Leigh was that tired by 7am, he decided to stay off work and slept alone in his bed while Emma slept on the sofa downstairs. Luckily for the couple, the man in black did not return and has not been seen to date at the house in Childwall. Now here's a strange thing: when I first heard of this account from Leigh, the story seemed tantalizingly familiar to me; I had definitely heard of something similar before. I spent a weekend looking through boxes of handwritten accounts and notes from years back, and then I found what I was looking for. In 2002 I received a letter from a woman named Sarah in Halewood. She had heard me on the *Pete Price Phone-in* talking about the paranormal and had decided to put pen to paper and tell me about a strange incident which had happened to her. Sarah clearly recalled the exact date of the unexplained incident – Tuesday 14 August 1984, and she could even remember what she was watching on television: *Play for Today* on BBC 1 – as well as the exact time she heard the knock at the door: 9.40pm. Sarah's husband Craig was working nights as a security guard on the university campus and was not due home until 8am, and so she nervously wondered who would be calling at twenty minutes to ten. She wasn't expecting anyone. Sarah opened the door, and there on the short path leading to the doorstep was a tall man in a black suit, black shoes, trilby – and although it was dusk, he was wearing a pair of sunglasses.

'Yes?' Sarah said to the alarming figure.

In a well-spoken but unidentifiable accent, the caller said: 'Can I come in? I've just been knocked down by a car.'

Sarah felt there was something quite odd about the situation and she said, 'Stay there, I'll ring for an ambulance.' Sarah then stepped back and just before she closed the door, the caller turned to look at a passer-by, and as he did Sarah had a glimpse of a very strange pair of eyes beneath the stranger's sunglasses. From a side view, Sarah could see that the man had huge bulging dome-shaped eyes that seemed dark brown, and these eyes did not look human at all. Sarah bolted the door once she had closed it and went to telephone the police. She did not mention the unearthly eyes of the visitor to the police operator but simply said a man had tried to gain access to her home under false pretences. About twenty minutes later, a car police car pulled up outside Sarah's home and two policemen knocked at the door. She explained how the man had called and had claimed he had just been knocked down by car, and the two policemen looked at one another, and one of them asked a question that sent a shudder down Sarah's spine: 'Did you notice anything about his eyes?'

Sarah told them how she had caught a sideways glimpse of the caller's eyes and that they had looked huge and domed-shaped. The policeman said there had been two previous reports of such a caller knocking on doors at houses in Halewood a few evenings ago. On those two prior occasions the strange-looking man had come out with the same story about being in some car accident. The police could not explain who the man was – or *what* he was for that matter, but they did advise Sarah to keep her door-chain on when she was alone in the house. She never saw the man in the sunglasses again but was always very nervous when she was alone and her husband was working nights. So there we have two remarkably similar cases (not including the two mentioned by the police) twenty-five years apart, both involving a strange individual with highly unusual eyes, wearing the same attire. Who is he and what is his reason for wanting to come into people's homes? These questions are still without answer, but there is another, more chilling question: could this strange entity call at *your* home some time in the future?

SMART ALEC

In May 1985 a poet named John Horngarth dried up. Writers sometimes get writer's block, and some of the most successful songwriters in the world often lose their creative mojo, but John Horngarth, a decorator (who saw himself as an interior designer) who hoped to become the Poet Laureate one day, had poet's block. He usually sat watching the passers-by at the window of a certain Bold Street café and studied the faces and postures of these individuals on life's conveyor belt. John usually had a knack of empathising with the 'Passing People of the Macrocosm' as he pretentiously termed them, and could almost feel their worries, their joy, their love, and their hate as they passed his window seat. The 18th century was all about the enlightened person, and the 19th century was all about science over religion. The Twentieth Century person passing the windows of the café was *Homo fuck-up* - a man or woman of many conflicting complexes, conditioned by the sado-capitalists to live in fear of natural armpit emissions and an empty toothpaste tube. Armpit hysteria had put a hole in the Ozone Layer and fluoride was dumbing down the population. These facts were fermenting into an epic poem as far as John was concerned. He felt he had truly tuned into this mid-Eighties *zeitgeist* and when he sat in the café window seat he would hold his pen like a divining rod and the words would flow like automatic writing, but since last Wednesday he felt as if his ship had hit a sandbank of self-doubt.

Sitting with John in the café today was Colin, his literary agent, and he was not impressed with John's latest doggerel. 'You promised me a poem for *Muse* magazine, and this – ' he ran his eyes over the blank verse attempt – 'is dreadful.'

'So you don't think they'll print it?' John asked in a broken voice, head tilted, peering at Colin sheep-eyed from under the brim of his fedora.

'Well, no.' Colin shrugged and the cheeks of his face rose, squeezed the bags under his eyes, and his forehead was corrugated; a grimace of discontent. He held his palms up as if he was about to catch someone, and tried to grumble, but he couldn't even get a word out. Then he said, 'Just a few weeks ago you were saying you had an idea for a concept book of verse that I could pitch to Chatto and Windus. And now *this*.' He looked at the pages pulled from the spiral bound notebook spread out on the table and said: 'I mean – ' and never finished the sentence.

'Ah, so what now?' John felt impotent, and a sense of panic was rising up from his stomach as he sat there. He could *not* go back to the 9 to 5 plane of existence after he'd had a taste of mild fame and full spiritual fulfilment in the poetry circuit. He thought of looking up suicide methods in the library, and wondered if the act of self-destruction would lionize him. He could also draw up a Will and leave his estate to his long-suffering wife Jill.

'I mean, is anything bothering you?' Colin asked, stirring his cappuccino. He then annoyed John by scooping the cream off the top of the coffee with the spoon and then licking that spoon slowly.

'No, everything's fine,' John said, averting his gaze from the literary agent's furred tongue. 'Just hit a dry spot. I'll be back to normal soon.'

'You usually just knock them out, John,' Colin told him, as if to say: go on, get back to the poetry writing, you just stick words on lined paper, it's not a Gore Vidal essay.

'I'll be back on form soon, Colin, sorry about this.'

A week later, John's over-tanned brother-in-law Lionel paid him a visit at his Aigburth home - with a bizarre gift from his latest Spanish holiday. 'I give you Alec Inteligente!' he said, thudding down onto his writing desk a weird plaster of Paris bust of a skull with a mortar board on its cranium. Engraved into the plinth were the words "Smart Alec". Lionel explained how he had bought the conversation piece at a Spanish flea market in Alicante for 200 pesetas. 'Smart Alec sits on your desk and gives you ideas,' Lionel chuckled, 'which is handy for budding Wordsworths with a mental block.'

'Who's been talking about my block, then?' John took a condescending sidelong look at his wife Jill.

'I haven't said a word, you paranoiac,' she told him, and she was telling the truth. She looked at the strange curio and didn't like it one bit. 'You're not keeping that on your desk, are you? How will *that* give you inspiration?'

'Well we've tried vases of roses and carnations on my desk and they haven't inspired me,' John sulkily told her, and he adjusted Smart Alec so he faced him.

'Never heard of a poet having writer's block, I must admit,' Lionel said in a flippant bouncy manner. 'proper writers, yeah, but poetry? I mean, it's just making words rhyme, isn't it?'

'Just making words rhyme,' John whispered, and held his forehead as he smiled. 'Here I am, pulling my hair out, agonising over whether I should use a semi-colon or a comma, begging the muse to help me put down my insights into the ironies and metaphysical nuances of life – and all along I should have just purchased the *Penguin Dictionary of Rhyming Slang*!'

'You said it, Dylan Thomas,' Lionel replied, and winked at a worried Jill before he left.

'Maybe you should write in the conservatory,' Jill suggested, 'you said you get inspired by the squirrels and the birds.'

'You know nothing about the mind of a poet Jill, and neither does your brother. He's a plumber; that Philistine can't take in anything beyond a dripping tap and a blocked toilet!'

'Don't be snobbish, John, it's not you!' Jill told him with a wagging finger, and she left his study in a huff.

As soon as the door slammed behind her, John gave a painful smirk and said to Smart Alec: 'Do you want to be my new muse?' And then he took up his pen and stared out the window until dusk fell. He watched the hair-thin crescent of the moon sliding ever so slowly down to the western horizon of suburbia's silhouetted rooftops, chimney pots and beeches. 'That's it,' John muttered, reaching for his Parker pen. 'The forces that move the moon and stars; the wheeling galaxies.'

But he couldn't get anything down on paper. He then did what every writer's block victim does – busied himself with anything but writing. He made himself a pot of coffee, listened to the radio, and dipped into a 1981 edition of *Pears Cyclopedia* and browsed through the Prominent People section while the unforgiving sentinel clock ticked on.

He looked up with tired reddened eyes at that draconian clock and saw that he had lost precious hours that were supposed to be dedicated to his writing. It was a few minutes past one in the morning. He vaguely remembered Jill's distant cry of 'Don't stay up too late. I love you!' and he hadn't even said that he loved her too. He felt so down now.

'John, do you want to be a loser forever?' said a weird-sounding voice in his Mind's Ear. John had heard strange snatches of phantom words and brief bursts of music when he was nodding off in his study on many occasions; that was all down to overtiredness, but this voice sounded too clear. He looked down at Smart Alec on his desk, and he felt goosepimples rise on his arms and a simultaneous shiver in his lower back.

'Yes, John, I'm alive, and I am smart, and I can teach you to be smart too.'

Although the voice was definitely in the troubled poet's head, it was obvious to him that the words had originated in that plaster skull with the black schoolmaster's cap on. 'Oh great, now I'm hearing things!' John yawned, but Smart Alec said, 'No! I am alive! Now, you really write for money don't you?' And John shook his head. 'No I don't, I write because I have this drive within my soul – '

Smart Alec butted in. 'And you also dream of being the big *I Am* down in Bloomsbury, being looked up to by the other poets, and you want the big fees and the ridiculous advances from the international publishers.'

John admitted he did want some financial returns for his work, but in a low whispering voice, he said: 'Money is not the sole driving force for my poetry, so you're not that smart, are you Alec?'

Smart Alec chuckled and replied: 'You're in it for the money, John, to thy own self be true. You can't lie to me, and you have no need to lie. You should have been a famous poet years ago, but your agent thinks too small. And, you need money to put yourself out there. You're not going to do that on a decorator's wages now, are you?'

'I'm an interior designer – 'John wanted to get that clear but the weird plaster bust talked over him again, and swamped his mind out.

'Here's how you make a thousand pounds a week…' Alec said, and explained the lucrative "Change raising" con-trick which only required a £20 note to initialise, and Alec told him exactly what to do, step by step, from asking the teller at the bank to change it, right through the distraction routine, until he ended up with ten quid more – and the teller would not even miss it. He went out the next day and pulled the trick at banks and many shops till he had £100. By the end of the week, John had amassed £1,060. He hid the money in a locked drawer in his desk, and he felt dirty over what he'd done. The con-trick he had pulled, the Change-Raising trick, was one of the most sophisticated routines known to the accomplished con artist, and it involved changing a quantity of money and changing it into an even greater quantity of money by confusing a person so they gave you more than they intended. This is accomplished by making that person carry out two cash transactions at the same time instead of just one, and even seasoned detectives will tell you that this con-trick - even when it is later explained to the victim in great detail - will rarely be understood. And yet John had pulled the trick off again and again.

When Jill had gone to bed, he unlocked the drawer in his study and browsed through all the five and ten-pound notes. Do I really need to worry about failing poems now? He thought.

'John, ' Smart Alec suddenly said. 'Put your little finger in my mouth.'

'What?' John smiled, thinking the thing was joking.

'Put your little finger in my mouth, John.'

John felt that Smart Alec - whatever he was - had a sense of humour, and he kept hold of the thousand quid in his left hand and he gingerly placed the little finger of his right hand into the half-inch black gap between the upper and lower teeth. Those teeth seemed to move apart slightly, and this scared John. He felt something grip his fingertip; it was like rubber lips, and they felt slimy, as if some mucilage was present.

'Oh!' John's finger was stuck, and he felt no pain, but blood was being drawn from his pinkie fingertip – he could feel his lifeblood being sucked down his finger, and he dropped the money as his hand grabbed the top of the plaster bust. 'Stop it!' he protested loudly, and feared Jill would hear him. He pulled his little finger out and examined the neat dark red pinhole just beyond the edge of the nail.

'Would you like to make a million, John?' Smart Alec then asked, and John, mesmerised by the promise of such a huge amount, slowly nodded.

'To make a million pounds, just take ten pounds and open a bank account. Then you simply -' Smart Alec hesitated, then said: 'Someone's watching us!'

John Horngarth's wife came into the study. 'I heard it speak,' Jill muttered. 'It's evil John, that million will cost you your soul!'

'We could live a life of luxury on that money, Jill!' John told her with a vacant look in his eyes and a silly smile on his lips. Jill pushed her husband back into his seat at the desk. 'No John! That thing is evil! I knew it from the first moment I set eyes on it! It's turned your brain!'

She reached out, intending to grab the bust, and she was afraid, and she saw the teeth move as it swore at her and threatened: 'You lay a finger on me you bitch and I will fuc – '

Jill screamed. She lifted the plaster bust and felt it move in her hands like a baby wriggling. When she lifted it, ready to destroy it, that plaster skull screamed and she saw a fleeting glimpse of red globular eyes in the black painted sockets. Jill smashed it on the floor. Blood, powder, pale white gelatinous goo and fragments of plaster went everywhere, and John Horngarth felt himself snapping out of a spell at that instant.

He hugged his wife, and cried and laughed, and then

in a garbled way he told her, 'I always said that you were psychic! Didn't I always tell you?'

Jill nodded, unable to speak because she was ready to sob. She had come so close to losing her beloved husband to that abomination in plaster.

'Thank God you *are* psychic! Thank God you heard his voice too!'

They went out to the hallway, and John went to fetch the brush and shovel from the cupboard under the stairs, but Jill told him not too. She didn't want him to go near the remains of that devil, but John said he'd be alright sweeping it up. When he went into his study, there wasn't even a trace of a particle of plaster or a stain from the blood he and Jill had seen spattered on the floor.

John Horngarth's writer's block eventually vanished, and he returned to composing poetry in the café window with a vengeance, but he never became the Poet Laureate, and in the greatest mental turnaround point of his life, he suddenly realised that he didn't want to be a part of that scene anyway. Years later, in the 1990s, John Horngarth and his wife were wandering around Quiggins one Saturday morning, when John felt a violent tugging to the arm of his mackintosh. It was his speechless wife, and she was pointing to a familiar plaster bust among a cluster of ornaments. It was a Smart Alec, and a girl of about fourteen was looking at it – and she had her little finger poking into its mouth.

'Don't do that!' John shouted to the girl, startling her. She withdrew her finger and looked him up and down with a scornful grin.

'John, let's get out of here,' Jill said, starting to panic.

John resisted her pulling and said, 'Maybe I should buy it and we can destroy it – '

'John! Let's go!' Jill yanked at him and he almost fell over. They left Quiggins and went straight home.

HARD KNOCK ANGEL

I've had to change a few names and details in the following story for legal reasons, but as far as I have been able to ascertain, everything described forthwith actually happened, for there are many witnesses to back up the testimony. Every story has a starting point, and this one begins one humid afternoon in July 2011 in a terraced house on Dovecot's Moss Gate Road. A man, just turned seventy, named John Stone, was coughing over the wash basin in the toilet of his friend's home when he spat out blood. He turned on the taps and washed the blood away. He wanted to ignore it, but he knew he should go and see the doctor. He had been getting a salty taste in his mouth for some time, and on such occasions when he had dabbed his tongue with a hankie, he'd see a pinkish stain. John eventually went to see his quack, and he referred him to a lung specialist. Tests were carried out, and John suspected the results would be bad – and he was right: lung cancer. John knew the day would come when he'd have to face the consequences of being a lifelong cigarette smoker, and a pipe smoker since he was in his thirties, and this was the day. 'How long have I got?' he asked, and had an urge to light up, even while he was sitting in the lung specialist's room with detailed X Rays of his lungs stuck to the lightboxes on the wall. The specialist, Mr Graham, went into all of the technical and medical talk, but John interrupted him and said, 'I just want an answer in plain English, Mr Graham; so, how long?'

Cornered by John's frank question, the lung specialist said: 'Maybe six months, a year at the most. It's metastasised, so – '

'And there's no treatment that might delay it?' John asked, squinting through his blue-tinted spectacles at the ceiling in a nonchalant way the specialist interpreted as the behaviour of a man in shock – but John was not your everyday man – not a man who knew panic, because of his background.

'No. Its terminal I'm afraid,' Mr Graham told him in a sombre low voice.

John Stone had lost his wife ten years before, and felt that was the only bizarre consolation in a way, because if Madeleine would have still been alive she would have been devastated by the bad news, and John knew without a doubt that his devoted wife would have wanted to die with him. But he had two daughters to tell - Natalia (who lived in Australia) and Holly who lived in Huyton. Natalia had two sons, aged 10 and 14, who loved John, and Holly had a 17-year-old daughter named Esmée, who also loved her grandfathers John and Barry, although she often argued with John in her early teens because he seemed to have a morbid fear that she'd become pregnant because she had a lot of boyfriends – all Platonic. Grandfather Barry was a little man, and a pushover as far as Esmée was concerned, but Grandad John was nearly six feet tall and a man with a hard reputation who was afraid of no one. So, John Stone went to Australia and he gently broke the bad news to his daughter and she sobbed in his arms. He made a strange promise to Natalia; he said that, if she ever needed him, nothing – not even death – would prevent him from being there with her. John stayed with Natalia and her husband and kids for a fortnight, then returned home to Liverpool. His other daughter, Holly, took the news of his terminal illness just as bad, but put on a braver face than her older sister. Esmée cried when she heard the news and ran up to her room, where she lay face down on the bed, pounding the mattress with her fist as she kept saying 'No!' over and over. John turned her over and calmed her down and told her to be strong for him. He made the same promise to his grand-daughter – he would always be around her somehow – always there to help – even after he had left this life.

Just before his health deteriorated, John visited his local priest and told him he wanted to make peace with his Maker. 'I did a lot of *wrong* things in my younger days, father,' he said. The priest told him no one was beyond forgiveness if they were really willing to repent, and John said a strange thing. 'I had a dream the other night, father; a strange dream it was too. I am not sure what your views on angels are, but I believe one visited me in my sleep.'

The priest raised a sceptical eyebrow.

'Well, this angel – and I couldn't tell you what he

looked like, but I know he was there as some powerful presence – he told me that as a type of atonement, I would be allowed back in this world from time to time, to help the needy – until I had earned my gold star type of thing, and only then would I be eligible to go to some state of Purgatory for a while, and then hopefully to the Good Place – to Heaven.'

'That's quite a dream, John,' the priest quipped.

'I have a lousy imagination, so I did not make this up, and ask anyone who knows me what my views are on religion and the supernatural, and they'll tell you I only believe what I can see with my own eyes – and I know that dream was some message from God, whether I or you, or anyone, believes it or not.'

The priest did not offer one word – not a single viewpoint – on the nature of John's dream, and this, to John, showed him how many priests, despite proclaiming the doctrine of the Resurrection and other metaphysical abilities, did not really believe in their own teachings.

John was cremated, and at the funeral, someone – some distant friend of John Stone – told Esmée that her grandfather had been a hard-knock years ago, and something of a criminal, and this shocked the girl. Many present didn't know about John's secret past, and thought it in bad taste that this aspect of the deceased man's life should be dredged up. Esmée asked her mother if it was true – had her grandfather been a criminal?

'Not the type you hear of now,' Holly told her daughter. 'He never hurt anyone; never mugged anyone or stole for from his own class. He robbed banks; tunnelled into them, but never used a gun.

Then came the strange rumours in the weeks after the death and cremation of John Stone: an old friend of John's named Harry said he had seen him standing outside the very building where his body had been laying in a state of rest at a funeral parlour in Huyton in the days before his cremation. The ghost had worn a flat cap, a black Adidas tracksuit top, and jeans, and he had been puffing on a pipe. But then John had vanished when Harry shouted over to him, and when Harry reached the spot where he had seen his old friend, he could smell the distinctive aroma of the tobacco John had smoked. More weird accounts of this kind circulated. A mugger had followed an old woman named May (who had been a neighbour of John) from the bingo one night, and the solid-looking ghost of John Stone had seized the mugger by the throat with gloved hands and had pounded the back of the cowardly crook's head against a brick wall until he dropped. The police believed the work had been carried out by a vigilante, and some heard that the vigilante had been the restless ghost of John Stone. A few months after the funeral service of the popular grandfather, Esmée was sitting in her bedroom one evening, reminiscing about John as she looked through her pictures of her and him on her phone, when she suddenly smelt that familiar scent of tobacco – the very tobacco her grandfather smoked in that funny-looking pipe of his. Just smelling this aroma had an uplifting effect on her. Then Esmée had an affair with a married man, and believed she might be pregnant. She got her best friend Rosie to buy a pregnancy-testing kit, and went into her bathroom with the test stick to use it. The result was negative, and Esmée smiled when she saw this. There was a rap on the door, and Esmée said, 'Come in.'

Rosie opened the door and walked in, but then looked past Esmée and said, 'Who's that?' before letting out a scream. The girl then ran out of the bathroom, down the stairs, and was about to run out into the street, when Esmée ran after her and asked her what the matter was.

Rosie's strange reply was: 'There was a man standing behind you in the toilet! And he went see-through! A ghost!'

'You're bullshitting me – 'Esmée said, understandably nervous, because Rosie was definitely not pulling her leg; she looked genuinely scared. Esmée asked her friend what the ghost was like, and Rosie's description sent a shudder down Esmée's spine.

'He had a cap on – not a baseball cap – an old man's cap, and glasses, like blue glass they were. And he had on a black tracky top – not sure if he had jeans on. Oh, and he had a pipe in his mouth!'

There was a pause and a slow dawning of realisation in Esmée's mind, and she said, 'Rosie, did you ever meet my granddad?'

'Barry?' the girl asked.

'No, my other one – John,' Esmée told her.

'No, why?' Rosie's eyes were wide, bulging, and she was looking past Esmée towards the top of her stairs, so afraid of the ghost coming down to her from the toilet.

'You just described him to a tee, 'Esmée said, with a sad look in her eyes. She realised that her beloved grandfather had been standing in that toilet, watching her conducting a pregnancy test; what must he think of her? She began to cry.

Esmée showed a picture of her late grandfather on her phone and Rosie's expression of pure shock said it all. 'That – that's him, Esmée! That's the man who was in our toilet standing behind you.' When the girls later went to the spot in the toilet, they could both smell tobacco, and yet Rosie's parents and older brother did not smoke. Esmée recognised the aroma though.

The married man who'd had the affair with Esmée suddenly telephoned the teenager and told her he could not see her any more, and when she asked why, he said: 'You should have just told me you wanted to end it instead of sending someone round to threaten me! Talk about an attention seeker, eh?'

'What are you talking about?' Esmée was puzzled for a moment. 'Who have I sent around? I don't understand – '

He hung up after swearing at her. Only then did she wonder if the person who had threatened her older lover had been her grandfather.

The ghost of John Stone was also seen in Sydney, Australia, where his daughter Natalia lived. Natalia saw his face reflected in her rear view mirror as she was travelling along the M4 Western Motorway in Sydney. She turned and saw no one there, but heard her father's distinctive voice say: 'Pull over now.'

Natalia pulled over, and seconds later a stolen high-powered car flashed past at over 100 mph, followed by two police cars. The stolen car clipped the side of a car travelling in the space close to where Natalia's car would have been, and the impact spun the car around, and the stolen car sped on, trailing sparks. Natalia's car would have been a few yards behind the car that was hit, and would have been knocked off the motorway with fatal consequences. Natalia sat there on the hard shoulder, naturally stunned at the supernatural warning she had heeded, and she suddenly smelt the very aroma of the tobacco her dad used to smoke in his pipe. Natalia's two sons also claimed they had seen their grandfather's ghost on Bondi Beach when they were swimming. He stood out because every single person was wearing shorts and a tee shirt, and he was wearing his familiar cap, a tracksuit top, jeans and boots. He even waved to the astounded teenagers, but when they went to talk to him he had vanished.

I have no doubt that a bond of love - be it between man and wife, a pet and its owner, or some bond between members of a family, or between the best of friends or lovers – remains intact, even after death. Too many times I have investigated and documented accounts where a loved one has made his or her presence known after they have left the physical world. Just think of all those 'funny things' which have happened to *you* over the years – those instances when you thought about someone you haven't seen in years, and you bump into them the same day or you receive a telephone call from a friend or relative you have not heard from in years after dreaming about them the night before. Some people dream of a person from their past, and the very next day they bump into that person in the street. Add up all of these strange incidents, and we see hints of a mysterious force which links us to those who we love or have great affection for. Some use the convenient word 'coincidence' – and perhaps some of these remarkable occurrences are down to pure chance, but not all of them.

I am told that the ghost of John Stone – the ghostly grandfather from beyond – is still being seen, still warning loved ones and helping those who need support and assistance.

THE SAURIANS

One humid summer night in the mid-1980s, a man in his sixties with wild-looking eyes, a prominent aquiline nose, and a shock of almost vertical Don King-style grey hair burst through the doors of a police station in Liverpool city centre and in a tone which could have been the product of RADA voice-coach, he told the young constable on desk duty that a 'deadly reptilian' was at large in the city. Feeling bored on such an otherwise uneventful night, the policeman airily asked the man - who gave his name as Jack Knight - if the dangerous reptilian was a snake, lizard or perhaps a crocodile, but Mr Knight grunted and slammed his fist down on the counter. 'Do you realise that our world is an open door to *them* because of idiots like you?' Knight almost cried as he spouted this question, and the constable's reply was, 'Aye-aye! Curb your lip dad or – '

Jack interrupted the caution with another thump on the counter. 'I've been hunting them for years, since the Sixties, and no, I'm not mad! I only wish this was all in my head! They look like us, but they are saurians! This city is crawling with them now! I've come here to report one of them! It's masquerading as some well known local entertainer in fact!'

'Oh God, I *knew* it was too quiet tonight – too good to be true...' the constable whined, and emitted a belly laugh when Jack named the local celebrity who was a reptilian 'infiltrator' in disguise.

'Look, Mr Knight, beat it before I nick you! Hear that? Beat it!' the policeman roared, and Jack Knight, self-styled Saurian-hunter, left in tears. The police deal with all sorts of cranks, time-wasters as well as sophisticated liars making bogus claims with an eye to compensation, and so we can't really blame a down-to-earth copper dismissing Jack Knight as a nut, considering his apparently outlandish claims. But let us now go forward to the early 1990s; the same policeman was now freed from his desk at the station and was out and about patrolling Liverpool at 2am on a chilly October morning when a lady of the night flagged him down on Catherine Street with a frantic semaphore waving of her arms. She seemed to have lost her voice for a moment as she pointed to a crashed Ford Orion which had mounted the kerb and impacted into a concrete lamp post. Then the woman gave a wheezing cough and managed to say that a man had staggered out the crumpled car, and his face had fallen off, and under that face was another face – a scaly face with huge black shiny eyes and a wide mouth of pointy teeth.

'What in God's name have you been taking love?' the policeman asked, but she swore she was not on drugs and said she didn't drink, and then she loudly urged the policeman to go after the 'thing' from the crashed car. 'It - it ran down there! Down there it ran!' she pointed to an alleyway, and so the constable turned to his colleague seated in the car with a slight smirk and said: 'I'm going to have a look; I've got to see this.'

'Well, there is a full moon tonight, mate,' said his

partner in the patrol car, handing him a flashlight.

The prostitute leaned into that car and showed the policeman seated there the St Jude medal she had fished out of her cleavage. 'I don't lie, alright? I might do some things which the law says is bad, but I'm very religious and I don't lie'.

'Alright, alright,' the cop in the car told her and gestured for her to back away and get her head out the vehicle. 'You've probably seen some guy in a Halloween mask.'

'That was no Halloween mask,' the streetwalker assured him, 'I'm not stupid; I know a mask when I see it and this was nothing like a mask.'

Meanwhile, In the alleyway, the constable spotted tiny spots of twinkling light about twenty yards away in the semi-darkness, and he walked to these peculiar lights and as his eyes got used to the dark, he saw a man's silhouette standing near the entry wall. The policeman turned on his torch and aimed the beam at the figure. It looked exactly as the prostitute had described; a human face hanging from a head with a weird inhuman face partly hidden by the dangling "mask" of realistic flesh. The policeman still advanced, thinking there had to be a rational explanation to what he was seeing. He came face to face with a nightmare; a man in a tweed jacket – but it didn't seem to be a real man, and his human face was hanging off like a mask, by sparking wires, and the real face behind it was – reptilian – that was the only way to describe it. The sparking wires had been responsible for the lights the policeman had seen from a distance. Unsure of what to do, the policeman froze, and the entity suddenly ran off at an incredible speed. There was something reminiscent of the way an insect suddenly bursts into a run when it's poked or faced with a threat; the legs did not seem to move like human legs but the limbs of something insect-like, and this really creeped the policeman out. All the same, the constable followed the thing, and when he turned the corner, he saw his colleague from the patrol car standing there. 'It – it went down there!' his partner said, pointing towards Blackburne Place, but the chase ended there because there was no sign of the thing anywhere. Just how the thing had gone to ground so fast was baffling.

When the policeman returned to the patrol car he saw his colleague sitting there, and he discovered that he *had not left the vehicle* earlier – so that thing had perhaps mimicked him somehow to throw him off in the pursuit through misdirection. The story was reported to sceptical seniors and a half-hearted attempt was made to trace the registration of the crashed Ford Orion, but the search only led to a man in St Helens who had been dead for 3 years. The car was searched for documents, and there were none anywhere in the vehicle. The policeman who had encountered something beyond his everyday experience subsequently recalled that night in the 1980s when the old man – who gave his name as Jack Knight – had told him about the "Saurians" – a word the constable had never heard before, and one which he looked up in his old dictionary at home – and the definition, according to *The Penguin English Dictionary* was 'member of a group of extinct reptiles.'

I published an abridged version of the policeman's encounter with the weird entity in the alley behind Catherine Street in my column in the *Liverpool Echo* and as a result I was very intrigued to receive several letters and emails from readers who told me about other alleged encounters with beings which bore a striking similarity to the "Saurians" I had detailed in my article. I got a letter from a woman named Millie in Bootle who told me about a strange story her late mother had often told her. One bitterly cold foggy day in December 1955, Millie's mother Jean was coming back from town on a double-decker corporation bus, and as it travelled past the Botanic Park and onto the bridge, the driver lost control of the vehicle on the icy road, and suddenly saw the headlamps of another bus coming towards him from the right. The bus headed for town hit the bus Jean was on and the woman was thrown out of her seat by the terrifying deafening impact thirty-six people from the crashed buses were taken to hospital that day, including Millie's mother Jean, who had sustained a cut to her forehead. While Jean was lying on the floor with two women – one of them a pensioner – on top of her, she looked up and saw a man climbing over the seats with a huge tear to his face, as if his flesh was paper, and through this tear Jean clearly saw green scaly skin. This strange man got to his feet and Jean watched him callously walk over injured men, women and children to get to the exit. When Jean later told a doctor in the hospital what she had seen he just smiled and said she'd been in shock. Jean told her brother and several other people about the man with the green skin under what looked like a mask made of cloth or thick paper, but her story was mocked and the same excuses – that she had been seeing things because of the shock of the crash – were used to explain away the strange incident. I also received a fascinating letter from a retired civil engineer named Richard, who read the account of the "Saurians" in my newspaper column. At around 2.20 am one morning in September 1989, 36-year-old bachelor Richard was travelling homeward to Ainsdale from Liverpool along Scaffold Lane, near the spot where the Ince Blundell Garage now stands. Two strange things happened at that unearthly hour; firstly, Richard saw that a car had broken down in front of him about 250 yards ahead, and as he neared the vehicle – a white Ford Cortina - he recognised its registration plate – it was the car of his former girlfriend Karlene. He pulled over and wondered at first whether Karlene was in the car with a boyfriend or whether she'd long sold the old car to someone else, but no, there she was with the bonnet up, shining a torch at the engine. Karlene didn't recognise Richard at first because he had grown a beard since he had last dated her some eighteen months back, but then she smiled with relief when she heard his voice. 'Can I help you there?' he said.

There was nothing wrong with the engine, Richard discovered; the battery was merely flat, so out came the jump cables from the boot of his car and he started Karlene's car via his battery. Once the engine of the Cortina was purring, the two former lovers chatted on the road, and Richard said he was going home after a long day attending a seminar on civil planning in Liverpool, and Karlene said she was returning from a visit to her cousin's house at Blundellsands. Karlene lived in Southport and was single at the time. There was an awkward pause in the conversation which was suddenly filled with the sound of raised voices and loud cracks. What the couple saw next astounded them. Something which looked like a man, only with a long tail like a kangaroo, came running from the hedge on the left of the road (which is officially the A565). The figure was in silhouette but Richard and Karlene could see that the strange running creature had webbed feet and strange hands that looked more like claws. It ran across the road, jumping over the low crash-barrier fence and crossing the central reservation, and as it did, the couple could see that the weird two-legged tailed entity had a greenish colour to it, and the body was devoid of hair; even the head was completely bald. The thing suddenly stooped, almost running on all fours as it crossed the second road and then it made an almighty leap of about twelve feet as it cleared another, smaller hedge, and bolted into the darkness of a field to the east. Then two men carrying rifles emerged from the same part of the hedge to the left of the road where the thing had come from. They wore dark woollen hats, jeans and what seemed to be Army surplus coats. One of the men was heavier and younger than the other, who seemed to be in his late twenties or early thirties. One of these men stopped on the central reservation and 'broke' open the barrel of what looked like an air rifled, to insert a pellet. He then aimed the rifle at the field to the east and Richard and Karlene heard a loud crack. The men shone torches into the field, and then came back across the lanes and saw Richard and Karlene watching them. One of the men, the older one, came over and explained that he was the son of a local farmer and that the thing he had been trying to shoot was a 'freak of nature'. The man said the thing had huge eyes that moved like a lizard, and had green shiny skin. It had been trying to grab chickens from a few farms in the area and the thing had been reported to the police but the authorities had never taken it serious. The other man then came over and backed up his friend's story, and he said that the thing was a mimic which would sometimes shout back phrases it must have heard somewhere, in parrot fashion. Richard and Karlene were very nervous at the sight of the air rifles and Richard said he and his 'fianceé' would have to be getting on, and wished the men luck in capturing the weird "Lizard Man" before he and Karlene drove off. Karlene went to Richard's home that morning and stayed there, and their romance resumed, albeit in very bizarre circumstances.

I told Richard that there had been several sightings of a reptilian type of creature quite similar to the one he had seen in places ranging from the outskirts of Hightown, to Maghull in the east, and the outlying areas of Southport – and even Preston. In fact the best documented sightings took place on Friday 16 May 1980, when scores of motorists reported what looked like a 6ft crocodile crossing the M55 motorway. One motorists even claimed to have run over the out-of-place animal's tail, and the police drafted in dogs to trace the animal, but it was never found. The *Sunday Express* and other newspapers covered the strange story and it was hypothesised that some lover of exotic pets had lost a crocodile but despite enquiries, the dangerous reptile had apparently vanished near that motorway. What are we to make of these reports of strange reptilians? Up until 66 million years ago, this world was ruled by the reptiles – the dinosaurs. Then some catastrophic event took place – some mass extinction, and the stage was set for man to become ruler of the Earth, but had that extinction not taken place, perhaps the dinosaurs would have evolved into something similar to ourselves; bipedal hunter-gatherers perhaps, and maybe we would have had two dominant humanoid species vying for the control of this world – the warm-blooded mammals and the Saurians, giving birth by laying eggs. There are billions of inhabitable worlds out there in space, and it is entirely possible that there will be reptilian-like beings on many of those worlds, some of them millions of years ahead of us in the evolutionary game. Is it possible that these reptilian humanoids could actually be among us, disguised as humans? It's possible, but let us also suppose that there are parallel dimensions – alternate worlds – where our history took another course, where the mass extinction of 66 million years ago never took place, and the Saurians lived on and evolved into intelligent human-shaped beings, then perhaps from time to time, these super-reptilian beings cross into our world…but that's a lot of maybes and what-ifs – perhaps time will reveal the truth behind the strange encounters.

NIGHT DRIVE TERROR

One summer night in 2000, a 50-year-old man named Terry was sitting up in bed next to his wife Janet at their home on Halewood Road, Gateacre, and he was trying to tackle *The Guardian* newspaper crossword. Janet put a bookmarker in her Maeve Binchy paperback, then placed it on her bedside unit, switched off her lamp and rolled over, facing away from her husband. She told him to try and sleep, but Terry was suffering from insomnia as he had a lot to worry about of late with the threat of redundancy and several debt problems hanging over his head. He put the newspaper on the floor beside his slippers, switched off the bedside lamp, and shut his eyes. He fidgeted; he turned, he sighed, and then he began to jiggle his right foot about until Janet eventually told him: 'You're not going to sleep, are you?'

His foot stopped. 'No,' came the muffled reply from under the covers, and then Terry resurfaced. 'I'm going to do something I used to do years ago to relax – a night drive – fancy coming along?' he said with great enthusiasm in his voice. It was a voice of the younger Terry – the fun person of long ago that Jan had fallen in love with. All of the worries of the world had kept that inner youth at bay for so long, but now he was back. But his eyes were still a bit bloodshot from lack of sleep.

'You're going for a drive at half-past-one in the morning?' Janet reached out and switched her lamp on. 'You're serious aren't you?'

Terry nodded and threw his legs out the bed. 'Jan, as you know, I have been restoring that old car – the Ford Zephyr – and I know if I took it out for a spin the drive would relax me. The doctor said I have to try and relax to get my blood pressure down, didn't he?'

'Yes, he did but, Terry, why don't you just read a book or do a jigsaw puzzle – or have a cup of tea?'

'So, I take it you're not coming with me then?' Terry stood up, hopped as he put on his pyjama bottoms, then shoved his feet into his brown suede slippers. He looked back at Janet with his droopy bloodhound eyes.

'I'm staying here,' she said, and shook her head, then reclined with the back of her hand on her forehead as she yawned. 'Don't go too far in that thing, it might break down.'

Terry bent over Janet and kissed her cheek, told her he loved her, and she told him she loved him, and he then went downstairs and got the keys to the Zephyr from the telephone table in the hall. Within the minute he was cruising along Halewood Road with the car radio piping out Mel C singing *Never Be the Same Again*. Already, Terry was relaxed, and all of his job and financial worries were evaporating. The Ford Zephyr, which Terry had restored almost from scratch as a hobby, was running perfectly, and he passed the old drinking fountain on the corner of Gateacre Brow and headed north up Grange Lane, where he began to actually yawn – so he wound down the window to admit some cool night air into the vehicle. Upon reaching the junction at Gateacre Park Drive, Terry went down to second gear and could plainly see that there was no traffic about, but as he was curving right onto the drive, an old white Triumph 1500 came rocketing in front of him and literally missed the bonnet of the Zephyr by inches. Terry screamed profanities out the wound-down window at the speeding relic from the 1970s. He then did a stupid thing: he gave chase, and did almost sixty trying to catch up with the Triumph. The white car accelerated and narrowly missed a hackney cab that was pulling out of the filling station. The driver of the Triumph then started to perform suicidal zig-zag manoeuvres between lanes and almost hit Terry twice, so he slowed down as he reached Barnham Drive, and here his senses returned; what was he thinking, chasing a reckless road-hog? He dropped to forty and breathed deeply – and all of a sudden, the white Triumph squealed to a halt about 100 yards ahead – and began to reverse. Terry just managed to swerve out the way in time as the car flew past him and screeched to an impossibly instant stop – as if it had no inertia. He stepped on the gas and tried to put as much distance between the insane driver and himself as possible, but that Triumph was already gaining on him as he flew along towards the Childwall Valley Road junction. Terry glanced down and with horror, realised he had not put on his seat belt. He wrestled with the strap and clicked it on, then with sweat exuding from his brow he watched the Triumph in the rear view mirror as it closed in. It was coming alongside, and so Terry slowed, but so did the vehicle giving chase, and now he could see the unbalanced driver; it was a woman with a mass of red curly hair. Her skin looked very off-colour, and at first Terry thought this was a trick of the highway sodium lamps. But as she matched her speed with his, he could now see that she was either wearing some weird mask, or she was not human, for her nose looked more like the snout of an animal. He turned left and went up Childwall Valley Road and then started to accelerate towards the Fiveways Roundabout. He felt goosebumps rising on his arms and the hairs on the back of his neck stood up as he thought of that weird face he'd just seen. He looked in the rear view mirror and the Triumph was so close he could see the driver laughing and throwing her head back. What on earth was she? Terry cursed as she began to tailgate him, and then, as he was approaching the roundabout, the fender of the Triumph made contact with his rear bumper. 'Stop it!' he yelled, but she rammed him and made him take that roundabout at nearly sixty, and his front right tyre sheered its walls against the kerb and Terry almost lost control as the sparking hubcap flew off. She rammed him again as he tried to get away down Queen's Drive Mossley Hill but the Zephyr began to overheat, and Terry detected the smell of burning with dread. He thought of Janet, and wished he'd listened to her advice about having a cuppa instead of taking to the road to relax. At the junction where Queen's Drive Mossley Hill meets Menlove Avenue, Terry mounted the circular grassy island and narrowly missed the ancient tree which has stood there for decades. He regained control and by now he could feel the old Ford Zephyr shaking. He coughed as wisps of smoke came from under the fascia, and still the unearthly nightmarish driver of the Triumph seemed hell-bent on driving him to his death. The Triumph moved in and now it was in constant contact with the Zephyr, and it was pushing Terry along at over 65 mph when Beaconsfield Road flashed past on his left. It all felt so dreamlike; Terry couldn't brake, or the Triumph would smash right through the Zephyr – and him – and he couldn't accelerate away from the car from hell because his car had lost power. He thought of jumping out the vehicle but knew he'd be flayed by the tarmac at this speed – if he didn't have his brains smashed out by hitting one of the many trees lining the route. 'Stop it! Stop it you bastard!' he cried, with tears in his eyes. 'Why are you doing this?'

Suddenly, he saw blue flashing lights in his rear view mirror; the police had seen him and were closing in! It looked like two patrol cars, but it was hard to see them because the mirror was shaking because the Zephyr was rattling along. 'Thank heavens!' Terry gasped, 'Arrest this idiot! Come on!'

The Triumph eased off, and Terry tried to get off the road, which was now Hillfoot Road. He did a stupid thing, but it was a dare – a do or die choice as far as he was concerned. He turned right, and drove over the central reservation – but so did the Triumph! The kerb hitting his wheels nearly threw Terry through the roof of the Ford Zephyr. The two cars screeched onto Springwood Avenue, and here, all power was lost in the Terry's car; it was now freewheeling and rocking violently, because one of the tyres had burst. 'Please don't let me die!' Terry cried over and over, and the white Triumph 1500 came alongside him, and he could see that the thing in the driving seat was not of this world, for its profile looked ghastly, with that snout and black bulging eyes. The Triumph bulleted off and the two police cars chased it – but it performed an impossible manoeuvre – it went *through* the railings of Allerton Cemetery and then faded into the darkness, out of reach of the police cars. The speechless officers examined the railings – saw they were perfectly intact with not a flake of paint amiss, and the rational men of the law stared into the deep blackness of that place of the dead. Terry came to a gradual halt, and he told the police about the sinister red-haired entity, but they never believed him; no one did, except Janet, and he never drove at night again. From the many letters and emails I receive from the public, I am of the opinion that the demon driver – whatever it is - still occasionally takes to the roads of Liverpool; bear that in mind when you're next driving late at night...

THE TAURED MYSTERY

In February 1971, a 27-year-old Hunts Cross woman named Juliet was being constantly badgered by her mother and two younger (and married) sisters - Marie and Frances - into meeting someone and tying the knot before it was 'too late'. The sisters both had children and Juliet's mother constantly reminded her that all of her friends were either pregnant or in serious relationships, but Juliet said she was happy being single; if she met someone, then so be it, but getting married and having kids wasn't the top of her agenda at the moment. The nagging continued however, with Juliet's mother talking about 'biological clocks ticking away' and Frances even cheekily arranged for Juliet to go on a blind date with a 31-year-old Whiston man named Blake Sutton, a driving instructor who had taught Frances to drive. Despite having grave reservations about dating a virtual stranger, Juliet enjoyed the blind date with the driving instructor, and she went on further dates with Blake. She began to see him more and more and by May she had moved in with him. At the end of May, she moved with Blake to Newton-le-Willows, where he set up his own driving school. In June of that year the couple went to Clarksons Holidays and succumbed to the travel agent's persuasive marketing patter and the brochure-blue seas of his glossy booklet. Blake and

Juliet decided on Alicante for a fortnight at a cost of £39 each. 'I can already taste the bean stews, paella and sangria,' Blake joked as they left the travel agent and walked out into a thin summer rain. A week later they boarded a rickety Dan Air jet at Manchester Ringway Airport, but when the plane was somewhere over Andorra, bad turbulence struck. Juliet was fine with the violent jolting of the craft, but Blake was looking in horror out the window. He said the clouds had changed to a bluish colour. The plane made a steady descent, and Blake clung to the arm rests of his seat and seemed to hyperventilate. 'It's alright, love,' Juliet reassured him, 'they must be flying under the turbulence.'

But it soon became apparent that the plane was attempting to land – in the Pyrenees! Now Juliet was gasping in fear too, but the stewardess calmly told the passengers they were coming in to Taured Airport – a place Blake and Juliet had never heard of before. Between the French Pyrenees and the Spanish Pyrenees there was a huge glittering and golden city twice the size of New York, with an airstrip adjacent to it, and Juliet and Blake could clearly see this out the aircraft window. Andorra should have been there, Blake estimated, and braced himself for landing.

'We booked a flight to Alicante,' Juliet told the stewardess, but only received a puzzled look from her as a response. The landing was perfect and the couple and about 120 other passengers disembarked into the Spanish heat, and the couple from Liverpool gazed in awe at the futuristic architecture of this city in the mountains – golden pyramids at least a thousand feet high, glittering mirrored towers and globes shimmering in the distance – but the most stunning object on the skyline was a gigantic replica of Rodin's "The Thinker" sculpture, which stood about a mile off, hazed by the summer morning mist. Blake estimated that this gargantuan statue was about half the height of the Eiffel Tower - about 500 feet tall. Why had he or Juliet never seen this wonder of the world before? To add to the enveloping mystery, spectacular blue and white delta-shaped aircraft also whispered across the sky, and some came to land on the immense landing strip in the distance. Even the hangars looked twice as large as any Blake had seen at Heathrow or JFK.

'Blake, where in God's name are we?' Juliet asked, clinging onto her boyfriend's arm.

'I've never heard of Taured,' he said, and looked down the line of passengers heading to a squat white marble building that he presumed to be baggage reclaim and customs. 'I'll talk to someone down there and see what's going on,' he added with a sigh.

'Blake, look!' Juliet yanked at his arm and pulled him to a stop as she watched the approach of three ominous uniformed men in black, all of them carrying firearms.

'These are not Franco's usual armed police,' Blake whispered to Juliet as he watched the trio of black-clad policemen with white helmets. These helmets looked exactly like the *stahlhelme* – the distinctive steel helmets worn by the German troops during WWII. 'Your passports please!' one of the armed policemen said in a strange accent that lay somewhere between Spain and France, and Blake, who was carrying Juliet's passport, slowly reached into his inside jacket pocket and produced what the armed cop requested.

The comrades on either side of this policeman watched the couple like a hawk.

'We're supposed to be going to Alicante, but now we've been diverted here – ' Blake explained.

The policeman scrutinising the passports seemed stunned, and he looked Blake straight in the eye without a trace of any emotion and sternly told him: 'You don't have permission to come here.'

'We didn't *want* to come here,' Blake told him, getting rather annoyed at this bureaucratic nightmare, 'we're supposed to be going to Alicante.'

The policeman handed the passports back to Blake and with a rude shooing gesture of his gloved hand, he told the couple: 'Go back to the plane! Go back, now!'

'Where *is* Taured?' Blake asked, walking with Juliet back to the apron where the Dan Air jet was parked. 'I've never heard of the place.' Blake waited for a reply but all he heard was the march of heavy boots on the tarmac.

'When did they build all this?' Blake asked once more, and he seemed agitated by the heavy-handedness of the paramilitary policemen, but Juliet, who was beginning to realise she and her boyfriend had somehow strayed into a place where they shouldn't have ever set foot, whispered 'Leave it, Blake, don't get pushy with these people, please.'

'Get on here and stay on here,' said the policeman, pointing at the airstairs leading into the plane.

The couple ascended the steps and both halted at the top of them to take another look at the breathtaking vista of Taured's skyline with the Pyrenees as a dramatic backdrop. Juliet noticed a sign on a hoarding near to one of the hangars which bore a huge blue disc covered with curved and straight white lines – a sort of symbol of the world globe, perhaps, and written across this in a squarish font was the word "TAURED".

The couple sat waiting in the jet for what seemed like an hour, and when the air stewardess appeared, they bombarded her with questions about the strange goings-on, but she said she didn't have a clue why the jet had stopped off here, and she claimed she too had never heard of Taured before. Blake and Juliet were the only passengers on the Dan Air when it took off. When the disoriented couple eventually reached Alicante, they enquired about Taured at the customs and were met with blank stares, and the couple later searched atlases but never found the place. I have collected many other reports of people who have glimpsed the mysterious nation of Taured, and it would seem that some Tauredians have occasionally strayed into our world, the most well-known case (among students of the unexplained, anyway) involved the arrival of a man (named Matt Lewis in some reports) from Taured at Tokyo's Haneda Airport in 1954. The authorities at the airport did not recognise the nation of Taured on the man's passport and detained him at a hotel near to the airport in case he was a spy. This mysterious individual had allegedly been interrogated about the whereabouts of Taured and claimed that it existed close to where Andorra exists on our current maps of the world – between the French and Spanish Pyrenees. The man from Taured was due to be subjected to more in-depth interrogation sessions to discover his 'true' identity but he vanished from a locked hotel room, and there was no indication that he had climbed out of a window or picked the lock of the hotel room door to effect his escape. It was as if the stranger had simply vanished as mysteriously as he had first appeared. There were other stories of strange Morse signals on the aircraft distress frequency spelling out the word "TAURED HK" being picked up at Haneda airport in August 1958 on the eve of a Japanese air crash in which a DC-3 of All Nippon Airways crashed into the sea after taking off from Haneda airport, bound for Nagoya. Among the passengers killed was a Howard Kriess, a businessman from Los Angeles. Some have mooted whether his initials – HK – have any bearing on the Morse signals picked up by the airport the day before.

There are many theories regarding Taured; some believe it exists in a parallel version of Earth where some city has been constructed between Southern France and Northern Spain, and that, under certain conditions – perhaps atmospheric conditions of the type which caused turbulence on the Dan Air jet bound for Alicante in 1971 – some dimensional gateway to the alternative world of Taured opens and planes fly into it. Some conspiracy theorists think Taured actually exists in our own dimension, but is somehow shielded from human prying because it is peopled by a secret society which is decades ahead of the rest of the world, and that the people of Taured are the real controllers of the planet – a bit like the fabled Illuminati. Obtaining evidence of Taured's existence – perhaps from satellite imagery – would allow us to make some progress on tackling a mystery which has haunted lovers of the unexplained for over half a century.

OLD SWAN'S BLACK-EYED CHILDREN

At a terraced house on Old Swan's Fitzgerald Road in September 1971, a 45-year-old man named Ernie was watching the television one evening around 6.45pm when there was a heavy knocking at his front door. Ernie answered it and his 9-year-old son Donald ran into the house in tears - and his hand was streaked with blood. The boy flew into the kitchen and put his injured hand under the cold water tap and turned it on. 'What happened to your hand?' Brendan asked his son, and Donald could hardly get his words out because he was so upset. He said he'd been playing with a 'cap bomb' toy on Prescot Road East when a gang of 'horrible-looking' children had chased him. One of the gang members caught up with Donald, seized him by the arm, and bit his hand deeply, drawing blood. Donald told his father that this boy and the others had horrible eyes. Ernie put Germolene on the deep cut on Donald's wrist and then got the first aid tin from the cupboard and bandaged the wound. 'Do any of this gang live round here?' Ernie asked Donald, because he intended to go and have it out with the father of the lad who had inflicted such a horrific bite to his son's hand. Donald was a very small child, even for his age, and the lad was quite inoffensive and trusting as well.

Just the week before a bully in the neighbourhood had robbed the lad of his sweet money when he was on the way to the shop. Donald said he had never seen the boys who had attacked him before and started to sob again – when suddenly there was a heavy knocking at the front door. Father and son went to the front room window and looked out and Donald shrieked: 'That's them!'

Three boys stood there – one on the doorstep and two on the pavement immediately in front of the house.

The frightened child then ran out of the house via the kitchen door, which led onto the backyard. A furious Ernie opened the door, and as he did, a passing neighbour – a Mrs Hammond-Davis – saw Ernie come out and shout at the children, and she noticed something which chilled her to the bone. Two of the three boys standing on Ernie's doorstep looked to be about 11 or 12 years of age – and they turned to look at her. Mrs Hamilton-Davis saw that the eyes of these boys, who she had never seen before – were jet black; their entire eyeballs were 'like blobs of melted tar', and their faces were 'white as milk' – that is how Mrs Hammond-Davis described these boys, which backs up the descriptions given by Donald, that they were 'horrible-looking' children. Donald ran all the way to his Nan's home on Derby Lane, where his mother Sheila was looking after her because she'd recently suffered a stroke. Donald told his mother about the strange gang, and she thought he was exaggerating about their 'horrible faces' and black eyes. However, when Sheila and her son went home to their house on Fitzgerald Road, they found the front door ajar and there on the floor of the dark hallway lay Sheila's husband – dead. The official cause of death was later given by the coroner as 'natural causes' but Donald thought the sinister black-eyed children were somehow responsible for his father's death. When Donald told me this intriguing story in 2012, he showed me the crescent-shaped scar on his wrist where one of the black-eyed kids had bitten him all those years ago. Donald never saw them again after that day and has no idea why they attacked him. Looking back on the incident today, Donald believes there was something satanic about the weird-looking children, and he is aware of the many other reports of the so-called black-eyed children in recent years in Britain and the rest of the world. Just what these black-eyed children are remains a mystery for the time being.

WITHER

Morgan's 50p Store was a very popular port of call to shoppers in 1980s Liverpool. As its name suggests, everything for sale in Morgan's cost 50p – and sometimes less too – and in the window there was a big sign which stated: 'Don't ask the price… Everything is 50p or less.'

Morgan's stood almost opposite Wades at 38 Bold Street (which happens to be a haunted address, but that's another story) and bargain hunters, cheapskates, lovers of kitsch novelty items and of course, the cash-strapped, all shopped at Morgan's, including a 44-year-old housewife from Knotty Ash named Connie. One afternoon in August 1982, Connie and her best friend Maude went to town together. Connie had on a pair of ankle-length boots which looked too big, and a pair of dark red stockings. It had seemed a good idea when she looked in the mirror, but now she reckoned she was getting some funny looks off other women. Maude assured her friend she looked great. Maude had to get a school uniform for her son at Hornes on Bold Street, and afterwards the two women called in at nearby Morgan's 50p store and Connie picked up a plastic pop-up telephone directory A to Z address finder with a graduated slider in the middle, and a shrink-wrapped pack of Smurf coasters. Maude bought a tiny trigonometry set – a flat tin containing clear-plastic ruler, protractor, try square, compass and pencil. Hopefully her son Eric would use it for his maths homework.

'Hey, isn't that lovely?' Connie pointed to an oval gold locket and chain hanging from a white plastic hook.

'I don't think that's for sale, Connie,' Maude told her, 'I think someone's left that there.'

'How could you possibly leave a locket on a hook, Maude?' Connie asked, lifting the chain off the hook.

'Maybe she's been trying some necklace on in here and she took that off and forgot about it,' Maude hypothesised.

'Don't talk daft,' Connie said, squinting at the locket. It felt like the real thing – 9 carat yellow gold, but Connie knew the manufacturers in the Far East could do wonders nowadays with their pseudo gold. She opened the locket with her thumbnail and saw it had just an empty oval frame – and Connie pictured the little photo of her husband Rod that would go in there.

When the women reached the checkout, Connie showed one of the women on the till the locket and said, 'That was hanging on a hook so I assume it's for sale.'

Maude looked at the lady on the till over her friend's shoulder and shook her head, then rolled her eyes.

'I can't see that being fifty pence,' the checkout woman said with a meek look. 'I think someone's mislaid it.'

'I *told* you, Connie,' Maude rubbed salt into her friend's wound.

'That won't be real gold, love,' Connie assured the woman, and felt so disappointed. 'I know real gold when I see it, I used to work in a jewellers.'

No you didn't, thought Maude, but said nothing.

'I'm sorry, I can't sell it for fifty pence,' the cashier told her. 'Someone might be missing this; they might have already reported it to the police.'

Connie wallowed in self-pity. 'Alright love, its okay, knew it was too good to be true – me finding anything…'

'Ah, it *is* lovely isn't it?' the girl at the till remarked, and she thinned her eyes as she looked at the locket close up. 'It's got a little drooping flower; aw, isn't that – oops!'

She dropped the locket and chain.

Connie stepped back and looked down.

The checkout lady got off her seat and searched the floor. Connie joined in, and so did Maude and a young male assistant. It was nowhere to be seen. As Maude was on all fours, the young assistant said to her; 'We can't go on meeting like this,' and flirted with her, then told the women how he was in a pub once when a gangster had flipped a £200 gold sovereign into the air to decide who was going to have the first shot in a duel. That sovereign went missing – just like this locket – and the gangsters finally left the pub, and the sales assistant then told his kneeling audience that the sovereign had landed in his pint of Guinness.

The locket was never found in the Bold Street store, and later that day, when the women reached Connie's home in Knotty Ash, they unloaded their carrier bags and Maude brewed a pot of tea. When Maude brought the cuppas in, she saw Connie sitting on the sofa, moaning about her feet feeling like 'two pots of jam'. 'I will never wear these stupid big ankle boots again', she sighed, and as she pulled the left boot off, the locket fell out of it onto the carpet.

'Oh my God, I don't believe it,' Maude gasped.

Connie was lost for words for once, and just looked at the locket laying on the carpet with its thin chain squiggly unarranged on the pile. 'So that's where it fell. What are the chances – '

'You must be meant to have it, Con,' Maude told her, plonking the teacup on the coffee table.

'You think so?' Connie asked, picking it up. She looked as if she had a little tear of joy welling in her eye. 'Ever since I was a kid, Maude, I was never the lucky one who found money or anything.'

'Well you've found something that might be worth something now,' Maude told her, and then she had a thought. 'You should go the jewellers and get it valued,' she suggested, and sipped her sugary tea.

'It might be hot,' Connie wondered out loud.

Maude almost spat her tea out. 'You've been watching too many American detective shows; *might be hot;* you're a case Connie.'

'*I* know its valuable – well, it's valuable to me anyway – so I don't need to go to Boodle and Dunthorne.' Connie undid the little lobster clasp of the chain, then put the locket on.

'Looks classy, Con,' Maude told her as she held her head back at a slight angle and looked down her nose. She always evaluated things that way.

'Doesn't draw attention to my cleavage does it?' Connie asked, and got up to look in the long wall mirror over the gas fire. 'I could get it shortened.'

'Looks perfect, Connie, honest,' Maude assured her. 'You going to put a picture of Andrew in it?' she asked, and gave a little laugh.

Connie's reflected face glared at Maude. 'Don't joke, Maude, these neighbours are nosy sods.' She indicated the woman next door with a wave of her thumb. 'She had the glass against the wall once; caught her when I was taking a letter of hers that had come to ours. '

'Go 'way?'

'Yeah, as I was passing her window. If she knew about me and you-know-who it'd be all over the neighbourhood.'

'So you'll be putting a little picture of your hubby in the locket instead then?' Maude asked with a mischievous twinkle in her eye.

Connie nodded. 'He's not bad, but well – '

Maude was honest with her friend. 'You can't make your mind up; I'm gonna start calling you Mary MacGregor.'

'Mary who?' Connie asked, jiggling and readjusting the position of the locket on her chest as she gazed in the mirror.

'Torn between two lovers, feeling like a fool...' sung Maude, reminding her of the Mary MacGregor chart hit from a few years back.

'Oh shut up,' Connie smirked and shook her head. She left the mirror, and went to close the door of the living room. She went to the window and closed that too. In a low voice she said, 'I'm not torn between anyone, but I know if Rod found out I was seeing Andrew he'd be gutted. I think he'd actually kill Andrew; I don't think he'd lay a finger on me – '

'He'd have to get through me first if he tried,' Maude said, grimly.

Connie smiled, appreciating her friend's words. 'I

should have just married you, never mind fellahs,' she laughed, then paused and said to her reflection in the mirror: 'But Roddy's not going to find out, and I told Andrew I'd only marry him if Rod had a heart attack or something and he's okay with that.'

'I'm different Con,' Maude began.

'I know, *you'd* tell Rod – but I'm not strong like that. I don't want the best of both worlds – haven't had a proper – you know – with Rod for a long time – but he loves me, and I love him, but I'm not *in* love with him.'

'We've been through all this before Connie,' Maude said, looking into the cup. 'It's all my fault in a way, taking you on that girly night out - you'd have never met him otherwise.'

Later that day, Connie found a picture of Rod from a few years ago. It was from a Polaroid snap and his face was small enough to fit into the locket. Connie cropped the photograph well so it was a fairly accurate oval. She put it in the locket, and felt so sad. Sad because she knew Andrew's photograph should be in that locket, and sad because the photograph she had chosen to put in the locket had been of Rod back when she loved him. She showed her husband the photograph and he seemed touched by it. 'Still love the bones of you,' he said that night as they lay in bed in the darkness.

'I love you,' she said back to him, and her throat closed with sorrow, because she didn't really mean it – not in the way it was supposed to be meant. She thought of Andrew. He would be with his girlfriend, Claire at this moment, lying beside her in bed, possibly making love to her. She had asked him to leave Claire, and he had said he would, but knew splitting up would break her heart. Claire was very clingy, according to Andrew, and was always telling him she'd had a nightmare about them splitting up. Connie couldn't exactly criticise Andrew for staying with his girlfriend because of the reason he'd cited; after all, she felt the same over Rod, only she also thought Rod would go on the rampage if he knew what was going on.

The next morning, Rod was up at 5.30 am. He was a tanker driver, and had a load to take up to Leeds. Then he had another job up there which would entail staying overnight – so he'd be gone for 36 hours. Connie thought she should call Andrew and meet up somewhere far outside of Liverpool. She was becoming more and more paranoid about the affair, and dreaded bumping into some old friend or acquaintance when she was with Andrew, who was ten years her junior.

Connie awoke at 7.30 am, and felt the empty space in the bed beside her, even without reaching out to it – she just knew it would be there before she even opened her eyes. She called Andrew at eight – before he set out for the school where he worked as a Geography teacher – and he said: 'Ah, yes, I'll get in a bit earlier then Miss James; thanks for telling me.' This was a code-phrase the couple had adopted which meant Claire was present.

Connie said nothing and heard him put the handset down. He rang her back at 8.30am and she told him she had to see him whenever he was free. He said he'd meet her in town after school – around 4.30pm, but Connie said she'd feel better if they could meet somewhere outside of Liverpool, and suggested the

Scarisbrick Hotel on Lord Street, Southport. Andrew said he'd be there around 4.45pm.

Connie boarded the train up to Southport that afternoon, and she kept watching everyone who was getting on, just in case someone knew her. At Formby station, a smart man in a tweed trilby and a mackintosh got on, and he sat across from Connie. She caught him looking at her over the top of the newspaper he was reading several times, and a worrying thought crossed her mind. Had Rod hired a private detective to shadow her? She dismissed the thought and recalled how, when she said the locket might be hot, Maude had accused her of watching too many American television detective shows. She delved into her coat and felt for the locket, then took it out and looked at it. She wondered what that drooping flower symbolized. She opened it – and got a shock when she saw Rod's photograph inlaid there, for he looked pale, and ill. At first Connie thought the effect might have been down to the old Polaroid snap being exposed to light; that it might have faded and gone off colour, but if that was so, how could it turn a smile into a frown? Rod had been smiling in the picture, and now he was louring and there were dark circles around his eyes. Connie rifled around in her handbag and located her reading glasses. She put them on and opened the locket again. Now she could see the uncanny change that had taken place in that photograph of her husband. At this point she was too shocked to link the gaunt, emaciated face of her husband with that wilting flower ornamentation on the front of the locket. When she got to the Scarisbrick Hotel, she showed Andrew the locket and he didn't take in what she was showing him because he was annoyed at her carrying a photograph of her husband around in the thing. This started them off on the wrong foot that late afternoon, but they soon made up, and Andrew somehow managed to book a room at the hotel at such short notice. They went for a walk along the beach, poured their hearts out and made insane promises of never-ending love, but every now and then, Connie would have the urge to check her husband's photograph in the locket, and would open it whenever she went to the toilet or when Andrew was going to get a drink. To Connie's eyes, the image of Rod looked as if it was steadily degrading, undergoing necrosis almost. She wanted to mention it to Andrew but knew he'd only 'get a cob on' if she even mentioned Rod. It was a night of joy otherwise, and they made love, and held onto one another all through the night, and every now and then Connie would drift into the waking world and think of that locket, and she also dreamt it contained a miniature skull.

In the morning, before breakfast, and before the couple decided they would each make their way back to Liverpool at different times, Connie said: 'I'd like a photograph of you. You have one of me.'

Andrew got up and went to his jacket. He took out his wallet and looked through a few photographs he had, including one of Claire, which he tried to shield from Connie but she glimpsed it and told him she had seen it. 'The only one I have – and I mean a recent one – is the picture taken of me and a group of teachers in Rhyl last year.'

'Oh, yeah, that'll do,' Connie sat up in the bed.

Andrew paused and gave a hollow, painful smile.

'Claire's on it – but she's right at the end so you can cut her off it if you want.'

Connie nodded, knowing that was what she intended to do. When Connie came home that morning at 9.40am, there was a knock at the door. It was Maude, and as soon as Connie let her in her friend told her, 'There's been murder here.'

'What?' Connie recoiled, knowing it would be dire news.

'Rod's been taken ill in hospital up in Leeds, Con,' Maude told her.

'Oh no – what do you mean taken ill? What's up with him?' Connie began to panic.

'They don't know yet, Con, stop panicking,' Maude told her, and watched her friend begin to hyperventilate. 'His sister's been down here on the bounce, wanting to know why you weren't at home. She said she'd been ringing you all night. I know she's Rod's sister but I can't stand her – she's such a stirrer. What's her name now?'

'Pat. She came down here? Oh my God – what-what did – I can't breathe!'

'Deep breaths Connie, come on,' Maude led her to the sofa and opened the windows of the living room. 'I told her that you went on a night out with your old mates from school, so you're covered.'

'I'll have to go and see him!' Connie tried to stand up but her legs felt tweak, and she sat down again.

'He's in St James's Hospital up there, and they think it might be a perforated ulcer. It just came on him yesterday, his sister said. She said he had to pull over – he was driving a petrol tanker.'

Connie swore and said: 'That locket! The locket's

done it!'

'What?' Maude asked, rather perplexed. She thought Connie was suffering from shock now.

Connie grasped the locked between finger and thumb, fished it from her cleavage, and opened it. She showed the photograph of Rod to Maude. Her friend's mouth slowly dropped.

'What's happened to it?' came the faint reply as Maude squinted at the almost skeletal face of Rod in the oval frame.

Connie pulled the photograph out and put it on the coffee table, and then she started to cry. She yanked the locket off, and threw it across the room, and Maude went and got it. She examined the chain and said 'You haven't broken it, Con, the lobster clasp just came undone.'

'I don't care, it's cursed, Maude! Get rid of it!'

'Cursed?'

'Take a look at that!' Connie pointed to the oval cut-out from the Polaroid snap.

Maude picked it up, and her eyebrows knitted in the middle as a puzzled expression formed on her face. 'Its gone back to normal now, Connie!'

Connie had a look, and she saw that her friend was telling the truth. It slowly dawned on Connie; if you placed a photograph of someone in that locket, they became ill, and this happened as their photographic likeness reflected that illness. Either that, or I am going insane, Connie thought.

Later that day, a call came through from Rod's sister, Pat. Rod had made a complete recovery and the doctors were now of the opinion that some rare allergy was to blame. He was so well he was asking for mash, onions and steak. More calls came through, and Pat eventually told Connie she was bringing Rod home.

A strange change came over Connie. She held that locket in her hand one night, just a week after Rod came home. She knew the locket had some power to slowly kill the person whose image it contained, and of course, Connie now had the photograph of Andrew with those teachers in Rhyl – and Claire was on that picture. In the dead of night, Connie cut Claire out the picture and placed her in the locket, and then she went to bed, and she became strangely aroused by what she was doing and made love to Rod the way she did so many years ago. He noticed the peculiar change in his wife's personality; not just the sexual side, but the way she began to go on about the moon being full and there was something strange in the way she looked at him – it was her eyes – they seemed to have darkened. He asked if she was wearing some eye-make up, but she just slowly shook her head. Connie heard about Claire's sudden illness on the third day after she had put the young woman's picture in that locket. Andrew could hardly get his words out when he called her because he was sobbing.

'If she dies, though, you'll be *all* mine,' she told him.

'What a horrible thing to say,' Andrew said, all choked up, and he slammed the telephone down on her.

Maude saw the locket on her friend when she visited one day, and asked to see it. She had a strange feeling about it forming in her mind.

'No,' Connie told her bluntly, and that was so out of character for her to talk like that to Maude.

'Connie, what's going on?' Maude asked, facing her

squarely.

'Nothing, beat it, go on.'

'Connie, I know you better than you know yourself, girl, now let's have a look at that locket."

'No,' Connie backed away from her into the kitchen – towards the cutlery drawer.

'Connie, something's happened to you since you started wearing that thing, and I want my old friend back.'

'Maude, get out of my house,' Connie told her, and felt for the drawer. She opened it and then turned, intending to get a knife, but Maude was upon her in a flash and she ripped the locket off her. Connie cried like a baby and followed her around the kitchen saying: 'I want it back! It's mine!'

'Go and sit down in there!' Maude stood in front of the cutlery drawer and pointed through the doorway of the kitchen to the living room, but Connie's eyes bulged and she kept looking at the locket. Maude pushed her friend back so hard, Connie fell onto the floor, and before she could get up, Maude was out of the house. She went into her own house and locked the door, and then she opened the locket and saw the ghastly picture of a white face with eyes sunken deep within the skull sockets. The face was so withered it was hard to tell its sex. Maude took the photograph of the horrid face out of the locket and put it on the laminate worktop in the kitchen. As Connie hammered on the front door knocker, Maude watched the photograph of the wasted face slowly return to a flesh colour. The dark circles around the eyes faded and after about a minute or so, Maude could clearly see this was a young lady – and she guessed who it was –

Claire.

Maude grabbed her coat and her purse and she sneaked out of the house through the backyard door and hailed a Hackney cab at the East Prescot Road End of Thomas Lane. She told the cabby to take her to the Pier Head, and there, on the landing stage, Maude pitched the accursed locket into the river. She had the weird sensation that something had been watching her when she had cast that malign piece of jewellery into the waters, and Maude sensed that the something watching her was very angry at her actions.

Andrew stopped seeing Connie not long after this, and Connie was heartbroken at first, but then a tectonic shift in her way of looking at life took place, and she actually realised she loved Rod. A week before Christmas that year, Connie and Maude were once again on Bold Street after they had both managed to get most of their Christmas shopping done. The women went into Morgan's and remembered the last visit when they had come across that weird locket. When they reached the aisle where they had found it, Connie and Maude could not believe their eyes, because there it was again. It could have been a mere replica, but somehow the women knew that this was not so, but how could a locket that had been cast onto the bed of the Mersey be here now, on that same white hook?

Connie and Maude turned, and they put baskets down which contained just a few items, and they walked out Morgan's 50p Store, never to return again.

EVERYWHERE ERIC

He came into the city centre pub that infernal day in June 1964 in a white vest, stubble-faced, wearing a crisp white cotton captain's cap with the black peak, yellow braiding and embroidered badge - supposedly given to him by the captain of the *Reina del Mar* passenger liner. In his mouth he sucked on a Havana cadged off Castro, and in his hands he held what seemed like a little grey dog with huge ears, big black expressive eyes and a very long tail which dangled from the blanket it was swathed in. It was a joey – a baby kangaroo – for the barmaid Julia. She thought it was a dog – till she saw the big hind legs. 'Oh Eric, how am I going to rear a kangaroo?' she asked as he thrust the marsupial into her arms. 'His mother was killed by hunters for meat, but this little fellah got away. Found him hiding in the bush. You can be his new old lady,' said "Everywhere Eric" as he was known – a man who said he could travel anywhere on earth – without going by land, air or sea – but just how this was achieved, he would not say. He'd been keeping up this 'act' for years, and while some said he was a canny hoaxer, others said they had bumped into him on their holidays, in places ranging from Cornwall to Canberra, and these encounters were often quite strange, because he was sometimes seen in two places widely separated within a day, and a case in point was the time, in January 1963, when a Mr and Mrs Richards of Litherland bumped into him in a sweltering Sydney during a fortnight's holiday Down Under. They wrote about the encounter with Eric in a postcard sent back to Liverpool, but the next day, Eric – or someone who was his exact double in sound and appearance – was encountered by the Joneses, a Liverpool family enjoying a skiing holiday in Switzerland. When Mr Jones later told Mr Richards about his encounter with Eric, Mr Richards said it was impossible, as he had met him Australia the day before.

Marty and Vic, two regulars at the pub, took great delight in catching out all of the liars and spinners of tall tales who frequented the pub over the years, and when they heard about the far-fetched stories concerning Everywhere Eric, they vowed to trip him up. Now, on this July afternoon, they had their chance.

Eric went to the toilet, and while he was gone, Vic said out loud: 'Has he gone to the khazi or will he return from Africa with a Zulu?'

No one thought the remark was funny, and Mr Richards approached the bar and tapped Vic's elbow.

'I *did* see him in Sydney though, Vic,' Mr Richards told the sceptic.

'You saw *someone* who looked like him,' Vic said, shaking his head and exhaling Woodbine smoke from his nostrils, 'why, he might even have a twin brother who's in on all this rubbish.'

'I saw him in New York,' an old man chipped in from the end of the bar counter. 'Saw him there in Times Square, as plainly as I see you now,' he pointed to Vic.

'So? What's so strange about that?' Marty – Vic's friend – asked.

'That day, he was seen in this pub, and they all vouched for it. Ask Julia or him – ' the old man pointed his pipe at the barman.

'Well you've been mistaken, dad,' Vic said without even looking at the old man. 'If you weren't mistaken, then they were mistaken in here. People make a mystery out of nothing. You can explain any mystery if you dig deep enough.'

'I'm not a liar,' the old man seemed annoyed at Vic's dismissal of his claim, 'I saw him in New York.'

Vic shook his head and stubbed out the Woodbine in the big black ashtray on the counter. He turned to face the old man. 'It takes about five days – sometimes longer – to sail from here to New York. The fastest they've ever done it is about 3 days, and they won the Blue Riband for that. Now, even if Eric went by plane, there is no way he could be in Times Square and a pub in Liverpool over three thousand miles away, is there? Unless he hopped onto a flying saucer!'

'He's back,' Marty whispered to Vic out the corner of his mouth as Eric returned from the toilet.

'You're a Doubting Thomas, sir,' the old man told Vic – who gestured for him to be quiet by placing his forefinger to his lips. Vic then walked around the corner, to a quiet part of the pub, and asked the barman if he had an envelope and a piece of paper.

'What for?' the barman asked, bemused.

'I need to send an important message to someone,' Vic told him, and offered him half a crown.

'Stop splashing your money around' the barman joked to Vic. 'What are you having?'

'Pint of bitter – and keep the change.' Vic seemed so serious all of a sudden. 'Oh, and have you got a pen as well?'

'I'll get you a writing bureau as well if you want,' said the barman, and he refused the change from the transaction and placed it in Vic's palm. He then went upstairs and returned with a writing pad, a biro and a little manila envelope. Vic thanked him and went to the toilet to write a little letter. He returned a few minutes later and took his pint round to the busy end of the bar, where Eric was regaling the drinkers with some story about an adventure in Brazil.

Julia interrupted the story, saying she was going home with the little kangaroo, who was becoming a bit of a handful. She was going to give him to her brother, a farmer up in Knowsley, because he'd have the space to rear the little thing. She kissed Eric and left.

'What happened to you?' Vic asked, nodding to the bandage on Eric's right upper arm.

'Alligator nipped me in the Florida Keys last week. My own fault for taking a short cut through a swamp when I was palatic,' was Eric's causal reply, and he delved into his pocket and produced pesetas, a dollar bill, a silver Japanese 100 Yen coin, a 25 kronur note from Iceland – anything but English money.

'Let me get you one,' Vic sneered, 'Younger's Tartan isn't it?' he asked, and Eric nodded. Vic asked the barman to line up this round and then he stood there with Marty and Everywhere Eric and produced an envelope. 'How soon can you get to New York?' he asked Eric.

'Tomorrow – sooner if it's urgent, why?' Eric replied.

Marty stifled a chuckle. This fellah's an absolute nut, he thought, but said nothing. He knew that this would be the day he and Vic caught Everywhere Eric out.

'Ever heard of McSorley's bar?' Vic enquired and Eric nodded and said, 'Was only in there a fortnight back with a friend of the late President.'

Vic smiled. 'Really? The joint's on East 7th Street, Manhattan, as I'm sure you know. You are to deliver this letter to Mr Antonio, he's a big noise in a certain Italian organisation. He's expecting this letter so don't let me down, or er,' and Vic did a cut throat gesture with his middle finger. 'Mr Antonio doesn't suffer fools gladly Eric, so you *will* get it to him, won't you?'

'Yeah, of course, if he's there,' said Eric. 'What do you mean an organisation?'

'You don't need to know, Eric,' Vic told him, 'you just make sure he gets the letter or he's going to be pretty upset.'

'What's in this letter, Vic?' Marty asked, spouting rehearsed lines, and Vic said it was an invitation for Mr Antonio to get a piece of the action in a dockside racket that would make millions for the 'boys on both sides of the pond'. Vic then told Eric: 'It's all above board, like.'

Eric then drank up, left with the letter, and Marty and Vic burst into laughter; Vic explained the prank to the barman. 'There's no Mr Antonio. There is a McSorley's bar, like, because I went there once when I was in the Merchant Navy, so I added that to make it seem more genuine.'

'I don't get the point of this joke though,' the Barman admitted.

Marty told him. 'Eric's a nut, that's the point. We know he doesn't go as far as New Brighton, never mind New York. We've called his bluff. He'll either come back with some cock and bull story about his encounter with Mr Antonio, or he might never show his face in here again because he won't admit he couldn't deliver the letter.'

'You two have been drinking in the Spanish House too long!' the barman said, rolling his heavy-lidded eyes, and he went to clean some glasses.

A fortnight later, five tall sharply-dressed Americans arrived at the pub. They asked for Vic, and Julia pointed to the pale-faced man cowering in the corner. The men walked over to him.

'Mr Antonio sent me,' said the American, offering his hand to a trembling Vic, 'I hear you have a business proposal.'

BEYOND EXPLANATION

The following collection of stories is but a small selection from a folder in my study which is labelled 'Beyond Explanation'. They are accounts of strange incidents and baffling phenomena which I have looked at from every conceivable angle in an effort to try and explain them. Perhaps a fresh pair of eyes and a different kind of mind can make a breakthrough with some of the mysteries presented here; maybe *you* can crack some of them.

Let's start with this old chestnut. Around 3 am on the Thursday morning of 31 March, 1977, a couple in their forties – George and Bridget - of Birch Road, Huyton, were having a heated argument about where to go on their holidays in April. George wanted to go to Alicante again, and Bridget was determined to holiday in Torquay, and George ended up storming out of his home in his pyjamas, yanking his harlequin poodle Daisy with him on its leash.

Bridget caught up with sulky George at McGoldrick Park, where something resembling a cat-sized rat with a polka-dot coat approached Daisy. Bridget gasped, stunned at the weird creature, and George, who had a phobia of rats – screamed unashamedly. A spectacled man in his sixties in a flat cap and a dark blue boiler suit approached, and years later, considering this man with hindsight, the couple realised that he was a dead ringer for the famous TV steeplejack, Fred Dibnah, both in looks and also in the clothes the stranger wore, because Dibnah usually wore a boiler suit, flat cap, and he also wore similar spectacles. Moreover, this stranger in McGoldrick Park also *sounded* like Dibnah (who had a Bolton accent). The man in the cap picked up the oversized "rat" and turned to walk towards something in a clearing. George and Bridget initially thought the big circular structure was the part of some fairground ride – perhaps the stripped-back hub of a Merry-Go-Round, but as the couple got nearer to the thing, they were astonished to see that it was a huge flying saucer on four legs – about sixty feet in diameter, and it had a union jack on the hull. 'What in God's name?' George said in amazement.

There was a hatchway in the curved underside of this craft, with a ladder leading from it. The man whistled as he went up this ladder into the saucer. Curiosity got the better of Bridget and George and they peeped into the hatchway. The man in the boiler suit introduced himself as Geoff in a Bolton accent, and warned the couple to get well away because he was taking off soon. George thought it was all a joke and asked if he could 'come aboard' what had to be some mock-up of a spaceship. Geoff seemed very annoyed at George's sceptical smirk and said, 'Come on then lad - and you lass.'

Bridget reluctantly ascended the ladder holding Daisy and she saw the polka-dot rodent in a cage.

Geoff nodded to him and said, 'That there's Barry, a Tiger quoll; picked him up Down Under.'

'Have you been to the moon yet?' George joked, and the hatchway was sealed by a whirring electric door. George thought that the spaceship would jolt about to give the impression of take off, just like the flight simulators often found in today's fairgrounds on their hydraulic legs.

Bridget felt her ears pop as the interior became pressurised, and she nervously urged George to come home with her. Then she said to Geoff: 'Well, we'll be going home now, I think.'

George laughed because Geoff never heard a word she said because he was so engrossed in strapping himself into a chair in a cockpit of some sort that was crammed with all sorts of dials, knobs, levers and red, green and yellow lights.

'Hold tight, Bridget, we're going to Mars!' George laughed.

In a low serious-sounding voice Geoff spoke into a microphone jutting from a control panel and his amplified voice emanated from a speaker grill by Bridget. Geoff's relayed question was: 'Where do you fancy going on *this* planet?'

'Let's go, George,' Bridget thought the man was unbalanced, but her husband called Geoff's bluff and quipped: 'Torquay would be fine.'

'Where was that, lad?' Geoff asked, via the intercom.

'Torquay? You know, that place on the coast of Devon?' George said, laying back with his hands behind his head. This game of charades had really cheered him up after that big argument with Bridget.

Everything shook, and Bridget screamed as a

tremendous g-force pushed her and George into the floor. Daisy yelped. The couple could feel the so-called 'fairground spaceship' thrumming, and their stomachs turned from a sensation of rocketing skywards.

Geoff laughed and said he had built the ship with money from a Pools win a few years back. He rambled via the intercom about being a self-taught engineer, and in some technical detail he discussed fuel cells, gyroscopes that rotated at the speed of sound and cancelled out gravity, and how the Ministry of Defence wanted his creation for military purposes. Bridget was hugging Daisy, and George was gripping his wife's ankle as he lay pinned down by the crushing inertia. He said his wife's name over and over again, and he thought the thing he was travelling in was going to crash. He and Bridget could not tell which way was up and which way was down; they felt completely disoriented and ill with acute motion sickness. And then at one point the couple and their dog floated up off the floor as they all experienced weightlessness.

'Whoo hoo!' Geoff cried through the intercom speaker during this taste of zero gravity. Then Bridget and George heard a loud buzzer sound and a red light in the ceiling flash on and off.

The parabolic trajectory of the ship brought it down fifteen minutes later, 200 miles away from Liverpool, on the green of the Torquay Bowling Club. As soon as the hatch door swung open, George and Bridget quickly vacated the vehicle with the poodle. George was violently sick behind a hedge, and Bridget felt as queasy but managed not to throw up. The poor poodle Daisy couldn't stop shaking.

The urban spaceman in the flat cap came down the

ladder, and laughed, then announced: 'This is Torquay. If you want to go home let me know now, or stay here, it's up to you.'

The couple backed away and watched the incredible Boltonian ascend the ladder into his home-made flying saucer in a very sprightly manner. George and Bridget hugged one another with Daisy squashed into Bridget's bosom as they watched the saucer rise silently off the ground. It's legs withdrew into its underside and within a minute it had climbed into the starry sky, where it was soon lost to sight. The disoriented couple found a police station but the story wasn't believed – especially with April Fool's Day so near. Years later, in the 1980s, George volunteered to have himself hypnotised by a professional hypnotherapist at a Rodney Street clinic after telling a specialist about the 1977 encounter. The hypnotherapist had recently used hypnosis on George to stop him smoking, and this so impressed George, he wondered if the hypnotist could regress him to explore his memory of that night in the flying saucer. When George was regressed, he saw that "Geoff" was not human at all, but some eerie grey-skinned entity in a dark blue one-piece suit. This weird being had a large globular head and massive black eyes. The creature that Geoff had called Barry (claiming it was a Tiger quoll) was some metallic spider-legged robot. There was also someone standing to the right of George, but he was a fuzzy shadow and George could not make out who or what this was. George later asked his wife to undergo hypnotic regression but she refused, as she had a phobia of being under someone's hypnotic control. Hypnotic regression has been used to extract information from the memories of people who have witnessed crimes and as a result, some of them have been able to recall details such as the registration number of a getaway car driven by a criminal after a bank raid. Hypnotic extraction of memories and possible enhancement of things partially forgotten is not wholly reliable, but its possible that George and Bridget where unknowingly abducted by something which chose to take on the form of someone resembling a down-to-earth likeable chap such as Fred Dibnah. But the problem is this: Dibnah never really came to the notice of television producers until 1978 – the year *after* the "close encounter" at McGoldrick Park. Perhaps then, if something was using Dibnah's persona as a cover, then that something may have either had foreknowledge of the future – or the thing was some form of time traveller. I have spoken to Bridget and George at length, and also interviewed relatives they told the story to over the years, and so far, I can find no answer that throws any light on their experience – it is truly beyond explanation.

In addition to being a ghost-chaser I am also an amateur 'psychonaut' – a Sunday sailor of the inner mind who endeavours to explore the human psyche through meditation and self-hypnosis, and at the risk of being sectioned, I can state categorically that the outlands and antipodes of the subconscious are populated by some weird but nevertheless real but poorly-understood creatures. They seem peculiar to us, and are occasionally glimpsed when a person has fever, chronic sleep-deprivation, a bad reaction to a medicine or narcotic, or an over-indulgence of alcohol resulting in the "DTs" (the delirium tremens), and in the old days, gas at the dentist sometimes fleetingly revealed these hallucinatory organisms. Although these psychedelic species may look as unreal as the duck-billed platypus did to zoologists (who declared the animal a hoax when first discovered in 1798), they are just as real as the weird Kuru laughing virus or the big-nosed proboscis monkey. I have amassed a huge dossier crammed with reports of these surreal creatures from the far reaches of inner space, and have noted how many of them have befriended children as "imaginary friends" – and some of these friends evidently get around from person to person. *Folie à deux* is French for "a madness shared by two", and also the name of a syndrome whereby two people experience the same hallucination. In Knotty Ash in 1950 a 5-year-old child named Rose was put in the care of her very strict Aunt Enid while the girl's mother recovered from an operation. Enid would cruelly lock Rose in the attic for up to two hours whenever the girl was deemed to have misbehaved, and one February afternoon during Rose's confinement, she heard strange jangling carnivalesque music, and a golden carousel horse came sailing through the wall. In a young-sounding feminine voice, the strange gilded filly said, 'Don't be afraid – my name is Diamonds – come and ride me!' and Rose shouted for Aunt Enid and pulled the door handle so hard it came off. She eventually calmed down, and after conversing with the friendly looking horse, the girl climbed on its back and it moved off in an up-and-down motion reminiscent of the funfair Merry-Go-Round. Rose noticed the red diamond pattern on the horse's neck, and Diamonds told her that her three sisters bore the symbols for hearts, clubs and spades. For what seemed a long time to Rose, she and Diamonds travelled through vast unknown lands, and Rose described these places and the strange animals and people there as shining with 'funny colours' and the houses and mountains there looked like the colourful stained glass in the windows of the church Rose attended. When Diamonds brought the girl back, she glided over the rooftops and came through the roof to the attic – to find the place dark. The police had been searching for Rose for hours after Enid had found the attic empty. Rose's story was not believed, and months later when she and her friend Poppy were playing in the attic one rainy afternoon, Diamonds visited again, but just when the children were going to climb onto her, the entity said, 'Oh! Someone's there!' and vanished, and the children saw Aunt Enid peeping round the door, gazing in disbelief. Diamonds never returned, and she was not a mere figment of two children's minds, or a *Folie à deux* – for Enid also saw her – so what in heaven's name was she? Yet another case that seems to be beyond explanation.

From fascinating beings of inner space we move next to the realm of the looking-glass…

One of the most powerful occult instruments is probably to be found within a few feet of you if you are reading this at home. I am referring to the mirror. There is more to the humble silvered looking glass than you imagine, and its power has been known to the occultists for millennia. Mirrors are the vital components in lasers which can be used in surgery – or to vaporize an incoming nuclear missile. Had the Nazis known how easy it is to make a carbon dioxide laser out of a glass tube, some gas, a few electrodes and mirrors, the Battle of Britain might have had quite a different outcome. During the siege of Syracuse (214-212 BC) Archimedes used an array of mirrors to focus the sun's rays on the attacking ships, and set them ablaze, and this early solar weapon was even reconstructed in 1973 by a Greek scientist who used 70 mirrors to train the heat of the sun onto a rowing boat, which burst into flames.

Place a mirror to face a mirror, peep over the edge of the glass at the breathtaking multiple reflections and you will glimpse eternity. This arrangement forms the basis of the Fabry–Pérot interferometer, a device used in telecommunications and astronomy – and it may also be used in a future time machine because of the "Casimir Effect" – the production of negative quantum energy between perfectly parallel mirrors. Such negative energy could be used to inflate wormholes to open up the past and future. The occultist already knows that mirrors can span the gulf of time, for they have been used to look into the future – and the past. In 1963, an Aztec obsidian mirror went up for auction at Southebys, along with many other exotic items belonging to the Maharajah of Jaipur. Bidding was fierce but Charles Phoenix, a wealthy Liverpool collector bidding by proxy, obtained the mirror for a princely fortune, and knowing its history, he knew the mirror was worth every penny. Phoenix knew that the Devil's mirror – known as the "See All" - had purportedly been owned by such seers as Nostradamus, Dr John Dee and Jacques Cazotte. Phoenix was a controversial collector of "Occultia", and amongst his collection he had alleged cuttings of the Tree of Knowledge (an exceedingly rare perennial psychedelic) mentioned in Genesis, a Persian bottle containing a djinn (genie), and the recipe to make "Soma" - the mysterious ancient Hindu immortality elixir. A sceptical friend of Phoenix was invited to dinner at his Crosby house one evening in May 1964, and when the table talk turned to politics, the circulating conspiracy theories about the assassination of President Kennedy seven months before came up, and Phoenix claimed he could use the "See All" – the Aztec mirror – to see the true assassin of the President. One of the group, a superstitious man, and a man who classed himself as a Christian, immediately left, but six stayed and were taken into the attic, where candles were lit as Phoenix quoted words in an unknown language from an ancient book. Within the long rectangular black mirror, clouds formed, and a young man appeared as a faint image which became steadily clearer. He was walking with outstretched palms and seemed distressed. Two well-informed guests instantly recognised him: they said it was the late Lee Harvey Oswald.

'Help me,' Oswald silently mouthed, and then grotesque shadowy faces appeared around him and he disappeared. The lights were turned on, and Phoenix explained that the person they had seen had been in a part of Hell. Some thought it was trickery, others suspected that a devious demon had created the illusion. There were further regular assemblies in the room at Mr Phoenix's house where the curious were supposedly shown many more visions of the past and future in the See All, and some of these spectral scenes in the mirror of obsidian were shocking, baffling, amusing and terrifying. On one occasion the assembled group saw what was apparently some unidentified future King of England on trial in a vast circular hall. He was a tall bald man with a long aquiline nose and he was flanked by soldiers with dark blue helmets and grey uniforms. The scene was, to the observers in the 1960s, reminiscent of the filmed scenes of the Nuremberg Trials. The time was undoubtedly some period in the future, for the clothing of the jurors, judges and barristers were very unusual in design and colour. Now and then, sound from this strange scene would come through the obsidian mirror, and there was mention of 'lie detectors' and all sorts of phrases that were gobbledygook to the 20th century viewers. Then, before the scene faded, someone announced that the 'former King of England and Wales has been found guilty of treason and will be deported to Canada.' This did not make any sense to the sitters in that darkened room in Mr Phoenix's home and it remains baffling today. Phoenix said he and his guests had also seen a future British 'President' who looked Asian, and he spoke English and what sounded like Hindi. The sitters in the 1960s also saw what seemed to be the aftermath of a nuclear accident – or possibly a deliberate attack – on Russia. This was a massive widespread area of destruction named "The Moscow Crater" which looked remarkably similar to the 50,000-year-old Arizona Crater which was created by meteoric impact. The Kremlin and many other areas of Moscow had apparently been turned to glass or vaporised by the intense thermonuclear heat, and many calcified bodies lay scattered about the perimeter of the crater, looking like latter day plaster casts of the Pompeian victims of the Mount Vesuvius eruption of AD79. There were many other weird and worrying scenes allegedly seen in the obsidian mirror, including a future civil war in the United States involving nightmare weaponry, but unfortunately the "See All" was stolen during a burglary in 1969. Its present whereabouts are unknown. How can an obsidian mirror allow a peephole into the past and future? It's currently inexplicable by the laws of today's science, but in the future, we may discover that there is more to the everyday mirror than meets the eye.

From mysterious mirrors we now plumb the latent powers of the human being, and in doing so we touch upon a character which has been labelled by some social anthropologists and local historians as an urban myth – the Green Jacket.

From time to time we catch glimpses of the superhuman that lies dormant in every one of us. Within that spiral staircase of life known as the double-helix of DNA, there are a myriad secrets about the powers this race possessed in the remote past, but subsequently lost, perhaps through laziness or mental stagnation. Ancient texts in cultures across the world say we can heal ourselves and others, that we can become fireproof (and history is full of accounts of mystics who could not be burnt at the stake, such as the Saints Cosmas and Damian of Arabia), and that we have an immense source of physical strength within us that could rival Samson. I recall a man of eighty who used to do handstands and also, with one hand, he would effortlessly lift a huge bar stool by gripping it at the bottom of one of its legs in the Vines public house, yet men a quarter of the pensioner's age couldn't make that stool budge. Then we have 'hysterical strength'; in the 1970s on Island Place, Garston, the jacks supporting a car a man was working under collapsed, and the vehicle began to crush him, but his 5ft 3 wife somehow lifted the vehicle off him and the man's friends pulled him clear in those vital seconds. There are also drugs in the pharmacopoeia of the modern biochemist which can quadruple standard human strength by stimulating the central nervous system and boosting muscle tissue, but it seems the most powerful drugs tend to bend the mind, so the chemically-induced real-life Hulk becomes hot under the collar and may even resort to crime, and this latter scenario allegedly took place in Lancashire and Liverpool in the early 1970s. There were widely circulating but strangely consistent rumours that military scientists were offering prisoners freedom if they would be willing to risk taking a top-secret drug which would turn them into a superman (and an ideal soldier) who would develop incredible muscle power and get by with virtually no sleep. The experiments that did take place involving the prisoners were an unmitigated disaster with the penal Guinea pigs going on the rampage and returning to crime. In August 1972, a terrifying rumour – later dismissed as an urban legend – circulated throughout Liverpool: the Green Jackets were in the area. These were skinheads who were not afraid of the police, the army – anything. No prison could hold them, they could not be subdued by anyone, and they lived for "aggro". Their Nietzschean motto was: "The only law is the law of the jungle". One of them had purportedly thrown a policeman up a tree in Wigan after swinging him around by his boots, and even the John Bulls – a much-feared gang of formidable skinheads – avoided the ruthless Green Jackets. Pupils were sent home early by schools that feared the Green Jacket invasion. On Dale Street around this time, there was a collision between a Hackney and a Cortina, and a policeman was taking a statement from the cabby when he heard a screech of tyres behind him. A police car was chasing a skinhead in a green army jacket, and he was outrunning the car. In his hand the criminal held a stolen handbag. That skinhead jumped high over the heads of the policeman, motorist and taxi driver like a modern-day Spring-Heeled Jack – a leap of over twelve feet - which is even beyond the capabilities of an Olympic high jumper. The skin laughed and avoided capture, and when the policeman enquired about the leaping lout, his superiors advised him to 'keep quiet' about the incident. Was the ultra-athletic outlaw unusually fit – or was he one of the fabled Green Jackets? I mentioned the Green Jackets one afternoon on BBC Radio Merseyside as a guest on a programme which explored urban legends. Callers swamped the switchboard and assured me that the Green Jackets were not urban legends and modern day bogeymen, but real and mysterious hard-knocks around which a mythos has now been woven. One shopkeeper named Alf called me on air and said he clearly recalled a gang of skinheads bursting into his shop in Anfield one evening in August 1972. He thought they were going to ransack the place and make off with the till, but the skins were taking refuge from the Green Jackets after a clash with them on Venmore Street off Walton Breck Road. This incident had taken place in the wake of the Manchester United v Arsenal game at Anfield. Two of the Green Jackets burst into the shop and assured Alf they were only coming for a 'bit of sport'. These fearsome young men had on police helmets they had pinched from the police, and they looked wild in the eyes. 'They wore green jackets of the type you could buy at the Army & Navy stores,' Alf told me, 'and they had on these boots that went up almost to the knees, all laced up. Like "bovver boots" but longer, and these fellahs were physically fit – much fitter than some athletes.'

The two Green Jackets pulled two of the skinheads from their hiding places behind the counter and dragged them outside. Alf could hear the screams of mercy from the skinheads and the sounds of heads being booted in. When he went outside, he thought he had two dead bodies outside his shop, because they were open-eyed yet inert, covered in blood and the blood had splashed all over Alf's van. In the distance he could see the Green Jackets running like the wind, and one of them jumped clean over the bonnet of a police car. The ambulance men tended the injured skinheads and said they had never seen multiple injuries like it – except in car crashes. I also received a call on air that day from a well-spoken man who did not want to give his name, and he claimed that the Green Jackets were out of control soldiers who had been chosen from prisons where they had been serving time for crimes of violence, but a few minutes into the conversation the line went dead and we lost contact with the caller. Another caller said there was a claim that the Green Jackets were some White Supremacy movement, but that simply wasn't so, because he recalled seeing black and white Green Jackets on the rampage at Wigan in the 1970s, and there was even a photo-fit issued of the extreme black and white hooligans in the local newspaper – possibly the *Wigan Observer*. With so many people reporting the terrifying antics of the Green Jackets, it seems unlikely that these mysterious yobbos were mere urban legends – so what lies behind the real origins of the Green Jackets? Were they merely glorified ruffians resorting to ultra-violence, or were they indeed the fallout from some disastrous experiment to engineer a superhuman soldier?

THE HUMLORTS

During the school summer holidays of 1976, a wayward 13-year-old girl from Huyton named Jenny Mandryn appropriated some money from her mum's purse and went to visit her eccentric old Uncle Winston at his Bootle home. Jenny recalled how her uncle predicted the big earthquake in Turkey last year and had said it would come about because of the moon's pull on the earth's crust, along with varying fluctuations from the sun's gravitational field. Everyone had laughed, but Jenny believed him, and thought he was a genius. Her parents and a few other relatives differed in their opinion of Winston Mackintosh, and all of them said he was a dangerous man without specifying why. Jenny had the feeling he had done something wrong a long time ago and whatever this was, it was still being held against him. As far as Jenny was concerned, Uncle Winston was a brainbox and a fantastic storyteller. Jenny wished he'd married because he seemed lonely, having only a green Rose-ringed parakeet named Jeffrey for company. Her uncle *did* have some odd beliefs though, Jenny admitted that. He told her some questionable things like: Harold Wilson was a KGB agent, Algebra had been invented by an ancient Persian mathematician who despised children, and Lord Lucan had been whisked from the long arm of the law by a global secret society which assembled in a hidden building beneath the Palace of Westminster. Jenny also conceded that her uncle's behaviour was a bit odd. He talked about deceased members of the family as if they were still alive, and the only chocolate he would touch had to be of the white variety – i.e. Nestlé Milky Bars and the odd white Swiss chocolate Easter Egg. Jenny forgot about that idiosyncrasy on this day when she told Uncle Winston she'd brought him a Topic chocolate bar. He reacted as if it was a hand grenade minus the pin, and he swiped the Topic from her hand before yowling 'Never bring that type of chocolate here!' And then he slung the chocolate bar in his wall safe and slammed the six-inch-thick brushed steel door.

'*Humlorts!*' shrieked the parakeet Jeffrey, high up in his cage, which hung from a hook in the ceiling which was once used to support a chandelier in Edwardian times.

'Shut up, Jeffrey!' Winston yelled at the excitable bird.

'The whole day has turned on me!' was Jeffrey's random response.

Jenny apologised, about bringing the chocolate and Uncle Winston eventually smiled and closed his eyes as he nodded vigorously, saying, 'It's alright, it's alright, we all make mistakes. Now, fancy going on an errand?'

'Yes, of course uncle, what do you want?' Jenny was

so glad to be back in his good books again.

'Just four packets of Oxo flavour Golden Wonder crisps, a quarter of Midget Gems, quarter of Pear Drops, a quarter of Pink Shrimps, a quarter of Sherbet Lemons, quarter of False Teeth, and erm – let me see – yes, a quarter of Flying Saucers, a quarter of Cherry Lips, a quarter of Chelsea Whoppers, a quarter of Fizz Bombs, a quarter of Kola Cubes, and just a quarter of Rhubarb and Custard, a quarter of Mojos, quarter of Cinder Toffee – did I already say a quarter of Pineapple Chunks?'

'I don't think so,' Jenny replied, knowing she'd never remember all these sweets.

Uncle Winston's eyes widened and he pointed his index finger at the ceiling. 'And a quarter of Acid Drops, a quarter of White Mice, and ah – let me see – a quarter of…Aniseed Balls. Shall I write all this down?'

'Yeah,' was Jenny's straightforward reply, and she smirked and whispered: 'Just write "A quarter of everything"'

'Not funny, Jennifer; not funny at all. No chocolate remember.' Uncle Winston took a small red pencil from behind his left ear and wrote the list in his spiral bound notebook, puckering his lips as he scribbled away. 'Maybe a bunch of bananas as well – lovely this time of year.' He muttered, then looked over at Jenny and told her: 'The fruiterer is right next to the sweetshop, dear, so you won't be going out of your way.'

Forty minutes later, Uncle Winston was snoring on his sofa with an undissolved flying saucer in his gaping mouth. Jenny felt sick with eating all of the sweets, but saw this as a good opportunity to go mooching upstairs in the attic, where, according to her mother, Uncle Winston had a magpie's nest of weird curiosities, including a little model village. Jenny got up off the big armchair and a loose spring made a metallic *boing* sound. She looked up at Jeffrey and whispered to him, 'I'll stuff you if you open that beak.'

The bird tilted its green head and watched her sneak out of the room and into the hallway. She crept up the stairs as softly as a ghost, and up in the gloomy attic she came upon at least a hundred doll's houses, but curiously, there was not a single doll to be seen in any of them. The one window of the attic was thick with dust and it was filtering out the light of the summer sun. There was a real sinister atmosphere up there, and the girl felt as if a thousand eyes were upon her. She thought she could see mice and spiders out the corner of her eyes, but still she mooched about.

'Who's your daddy?' she heard down below, and cursed that parakeet. She had to move quickly now. Jenny decided she was having one of the little houses, and she wheezed as she carried it out the attic, trailing cobwebs behind her as she went. She rested on the landing, then slowly dragged it down the stairs, step by step. Every now and then she'd hear some screechy phrase from Jeffrey, but she persevered, and eventually reached the hallway with the model house. She hid it in the back yard, regained her breath, then went into the kitchen and washed her hands. She cadged the taxi fare off Uncle Winston when dusk fell and she was soon home with the strange old gothic-looking miniature house. She installed it in a corner of her bedroom and planned to buy some suitably sized dolls for it. Jenny's mother, Jo, laughed when she saw the doll's house and told her daughter she was too old for it, and that she should give it to her 7-year-old cousin Julie.

Strange things happened not long after this; shadowy, twitchy things were seen out the corner of Jenny's eye, but whenever she would turn to see what they were, they'd flit away, and her cat Bill kept hissing at something Jenny couldn't see. She had a feeling that these spooky goings-on had something to do with the little house she'd stolen from her uncle's attic, but she didn't want to believe her gut feelings. On the following evening she was watching TV with her parents and younger brother Gerry, when she suddenly felt peckish, and so, as the family were nonchalantly concerned with the stretched innuendo of *Are You Being Served?*, she sneaked into the kitchen, where she located the box of Week End chocolates her mother had received for her birthday. They were in the bread bin. Jenny carefully lifted the cardboard lid and rustled the silky sheet covering the tray of chocolate assortments. She chose a soft almond toffee, a chocolate cherry cup, a montelimar, and chocolate cracknel, and then she closed the box silently and replaced it in the bread bin. She read a comic as she lay on the bed, and listened to the radio. She began to eat the purloined chocolates without so much as a trace of guilt, and saved the chocolate cherry cup for her last little treat – but the cat Bill jumped up onto the bedside cabinet and for some reason known only to him, he curled his paw and deliberately knocked the last chocolate onto the floor. Jenny bawled at him and got up off the bed, and the felid ran out of the room. She felt something squelch under her left bare foot, and looked down to see the innards of the chocolate cherry cup smeared on her big toe. She cursed softly and went to wipe it off in the toilet with some tissue before wandering back to the bed. She lay on her side, reading the panels of the comic, and her eyelids felt as heavy as lead, and then nothing. She awoke in the morning to a sharp pain in her big toe, and told Bill to stop it – but it wasn't Bill gnawing on it to get attention. Jennifer sat up and looked down towards her feet. The end of the bed looked sort of in soft focus because of the sleep in her bleary eyes, but she could still see something down there. A spasm of fear lanced through her stomach as Jenny thought she saw what looked like a tarantula on the white enamel rail at the bottom of the bed. If it was a spider it was missing half of its legs, because Jenny could only see four black legs sticking out, and these did *not* look like spider legs at all – more like long wobbling wavy tentacles, and the head of this strange matt black creature was chomping on her toe. Jenny screamed, kicked the thing away, and it landed with a clatter on the thin carpet. The girl hopped out the bed and flew to her shoe rack to choose one of her big platforms. She then walked round the bed with a strange tingling in her stomach as fear got the better of her. There it was. That was no spider with four legs. It was some sort of little man, about six inches tall, and his arms, legs and even his torso were moving with a wavy snake-like motion. The head was small and globular and two gleaming eyes were looking up to her as if they had been mounted by Cartier; they scintillated and flashed red, royal blue, yellow, gold, green and purple, and the weird arms – twice the length they should be, waved in the air. She could see the little triangular mouth open and close with a faint clicking sound, but she could see no teeth or fangs. Jenny let out a scream in an effort to vent her fear, and she dropped to one knee and she slammed down that platform on the little black humanoid.

Bang! Bang! Bang!

She swore with each smash of the platform heel and sole, and saw the poor thing go flat and embed into the carpet. She stopped hitting it and everything felt dreamlike, because things like this did not happen everyday. It all felt unreal, as if she hadn't awakened yet, but it was real, and now that little invader of her bedroom was peeling itself up off the carpet. As Jenny watched in horror, it sprung up and darted under the bed.

She felt so vulnerable now, looking down at her bare feet. She could see the red mark on her big toe, and she recalled that was the toe that had accidentally squished the chocolate cherry cup last night, but she didn't link this with the weird entity yet.

'What's all that banging?' Jenny's mother said, downstairs in the hallway.

'Mum! Mum!' Jenny fled from her bedroom and went downstairs to tell her mother about the creepy black entity, but before she could get the chance to utter a syllable, her sour-faced father intercepted her and asked, 'Have you eaten all the chocolate olivers?'

Jenny shook her head, trying to get her words sorted in her brain so she could talk sense and tell everyone what had just happened.

'What a gannet you are, Jenny!' her father told her. 'You nicked some of your mum's chocolates last night and now you've walloped down a whole tin of *my* biscuits!'

'They're not *your* biscuits dad, they're everyone's' Gerry informed his father, 'and why do you always blame Jen for half-inching everything in the kitchen, eh?'

'Well who else could it be eh? The Cookie Monster?' Mr Mandryn yelled to his son.

And Gerry yelled back: 'You're not even funny, dad, and you get everyone down with your constant criticisms and accusations!'

'You don't exactly light up a room yourself, you miserable little long-haired jangler!' retorted his father, deeply hurt by his son's remark.

'Excuse me – ' Jenny was ready to speak.

'Jangler?' Gerry returned a puzzled look to his perturbed father.

'Yeah, jangler! I heard what you said to your mum about me behind my back!'

'Shut up! Shut up!' Jenny screamed, silencing the argumentative males. When she began to babble about the little six-inch-tall shadow man with undulating limbs her dad and brother assumed she was pulling their legs, but then a few minutes later, Jenny's mother saw one of the things her daughter had tried to describe, and it was in the fridge, eating her Fry's Five Centres plain chocolate bar! It had neatly removed the silver foil and paper wrapper first. She screamed, and Jenny ran over and yelled: 'That's one of them! I told you!'

When Jenny's father saw the thing he went cold, for he was terrified of anything which looked remotely like a spider, and he backed away to the doorway of the kitchen. 'Call the zoo!' he gasped, and his face was now white as snow.

'I think you call the Health Department,' his wife said, watching the fridge door slowly close itself.

'Never mind all that, call the police,' Mr Mandryn stumbled backwards into the hallway, and then he asked, 'What the hell is it anyway?'

'Its like a little man, and they bite!' Jenny told him. 'It bit my big toe. And they run faster than your eye can follow them.'

By 5pm the wormy things were all over the house, and Jenny and her mum hit them with rolling pins, pressed them with combined fists under a flat-iron, whacked them with a dustpan and dropped a telephone book on them before jumping up and down on them – all to no avail – they were indestructible.

'Winston!' Jenny's dad – now chain-smoking and rambling - suddenly realised where they had come from after his daughter had told him about the doll's house. He drove to Winston's Bootle home and berated the old man about the things that had infested his house.

Winston buried his face in his hands and then looked at Mr Mandryn through splayed fingers. 'She must have taken one of the model houses from the attic! Oh dear!'

Winston turned up at Jenny's house with a long thin cane with a green goldfish net at the end – and some onions. He explained that the 'little chaps' were Humlorts - 'endangered' sweet-toothed Welsh imps he had kept in his little houses for company. They hated onions (and leeks), and he used the pungent bulbs to herd them one by one into the nets, and then he put them in the doll's house, where a few squares of milk chocolate – which made the Humlorts euphoric but hyperactive – were placed. Six of the seven Humlorts were captured, but the seventh one's fate is unknown, and presumably it is still at large somewhere – perhaps still in Huyton, for according to Winston, the things live much longer than the laughable human lifespan of three score years and ten. This missing Humlort might just be responsible for the unaccountable loss of the occasional chocolate digestive or that crème egg you swore you had. In Lancashire, the Humlorts were often mistaken for dobbies, boggarts, mischievous fairies and goblins, but tradition says these little entities mostly stay in North Wales, and hundreds of people vouch for their existence. The Humlorts were as real and menacing to the old folk of England as the deadly False Widow spider is to the people of today. Just why the things have a fondness for chocolate is unknown, but the substance was originally classed as a drug when it reached Spain in 1529 (brought back by Cortes) because it seemed to mellow the taker and it was also highly addictive. Recent research undertaken by the University of Aberdeen suggests that the consumption of two chocolate bars a day may be beneficial for our health by lessening the likelihood of strokes and heart disease by 11%. *Chocolatl*, as the Aztecs called chocolate, was used originally for ceremonial purposes, and those ancient peoples believed that the great god Quetzalcoatl was cast out from the company of the other gods for sharing the secret of chocolate with the human race. There is evidently more to chocolate than meets the tongue – both from a medical and metaphysical point of view, and therein lies a possible clue which may link the craving of the Humlorts with the food of the Mesoamerican gods.

COLD CALLER

The following strange story came my way many years ago after I had been a guest on a four-hour programme about the supernatural on Radio City, Liverpool's independent radio station. A man in his sixties named Barry told me how, in the 1980s, the people of a certain neighbourhood in Liverpool were persecuted and insulted by a mysterious and rather malicious man who would telephone people and tell them that he knew their darkest secrets and what their friends, spouses and family members were doing behind their backs. The authorities and a telephone company tried to trace him, but the creepy culprit always seemed a step ahead of everybody. The peculiar story begins in at a hairdresser's salon in North Liverpool in October 1995. I have agreed to change the names in this story to comply with issues of privacy, but otherwise, everything else is factually correct.

It was autumn, and leaves lay scattered about like unopened letters on the pavement which runs along the row of shops. A popular hairdresser named Lindsey had not long opened her salon that morning when the telephone rang. She answered it, assuming it was either a client wishing to book an appointment with her or someone who had never been to the salon before enquiring about some style or service, but instead a man's voice she had never heard before spoke. He did not have a strong local accent but Lindsey could tell he was a Liverpudlian – or he was some actor who could imitate the Scouse accent in a subtle way.

'Hello Lindsey, I see you're doing very well for yourself,' he said. There was no background noise as he spoke, Lindsey recalled that much.

'Hello, Lindsey's Salon. Can I help you?' she replied, ignoring the opening line. She wondered if it was an ex, or maybe a schoolfriend who had seen her in the salon from a passing bus.

'How could you do what you did, eh, Lindsey?' the stranger said, and he had a sort of mocking quality to his tone.

'Sorry? Who is this?' Lindsey asked, believing by now she had been contacted by a nuisance caller.

'You got rid of that baby, you cold, selfish cow,' the man said, and there was anger in the timbre of his voice.

Lindsey went cold inside. Seven years ago when she was twenty, her boyfriend Adam – a man she had worshipped – suddenly upped and left her, and moved in with another girl down in London. Lindsey's world fell apart, and she turned to drink and drugs to get through those horrible days. A friend who had gone to college with her – a 19-year-old named Alex, had been there for her during the time. He had been her rock, but he ended up falling for Lindsey, and somewhere along the line the relationship ceased being platonic, and they slept together. Lindsey became pregnant, and at seven months, Adam turned up again. He gave Lindsey an ultimatum – terminate the pregnancy or stay with Alex. Alex begged her not to have an abortion, but Lindsey was confused. Her love for Adam blurred her common sense and judgement. Alex tearfully told her that by law it was only possible to have an abortion during the first 24 weeks of pregnancy. There was a huge row with Lindsey blaming Alex for getting her pregnant in the first place. 'I didn't love you in that way! You took advantage of me when I was at my lowest ebb!' she had claimed. Lindsey could remember the whole tragic script as she held the phone in the salon. That caller had brought the whole sordid episode out of mothballs. She had gone with a cousin to an abortionist in Bournemouth and had almost bled to death during the botched 'procedure'. Then Alex took an overdose. They say he didn't mean to end his life – like a lot of people who get lost wallowing in self pity – but he died without regaining consciousness. She went back to Adam in a terrible state, and he had the audacity to say she looked 'rough' – that her fingernails were dirty and that she'd let herself go. He left her again – for good – three months after that.

She held the phone with a tear in her eye.

'What a selfish cow,' said the wicked caller, and then with real venom in his voice he said, 'and I think its time your customers knew about your history.' Then there was silence. The line was dead.

'Linds – what's up?' Kayla, her 19-year-old trainee hairdresser asked. She was a very caring and empathic girl, and she had a mug of coffee for her boss.

'Nothing,' Lindsey told her and put on a brave smile. She wiped the tear away and took the coffee from her as she said: 'Crank caller. Real far gone one too.'

'You sure you're okay?' Kayla's big brown eyes probed her face.

'Yeah, don't you worry,' she said, sipping the coffee.

'Ew, you've put real sugar in that Kay,' Lindsey said, stretching the sides of her lips down in a comical grimace.

'I don't even know why you're dieting for,' said Kayla, 'you look fit.'

'I want to get back to size 12,' she whispered.

Around this time, Karl, a 16-stone bulleted-headed butcher of 35 years was admiring the neat display in the window; from all the varieties of sausages, chops, pork pies and home-made burgers to the huge joints with their red white and blue rosettes of British quality. Karl's younger brother Paul broke his spell by telling him that the kids outside were rubbing out the letters written in white paint on the windows again. 'Oi!' Karl shouted at the schoolkids and they ran off to howls of laughter. They had changed 'Freshly Made Sausages' to 'Freshly Mad ages' by erasing some of the letters, and other edits of the window writing bordered on the obscene. Paul suggested writing the words back to front on the *inside* of the window so the pesky kids couldn't rub the letters out. Karl told his brother to do this, seeing as he had suggested it, and as Paul got to work in the window, the telephone rang. 'Karl answered it. Karl's butchers.'

'Hello Karl, I see your doing well,' said a stranger's voice.

'Who is it?' Karl asked, sensing a wind-up was in the offing.

'Well, you've gone from one joint to another haven't you, eh?' said the unknown caller. 'Used to sell cannabis, and now look at you with your silly white trilby and that striped apron.'

Karl was a little stunned for a moment, but then he

became angry. He *had* sold cannabis resin and pills a few years ago, but then he had done time – just a few months – and now he had turned his back on all that. Karl thought the caller sounded like someone he had shared a cell with in Walton nick – a guy named Jimmy – he was almost sure of it, and so he had it out with him as Paul gawped at him from the window with a paintbrush and pot of paint in his hand.

'Long time no speak, eh Jimmy?' Karl beamed a smile but it had so much anger in it and his cheeks flushed.

There was no reply – not even a whisper or a tracery of faint breath against the telephone mouthpiece.

'It is *you* isn't it bollock-brain? Still knocking over old ladies for their pensions eh?'

'My name isn't Jimmy,' the caller assured him in that mocking tone Lindsey had experienced earlier that morning. 'Karl, I have a cutting from the local newspaper here – from a few years back, and its all about you.'

Karl felt both angry and sick. He had a blood pressure condition and now he was seeing blue lights in front of his eyes.

'So what I'll do, Karl, is this: I'll pop round the library and use their photocopying machine and make about twenty enlargements, maybe more, and I'll post them all over the place to let people know about your past.'

'Who are you, you little grass?' Karl asked, squeezing the handset.

'I can't give you my name because you'd only stop me from bothering all the people like you with their little secrets. Bye bye Karl.'

Karl swore, and his brother asked who the caller was. 'How do I bleedin' know?' Karl yelled back, and at that moment an elderly woman – a regular at Karl's butchers – came into the shop, and she seemed shocked at Karl's outburst. 'Sorry Mrs Stafford,' Karl told her in a meek voice.

About a quarter of an hour after this, Clive Telford, a 56-year-old man whose expertise lay in the field of personal injury, received a very personal and very injurious call from the sinister shit-stirrer who obviously derived so much pleasure in causing trouble or discord over the telephone. The mysterious know-all called the firm of solicitors Telford worked for, and the secretary, Suzi, answered. 'Good morning,' she greeted the spiteful caller, 'Bardley David and Klein; can I help you?'

'I would like to talk to Mr Telford – Clive Telford.'

'Is Mr Telford expecting a call from you?' Suzi asked, robotically, a routine she did many times six days of the week. She glanced down the list of people who had booked appointments with the various solicitors of the firm.

'Yes.'

'And what's your name, sir?'

'Michael Burgess,' said the caller.

Suzi hummed. 'Can't see you on the list here. Can you hold the line a tick?'

'Yes.'

The intercom chimed pleasantly on Clive Telford's desk as he clinked the china cup of Earl Grey on the saucer. 'Yes?' he said, pressing the mustard-coloured button on the Tandy intercom.

'A Mr Michael Burgess on the line for you Mr

Telford,' Suzi told him.

Telford's stomach somersaulted and he felt his heart palpitate. 'Mr Burgess?'

'Yes, he said you're expecting his call,' said Suzi, 'but he isn't on my list here.'

'I – I wasn't – er – I well, er - put him through anyway,' Clive stammered, and he knocked the cup of tea over and the Earl Grey flowed across two unopened manila envelopes.

'Hello Clive,' said the enigmatic voice.

Clive Telford knew immediately that this was not Michael Burgess - a man he had worked with for many years - because Burgess was very well-spoken and was not a local, unlike this caller. 'Who *is* this?' Telford asked, relieved in a way and yet still baffled as to why someone should impersonate a former business partner.

'Well I'm not Michael Burgess as you have guessed, but I happen to know about the affair you had with his wife, Tiffany.'

Upon hearing the name Tiffany, time seemed to stand still, and the ticking of the electric clock on the office wall somehow increased in volume for a moment. 'What on earth are you talking about? Who the hell are you?'

'You giving it to Tiffany in your partner's bed when he was away on business – that's what the hell I'm talking about, Clive.'

'Stay there! Stay right there!' Clive began to panic and stood up then sat down, and he said, 'I'm calling the police now, and I shall report you! You-you'll be traced!'

'And you even slept with his daughter, and she had

just turned eighteen that day,' said the voice on the phone, and then he tutted.

'What do you want?' Clive's hand was shaking now, and he suddenly noticed that the spilt tea had trickled onto his lap, creating a stain between his legs. 'Is it money you want you bastard?' he whispered now, and he stood up, tip-toed to the door of his office, dragging the telephone off the desk by its lead. He made sure no one was listening outside. There was only the short carpeted corridor and the door with the frosted pane of glass leading to the reception where Suzi sat.

'What a horrible, dirty bastard you are,' said the voice, full of disgust. 'Sleeping with the wife of the man you worked with for years, and even sleeping with his teenage daughter. People like you should be shot against a wall; you wouldn't be missed.'

'Oh, and dirty blackmailers like you are alright are they?' Clive picked up the phone and carried it back to the desk, and he seized the hanky in the top pocket of his blazer and dabbed the perspiration on his face.

'Who said I wanted money?' came the unsettling reply.

'Well what else can you possibly want, eh?' Telford asked, and began to take deep breaths.

'Satisfaction,' was the unexpected reply. 'I want to write a long, long letter to your old friend Michael Burgess, and I want to tell him about everything you did to his wife and daughter. Bye.'

That afternoon, Karl the butcher called at Bardley David and Klein solicitors and to Suzi the receptionist he said, in rather an awkward fashion, that he wasn't really sure who he should see for advice. Then he looked at the types of solicitor on a faux gold plaque on the wall and said: 'Personal Injury; yes that's it.'

At that moment, ruffled Clive Telford came into the reception area, and he told Suzi he might be leaving a little earlier because his wife wasn't feeling too good. He then lingered, deep in thought, looking out the plate-glass window at the street, at the people milling by, and he wondered who that caller had been, and why did he want to ruin him? As he stood there, he heard a snatch of the conversation from Karl as he addressed Suzi.

'Well, I got this anonymous call this morning you see, and I don't want to go into it all now, I'd rather see a solicitor. The gist of it is the caller said he was going to expose my past you see, because er, well I have a criminal record, I mean I'm clean now and I have me own business but – '

'Excuse me,' Clive interrupted the conversation between Karl and the receptionist.

'Yeah?' Karl turned to face him and saw he had to be one of the names on that plaque because he was so immaculately dressed and groomed.

'Did you just say you received an anonymous call this morning?' Clive asked, his head turned so he presented his right (and best) ear to the butcher.

'Yeah, why?' said Karl.

'Maybe I can help,' Clive told him, 'I'm a solicitor see. Would you like to come through to my office now or do you – '

'Yeah, thanks,' Karl nodded, and smiled as Clive held out his hand.

'Clive Telford,' he shook Karl's hand weakly and opened the door to the offices.

'Someone said I get the first half hour free – ' Karl said, taking his flat cap off.

'Don't worry about that yet, this is all free, come on,' Clive led him down the corridor to his office and directed him to take a seat.

'This might just be someone arsing – er, playing a prank on me Mr Telford, but er, this morning, about – let's see – about twenty to ten, I got a call, and this fellah said er, "You've done well for yourself, selling joints" – cos I'm a butcher like – '

'And this was a call made to the shop?'

'Yeah, to the shop.'

'Do you run that butcher's shop down by the parade? Oh you're the Karl on that sign above the shop – of course,' Telford realised, recalling the shop he'd often driven past.

'Yeah, that's me,' said Karl with a nod, and he went on: 'So yeah, the caller said "You've gone from one joint to another haven't you?" because I got done – years ago – for selling cannabis, and I did time – '

'Just for selling pot?' Telford seemed surprised.

'And tablets and stuff,' Karl explained. He went into the details of the nasty caller and his threat to put the enlarged photocopied newspaper reports about Karl's past crime all over the place – in an effort to ruin him.

This really struck a chord in the mind of the solicitor, but he could not say *why* to someone like Karl; after all, he *did* have a criminal record, and while he might be the most honest man in Liverpool, it was equally possible that he could use the information about Telford's dalliances to a financial advantage. 'Karl, do you have any idea who this man might be? I mean, did his voice sound familiar? Do you have any enemies?' Telford asked him.

'Not really, I thought it was this fellah who was my cellmate in Walton, but it wasn't him. It sounded like him at first but then I thought, no, it can't be him because he er – well, his name was Jimmy – and he's thick as two short planks, and he couldn't string a sentence together. I haven't a clue who it is and it's doing me head in.'

'You see, there's a problem here, Karl. You've done your time, and you're obviously a reformed man, but the articles about you – detailing your drug-dealing, to put it bluntly - are still accessible to any Tom, Dick or Harry in the archives of the Central Library in town – and that's perfectly legal. A man might kill someone and do his time and become a born-again Christian and go on to become a minister, but the gory details of his murderous past will remain in the newspaper archives for any member of the public to delve into if he or she should wish to.'

Karl put his cap back on his bald head and his face turned red with rage. 'So I'm wasting your time and there's nothing I can legally do about this – well, what is he? A blackmailer?'

With a far-away look, Clive Telford slowly shook his head. 'No, because he hasn't demanded money in return for withholding that damaging information about you, but I would dearly love to find out who he is, believe me.'

'Why? What's it to you?' Karl wanted to know.

'Oh, I might be a solicitor Karl, but I do have a heart you know, and I mean, I don't just see you as a potential client, but as a man who has gone straight in the world, and is now threatened by this faceless, gutless coward hiding behind a telephone. It's not all about money you know?'

Karl thought this compassion was way out of kilter for a solicitor, but he was already confused and his mind was scrambled. He'd been racking his brain, trying to work out who that caller had been.

'So, keep in touch, and call me on this number – ' Clive scribbled down his extension on a little Bardley David and Klein appointment card. 'If he calls again or you think you might have worked out who he is – call me, and we'll take it from there.'

'No fees or anything, like?' Karl was puzzled as he took the card.

'No, no fees at all. Let's find out who this bastard is, eh?' Clive said, hauling himself out his chair.

On the following day, the butcher's shop closed half-day because it was mid-week, and Karl went to sit in the café just across the road from his shop at half-past noon. He saw Lindsey from the salon come in. She was a girl he'd admired from afar, and although he had served her a few times in his shop, he had never really talked to her socially. He noticed that she appeared to be crying. She sat at a table in a corner and ordered a coffee, and he heard the waitress say to her, 'No croissants or bickies today Linds?' Lindsey didn't feel like eating, and she shook her head, unable to even reply to the waitress because she was obviously distressed by something. The waitress had seen this before in other customers from time to time, and never pushed them to find out why they were upset, so she wisely went and made the coffee without saying another word to the hairdresser.

Karl had to go and talk to her. He could see she was

dabbing her red eyes, and he expected her to tell him to go away, but he went over anyway. He stood at her table and said, 'Hiya. Last time I talked to you, you were telling me black pudding should be banned.'

She smiled for a moment, and nodded, then managed one little laugh in the midst of her personal hell.

Karl cleared his throat with a cough and said: 'Do you want me to sit with you for a bit? I'm not trying to cop off or anything like that, just don't like seeing anyone cry.'

She shook her head.

'Alright, but I'll just be over there if you want to talk to anyone or discuss black puddings,' said Karl, and then he turned and walked away. He heard a noise. It sounded like a strangled coughing sound coming from the waitress - who looked at him, then nodded towards Lindsey – meaning 'she wants you.'

Karl turned and Lindsey said, 'Yeah, sit here.'

Karl sat at her table and folded his arms, He looked out the window to create the impression he was not scrutinising her.

She eventually told him about that phone call, but she didn't say what the anonymous caller was threatening to divulge. When Karl heard her account, his throat dried up, because he wondered how he could tell her about his encounter with this ubiquitous telephone tormentor – it would mean telling her he had a criminal record. He was going to keep it secret at first, but then he came out with it. Lindsey thought he was just joking at first – perhaps to make her feel better – but Karl said he was deadly serious and that he would dearly love to get his hands on whoever was behind the threatening calls.

Lindsey was not tearful now. Her eyes were clear and bright again, and not reddened. 'Karl, do you swear before God that you really did get an anonymous call from someone saying they'll bring up all your past?'

'Well I believe in God, Lindsey, He got me through a lot of crap, and yes, I swear before Him that what I have told you is the truth.'

Somewhere along the line, Lindsey told her best friend Ashley what had happened to Karl the butcher, and how it had happened to her, and Ashley then told her that her father had received one of those calls just over a week ago. Ashley was not kidding and was not the sort to make up stories. She told Lindsey that her father had photocopied his tax disc and altered the date because he couldn't afford to pay his car tax, and a month later he received a call from someone who said they'd report him to the police for forging the disc. The weeks went by and more and more people in this one area of Liverpool were receiving the weird calls from a man who seemed to know every little indiscretion big and small, every little misdemeanour and major crime – and there was a pattern emerging – he never followed through with his threats. No photocopies of those articles detailing Karl's criminal past were ever posted about, and the secret of Lindsey's abortion remained a secret, and so did the underhand sexual exploits of the personal injury solicitor. All sorts of people were accused of being the anonymous persecutor, and a few people came to blows when accusations were hurled about, but no one ever got to the bottom of the mystery. I heard of a similar case further back in time, in Germany in the

1970s. An anonymous caller telephoned dozens of people from all walks of life, and threatened to expose a whole graveyard of skeletons in all their closets. The police investigated the matter, and the mystery deepened because the caller could not be traced, even when the police wired up sophisticated electronic devices to various telephone lines. And then a psychiatrist visited the police one day, and he said that he had studied a similar case in Belgium. He drew up what is known as a Venn Diagram, and filled in the names and places of the 'victims' of the creepy caller, and eventually, one person remained in every single circle of the Venn Diagram, and this was a rather shy, retiring man who was henpecked by his wife and was too timid to stand up for himself. The man in question was a night watchman, and slept during the day, and whenever he was asleep, his wife would receive calls from someone with her husband's distinctive accent, and she eventually realised that somehow, when her husband was asleep, his unconscious mind was able to call her at work and insult her. It was as if all of the things the man could not dare say during his waking hours were somehow being vented as he slept. The man himself later recalled dreams in which he was dialling his wife and accusing her of all kinds - and this man then recalled he'd had similar dreams where he telephoned people in his dream and tormented them by threatening to divulge their shameful secrets. The German police were open-minded and intrigued by the psychiatrist's account, and so they allowed him to use his same technique with the data from their case, and again, the culprit was found: a disabled factory worker who slept of a day. He knew all of the victims and had been privy to secrets they kept from even their closest friends. So, was this the case in Liverpool in 1995? Was some repressed man who knew Karl, and Lindsey and Clive Telford, and many other people, somehow calling them via the telephone network with his subconscious mind as he was asleep, and is that why no one could ever trace the weird calls? The culprit – whoever he was - suddenly stopped in January 1996, so perhaps he died or maybe he was confronted by some suspicious individual and he quit as a result. Then again, perhaps the caller was dead when he made the calls, because there have been many documented accounts of nuisance calls from beyond the grave, and I have written about these 'phonecalls from the dead' in several of my books. We may learn more about this phenomenon one day – hopefully not from first-hand experience...

Printed in Great Britain
by Amazon.co.uk, Ltd.,
Marston Gate.